This Too
Shall Pass

This Too Shall Pass

Reflections on Faith, Psychology,
Black Lives Matter, the Pandemic, Ethics

Reverend James R. Squire

MILL CITY PRESS

Mill City Press, Inc.
2301 Lucien Way #415
Maitland, FL 32751
407.339.4217
www.millcitypress.net

Paperback ISBN-13: 978-1-6628-3651-0
Ebook ISBN-13: 978-1-6628-3652-7

Acclaim for *This Too Shall Pass*

"Jim Squire's book is extraordinarily timely and very current on issues of the day. He is on the mark in virtually every essay. This is a book to be read many times to keep our moral compass on track."

—Richardson Merriman,
Fiduciary Trust International,
Vice Chairman Radnor,
Senior Portfolio Manager.

"The Reverend Jim Squire's collected writings here are exquisite. They come from the heart, soul, and mind of an experienced and skilled ethicist. He is a teacher, thinker, and sensitive man, as he ponders the many ethical issues facing our world today."

—The Reverend Alexander McCurdy, PH.D.
received his diploma in Jungian Analysis at the Berlin Jung Institute. He practiced in Rome, Philadelphia, and New York and was a visiting lecturer in the Department of Psychiatry and Human Behavior at Jefferson Medical College.

"*This Too Shall Pass* is a collection of lessons and stories that enlightens, engages, and inspires. Rev. Squire leverages his rich foundation in counseling, teaching, and spiritual leadership to speak with a passionate and empathetic voice. He fuses current events, daily encounters, and ethical dilemmas to create a compilation of passages relatable to readers of all backgrounds and beliefs. *This Too Shall Pass* is my go-to read when I am seeking a conversation with a friend, a helping hand, or an insightful perspective on the everyday experience. Whether read from start to finish, uninterrupted, or one entry at a time, it adds both a thoughtful reflection on the big picture and a renewed appreciation for each of life's individual moments. It is a timeless treasure trove of actionable readings not to be missed."

—*Christy Rivard,*
Episcopal Academy, '10,
Harvard Class Day Speaker, '14,
Physician Assistant.

"These posts have been a great encouragement and piercingly clear insight into the lives we've been living as individuals and communities. Jim's insights and careful writings have been both an encouragement and a light in the midst of shadows."

—*The Reverend Frank Allen,*
Rector of St. David's Episcopal Church
in Radnor, Pennsylvania, a large church in the
Diocese of Pennsylvania.

"Jim uses his observations of everyday events as a method to unravel complex issues that are always discussed in everyday language. He seamlessly weaves diverse philosophical, ethical, cultural, and religious teachings in his essays, enlightening the reader about varied perspectives on the issues at hand. I look forward to every post and admire his ability to write so easily with such insight."

—*Gina Whelan,*
art conservator, specializing in the treatment
of historic textiles and artifacts.

"Reverend Jim Squire is truly eloquent and a prolific writer with great insight. He discusses relevant issues with personal stories which will inspire all to be better human beings. Bravo!"

—*Anita Millici,*
Dentist

"I grew up listening to Reverend Squire's sermons three times a week for twelve years as a child and young adult. Now that I am older with a family and three kids, trying to deal with work, childcare, a global pandemic, and massive civil unrest, every single time I get a new post from Reverend Squire regarding his view of events "of the day," it's the first thing I read. It helps me, personally, to keep grounded and focused on that light on the distant shore. His writing is compelling, relevant, empathetic, and infused with his moral teachings from a lifetime of service to the community in which he lived. I am grateful that I've been able to rediscover his writings and lessons after decades of being away."

—Ben Prusky,
Episcopal Academy, '92,
CEO of Freedom Merchants Corporation

"Ever since the Reverend Jim Squire began posting his thoughts, we've been hooked. It takes but a day after a local, national, or international event occurs for the Rev. to digest and process the event, then shows how this impacts us as individuals and members of the human race. He has this incredible knack to express his analysis while inspiring his followers with powerful insights and provocative storytelling. Surely, his many years of counseling families in crisis and motivating our youth have endowed him with gifts of knowledge and wisdom. Thankfully, he shares this with us, helping us to grow each time we read his prose. He makes us think; he makes us feel!"

—Frank Matarazzo,
Dentist

"Reverend Squire's essays cut through the fog of digital information overload. Don't set sail without this moral and ethical compass. While the general media offers many commendable news commentators and analysts, in-depth thinking is wanting. Jim's thirty-eight years career as an independent school chaplain intertwined his knowledge of classical philosophy and theology with leading and teaching students has created his unique perspective on life. Jim's book now offers a sound interpretation of news and current events."

—Joseph Pratt,
CEO of Alpha Vest Capital

About the Author

The Reverend James R. Squire has spent thirty-eight years teaching ethics and biblical studies as the head chaplain at the Episcopal Academy in Philadelphia, Pennsylvania. He also specializes in bioethics, faith development, positive psychology, diversity work, and the development of student leaders. He was chair of the Religion Department. After the 9/11 attacks, he created a national conference on "Understanding Islam."

Squire has served as chief pastor to thousands of people who make up the school community. He was a founding board member and counselor at the Marianist Counseling Center in Chester, Pennsylvania. He has served on the board of the Middleton Counseling Center in Bryn Mawr, Pennsylvania.

He holds degrees from West Chester University, Berkeley Divinity School at Yale University, and Duke University where he was the Jarvis Traveling Fellow to Duke from Berkeley. He was among the first in his family to attend college and values his work as a laborer in a steel mill to pay for his college education as one of the most valuable learning experiences of his life.

His first book, published in Spring of 2017, is *Watch Your Time: An Interfaith Spiritual and Psychological Journey*. He has developed an innovative approach to counseling called Lever Therapy for everyone who wants to help another in distress. That model is on his website, www.revsquirecounseling.com, as well as his blog. He still remains a counselor to those in need of assistance.

His second book, *The Times of My Life*, is a memoir and was published in the fall of 2019.

Table of Contents

For Vicki, Thaddeus, Meredith, Joanna, Adam, Courtney,
and Spencer

For the Episcopal Academy

For all those people who have raised awareness that
black lives matter

For all the medical community, first responders, essential
workers, and others who made a
difference in helping others during the pandemic

For all those who suffered loss during the pandemic

For all those who seek justice at home and in far-off lands,
paticularly those who are making the vaccines available
to all in need

For all who see the world as a global village and care for
the earth, our island home.

Acknowledgments

The *Shema* is at the heart of Judaism and Christianity. It also speaks to the importance of relationships in the religious experience. The word *Shema* is the Hebrew word, meaning, "to hear." Jesus is asked, "Which commandment is first of all?" Jesus answered, "The first is, hear O Israel: The Lord our God, the Lord is one; you shall love the Lord your God with all your heart, with all your soul, with all your mind, and with all your strength." The second is this, "You shall love your neighbor as yourself. There are no other commandments greater than these" (Mark 12:28–31).

When Harry Stack Sullivan, founder of the Interpersonal School of Psychiatry, was asked what made an individual mature, he didn't let a millisecond go by when he answered, "It is the ability to put another person first." A sacred goal that we have as human beings should be to help the people in the world to have a better life.

I want to acknowledge three people who have done the above in three different "times of my life." These three people share an important theme that relationships are important to them and they have the motivation to always put others first and empower the lives of those around them to make their good, better, and their better, the best that it could be.

First, there is David Spence who is one of my oldest friends. We went to school together from first grade through graduation from high school in a struggling working-class community. David wrote the foreword for my memoir, *The Times of my Life*. David was a gifted student. He became a chemical engineer in his professional life. There were times when I was struggling with a math or science problem in school. He would always take the time to help me out, and he did this without me asking. It was just part of who he was. He was patient in his providing help to me and any others who needed assistance.

Second, there is Richardson Merriman who is the chairman and founder of Pennsylvania Trust, now Fidelity Trust International of Pennsylvania, who has been a long-standing friend first during my days at the Episcopal Academy when he was a parent of one of my students. He is the very embodiment of an advocate. His support made it possible for me to start a robust bioethics program and a National Conference on Understanding Islam after 9/11. He also made it possible for a copy of my memoir to be sent to every Episcopal school in the nation. Rich is someone who is "all in" in his work, his life, his faith, and his friendship. Everyone should be blessed to have someone, such as Rich, in their life who said to me, "I support you, 100 percent!"

Third, is my newest friend, Dr. John Crosby, who received copies of my blog via email and would offer comments from time to time. Since my oldest friend wrote the foreword to my last book, I thought that it would be appropriate to ask my newest friend to write the foreword to this work, *This Too Shall Pass*. John is the author of *Built to Help Each Other,* with Richard Caruso.

John is the founding director of the Uncommon Individual Foundation. He has developed with his partner, Richard Caruso, a foundation that has cutting edge systems of mentoring others. Richard Caruso started Integra Life Sciences, the ground-breaking medical company that produced the first artificial skin for burn victims.

Prior to John's work with the Uncommon Individual Foundation for mentoring, he was the superintendent of schools in Pennsylvania for twenty years. Under his leadership in the Radnor School District, the *Wall Street Journal* and *Consumer Reports* wrote that it was one of the nation's best school districts. John's wife, Marlene, was a teacher at the Episcopal Academy.

These three individuals have helped those around them to strive to be the best that they could be, and I am grateful their efforts include me.

Foreword

This Too Shall Pass is a captivating book by the Rev. James R.
Squire, who recently retired after thirty-eight years as head chaplain
of Episcopal Academy, a prominent independent school on the
Main Line, twenty-two miles west of Philadelphia.

Eloquently written, instructive, and above all timely, it's a must-
read collection of 211 essays for those who want to be grounded
in the ethics of making good and just decisions. What's at stake
is your moral integrity and commitment of honoring your values.

Deep thought is needed in making decisions of right and wrong,
and Rev. Squire uses simple, straight forward language to show
the human struggle in making the best decisions. President Harry
Truman, whose presidency included the decision of dropping the
atomic bomb, said he had no trouble doing the right thing. He had
trouble knowing the right thing to do. Such momentous decisions
are not black and white, but cloaked in gray. With Jim's expertise
in ethics and bioethics, he cuts to the chase of how ethical decisions
depend on the specific circumstances of the right thing to do.

Jim Squire is a prolific writer and analyzes current events and
makes critical observations on political and cultural decisions
that are correct or terribly wrong. He encourages readers to think
more clearly and to make judgments that live up to their beliefs
and values. He covers the most important themes in this book,
including human nature, Black Lives Matter, as well as the trials
and tribulations of the pandemic and how to move forward through
such challenges.

His thirty-eight years of experience in teaching biblical studies,
ethics, and bioethics to Episcopal students, counseling parents,

faculty, students, and alumni and proclaiming the worth of a person's life in chapel talks, eulogies, and memorial services open our eyes to a life well lived. It compels us to mirror such lives so we reflect the same virtues and attributes that guide our moral and ethical compass.

Thinking deeply is lacking in magazines, newspapers, videos, television, and social media. Jim looks through his lens of expertise, and he also brings the wisdom of others to the table: Aristippus, Dietrich Bonhoeffer, C. S. Lewis, Martin Luther King Jr., Victor Frankl, Ellie Wiesel, John Stuart Mills, Jean-Paul Sartre, Friedrich Nietzsche, Thomas Hobbes, John Locke, Jean-Jacques Rousseau, St. Augustine, and others.

These writings blended with disciplines of philosophy, psychology, and theology helped Episcopal students explore the nature of interpersonal relationships and the concepts of love and justice that are the pillars of ethical thought. Rev. Squire's courses became some of the most popular and essential classes at Episcopal and provided students with a strong moral and spiritual foundation for their entire lives. Jim Squire wants your behavior to match your beliefs, particularly when others aren't looking. As Harvard professor and Pulitzer-Prize winner Robert Coles, in just *eight* words, summarizes his book, *The Moral Intelligence of Children,* "Do as I do, not as I say."

As a retired superintendent of Radnor Township School District, rated as one of the nation's best, and as the founding director for thirty-five years of the first nonprofit educational foundation solely devoted to mentoring, I am very interested in ethics, faith, and justice. I was hooked, and each morning when Jim posts his essay, it is the first thing I read. The titles are eye-catching: *Ethics and the Impeachment Decision; Justice, Kindness, Humility; An Ethical Guideline That Works to Create Justice; Lying in Politics; Bill and Melinda Gates; The Biology of Racism;* and many more listed in the Table of Contents.

Over his long career as head chaplain, Rev. Squire has become a beacon of light, encouraging young people, colleagues, and all who know him to find success and happiness in their lives. I was incredibly blessed to meet and have lunch with Jim Squire on May 13, 2021. After seeing the goodness of this man, I am proud to call him a good friend and one I intend to emulate. You will too when you read *This Too Shall Pass* and be inspired by the wisdom he imparts of faith, justice, and reason.

—*John C. Crosby, EdD*
May 17, 2021

Preface

This Too Shall Pass is what several religious traditions indicate was inscribed on the inside of the ring of Solomon as an example of universal wisdom. It is a truth that has empowered others for centuries. I wrote posts, including one about the title of this book, throughout the pandemic. I wasn't looking to put the posts in a book when I started. I was reflecting to myself and would share them with others about the pandemic, Black Lives Matter, politics, human nature, and the importance of faith.

I received an email one day from those who were on my email list that they were helped by what I had written. One of my former students wrote that it "was the only thing that he consistently reads," which was similar to feedback that I was getting from others. My friends encouraged me to develop a blog and to post the essays on Facebook so that others could be helped as well.

A member of my family, Meredith Rainey, who is a computer wizard, set up the technology for me to put up my posts on the Facebook social media platform. The posts were written throughout a terrible period where all of us tried to make some sense of everything that was going on around us. I never sat down with the thought that I should write something on any given day. I first had to be inspired by something that I read, heard, or experienced with another person.

During this period, I had several medical challenges. The procedures that influenced me the most were two hand surgeries that I thought would stop my ability to type on a computer. The cast left my fingers free, so I just struggled a lot at first with pain and getting the fingers to work and found that typing was like a form of physical therapy for my left hand, my dominant hand. All of this underscored a central philosophy that guides me that "life is to be enjoyed or learned from." Suffice it to say that I have learned a lot from this terrible year as I know that you have.

The posts are sequential in this book and not organized by theme. This was the way that I experienced these thoughts, as I made my way from one day to the next. I thought that it would be important to do it that way so that you could see how my thinking process was developing over time. Hence, you may see a very limited number of essays that repeat a theme or thought that was cited before.

I also have a theology that I never do anything, such as writing this book, that is not done in the interest of helping others. I thank all of those who have inspired me. I hope that this helps you, the reader, in other challenging times. The inspiration that we found on a daily basis living through this challenging time can also be universal in nature, and good for all time in every situation, such as the title of this book, *This Too Shall Pass.*

A Note to the reader: As indicated above this book contains a sequence of blogs that I wrote over the course of a year. In a way they were a journal of my thinking as we moved from one day to the next day during the pandemic. They are organized from the first written to the last in this book. You will find references to videos or online information on some of the posts. Please go to my website at www.revsquirecounseling.com where the posts are listed in the same sequential manner. There you will find on my blog the link to any of videos or online articles that are referenced in this book of posts.

Post 1.   Ring of Wisdom

The biblical record states that Solomon was the wisest of all men. The story that many know about him in gaining this recognition is found in 1 Kings 3:16–28. In this passage, Solomon must determine the real mother of a baby claimed by two women. He sent his servant to get a sword. He said that he would cut the child in half and give each woman half of the baby. One of the women pleaded, "Give the child to her!" Solomon responded, "You must be the mother!"

There is another story about Solomon's wisdom that is not as well known. Its origin has been speculated to come from several different possible sources. Some believe that its author was Rumi, a Persian poet, Islamic scholar, and Sufi mystic. Others feel that it is part of Jewish folk lore and was found first there. We know that Lincoln used the famous phrase included in Solomon's Ring story in an address before he became the sixteenth president of the United States.

I will paraphrase the story of "Solomon's Ring." Solomon's chief of the army was an arrogant man. As the story goes, Solomon gave him a task to introduce humility into the army chief's life. He asked him to find a ring with an inscription, "that would make happy people, sad and sad people, happy." (Spoiler alert) If you don't know the story, stop and think of a possible answer.

The officer came upon a merchant who was putting out his things to sell. He asked, "Have you ever heard of a magic ring that is inscribed with words that makes the happy wearer forget his joy and a brokenhearted man forget his sorrows?" The merchant replied, "Yes!" He then showed the officer the ring inscribed in it were the words, "This Too Shall Pass."

The inscription did as the king requested, making happy people sad and sad people happy. The inscribed words did something more. They spoke to the impermanence of life and that what was really important was to live life as though today were the last day of your life. The message of the inscription was also to realize that things and external acclaim are not as important as the people around us. Live in the moment! Focus your love on others!

Heraclitus, a Greek philosopher, offered a corollary to the inscription when he stated, "You can't step into the same river twice." You change and the river changes. That is the nature of life.

The 2020 winner of the Icon Award for the Peoples' Choice Awards was multi-talented Jennifer Lopez. She began by acknowledging the difficult journey for all of us this year. The COVID-19 virus touched every part of the fabric of the world. She went on to say (I paraphrase), "Before the pandemic, people were focused on what one could achieve as successes, and what awards could be won. People were obsessed with things. The pandemic taught me a lot, namely that your character and the people who you love and who love you are what is really important and what will last."

If there is one phrase that fits as a perfect theme to describe what we all could learn this year, it is what was inscribed in that ring requested by God's wise man, Solomon, "This too shall pass!" — both the good and the bad! Remembering that phrase could help us move through this year of struggle and disease because it is a universal truth that binds us all together.

Post 2.   Never Let a Crisis Go to Waste

In an article by Larry Platt in the *Philadelphia Citizen*, regarding developing an equitable work force, he quotes Warren Buffett who said, "When the tide goes out, you can see who is swimming with no shorts." A bad market, in essence, reveals bad business.

One of my favorite sayings is, "Never let a crisis go to waste! Learn from it." The metaphor was first used by Churchill. What if our shorts were our strengths and when they are off when the tide goes out (in our case a medical crisis), we can be left with only the picture of what embarrasses us, our self-perceived weaknesses.

Let's put our shorts, our strengths, on. You can do this by going to the Penn Center for Positive Psychology website and doing a questionnaire, the VIA Survey of Character Strengths. It will determine your strengths in rank order and describe them. It is free and will take you about thirty minutes. Then, once you know the top five, use them in your interactions. Pay attention to them. The website is loaded with other information that you may like to see.

Those who have read *The Times of My Life* know that positive psychology and this exercise are part of the ethics course that I taught. Students found the exercise to be very enlightening and empowering once they acted on their identified strengths and used them in daily life. They didn't allow them to go to waste. They became part of their decision-making and path through life.

"The Lord is my strength and my shield; my heart trusts in him, and he helps me" (Ps. 28:7).

Yesterday Vicki and I video streamed the worship service at St. David's Episcopal Church in Wayne. The worship streaming occurs on Sunday mornings at 9:15. Go to the church's website and you will see a link that will take you to the worship service.

Post 3. Why Do Some People Survive Hardship?

As we move through our time coping with the pandemic, let's consider some of the approaches that are mentioned on www.revsquire-counseling.com. There you will find a link to the book, *The Times of My Life*, and a description of Lever Counseling. I am currently reading Erik Larson's, *The Splendid and the Vile: A Saga of the Churchill Family, and Defiance During the Blitz*. Lives were at stake during the Blitz, as they are for us now with the virus. There was so much that was uncertain for the British, as it is for us now. When and where would the next bomb be dropped?

There are parallels between Larson's book and what I cover in my book. One example from my book, Logotherapy, is also seen in Larson's work. It was created by Victor Frankl who endured imprisonment in a camp during the Holocaust. When he was freed, he raised the question of why some survived and others didn't. Through countless interviews with survivors, he identified two things that would be important to us today to survive COVID-19. First, he noticed that the survivors of the camp had a sense of identity. They knew who they were. Second, they had a sense of destiny and could identify what it would be like when they were freed. Frankl also discovered that he and his fellow survivors remembered their loved ones, picturing them during better days.

During the Blitz, the British did the same thing. They had a clear identity of being both British, a national identity, and beyond that, their sense of personal identity. We should stand before a mirror and ask ourselves who we are and dream about what our future will hold, supported by memories of our loved ones. Having a sense of destiny or future is important. Let's consider the words of a wonderful hymn, "Be not afraid, I go before you always, come follow me, and I will give you rest."

Post 4.   Five to One

During this required time at home, we have the opportunity to reflect on things that are usually not part of our conscious thinking. Have you ever thought about how you make decisions? How many times do you say, "I did that because it felt right?" There are many factors that impact our decisions. One of the central issues involved in decision making is ethics, "Why do I do what I do?"

Two factors guide our ethical decision-making and these are not necessarily in our realm of consciousness. One involves our core personal value and the other involves our core interpersonal value.

Take a piece of paper and write down the ten things that get you up in the morning or what give you meaning and purpose in life. Try not to think about this. Do this by free association, so that you get the most honest answers. Now read through the list reflecting on each item. Next cross through five things that are expendable. Look at the remaining five and cross off three that you could live without. You are left with two. This should be a difficult choice between two important things that give you meaning and purpose in life. These things are what excite us as we start each day. Now, choose just one of the remaining statements. This one is your core personal value.

The other part of ethical decision-making is your core interpersonal value. This is what you value as the most important ingredient in your relationships. For example, you may choose "trust" or "kindness to others," as your most important interpersonal core value. During this time of being at home reflect on how these two values shape your decisions.

Post 5. A Post-Easter Reflection on Jesus, Richard Nixon, Elvis, and Avatar

What do the movies *Elvis, Nixon,* and A*vatar*, tell us about the experience of the disciples the days after Jesus' Resurrection? The scripture post-Easter is about who sees Jesus and who doesn't in their initial encounters with Him. Doubting Thomas embodies this theme of the need for "seeing and believing." He needs to see the holes in Jesus' hands before believing.

The movie, *Avatar* was released in 2009. The theme song was "I See You." One of the verses is:

I see you
Walking through a dream
I see you
A light in darkness breathing hope of a new life

Now I live through you and you through me, enchanting
I pray in my heart this dream never ends
I see me through your eyes.
Now I live through you and you through me.

This is what the disciples realized when Jesus appeared to them after the resurrection. They were seen by each other in a profound way, and they, in turn, saw who He was, the holy one. This is the power behind Christianity. That power enables us to see and be seen for who we are, our flaws and good things. What does this have to do with our daily lives?

One way this power is seen is in the fictional account of a real life encounter between Elvis and Nixon in a movie by that name released in 2016. Two of Elvis' friends accompany him on his journey to meet Nixon, as Elvis desires to request an FBI badge so that he can do some good in the world.

It was not the exchanges between Nixon and Elvis that got my attention, although those exchanges are laced with humor and memorable lines. Rather, it was an exchange between Elvis and his friend that caught my attention. Elvis is one of the most recognized figures around the world. As he tries to give his friend an expensive gift, the friend refuses it. Elvis states that everyone knows him as a singer, a phenomenon, a personality, but his friend knows him as the "Memphis Elvis." "You knew me before all of that. You know everything about me. You have seen it all! The other stuff doesn't count." It is a poignant moment.

There in the oval office, a symbol of worldly power, we see worldly power eclipsed by the importance of being seen and loved for who we are, warts and all. That is what the Resurrection has given us, a spiritual power. "I pray in my heart that this dream never ends." It doesn't. That dream is there for all time. A new vision, a new way of seeing, "I see me through your eyes," both now and in life eternal.

Post 6. The Tortoise and the Hare

The story of the tortoise and the hare is an excellent commentary on where we are today with COVID-19 and the Black Lives Matter Movement. We all know the fable of the tortoise and the hare. They race. The smart money would be on the hare as he is lightning fast and gets off to a fast start. The tortoise is slow but steady. During the race, the hare literally runs rings around the tortoise, but the tortoise wins because he is slow but steady to the end.

This image applies in an election or sports when we hear after a loss of a person who made a big splash or team but didn't know how to finish. They are good for the short run but not for the long haul. The importance of grit is well known, but not enough has been underscored by researchers about the long haul or comeback and its relationship to grit. I think there is something that has been left out. Referring back to the fable, it isn't how you start. It is how you finish, whatever the task may be. Let's link to grit the importance of pace and someone who is in it for the long haul. Let's begin to celebrate the "closer."

How many times in the Philly sports world or our own professional lives do people arrive on the scene with a lot of fanfare, bells, and whistles, who do well in the beginning but seem to run out of the ability to get the job done?

There is currently a contrast between the Black Lives Matter Movement and the time of COVID-19. Everyone thought that there would be a few local, if not global, protests. No one seemed to grasp that this was going to be a global phenomenon that, at this point in time, seems to be a movement for the long haul, possessing a fast start, then pace, and certain outcomes coming into view to make things more equal among the races in the end.

I write this as numbers spikes of the virus have occurred because areas have opened too soon and were filled with people who gathered in close proximity without masks as they couldn't wait to get outside with some declaring, "I've got to party!"

7

I would put my money on people, like our troops away from their families, John McCain in his five-year imprisonment, Anne Frank in her self-imposed hiding from the Nazis, who did the long haul. It is why we often hear about the teams that come from far behind to win. This is the reason why "Rocky" was such a hit for it slid into the national consciousness. He was a closer.

Clearly, with COVID-19 and Black Lives Matter, we are either part of the problem or part of the solution. Maybe we need a cause bigger than us to help us seek justice for all and a state of wellness for our nation and the world. Maybe the closer is what is best for a team or a group of people wanting something and about "we"— and not about "me."

Grit, pace, the long haul, and the closer are some of the secrets of success. Ask any runner who goes out too fast as he looks good out front but is pretty ugly at the finish line, when he is passed by someone who knew about these markers of success, such as pace, the long haul, and the closer. We have to choose between being a "flash in the pan" or a "closer."

Post 7.   August 18th

It is August 18th. This is a date that never goes by without my thinking way back to my high school football days. It is the date that we left for football camp at Camp Conrad Weiser. I always felt caught between dread and excitement, but it has given me a key to what really motivates me. It is about discovering a truth that has guided me and others throughout our lives for centuries.

I would do all the required summer training exercises, such as running and weightlifting, but that did not change my reality, I was a 5-foot, 10-inch, 121-pound lineman. My neighbor and teammate, Bernard Smondrowski, was a 6-foot, 6-inch, 230-pound tackle. We were quite a contrast, walking to practice each day. Today, we have a word to describe me—undersized. I was among the smallest players on the team. We took a beating. The spirit was willing, but the flesh was weak. For me, the spirit was willing, but there was not enough flesh to make a difference.

We were at camp far from home to create bonding and to go through three practices a day that were exercises in controlled violence. Bear Bryant, legendary football coach at Alabama, would have been smiling. I was injured during the camp and could hardly walk but returned to practice when we arrived home. Being unskilled and undersized is a deadly combination for a want-to-be offensive guard and defensive middle linebacker. No matter what I did, I would be relegated to the practice squad.

So, why did I continue? I don't think it had anything to do with grit, resilience, or perseverance. I know, without a doubt, thinking back on it every August 18th since then, that it had to do with my desire to be a part of something that I valued, that was bigger than me, where I felt that the team was more important than anything that I did. There was nothing pleasurable about it, but I did get the respect of the team as they always pulled for me. I graduated valedictorian of my high school class and was surprised to receive the scholar athlete award as well, since I never got off the practice squad.

What does this have to do with the pandemic and the Black Lives Matter Movement? Can you imagine Jesus' disciples being frustrated by the requirement to wear masks, to social distance, and to wash their hands to bring their message to the world? Can you imagine an essential worker saying, "This is just too hard?" Can you imagine a member of the Naval Academy saying that he just couldn't comply to be in the military of our nation? I was a harsh judge, reading in today's paper about the hundreds of students who attended a party at a Georgia college before school started with no adherence to healthy guidelines. I have had it with those who cry "personal freedom" and "nobody is going to tell me what to do. I am going to party." It is the same for those who criticize the protesters. They share something with the looters, and people who have chosen violence.

I have not seen the real issue until now, as I sit here and think about what August 18 means to me. I believe that the refusal to wear masks and adhere to the guidelines, the people who loot and are using this as a vehicle for personal thrill and gain, and those who criticize what the *real* protesters are trying to do have never had an experience that made them see that the welfare of the group is more important than the concerns of the individual. I don't believe that they have had an experience that has significantly impacted them to sacrifice for others. Such an experience can set a pattern for life and can create a place where true joy can be found. I guess I should feel sorry for them. I know that I didn't understand that pattern when I first arrived at Camp Conrad Weiser. The important thing is that having that date pop up every year guarantees that I know it now.

Post 8. Churchill and Cuomo Are Examples of Great Leadership

I was reading the *Philadelphia Citizen* newsfeed when I was struck by two articles. I will send out the second article tomorrow to keep this short. First, in Larry Platt's article, he recommended Erik Larson's book on the life of Winston Churchill during the blitz, as a great read *The Splendid and the Vile*: *A Saga of the Churchill Family, and Defiance During the Blitz*. It is a great read particularly in a time of crisis with COVID-19.

I mentioned Larson's book in an earlier post. Platt's article centered on how great leaders, such as Churchill and Andrew Cuomo, are able to use language effectively. It was Cuomo who said, "My mother is not expendable." Cuomo balances human life with the scientific knowledge that would point to approaches to deal with COVID-19.

Platt went on to quote President John F. Kennedy, "Churchill mobilized the English language and took it into war." Churchill's memorable words speak to challenges and hope. They underscore that powerful words are just as important for all of us in this time of quarantine. When I read Churchill's words to the English people during the blitz, I feel as though I could take on anything.

Google those words and see what I mean. Words matter. As Sartre, the existentialist philosopher, put it in his play, "No Exit," we can lift up and tear down with words. He used the expression that "heaven and hell are (the words spoken by) the others." What power! What responsibility!

The author of the Gospel of John, the last gospel written, must have had his world and ours in mind when he began with, "In the beginning was the word, and the word was with God, and the word was God" (John 1:1–3).

Post 9.   The Death of George Floyd

Personal and Institutional Racism

I think there are specific things that we should be doing to move forward as a nation. Flowery language will not change a thing. Specific language will.

Adopt the Stanford Rule. There was a study done at Stanford University. Teachers were told that a gifted group of students (Group A) were academically challenged. In another group, teachers were told that an academically challenged group (Group B) were gifted. Group A performed at a low level, and Group B performed much higher than expected. How people are seen is what they become. Whoever you see as your enemy will become your enemy and whoever you see as your friend will become your friend. Change how you see "the other."

The Golden Rule has been absent. Do for others as you would want them to do for you. This is what love and justice look like. What specific gestures reflect those two pillars of ethics in our lives?

Empathy counts. Regard everyone you encounter as though they are a member of your family or the human family. Think this is impossible? No. If you repeat empathetic behavior over and over (a habit of the heart), you will begin seeing people that way. Perhaps Aristotle's great thought gift to us was this idea.

All anger is based on a failed expectation. Get clear expectations from the protestors and the agents of the government. Talk about what is doable.

During this past week, police officers were killed or injured. The head of the Juvenile Law Center in Philly, when kneeling with her hands behind her back, was approached by a police officer who sprayed her directly in her face with pepper spray. During another TV moment where a member of the press was filming the protest, a policeman went out of his way to knock the person down in a violent fashion. This reflects a small number of police. Task forces are fine, but it would be preferable to do a better job of screening applicants and to train police officers in de-escalation techniques. Derek Chauvin had eighteen complaints against him that were based on prior offenses while he remained on the force. The police union needs to buy into this on the front end of hiring decisions. Unions can work for or against the good.

The debate this week about punishment for Chauvin and the other officers who were present and did not intervene is a source of anger. Some want *Lex Talionis*, which doesn't mean an eye for an eye or retaliation. It means the punishment needs to fit the crime. Focus on justice. In ethics, failure to act to right a wrong is seen as a choice to act in the wrong way. There is no ethical neutral ground.

People pay attention to what you do. People remember how they felt after an exchange. If you were called a "thug," how would that make you feel? You wouldn't forget it. If you were a police officer risking your life on a daily basis, and someone called you a killer, how would you feel? You certainly would not forget it. No one wants to be dominated. But let's consider the looters.

There is a saying in group dynamics that crowds make good-intentioned people, such as the peaceful protesters, better, and bad-intentioned people, such as the looters, worse. The gap between the rich and poor in our nation is greater than at any other time in history. This gap plus the pandemic emphasized awareness of racism and classism, and COVID-19 drove the looters to unlawful actions. They knew what they were doing was wrong.

Unlike some of the past marches and protests after the taking of black lives, this one feels much different. The words that come quickly to mind are "pay me now or pay me later." We are running out of "later."

You don't die the day that your heart stops. You die the day when you refuse to do the right thing.

Don't hold up a Bible for all to see. Hold it in your heart for all you do!

Post 10. An Honorary Doctorate

I just saw in the news that a yellow Labrador retriever, named Moose, has received an honorary doctorate degree from Virginia Tech Vet School for his work as a therapy dog, helping those in need of psychological support for over 7,500 counseling sessions.

I, too, have a therapy dog, a yellow lab, by the name of Sadie! I often let people know that she is a therapy dog because after her initial greeting of you, you will need therapy. She is six but acts like a puppy. She can literally jump high enough to kiss your forehead, which she has done as she has unbounded energy. She loves people and food. If I forget to keep an eye on my sandwich, she will eat it quickly. She doesn't bark much, so if a burglar entered our house, she would lick him into submission.

Sometimes, she doesn't come when I call her repeatedly, but when she hears the crackle of the pretzel bag when she is far away, she is instantly by my side, sitting, looking at me with her beautiful brown eyes, and I give in! When I leave the room and come back, her greeting is like I have been away for a year. She's a mystery, as she will dive under the water on the Chesapeake but has to be forced to go out in the rain.

Maybe we can learn something from Sadie that would warrant a doctorate degree—unconditional positive regard, joyful in every way, and when I am having a bad day, I take one look at her and then I smile. She immediately forgives and forgets immediately any injustice that comes her way. She doesn't harbor grudges! She won't tolerate anyone who raises their voice, as she is immediately there to act as a mediator, even if it is not a fight.

A doctorate degree? Maybe that is not enough! Certainly thoughts, however, to keep in mind during our lives during these COVID-19 days.

Post 11.   The Parable of the Light Switch, Part 1

We recently had the worst storm that either Vicki or I could remember encountering. Wind and rain and massive damage in our neighborhood included trees down and some limbs hitting roofs. There was debris everywhere. It looked like the London Blitz. As I understand it, it was a sheer wind coming in sideways, which happens on rare occasions.

We went to the basement and could hear everything that was happening. We lost power and were told that it would be out for three days. We were feeling a bit like Job. First, we had COVID-19, then the killing of George Floyd and the looting, and we were thinking, "What else could occur?" And it did, a storm the likes of which we had not seen before. Since there were trees across our drive, there was no outside contact, no cell phone, TV, or internet.

My first thoughts were self-centered in the form of "Woe is me." I don't know when it started, but quickly my attitude and prayer life changed too, "How did the people who have endured the worst storms here in our nation and around the globe get through their challenges with the weather?"

Puerto Rico and Hurricane Katrina first came to mind. Then a change occurred in me to ask the more important question, "Why not me?" With a change in attitude, it changed the whole experience for me to asking how I can help and reaching out to people in need with real problems." It was empowering.

We spent more time than usual without power and in darkness. Something very profound happened. As I would enter darkened rooms, I would turn on the light switch. I did this for three days and began to feel stupid for doing this. We had water in our basement where I committed the final stupid action. I plugged the wet vac into the outlet, and it didn't turn on. My wife started to laugh hysterically. I realized then that we had no power.

This light switch issue provided me with one of the most important insights that I have seen in moving forward during difficult times. Keep in mind that Jesus taught, for the most part, in parables for attitudes and actions that were very important for him. They were words for us to live by. I will tell you what I learned from this issue with the light switch in my next post. Could you write a parable using this story regarding what you feel to be essential in life?

Post 12. The Parable of the Light Switch, Part 2

I am following up on the parable of the light switch that I introduced in my last post. We constantly turned the switch on in the dark when there was no power during a recent storm. This habit is like any habit of the heart. It is fixed in us when it is done over and over. What brings the habit of turning on the switch to have light or goodness in our life is power. For me, that power is Jesus. For you, it may be something else. The important thing is for you to name it!

Second, this parable speaks loudly about how you view the way life is or reality. My initial response to damage after the storm was "Why me?" This response leads to despair. But then I was reminded of a book title written by Gilda Radner, a comedian on *Saturday Night Live*, who was battling ovarian cancer. The title was *It Is Always Something*. That view connects us to the way life really is and to hope. I know that I am at my best when this attitude is front and center for my spiritual eye to see.

Being in the dark after the storm can leave you feeling isolated. COVID-19 did this for many, as well. Make whatever effort is necessary to stay connected. I learned something important that I found in working with a large number of people over a lengthy period. There was research to support the importance of connection. Patricia Hersch wrote *A Tribe Apart*. She studied a group of eight teenagers for three years and came up with an important finding that would apply to adults as well.

If you have just one adult friend (ideally several) to talk to about a concern, you will be fine in navigating the seas of adolescence. It can be a parent, grandfather/grandmother, coach, teacher, and so forth. She didn't emphasize adult connections, but I have seen a good number of peers can do this with a trusted adult(s) as well. If you are married, it could be your spouse. You have to have at least one.

Remember the AT&T slogan that improved their marketing: "Reach out and touch someone!" It is a slogan that goes well with "It is always something."

Post 13.   Let's Be Aware of the Quo

Part 1 *Quid Pro Quo*

During my years of taking Latin, a course that I loved, I knew that it was helping me with English grammar and definitions of words, for there are strict grammar rules in Latin and many root words in the English language are based on that ancient language. But its importance seemed to stop there, until now. Then a Latin phrase, *Quid Pro Quo,* seemed to dominate political discussion during President Donald Trump's impeachment trial. The phrase means "I will do this for you if you will do something for me." It was an integral part of the national conversation. Who knew that I would be hearing so much Latin in our national discussions?

Our relationships with others have become more transactional in nature. There is a school of counseling that I studied that is even called transactional analysis. That is a different way of looking at "I will do this for you if you do something for me." Think about how much you and I do this in our relationships. I think that the ultimate form of relationships doesn't have the "*Quo*" when we act and expect nothing in return. "No strings attached." How often is that how our relationships work? I would suggest that you and I do more to promote "no strings attached," as our culture is full of transactions.

Let's take a look at our prayer life, whatever your religious orientation. I find myself praying to God with the transactional approach usually in times of great trouble. I bargain. "Lord God, if you just would do this one thing for me, I promise that I will ..."

There is that phrase in our culture, "There are no atheists in foxholes." Since gratitude shapes our prayers and actions in the strongest way, let's pay more attention to our prayers that begin with "Thank you." For that matter let's increase those "thank you(s)" in our daily conversations. I think that it would make a great difference for the better in our daily lives. Remember when your mother taught you to "always say please and thank you." She knew what she was talking about.

Quid Pro Quo was the foundation of evolutionary biology where cooperation was needed to survive. Our whole nature of evolution couldn't have occurred with only "survival of the fittest."

Part 2 The Death of George Floyd Contrasted with Denzel Washington's Interaction

There is one place where *Quid Pro Quo* helps us in extraordinary ways. It is the basis of many moral codes. "Do unto others as you would want them to do unto you." This is a form of transaction and one that is needed in our nation at the moment more than ever.

Equality for all is our goal. However, that has to go hand-in-hand with how we treat one another. I would call this a sacred transaction. Who could say that George Floyd was being treated the way that the police officer would like to be treated? Who would like to have someone kneeling on our neck after we are thrown to the ground and have our friends just look and do nothing? I bet that never crossed their mind. That is a major part of the problem for how different that arrest would have been if honoring Mr. Floyd would be their first inclination and not a distant thought.

If you think this is naïve, watch the video and Denzel Washington's interactions in an arrest, and you will see how it should be done. It is a sacred transaction.

"Denzel Washington's Intervention Video" can be found on my blog on my website under the title of "Let's Be Aware of the Quo."

Post 14. Pockets

The world has seen the killing of George Floyd multiple times. He was a black man who was killed by Derek Chauvin, while his fellow officers were watching. It was the nature of the killing that added to the sheer horror of the event. As many times as I watched it on the news, there was something else that was horrific in the killing of George Floyd.

Finally, it dawned on me. It was that Chauvin's hands were in his pockets. For me, this communicated two things. We put our hands in our pockets when we are watching something in a casual manner that is not important. It was a stance that we take when there is not much on the line, just another day at the office. It was a though he was just taking a break from important police work. Second, it communicated that Chauvin was in control. It reminded me of that moment in our youth when we learned to ride a bike, and we shouted, "Look, Mom, no hands." We got this riding the bike thing down and under control.

When I thought about it, I don't think that when I was talking with someone where there was a lot on the line that I or the other person had their hands in their pockets. There is a whole school of thought referred to as nonverbal communication where the person's body language can tell you a great deal about what the other person is thinking and feeling.

Casual and controlled gestures by Chauvin makes this crime more heinous. If we add to this the suffocation of Mr. Floyd, we are in a whole new dimension of evil. When dealing with end-of-life issues in an ethics course that I taught, the question would be raised, "What is the worst way that any of us would want to die?" The response, for the most part, was to struggle to get that last breath. That phrase, "I can't breathe!" takes on a whole new meaning.

Post 15. Coffee, Decision-Making, Black lives Matter, and the Pandemic

I learned from an Episcopal Academy parent that Todd Carmichael, Founder and CEO of La Colombe Coffee, would be a great speaker for our community to hear, particularly as it relates to a different way of making decisions. I invited him to come and speak. He got off to a right start by bringing me a box of different kinds of his gourmet coffee. He knew that I love coffee! Todd is a businessman, adventurer, an agent of social justice, and a modern-day guy who seems to be more like Indiana Jones than the more traditional successful businessman. He is the first American to complete a solo trek across Antarctica to the South Pole with no assistance, capturing the World Speed Record in a total time of thirty-nine days, seven hours, and forty-nine minutes.

He had the community in rapt attention as he described his many adventures, exhibiting a model for how to live every moment of your life with gusto. He included the reason that I brought him in, namely how he made decisions on the ice as well as the business world, his personal life, and as a champion of social justice. He said everyone sets goals at some time in their life. It is obvious he wanted to arrive safely at the South Pole. But he indicated that no one thinks about setting a key specific mark of when to stop or change course. People tend to barrel forward without thinking when a change of direction is what is needed. Changing and clarifying the new direction can be more important than anything in reaching the ultimate goal.

His wife, Lauren Hart, sang the National Anthem before Flyers games. She had been diagnosed with Non-Hodgkins Lymphoma. They agreed that he should go ahead with his quest to set a land record to reach the South Pole by walking across Antarctica. There were several reasons that he identified that he would stop and change course or come home. He contacted Lauren every night by cell phone. If her cancer returned, he would immediately come home.

Factoring in specific items for when we would change course means we would no longer move forward in a period of "drift." You don't wait long with no change to have clearer expectations to reset to get to the identified goal.

The Black Lives Matter movement needs to ask themselves what they want in specific terms. They have the world's awareness, but what do you want with specific demands that can be addressed at a national level to get a win for the movement and the nation to talk and negotiate. We want justice to be too general. What does that look like in specific terms? That is what John Lewis did that ultimately led to the Civil Rights Act.

The approach to saving lives in the pandemic needs to be approached differently. We are just drifting through a daily progression of data and increased death. We need a negotiation where national leaders say when we reach X, we need to change course, such as required masks, social distance requirements, and handwashing and limiting the number of people who could gather together. It has to be the law of the land. *Put teeth in the course change*. This should have happened long ago. COVID-19 is not going to just go away!

If you love the taste of coffee, check out La Colombe. After his address, many members of the community told me that they never thought about decision-making the Carmichael Way. Time for our leaders "to be like Todd." The stakes are higher and more perilous than a land record trek to the South Pole.

Post 16.   Are Golfers the Most Truthful People in the World?

I don't play golf, but there is something that we can learn from the better angels that walk from hole to hole. Dan Ariely is the author of *The Truth About Dishonesty: How We Lie to Everyone Especially Ourselves*. He dives deeply into truth and lies.

He writes about the 1925 US Open. The golfer, Bobby Jones, noticed that his ball moved ever so slightly as he prepared for his shot from the rough. No one saw, no one would ever have known, but he called the stroke on himself and went on to lose the match. When people discovered what he'd done and reporters began to flock to him, Jones famously asked them not to write about the event, saying, "You might as well praise me for not robbing banks." The point was that Bobby Jones would have known. Unfortunately, the culture doesn't encourage this kind of thinking, particularly among politicians who move from insider trading to spending government money on nongovernment things.

Ariely makes several key points. We assume that others are telling the truth because that takes less energy to do, but if a person has a reputation as a liar or cheater, we assume the opposite. We find ourselves caught in a dilemma where "we want to feel good about ourselves but also benefit from dishonest behavior." Simply put, what is the cost/risk/benefit analysis of our actions. We lie to ourselves and others with "little white lies." The truth may not seem as exciting, so we add value-added examples to our stories.

We also don't tell others how we really feel about what they are wearing. This would defy social graces that have us avoid saying what will make another feel badly.

There are two ways that can help us come down on the side of truth. Ariely did a study that people who read the Ten Commandments before an opportunity to cheat seldom did so, compared to a control group who did not read the Ten Commandments. He is a great advocate of having short phrases that are quickly reviewed in our minds before we are tempted to lie, such as "Honesty is the best policy," or if your school has an honor code to write the required statement, "I will not lie, cheat, or pass someone else's work on as my own" at the top of your test.

Second, there is a phrase that I came across years ago called "O happy guilt." It was used first during the medieval ages but is certainly true today. We would do anything to avoid guilt, rejection, and vulnerability. Guilt can be a powerful force in having us tell the truth or not to cheat. Unfortunately, we have a counterthought in place that works against happy guilt. "Everybody does it, so I must do it to make things equal and fair."

My father used an expression that helps to bolster the short phrase and O happy guilt solutions to lying or cheating. He was a man with a sixth-grade education and a Ph.D. in how to live doing the hard right and not the easy wrong. He would say, "Your name is all that you have at the end of the day. Don't do anything to smear it."

Post 17.   Gratitude Is the Key

We are living in uncertain times as we fight against the Coronavirus. Much has been written about it, including the recommended size of groups and distance to keep from one another. We are asked to stay at home. We need to also think about how we support one another and a key ingredient to make our way forward. That ingredient is gratitude even in these worst of times. It is also important to know how we should talk with one another in a way that helps others.

I have two sources that may help you with the gratitude and helping another piece. My website (1) gives help in making it possible to live through these times and how to help one another in conversation, and (2) I spoke at the burial service for Joanne Bagnell about gratitude on March 7, 2020 at the Episcopal Academy. She is the mother of Bill Bagnell, '82, an alumnus.

Thank you, Joanne

Thank you is said to be the greatest prayer that we can say to one another, to God, and His son our Lord, Jesus Christ. It is the basic statement of gratitude. Bill, her son, wanted to make this service today a celebration of Joanne and a big thank you to what she meant to him and so many others.

Gratitude is the basis for everything that is good as well as everything that is holy in ethics, psychology, and theology. That is the starting point for the good life that Joanne led, the good moral life.

I have talked with Bill about his mother over the years, and he shared with me notes that he received recently after her death. The notes, sometimes with different words, described her as someone who lived Episcopal Academy's stripes, our values, which are self-control, faith, honesty, kindness generosity, gratitude, courage, and sportsmanship, particularly on the golf course. She was also tough and patriotic.

Thank you, Joanne

One person referred to her in a note as being elegant, and I want to stop here and look at that characteristic a bit more closely. She had such a presence experienced most vividly felt when she would be talking about Bill or her beloved Reds.

Bill was a "bit edgy," they are her words, not mine. When Joanne and I would talk about that aspect of him or other things that he was doing or not doing, I felt that I was with someone with the presence of a very famous person such as a movie star, a politician, her personal friend Barbara Bush, or perhaps royalty, someone who was important in the public domain. She didn't try to be this way. That is who she was. It came by her naturally. She could be no other.

I chose the beatitudes as a reading for the Gospel today because of that verse, "Blessed are the meek for they shall inherit the earth" (Matt. 5:5). It is not what you think. Meekness does not mean weakness. When I was on the staff of St. James Parish, Montego Bay in Jamaica, some years ago during the summer, the people would describe Queen Elizabeth with the proclamation, "She meek," meaning they were quick to say she is royalty. Think of Joanne and immediately you can feel her elegant, if not royal, presence.

Thank you, Joanne

Joanne lost the love of her life, Reds Bagnell, too young. She never married again. Reds set a high standard. I was out of the country when I learned of Joanne's death. I told Bill that the first thing I did was to go to my computer and look up Reds Bagnell, running back par excellence from Penn, one of the best in the nation. I watched a video of him running seventy-four yards down the field, weaving in and out of the opposition, and scoring a touchdown against Navy.

When I finished watching, I thought to myself what a strange thing to do. What was the source of that action? My thoughts and prayers should just be about Joanne. I did it because Joanne and Reds were inextricably linked. I don't think that she was aware of how much she referenced him in our conversations.

In a letter to Bill on his thirty-fifth birthday, Joanne indicated, "I know that I speak for myself and your dad." She went on to say, "A more loyal, loving, caring, decent son I could not have wished to have. Since I have been alone, your attention and energies have doubled. That's been a very big factor in my survival without my sweetheart. Happy birthday, son! I see so much of Reds in you (always her reference point). I love you very much."

Mom

Meekness in its original meaning meant, among other things, to "accept the hand that you are dealt," not to like it but to accept it. We see that meekness and gratitude again in her own words in a letter to Bill, perhaps the biggest takeaway that she gives us as a gift today of her life. Her words, "With every great love or pleasure comes pain with the loss of it, but it's worth it," gratitude for what she had, and meekness, accepting the hand she was dealt.

That's something this elegant lady had in her soul each and every day of her life.

Meek—gratitude
Thank you, Joanne Bagnell
Thank you, Francis Reds Bagnell
Together forever. Together forever
In internal life with our Lord. Amen

Post 18.   Mssssssssssssssssssss. Engle

During this time of COVID-19 and Black Lives Matter protests, there is a quotation from Dr. Martin Luther King Jr. that appears quite frequently in the media, "I am convinced that men hate each other because they fear each other. They fear each other because they don't know each other. They don't know each other because they don't communicate with each other. They don't communicate with each other because they are separated from each other."

It was a Friday afternoon, after completing co teaching a course on diversity with our Director of Diversity, Courtney Portlock. We finished a two-week deep dive into the issues regarding racism and the other "isms." We ended by taking the class to see the movie, *Selma*.

When I returned to the office that Friday, I received a phone call from a representative of the fiftieth reunion class, who told me that the unanimous choice of the class was Clemmie Engel to address the Alumni Day Chapel. Among many things, she is transgender, an award-winning attorney, and someone honored by the LGBTQ community. This all-male class was very fond of Clemmie, as she was a great scholar, athlete, and classmate. The person who called me went on and on in glowing terms about her. I asked him to introduce Clemmie at the Chapel service with the same glowing terms. *I did this for I believe that all the "isms" are removed once you get to know someone. They are no longer a label but become a person you know and value.*

A few weeks before Clemmie spoke, the Vestry and I had Joan Mulholland speak in Chapel about social justice and the Civil Rights Movement. She is the white woman, who was photographed with black people at a Woolworth lunch counter with ketchup being poured over her head. She was beaten and berated. She took a stand and paid a price, including her parents disowning her. Her theme was "Civil rights is something that should never be taken for granted."

A few weeks later, Clemmie was introduced by the representative from the Fiftieth reunion class at the Alumni Chapel that underscored how she was unanimously chosen by her classmates. Clemmie picked up where Joan left off with the beginning of the Gay Rights Movement at Stonewall. Clemmie also spoke about her struggles as an attorney, such as when one judge who always asked her in front of the courtroom the question, "Is Mssssssssssssss Engle ready?"

There were some in the school community that were not happy with me having Clemmie speak. I invited them to come and hear what she had to say. When she finished, there was a standing ovation by those gathered in the Chapel. I could see that some members were seated in protest.

Two things in diversity work: (1) Always take a stand but listen carefully and respectfully to those who disagree with you, and (2) Is everyone paying a price? What is the price that you and I are paying? Is it worth it? Is it making the world a better place?

Clemmie's video can be found on my blog on my website under the title "Mssssssssssssss. Engle"

Post 19.   Don't Throw the Baby Out with the Bath Water

"Don't throw the baby out with the bath water." It means keep what is good and get rid of what is bad. I read Larry Platt's article, "Defund the FOP," in the *Philadelphia Citizen*, and I said, "That's the answer" (Full disclosure: I think the police are courageous and caring). Get rid of the police unions and keep the police. Are unions good or bad? They are both. I have experience with unions, which I recounted in my memoir, *The Times of My Life*, reflecting on this.

When I was in tenth grade, my father had a crippling stroke. It took a year before he returned to work. He was a member of the Meat Cutters Union. If he wasn't a member of that union, I don't know how we would have survived. However, the sixty percent of his salary that he earned for disability wasn't a lot! When I worked during the summer at a steel mill to pay for college, everyone had to join the union. I still have the badge to prove it. I made lots of money. Yes, the work was brutal. The mill closed as the workers' union made excessive demands on management. Later in life, when I was talking to the owner on the mill, he indicated that when the workers arrived for work and the gates were closed and locked, they asked why. The mill closed because of the union demands.

When I was substitute teaching in the Philadelphia School System, one of the schools that I was in was also the school of the leader of the union. It was as though I were an undercover reporter. I never saw him doing any planning for class, but I did hear a lot of conversation in the faculty lounge. The talk was not about making students' lives better. It was about teachers making more money (Full disclosure: I don't believe that there *is* a salary that is too high for a teacher.).

Platt writes about several models of where the police and communities are working to make things better where they honor one another. It is called "Ethical Policing Is Courageous." The one that we have heard the most about is in Camden, New Jersey. They disbanded the union first. There are similar programs in New Orleans and Eugene, Oregon.

Derek Chauvin had seventeen complaints against him for excessive force and suspect behavior before he killed George Floyd. Garrett Rolfe had twelve complaints against him for excessive force and suspect behavior before killing Rayshard Brooks. Want to guess why they could be excessive for so many times that establishes a pattern?

"In the meantime, you can pass as many bans on chokeholds as you like, but as long as police unions control how bad acts are or are not dealt with, you won't be transforming many para military organizations. Because, as it stands now, police unions still have political clout. If you protest anything start with that. No wonder we have the Guardian Civic League, a Union of Black Officers.

If you were black, would you want to pay dues to the police FOP (Fraternal Order of Police)?" — Larry Platt, "Defund the FOP," *The Philadelphia Citizen*.

Post 20.   The Student Teaches the Teacher about Learning

The issue of waiting comes into focus, as we consider the Black Lives Matter movement and the pandemic. First, let's consider waiting and the pandemic. There is an oft-quoted experiment known as the Marshmallow Experiment, which was done at Stanford that studied the power of waiting. The design is simple. A marshmallow is put in front of a young child. The child is told that if he can wait to eat it, he will get two later on. The experiment revealed that people who could wait have more success in life. There is something about that experiment that always bothered me, and I could never figure out why.

Connor Boyle was a senior warden of the Student Vestry at the Episcopal Academy where he worked with me in leading the other members of the Student Vestry to shape the moral culture of the school by planning and leading worship services. He is now a researcher at Penn, in the Department of Medical Ethics and Health Policy. He co-authored an article with Ezekiel J. Emanuel who is vice provost of the Global Initiatives at Penn. It explored the issue of waiting and appeared in July 28, 2021's *Philadelphia Inquirer*.

When you are the product of a struggling community as I was in my youth, you are destined to see everything through the lens of class whether you like it or not.

The last paragraph of their article opened my eyes as to what was missing for me in the Marshmallow experiment. Connor and his supervisor wrote, "Appreciating the full arc of the Marshmallow experiment means not only choosing to endure a little longer but working to help Americans for whom the choice to wait is most difficult." Those with financial resources have an easier time waiting than someone who is wondering if funds for the next meal and housing will arrive.

I called Connor this morning and thanked him for solving the problem that I had with the Stanford experiment, that class and money can influence waiting. Yes, I told him I was bursting with pride to have a former student tell me what I found missing.

There is irony in the opinion section of today's *Inquirer*. Below Connor's article there is an article by Will Bunch entitled, "We Can No Longer Wait." The article centers on the lack of swift justice for Breanna Taylor. It has been months since her death. The three police officers who were involved in her death are still going to work in their blue uniforms. The Reverend Dr. Martin Luther King said, "Injustice anywhere is a threat to justice everywhere."

Connor's message can be found on my blog on my website under the title of "The Teacher Teaches the Teacher About Learning".

Post 21.   Honorable People Shape Us

Ever since I was a teenager, I have heard the expression, "You can measure the character of a person by the friends that he keeps." My experiences in life tell me that is true. Good people make good-intentioned people better. It is the basic dynamic of any support group. We have the "Swamp" in Washington with more former members of the current administration convicted of high crimes than in another other administration in the history of the Presidency.

Let me offer two optimistic examples to counter the Swamp and to demonstrate that expression from my adolescence.

I was asked to be part of an evaluation team at the Gilman School in Maryland. We spent four days there investigating all aspects of the school. I titled my report, "The Four Quarters." I would go running every day that we were there late in the day. I would change in the locker room and then head out for the open road. There were four quarters on the bench where I changed. Those same quarters were still there at day four. I met with the senior students, and I asked them about those four quarters. Their universal response was heart-warming. Gilman is a high school lacrosse powerhouse. There are expensive lacrosse sticks left all over the place.

The spokesman for the group said, "We are not perfect, but there is an unstated rule here at our school. No one touches anything that doesn't belong to them. Nothing is ever stolen." That idea led to powerful ethical action. Those four quarters would be on that bench until the rightful owner retrieved them.

Second, honor codes had their beginning in the military academies for what should be an obvious reason. If you were on the battlefield and your life depended on your fellow soldier doing what he said he would do, you wouldn't have time to second guess him. Likewise, the honor code of never leaving anyone behind spoke, in concrete terms, to how each soldier would conduct the business of war and underscore the importance of every human life. I would risk my life for you. There is another part to their honor codes that underscore the importance of honesty. You will not lie, cheat or steal nor *will you tolerate anyone who does*. People have been expelled from the service academies not because they cheated but because they knew someone who did and did not make that dishonesty known to the Honor Committee. That is hard to do, but what is harder is going to war, thinking that you may have a dishonest person having your back who may or may not be good to his word.

My oldest son attended Princeton University. Princeton has one of the first honor codes in the nation established in 1893. When you receive the "book," which describes the code and when the student signs off on it, you know that you are entering a school that prides itself on honesty. You promise not to cheat on examinations, tests, or quizzes that are conducted in your classes.

That's the type of person we should want to be around. Too bad some Washington politicians haven't discovered those words that were first said to me when I was a teenager!

31

Post 22. How To Be An Anti-Racist

I have just finished examining the work of Ibram X. Kendi who wrote, *How to be an Anti-Racist*. He was a professor at American University and has moved to Boston University and Harvard to continue his work on racism. Why did a book about racism immediately take me to a course that I took at St. George's College in Jerusalem? One evening we had the chief rabbi of the area talk about the history of the Jewish people in Israel. The next night we had a PLO officer talk about the history of the area from the Palestinian perspective. There was no common ground in understanding the history. Each saw it differently. How can you have peace with that as the background? They agreed on very little of the pertinent information.

The same basic issue is true for the Black Lives Matter movement. A lack of common ground is true for this movement as well.

Kendi's point is that we need a common definition of racism. "Right now, racism is limited to what one person does or says to another. Racism needs to be seen as racist policies that lead to racial inequity that is substantiated by racist ideas." That has to be a larger part of the discussion as important as the person-to-person exchange is. Once that is completed, we can make significant progress. What I have taught is that ideas always precede action as a basic tenet of ethics.

He makes the case for two kinds of racism. Segregationists believe black people are inherently inferior by nature. People who believe in "assimilating" black people believe that black people are inferior because of nurture, having been raised in broken, low-income homes. Liberals believe that you can civilize black people by nurturing them to get out of these broken homes and join the middle and upper class. He also indicates that middle and upper-class black people make it difficult for the vast majority of black people, for white people can say, "If they made it, so can you."

He also deals with the issue that stops the racial movement from moving forward. It is the following logic: If I am a racist, I am not a good person. We know that the overwhelming number of us are good white people. Even he has racist ideas moving about in him. Anti-racism asks that we try to "do something" about the racial systems in place, like making sure that we vote and many more.

Those are basically his ideas, but here are mine with which he would agree as the heart of the problem. It is classism that is also based on human nature. We like to give a little and get a lot. We like to hold on to our "stuff," aka money and not give it to others. We are competitive. These are generalizations, but I think hold true for a good many white people. If this is the case, then we can feel threatened by the progress of others, particularly if they are not white. It is worse if we are white in the lower socioeconomic class.

There is an additional issue that was certainly in a group of which I was one on my journey from nobody in the lower class to somebody in the middle/upper class. I never looked around and said to myself, "How can I help someone else get there with me?" It was hard enough for me to get out, but because of educational opportunities where I enjoyed great success and as a result of very hard work, I was was lifted up. But few people say that if I could make it, anybody else could too. I am white, and there were systems in place that helped me that I didn't even know about at the time.

Post 23.   Where's the Beef? Part 1

"Where is the beef?" is the iconic marketing tool used by Wendy's, implying that there was something missing from traditional fast food burgers. You got more beef at Wendy's. This is a truth in counseling as well. Pay as much attention to what someone is not saying as to what they do share. What more do you need to know about them in order to direct the counseling process?

What is missing?

For example, what we know about COVID-19 is clear in terms of prevention. We have guidelines for how to prevent it. We need to know more to create a vaccine. That important knowledge is missing.

"Where is the beef?" plays a role regarding so much important stuff in life where key pieces are missing.

Several people who knew I was committed to diversity work suggested that I read *White Fragility,* by Robin Diangelo. It covers issues essential to understanding the Black Lives Matter movement. Understanding promotes forward movement. She presents an in depth analysis describing the ideas that precede action necessary for any movement to go forward. This has been true throughout history. I am a white male. I have had the opportunity to work with two of the best diversity trainers, Courtney Portlock and Walidah Justice. Diangelo is a college professor, author, and an expert on race matters whose insights are terrific. However, she weaves information that is hard to engage when we have those basic questions like, "But what about____?" I want to ask a few "Where's the beef?" questions. For me, what's missing?

When a friend of mine who has no filters finished my recent memoir, she stood in my kitchen and said, "OK, I get it. You grew up poor, and your parents had little education." After reading 389 pages, that was her summary. There is more "beef" in it. Racism is crucial to discuss, but what about classism, which I am passionate about correcting as well? Who is your target audience for "white fragility?" What about the importance of education? What about money as power and choice? How do we embed anti-racism in the culture of a school, community, nation, and world?

Diangelo has two paragraphs about class in her book. We learn that she grew up in poverty and was embarrassed about that. But she always knew she was white, and it was better to be white (pp. 19

and 66). She addresses, "Where Do We Go from Here?" in twenty pages at the end.

Here is what I want to know and what I also value. I have a series of "Where's the beef?" questions about classism, education, and an author's target audience that I would like to raise. Your target audience is the first question that a publisher will ask you as any author/academic knows. What personal experiences have shaped your views? I always believe that if you provide analysis of a problem, you must provide possible solutions. Part 2 will be my next post and will address the "Where's the beef?" questions that are important to me.

Post 24. Where's the Beef? Part 2

What was missing for me in Diangelo's book, *White Fragility*, is that I wanted to know more about class as it relates to racism, her education, her target audience, and her personal experiences that informed all that is contained in her book. One of the desired outcomes that I wanted for my children was to have opportunity and choices commensurate with their ability. Class is determined by factors, such as where you lived as a young person and where you live now, a work ethic, money to have options, and education. Class is a difference maker no matter what your race. A white person from a low economic class has a different experience in life than a wealthy black, Hispanic, or other minority. If access and opportunity coupled with equality are the goals, class is a big player. It is difficult to achieve for any race without economic power.

White Fragility is written by someone who is a gifted writer and someone who can make a compelling argument regarding the ingredients of racism. Where did she go to school to hone these gifts? I believe that education is the great equalizer, no matter what your race. In our nation, the poor, regardless of race, have an almost impossible challenge. The system is rigged against the poor. I grew up in an underserved family. I was competitive and focused that trait into my education. I realized at some point that education was a way out! No matter what your race, you need a skill, such as gifted academician, athlete, or prodigy of some discipline, like music, to name a few. The adage is true that the way to Carnegie Hall is practice, practice, practice.

We need to pay attention to our target audience to really make change at a grassroots level.

White Fragility is an erudite piece. I read it as though I was dining on a fine meal. I am not sure that a blue-collar worker would pick it up to read. It has great content, but who is accessible to the ideas? We are not a culture of readers of theory.

When I had a draft ready of my first book, *Watch Your Time*, I gave the draft to someone who has changed the course of psychology and is one of the smartest people I know. I also knew that his feedback would be honest and direct. He indicated when he got back to me that he thought the book was too much head and not enough heart. He went on to say that I have an abundance of stories that could inform the theory. This person's culture-changing ideas were based on his experience watching his daughter work in his garden. It is this experience that shaped his ideas. More important, it is the effect rich experiences have on others that brings others to read what we have written. Michelle Obama was responding to a student, when she said, "Forget the stats. Tell your story."

I indicated in Part 1 that if you raise a problem, come with the solution as well. When you are reading *White Fragility*, read Michelle Obama's *Becoming* at the same time. You will get a blend of experience with theory. You can also hear her story in the Netflix documentary, *Becoming*. Everyone is reading or watching it.

Post 25   The One/Two Punch

We are all familiar with filling out a survey where we check the boxes of some of those parameters that define us. When it comes to the issue of race, it is an easy choice for me because white is such a norm in our country. But when it asks for socioeconomic group, the question always stays with me much longer before I answer. A lot of my feelings put me in the low socioeconomic group, even now, when my life's work has lifted me up in that category. Even now, when I have all of the trappings of the higher socioeconomic strata, I retain those feelings of economic insecurity because that is one of the dynamics of class.

When you grow up in an underserved culture as I did, you are always thinking about money. That orientation stays with you, no matter how much wealth you accrue. People who come from a low socioeconomic group always have money on the mind.

I like to think about this as the "Great Depression Syndrome." People who have gone through the depression always had over-stocked food pantries later in life. They thought that with one bad financial moment, they would be back in the food line again. Costco patrons have to buy everything in bulk. We have friends who shop at Costco. They have large pantries in their homes they call "Costco Closets." This would be the kind of thing that people who went through the Great Depression would have loved to have had later in their life as "a lot is never enough" to combat that worst fear of when the next meal would be had.

The Black Lives Matter movement has helped people to focus on the issue of humanity. These folks are my brothers and sisters. Black Lives Matter reveals the pain that has been there for over two centuries. The pain is always there but becomes more focused during times, such as the present. It is heartbreaking to witness businesses and livelihoods destroyed. There are so many lacking resources to save their businesses. You can bet that they are constantly thinking about money. That pain is particularly great for those who have dedicated their lives to working their way into a degree of financial security. Listen to the people in line for food. I hope and pray that their future lives will yield happiness and financial security. But there is a truth that needs to be told. They will never forget this point in time, no matter how much they gain back. It will form and shape their lives forever.

Imagine a black person filling out that survey. They have to pause twice if they were or are in a low socioeconomic group. Skin color matters. Money and security matter. The "one/two punch" is a boxing phrase to describe a tactic that can result in a knockout. That combination of class and race can put our black brothers and sisters on the mat unless we can effect positive change that is specific to make their lives better, that their lives matter.

Post 26.   Lessons Learned on the Chesapeake

I learned a valuable lesson from my neighbor on the Chesapeake, patience. Before you build a home on the bay, you must first dig your well at the edge of the beachfront property. The house is built after the well is in. That goes in first. For the most part, there is no public water on the properties that drain directly into the Chesapeake.

Our neighbor who was ahead of us in building his home was a high-powered fellow at DuPont. His home was finished as we were clearing the land and starting our building process. He was the person who led Dupont to have a footprint in China, which was not easy to do. Today we would call him a "hard charger." He was very frustrated that his well was not being drilled, so he tells this cautionary tale about his experience, which is followed with a hearty laugh.

When the well driller wasn't getting to his property, he had several lawyers from Dupont go to the well driller to make him aware of Bob's rights and well driller's responsibilities. The attorneys appeared in the well driller's office, which was a small operation. The well driller was sitting next to a wood-burning stove in a rocking chair and was listening attentively to the lawyers' comments. He then stopped rocking and said, "Thank you for making me aware of my legal obligations. I was going to drill that well in June. Now I will wait and drill it in August." The lawyers' mouths dropped open. They didn't know what to say!

What worked in China was not the way business was conducted on the Chesapeake when dealing with the people on the Bay. They are rugged, independent thinkers. My family and I literally built our home with our own hands under supervision of a friend. I remembered our neighbor's experience. When I had a subcontractor do some work for us, I had difficulty getting him to do the job. I said nothing. When he appeared, I did ask him what delayed him. He simply said, "It is hunting season." No apology. The implication was I should have known better.

I am not very good at patience. Although I hate to admit it, I am a bit like my neighbor. I am still learning that lesson, and that includes seeing the positive when you are waiting and "knowing your audience."

We recently lost some trees on our Newtown Square home during the derecho storm six weeks ago. Our tree person is just getting around to removing the trunks that were left. What I try to say on my better days is that the tree person didn't get up in the morning and say, "I think I will frustrate Jim." When he apologized for taking so long getting to them, I simply said, "What I will remember is that you were here the first thing the next morning after the storm, clearing debris and the bigger tree trunks." He said, "Thanks!" It made his day!

Patience can work for or against us as we deal with the pandemic and Black Lives Matter. Some would say we have been patient long enough. We want signs of resolution. Times up!

Post 27.   Choiceless Choices and the Way Forward

We have difficult choices before us as a nation. They are choiceless choices, meaning we wish that we were clear of what is absolutely right or wrong. Some of these choiceless choices are to open schools versus to do what is safe for children and adults, opening the economy versus keeping people safe, staying in versus going out, masks, social distancing, handwashing, and six feet between people versus not doing that, allowing sports to have a season versus protecting participants, putting self and family members at risk, supporting Black Lives Matter versus concern for people protesting and the spread of the virus in groups and protecting business and other places.

Systematic ethics is needed to make these decisions in a thoughtful way.

The utilitarian perspective says that we should choose what is the greatest good for the greatest number. This system requires us to identify our primary group. Groups could be nation, family, or race and then to decide what is best for my primary group.

The *Via Media* (meaning the middle way) frames the decision as what is wrong but necessary or the lesser of two evils. This is often held by mainline Christian groups.

The Jewish ethic has the "law of the pursuer," whereby what is pursuing you is a threat to you, must enter into the equation. Which of the decisions above is a personal threat to you?

The Roman Catholic ethic includes the biblical record and natural law as its requirement where the value of human life is the first priority. They are against anything that interrupts the natural continuum. This is why this ethic is against abortion and capital punishment.

In addition to the above perspectives, we have "what feels the best to you." Feelings are your feelings, and you shouldn't have to defend how you feel with others indicating, "you shouldn't feel that way."

We also have the "reasonable person" standard. You can pick any number, but if ten people were in a room and see the right decision in the same way, that is a good decision. This assumes a degree of diversity in the group. This approach is the basis of our legal system, whereby the jury has to reach a decision regarding a particular case that they are deciding.

The slippery slope argument focuses on the decision and unforeseen negative consequences in the future.

We have read and seen a great deal that identifies the various choices that need to be made. I have not seen a "thoughtful" response to determine action. I think the above decision-making models could help people make the best decision. At least when the decisions are made, you can use the above models to help you identify why. There is an important theme that is needed no matter what is decided. We can tolerate (meaning to move forward, not necessarily agree with) what we *understand*.

Post 28. Cost/Risk/Benefit Analysis

There was an opinion piece on July 21, 2020, in the *Inquirer,* by Janet Bednarek about the current plight of the airlines. The US airline industry has two historic obstacles: fear and fares. They had the same plight after 9/11. Back then the FAA, Congress, and the White House were all on the same page. Today, there is a mishmash of policies and the thought, 'Why fly if you have nowhere to go?'

After 9/11, we were united, and the airlines and airports made adjustments so that people felt safe. Today, we are living in a partisan world with fear and being scared are part of everyday life.

Fares are an interesting dilemma for airlines to solve. They have the same way of approaching fares as we do each day of our lives. It is referred to as cost/risk/ benefit analysis. Each day of our lives, we enter into the same equation that the airlines use. What is the price that you and I are paying? More importantly, is it worth it? What is the cost?

Essential workers have used this formula in their daily deliberations as well. What price are our patients paying? What price are we paying as helpers in the pandemic as we may bring this virus home to our families? What is the risk to me? For essential workers risk, cost, and benefit to me or others guides our actions during this uncertain time of the virus. It takes courage to address these concerns.

Our most valuable possession is time, not money. If you listen to people who come out of the hospital after beating COVID-19, they are grateful that they have time now to engage the rest of their life.

There is a story regarding the headmaster of Eton, the fine British prep school, who was confronted by a very angry parent who did not feel her son was progressing enough. She laid that responsibility at the feet of the school. Her emotions emerged in an angry question, "Just what are you preparing him for?" The headmaster took the wind from her sail by responding to her with, "We are preparing him for death!" The boy was wasting time and was unfocused. The headmaster wanted him to appreciate the time that he had on this earth and to use it better.

Someone who spoke eloquently regarding the formula of cost/risk/benefit ratio was Dietrich Bonhoeffer who was a German pastor, theologian, and anti-Nazi dissident. He was imprisoned in 1943 and hung on April 9, 1945. He paid the highest price for his convictions. In his book, *The Cost of Discipleship*, he indicates how he paid the highest price for his convictions. His decision to stand up to Hitler was the cost of his love for the Gospel and for the people of Germany.

What is the cost to us in living our lives during this time of uncertainty? Is it preparing us to love and assist others as our essential workers do? They are rightly referred to as heroes for our time. John Lewis comes quickly to mind as well.

Post 29. Deal Maker or Brick Thrower

The American people desperately need a deal struck by the Democrats and Republicans in Congress to provide additional aid to those who need financial help and rent due. One of the key figures making the deal for the Republicans was former White House Chief of Staff Mark Meadows, who as a conservative member of the House and the former Chairman of the Conservative House Freedom Caucus, was in a difficult spot for he is known as a "brick thrower and not a dealmaker." He has historically been critical of dealmakers in both the Republican and Democratic parties. He found himself having to cut a most important deal to make with the Coronavirus Relief Package.

There is a cautionary tale here for those who are Monday morning quarterbacks. Namely, at some point, you could be in the role that you are constantly criticizing.

I am at my best when I act on an important question. What would our community or nation be like if we treated everyone like our very lives depended on one another? If history repeats itself, I don't think that we can depend on others to adopt this point of view. We can't get everyone to wear masks, keep six feet apart, or wash our hands. We know that we should treat others as we want to be treated. When I asked a former member of our security staff at the Episcopal Academy, Mr. Thomas Hunter, what he thought was the reason for ignoring these guidelines. He quickly replied, "Those people are stupid." That comes from a very astute person with a "man of the people approach." So, how do we make people smarter?

Nobody has discussed a decision-making model for treating COVID-19 patients. The guideline now is if they show up at the hospital, you have to treat them. What about the risk to the medical staff and their families? We already have decision-making models. One is already used in facilities that have been overrun with cases with no space left. We treat the ones we think will survive. This was the controversial policy during Hurricane Katrina at Memorial Hospital in New Orleans that Sheri Fink wrote about in *Five Days at Memorial*.

This raises one of the most difficult bioethical questions. Consider for a moment if we were acting in a utilitarian ethical perspective, we would do "the greatest good for the greatest number of a group." If we know that thirty people came down with the virus through tracing after they attended a party with no mask, social distancing, and hand washing, should they be treated before thirty people who got the virus as part of the general contagion? We have limited resources so that only thirty could be treated. We have all seen the party pics. Choices have consequences! This is a classic bioethics case study. In reality, we don't have a limitless supply of people and product to treat COVID-19.

I am tired of people saying masks are stupid, then get the virus and change their conversion to "I was wrong. Wear a Mask." In the meantime, they have put medical people and others at risk.

There is a disconnect between reality and action. Right now, the burden is on the essential workers. We need to shift some of that burden to the patients who did not adhere to guidelines. What would our nation look like if we treated everyone as though our lives depended on it? That's the question that needs to be asked. That's where we are right now. If people acted responsibly, we would be out of this by the fall, according to the experts, with fewer deaths. We need a plan to get us there, a policy that you need to follow the guidelines or face an unpleasant option.

Post 30. Are You Lonely Tonight?

There is an important truth that needs to be highlighted that was revealed by this pandemic. We live in a culture of constant stimu-lation. We are not at ease (diseased) when we are isolated and feel alone. It is captured by the title of one of my favorite songs by Elvis, "Are You Lonely Tonight?"

There is a big difference between solitude and loneliness. Loneliness is a feeling of being isolated. One *feels* that something is missing. Solitude is the state of being alone without being lonely. It is a pos-itive and constructive state of being engaged with oneself.

It hasn't dawned on the Russian government that they could take over our country without hacking our elections. They could require people to be in their homes, alone or not talking with a family member, with no devices allowed, not indicating when this period of time would be over. I am afraid a good many would walk out their front doors with their hands up.

What an opportunity to be aware that we need to become friends with ourselves and/or ourselves and our God. That is one of the lessons that the pandemic has taught us.

There is a movement throughout our nation referred to as "mindfulness studies." It is required in certain medical schools, in businesses, and other places where attention and the importance of a sense of our inner being are required. The simple version is that you focus on your breathing and put everything else out of your mind. It sounds simple, but most people find it very difficult to do in our sound bite and constant stimulation culture. The meaning of FOMO is clearly a dis-ease and makes us uneasy. It stands for "fear of missing out." What are we missing? I believe that it is stated in the definition of religion which is derived from the Latin word *ligio* which means "to connect" like our ligaments in our body. Religion is that holy connection among self, others, and God.

We often forget that prayer is a way to make friends with our God, for prayer is a conversation with the holy one. I was given a shirt that had "Prayer Is the Ultimate Connection" printed across the front.

"Are you lonely tonight?" This could be one of the most important questions that comes out of this pandemic.

Post 31. When Fear Knocks on the Door; Faith Says No One Is Home

There was an opinion piece on July 21, 2020 in the *Inquirer* by Janet Bednarek about the current plight of the airlines. The US airline industry has two historic obstacles: fear and fares. They had the same plight after 9/11. Back then the FAA, Congress, and the White House were all on the same page. Today there is a mishmash of policies and why fly if you have nowhere to go? After 9/11, we were united, and the airlines and airports made adjustments so that people felt safe.

Today we are living in a partisan world, and fear and being scared are part of everyday life. There is a difference between fear and being scared. Being scared is something that we usually have some choice over. It is why Stephen King has so many readers. When asked why he thought this was so, he responded by saying that his books sold a lot for the same reason that we slow down when driving to see an accident that has occurred. We like to get close to being scared. We are scared when we choose to ride that roller coaster, which says that you should not get on if you have a heart condition.

Fear, on the other hand, is a condition in life where we haven't chosen the circumstances that surround the condition. We are living in fear with the virus that we have not chosen and could kill us. Our essential workers go to work each day afraid. It is uncertain if Black Lives Matter will turn out well for protesters, police, and black people and everybody else. This was not so much a choice as timing and history merged. For both of these events we know that life will not be the same going forward.

Being scared focuses on specific events. Being afraid is a way of life. It is worth noting that "Be not afraid" is mentioned 365 times in the Old and New Testaments. Jesus walking on the water, and Psalm 23 are the two most familiar passages although Jesus uses the phrase, "Be not afraid," or a variation in countless other situations. In Psalm 23, the King James Version, we say, "Yeah though I walk through the valley of death I will fear no evil ...."

There are few mentions of faith by the media today, although that, in my opinion, may be key to our security and hope. We only hear the importance of the religious quest when we are given notice of when houses of worship can be opened to how many people at a time. One of my favorite hymns has the refrain, "Be not afraid. I go before you always, Come and follow me, and I will give you rest."

As I passed a restaurant in the city there was a sign in the window that stopped me in my tracks. It said: When fear knocks on our door, our faith will indicate that no one is home."

Post 32.   God's Minute

Elijah Cummings, a Democrat from Baltimore who served in the House of Representatives, died in October of 2019. A prophetic voice, he recited a forty-six-word poem in his very first speech to Congress. The poem was a guidepost for him, and I find it to be inspiring. It has two titles: "Just a Minute" and "God's Minute."

> I have only a minute.
> Sixty seconds in it.
> Forced upon me, I did not choose it,
> But I know that I must use it.
> Give account if I abuse it.
> Suffer, if I lose it.
> Only a tiny little minute,
> But eternity is in it.

Each and every time I read this poem, I see something different that moves my soul. The poem is familiar to some. I have found that reading each line multiple times takes on the role of a meditation.

When we think of people who influenced the Reverend Dr. Martin Luther King Jr., one of the first people who comes to mind is Gandhi. Certainly, Gandhi's nonviolent philosophy influenced King, but there is another person who perhaps had greater influence on Dr. King, the Reverend Dr. Benjamin Mays, President of Morehouse College from 1940 to 1967. Dr. King attended Morehouse and had an enduring relationship with Dr. Mays. It was Dr. Mays who was chosen to give the eulogy at the public service five days after Dr. King's death. He was the only speaker. Dr. King's short life is filled with events that can be summed up in that short phrase, "But eternity is in it."

In reading about Dr. Mays, I have been struck by the short pithy words that he wrote such as "Not failure, but low aim is a sin." It was Dr. Mays who wrote the words of "God's minute."

As the short poem was a guidepost for Elijah's Cummings' decision-making, we too can select a short Bible passage, poem, or phrase to guide our decision-making during this challenging time of the pandemic.

Post 33. Intersectionality

Intersectionality is an important ingredient in social justice work that means doing something positive for groups, such as black people, Jewish people, gay people, and the issue of class as examples. It means that we are required to lift up other people or groups that are not part of our self-identified group. For example, if you are black, you should also seek justice for those who are gay or women. Privilege can be granted to us if we are just all about us as our priority.

An example of something that is addressed by intersectionality was the recent incident where the head of the NAACP in Philadelphia, Rodney Muhammad, posted an anti-Semitic image on social media. He was confronted for this by *both* the black community and the Jewish community with the common language, "We are all in this together."

A biblical verse that speaks to intersectionality is St. Paul's description of the Christian community. We all need to be lifted up and play a role as he uses the metaphor of the human body to describe the importance of each of our roles in comprising the whole. "So just as the body is one and has many members (such as hand, ear, etc.), and all the members of the body, though many, are one body" (First Corinthians 2:12).

This idea of intersectionality plays a role in how we deal with the importance or unimportance of other people's views. I put it in the following words in my recent memoir, *The Times of My*

Life, "We will not major in minor things We need to be aware of the fact that what is important to one may not be important to another. One of the ways of empowering a relationship is to take seriously what the other person takes seriously, to honor those things that may not be important to us. It is equally important to identify issues that are regarded with mutual importance to be the focus of our communication. Overlooking something that both parties feel is important, while caught in the swamp of the trivial, is unhelpful." I found myself often dealing with a life or death issue within our school community. Soon after, I might be speaking with a student, whose greatest concern would be which college would accept him, whether they would win a tournament, or how well they performed on a test. All circumstances are relative, and we should never judge someone's concerns as more or less important than ours."

That is intersectionality in relationships. For example, people in the pandemic are to be aware of what government should do and the government position should be aware of what the people want. Neither view should be dismissed by the other. Both groups need to be aware that what is important to the one may not be important to the other. Both groups need to pay attention to this reality and not be dismissive of the other's views.

Post 34.   The Man in the Red Bandana

We studied choices in my ethics course that I taught to thousands of high school students over thirty-eight years. Ethics is about choices and the life events and people that shape our choices. Ethics is about choiceless choices as well, choices that we would not want to make, but we feel are the only way forward. Ethics is about hard choices!

I became friends with Dr. Chaim Potok, a Jewish author, who is best known for his novel, *The Chosen*. He was an academic, and in his culture, it was understood that he should write academic works. His novel, *The Chosen*, sold 650,000 copies. He went against his culture and family to become a writer of fiction that contained stories of hard choices people feel compelled to make. One day when we were talking, I asked him where he got the courage to go against the pressure of his culture to become a novelist. He smiled and said, "I wish I had a choice. I had to do it."

Courage is at the heart of choiceless choices. When I talked recently with someone battling cancer, I commented that I admired his courageous battle against this disease. He said, "I wish I had a choice." Tough chemo and surgery were required to battle his disease. Courage was present there.

Choices can overwhelm. Barry Schwartz wrote *The Paradox of Choice*, indicating that we have too many choices. There used to be only one brand of ketchup. Now, there are many. Students choosing a college are sometimes overwhelmed by the number of options they have. I believe that choices are shaped by different forces throughout our lives. I often indicated to my ethics class that their choices were being shaped right in the present. If you cheat as a high school student, you will more than likely cheat as a way of life. I have seen over and over again where the seeds of courage inform someone's life choices. The important thing to remember is that we are all capable of a courageous act at any time in our lives.

The ultimate act of courage is to save the life of another. Jesus said, "There is no greater love than for someone to lay down one's life for his friends." My ethics students have informed me that a video I showed in class remained a source of inspiration for them. Watch it and you will see a sample of the origins of a courageous choice. My students would tell me that when they had to make a tough choice later in life, they thought of the video below. *The Man in the Red Bandana* comes with the *warning*: YOU SHOULDN'T WATCH THIS IF YOU WANT AN EASY WAY OUT IN LIFE WHEN FACED WITH A DIFFICULT DECISION. THIS VIDEO WILL INSPIRE YOU TO TAKE THE HARD RIGHT AND NOT THE EASY WRONG. THIS MAY HELP YOU CHOOSE THE COURAGEOUS WAY.

The movie, *The Man in the Red Bandana,* can be found on my blog on my website under the title of "The Man in the Red Bandana."

Post 35. Why Are All the Black Kids Sitting Together in the Cafeteria?

When my son was a student at Princeton University, my wife Vicki and I became co-chairs of the Princeton Parents Association of the Philadelphia Area. We were receiving news about the issues that Princeton was dealing with at the time. I remember that one of the mailings that we received was a concern that although Princeton was admitting more black students, the university was struggling to find ways that the students could be more integrated in the life of the school. They always seemed to be seated together at meals or joining the same clubs. The university was very interested in all students having cross-cultural communication.

There is a classic book revised and updated in 2017 that addresses the psychology of race. It is *Why Are All the Black Kids Sitting Together in the Cafeteria?* Its author, Dr. Beverly Daniel Tatum, recently retired as president of Spelman College. The title is catchy, like pop psychology. Don't be fooled. The content is a brilliant blend of theory and personal experience. If you want to understand the Black Lives Matter movement, read it! It is all there.

The book and my ethics course intersected at many points. For example, we study friendship in ethics. We see that friendship is found in shared experience or shared purpose. Students told me that they often take their problems to their friends and not to an adult because their friends know what it is like to be them. Black students are very aware of their blackness. Dr. Tatum reflects that black students/people are often seen in a warped sense of who they really are. They are trying to figure out who they are, so they have to also reject stereotypes given to them. Dr. Tatum refers this process as "oppositional" identity. "When feelings, rational or irrational, are invalidated most people disengage."

One of the things that were important for me to know about was the complex process of identity formation in black people. The other thing was that Dr. Tatum makes a point about the election of Barack Obama as president and Michelle Obama becoming first lady. Obviously, I knew how important this was for our nation, but they also became role models for people to see two black people who were kind, cool, and who demonstrated the power of getting an education as a stepping stone to success.

I had an experience in Paris, of all places, that helped me to understand why all the black kids sit at the same table in the cafeteria. It is a metaphor for that black experience. Paris is a city where the French people love to speak French to people who they encounter, more so than in any other country where I have traveled. One day, I heard some Americans talking nearby. I found myself gravitating to them just to feel as though someone knew what I was talking about and share some stories of some places I had found to be terrific locations to visit in the city. If there was a cafeteria table there, I am sure that I would find myself with fellow Americans whom I could literally understand and who could understand me. It's important to feel that safety and understanding. It is no different for black students during lunch!

Post 36. A Log in the Eye: A Cautionary Tale

Jesus said, "Why do you see the speck in your friend's eye, and do not see the log in your own eye?"

I am writing this from our home on the Chesapeake. Our neighbors have been great friends. Paul is a retired architect, and Gail is a retired psychologist. They both have been great adventurers. They have sailed their boat over a lot of open water, such as to Central

America. Recently they flew to Bhutan, a country near India where they hiked to remote sites to fully experience the area.

Gail is a triathlete who has won many races in her age category as a retired person. She trains hard for these races and is very experienced with this kind of challenge. She was about to complete a triathlon a year ago in May when she ran into trouble in the swim part of the competition and was near the finish line. She had trouble swimming. A race official in a kayak made his way to her and asked if she needed assistance. She told him "no" and waved him off. She drowned. Attempts to revive her were made on the beach. She was taken to a hospital where she died a few days later. Friends, family, and neighbors experienced grief and frustration that she should have asked for help when it was offered. Vicki indicated when we are driving to our home that she thinks of Gail when we get close to our place.

Earlier this week, I went out for a fast walk or slow run. I am not sure of the category. I do know that I give it everything that I have as I race against my own best times on a particular route. The weather app said that it would be hot, but a cloud cover would come late in the day, so off I went. The clouds never came. I am beyond the age of retirement as Gail was as well. I was about twenty yards from the end of the run when I shifted up a gear. I have never had an experience like I had then. I knew I was in trouble as my brain said stop but my legs just continued on. I felt like I was driving a car with no brakes. I did manage to get off the road and into the grass where I went down and bounced across the turf like a beach ball. I never lost consciousness. I called Vicki on the cell. She asked where I was and that she would be there soon.

A man in a blue truck stopped and asked if I needed help. I said, "No!" A woman in a car stopped as well, and I waved her on. Another person indicated that there was an EMT down the road. I said, "No!" Vicki arrived, assessed the scene, and went to work helping me to get turned over. I got to my hands and knees. The man in the blue truck was the modern-day good Samaritan as he came back with a cold bottle of water and expressed his frustration that I wouldn't take any help. I was able after some time to get into the car to be driven home. It took several days to recover.

We have been taught rugged individualism in our country. Everything has an upside and a downside. At times, it is difficult to get the log out of my eye, particularly when I saw the speck in Gail's.

Post 37.   The Immortal Life of Henrietta Lacks

August 1, 2020 was the 100th birthday of Henrietta Lacks, a black woman of little means whose cells are responsible for research resulting in medical breakthroughs. Cells from her could be one of the reasons that a COVID-19 vaccine is discovered. She lived in the Baltimore area in 1951 and was taken to John Hopkins Hospital to a separate division for black patients for treatment for cervical cancer. She died at the age of thirty-one. Doctors at Hopkins took her cells to use for research without asking permission. Her cells never die when kept under proper conditions. They are called HeLa cells, the first two letters of her first and last names.

These cells were different from other cells that researchers used for they replicated amazingly. They have been used in research all over the world and are still the cells that are used today by scientists. Some argue that she has given science and physicians the most important gift that they have ever received as her cells are responsible for many medical breakthroughs. Others refer to her as the mother of modern research. The gift also became a driving force for bioethicists around the issue of consent. No one gave their consent to have these cells taken, including Henrietta Lacks or any members of her family.

We take for granted that each of us must give consent for any procedures that we have done by medical doctors or in clinical trial participation. We are told what will happen in the procedure, the side effects, the risks involved, and the expected outcome. When this occurs, think of Henrietta Lacks and her gift of today's requirement to consent all patients. Why hasn't her name become a household word?

Rebecca Skloot revealed Henrietta Lack's story in her book, *The Immortal Life of Henrietta Lacks*, published on March 8, 2011. Skloot had difficulty getting permission from the family of Henrietta Lacks to write her book. This was due to mistrust of the medical establishment in the black community because of unethical trials have been perpetrated on black people in our nation where consent was not given. In the Tuskegee experiment, sponsored by the US Public Health Service, black men were experimented on to observe the progression of syphilis while withholding known treatment. Some died, and others gave the disease to their wives.

I had already read Skloot's book when I was invited to attend a lecture she presented, addressing researchers, bioethicists, and physicians at Thomas Jefferson University Hospital. Several hundred people were present. There was standing room only. Skloot asked the audience how many in attendance had used HeLa cells in their research. I was seated in the front of the room, so I had turned around to see every hand in the audience go up.

Medicine owes its progress to a little-known black woman who lived in an underserved community. Another example of Black Lives Matter intersecting with the pandemic.

Post 38. How to Care for the Narcissist in Your Life

We have heard the term "narcissistic personality" frequently in the course of conversations about Donald Trump. I have had a good number of narcissists in counseling. They are very difficult to assist to get to a better place for themselves and those who are in their social orbit.

One of the experts on narcissistic personalities is a lawyer, Rebecca Zung, who has had to deal with them a great deal in her legal practice as they are often involved in divorce proceedings. Zung states on her website what creates a narcissistic personality, the traits that make them difficult to deal with, and what you need to know to survive a relationship with them. She is regarded by some as "the best lawyer in America."

To paraphrase Ms. Zung, Esq, "Narcissists deny, deflect, devalue, dismiss, and gaslight others making you feel crazy. They lie, manipulate others about everything, intimidate and triangulate shifting any blame to someone or something else. They can't apologize for anything." Bullies are narcissists.

How can you possibly feel any degree of empathy for them as they often engender anger, frustration, and strong dislike by others? But empathy is needed for any change to occur. Narcissistic personalities have very little sense of self or values. This means that they cannot sense affirmation from within themselves. They crave external affirmation from others. If you can see them as people with a hollow core, where they do anything to get that sense of self that is within "normal" people, this will be helpful to you. If you see them as fighting for their very psychological survival, that is what it is like to be them.

Their external manifestation of self is so off putting that most people will reject them. External affirmation is the very air that keeps them psychologically alive. They can't get enough of it. Narcissists don't respond to honest feedback. They have a powerful need to control for they need to control responses to them because their internal affirming voice is not loud enough to not be threatened. If you want to see how feedback can happen in a real exchange, go to an online interview that Barbara Walters had with Donald Trump on August 17, 1990. There is a paradox that they act so callous, cool, even cruel, because they are so afraid.

I have also learned that if you stay with a person long enough, then you will be able to see the good in them. It can feel like an eternity when you can finally see the good that is in a narcissist. What will also help is to be aware that we all possess narcissistic personality traits within us. Fortunately, we can keep them in check. Our posture should be humility in trying to help them, realizing "There but for the grace of God go I."

Post 39.   The Nuremberg Defense and the Reasonable Person Standard

We have had numerous excuses why there have been excessive approaches by police to citizens during this time of Black Lives Matter and COVID-19. One of the examples of this excessive use of force in Philadelphia was when police chased peaceful protesters off the I-676 and drove them up an embankment. During this police action, the police used tear gas and beat the civilian population. One protestor was kneeling with her hands behind her back and was sprayed with tear gas directly into her face. It is now the end of June, 2020. This event happened weeks ago. The mayor and police commissioner recently apologized for this overreach.

I was struck by the fact that one police officer said, "I was just doing what I was told!" We call this the Nuremberg Defense in Ethics. During the trial in Nuremberg, a number of the Nazis who were being tried used this as their defense: "I was just doing what I was told."

The problem with this defense is that you could indicate that you must do what the command chain tells you to do, but at what point does your ethical nature take over and stir you to feel that what you are doing is wrong. It is obvious that the policeman who shot tear gas into the face of a kneeling woman who was vulnerable is not right by most standards of behavior. We call this the "reasonable person" response. If twelve neutral people saw that this is wrong, then it is wrong. When I would tell my father that I did something wrong because others were doing it, he simply said, "Would you jump off a roof if someone told you to do that?"

There is an exercise in Holocaust education to demonstrate that people do what they do when an authority speaks. It is based on an experiment that was done by a high school teacher in 1967. A variation of this experiment addresses why the Nazis were able to do what they did with little or no corrective action from the German people. Simply stated, a teacher enters a classroom. He then orders the students to be completely silent. He then states that the students must move from their classroom to another. This is repeated over and over, and the students obediently do what they are told. After many moves to different classrooms, a student or a small group of students will say, "Wait a minute. This is crazy! What's going on?" The lesson learned is people respond to an authority figure, particularly if it is a person who they trust.

This is a central issue in the police and community lacking trust in one another, which is the power leading to protests and police encounters. The police have had experiences where they were attacked by members of the community. The community has enough examples of police brutality to destroy trust there as well.

What I think is needed is ethical action where we balance "I was just doing what I was told" with "the reasonable person standard." This will demonstrate why there is so much division today. Notice that this will only be resolved by *trust*. You can have many bills going through Congress that emphasize proper behavior by police or protesters, but it will not resolve the issue until *trust* is established first. That will be done when each group has empathy for the other.

What is it like to be you? As policeman? As a protestor? This is the mediation that is needed.

Post 40.   Are Smart People More Ethical Than Others?

Do smart people make better ethical decisions? There was an article in the *Inquirer* (July 5, 2020) by Janice Armstrong that students in top-tier schools (Masterman and Central) used social media to vent ugly, hateful views of their female and nonwhite classmates. There was a strong letter to the editor that perhaps intelligent people are just like everyone else in making or not making ethical decisions.

There are a couple of views on this correlation. The writer of the letter indicated that students needed to listen to the ground-breaking musical, *South Pacific*. Lt. Cable says in the musical that "Racism is not born into you. It happens after you are born." The letter went on to say that maybe young Philadelphians should pay attention to Cable's song, "You have got to be carefully taught." The letter suggested that students need to attend support groups so that they experience first-hand the impact of their comments on others.

Robert Coles, a professor at Harvard, reflected that he was appalled to learn that one of his A+ students in his ethics course was treating the cleaners in his house very badly. This would support the view that you "have to be carefully taught." There is no one better than Coles in covering ethical issues. The letter and Coles' stories indicate that intelligence and ethical decisions may not go hand in hand.

I want to focus on the support group recommendation of the letter. I taught Ethics for thirty-eight years at an elite, independent school. I am sure that all of my students did not make ethical decisions in their lives, but I have also heard from many of them how my course guided them in doing the hard right and not the easy wrong.

One of the goals in the course that I taught was to make ethical decisions become second nature. This is what elite athletes strive to do. For example, in basketball, you get better by practicing a shot over and over again. When you enter a game, this shot would become more available to you. Ethical behavior has to be caught as well as being taught. It has to become a matter of the heart over just the head or knowledge. Aristotle made it clear that good deeds must be done over and over to achieve ethical action.

If the Harvard student in Coles' class had experience in doing the right thing in the treatment of his cleaning lady, he and the cleaning lady would have had the possibility of a better experience for them both.

The letter to the editor had it right. You have to have experience of both the head and the heart to translate ideas into action. I provided both in my ethics course.

Post 41.   So, What Did I Miss?

In the hit musical, *Hamilton*, there is a song sung by Jefferson when he reflects on the kind of things that he didn't experience in America when he was ambassador to France living in Paris. He sings a song that bounces around in my mind. Its refrain is a catchy tune, "So what did I miss?"

I was thinking of this song as I was watching a lecture by Robert Watson before reading his book, *The Nazi Titanic*. He said that there is more about history that we don't know than what we do know. He referenced the Law of the Unread. Ninety-nine percent of any books written are gone. He reminded me of walking into my first class at Berkeley Divinity School at Yale when my first teacher was the Rev. Dr. Edward Rochie Hardy, the New York Wiz Kidd, who was only twenty-six when he earned his fifth academic degree. He matriculated at NYU when he was five years old. He gave us a ton of reading assignments and a thick main text and then said, "I will be lecturing about the historical record that is not in these materials. You are responsible for both the readings and what I will be lecturing about in class." That is exactly what he did. It was fascinating!

Robert Watson found a series of letters where he connected the dots about an unknown event during the last week of the Second World War. He also interviewed hundred(s) of people and read other primary sources that indicated a killing of Jewish holocaust survivors who were put on a ship during the last week of the war. They were bombed by the British who did not know what this ship contained. All the records were sealed about this tragedy until recently. No historian or Holocaust scholar had ever heard of this significant historical event. They missed knowing about the single bloodiest event during the Holocaust. "So, what did I miss?"

One of the things that is helpful in doing counseling, whether in person or on the phone, is to ask yourself after the session the question, "So what did I miss?" This question is particularly important when there doesn't seem that much progress has been made in the counseling after a good amount of time. There is a certain hubris in not raising the question for you have to admit to yourself and the person who you are helping that you have been on the wrong course and a shift in the approach needs to take place.

"So, what did I miss?" is an important question to raise and to do so with humility. I am sure that the researchers for the COVID-19 vaccine must be raising that question each day as they are working on a successful vaccine. The Black Lives Matter movement is raising that question frequently when the lawyers, investigators, protesters, police, and members of the community at large seek the truth of what really occurred in an exchange between police and someone who is a victim. This question has been a mantra by the families of those who have died.

"So, what did I miss?" during the pandemic and the Black Lives Matter movement is a question that could lead the way back to some degree of a new normal.

Post 42. Whoever Thought That You Would Be a Politician

Whether we like it or not, we are all politicians, for politics is about the distribution of power. Who has it? How do I keep it? How do I get it? In terms of everyday power found in our relationships with others, we are either one up, one down, or equal to another. For example, when we go to see a doctor, we are in the one down position. When we are the know-it-all, we find ourselves in the one up position. The goal is to have relationships with shared power for they empower one another and move the relationship forward.

We should strive for relationships that are not transactional. We have heard over and over that Latin phrase, *Quid Pro Quo,* that means I will do this for you if you will do that for me. Now let's look at a variation of a transactional relationship that could translate to all of us entering more fully into the golden rule: Do unto others as you would like them to do for you.

A prominent politician of the twentieth century was Tip O'Neill, Speaker of the House of Representatives, who coined a phrase that would be helpful to all of us making our way through life: "All politics is local."

During one of Tip's first political campaigns, he realized that the woman who lived across the street from him when he was a boy did not vote for him in his campaign. He shoveled the snow off of her sidewalk every time that it snowed, and he did it for free. So, with anger and curiosity, he made his way to the woman's house and asked, "Why didn't you vote for me?" As the story goes, she looked at Tip and said, "Everybody likes to be asked." He had taken her for granted. That lesson played out each day of his political life as the key to his great success in politics.

What is the difference between the golden rule/all politics is local and people who seek power over others in relationships with strings attached or transactions as the basis for the exchange?

When considering "All politics are local." we are focusing on the relationship itself and *never take for granted* the people whom we are with. We look for a shared experience. We *may* benefit from these relationships, but the intent is shared power. No one likes to be taken for granted. It is not what you can get. It is what you can give. It is characterized by that expression that you "may be one person in the world, but you may be the world to one person."

Post 43.   So You Want to Talk About Race

So, You Want to Talk About Race is the best-selling book written by Ijeoma Oluo. Quite frankly, I am surprised that it was read by so many people. Why would someone read a book that the author writes is guaranteed to challenge you, make you angry even make you uncomfortable, and turn your understanding of the world upside down. They should have a warning on the cover to "Read at your own risk" or "Not bedtime reading."

There was some reverse psychology operating here for people like me who are incapable of not reading it when such a curious introduction puts down the challenge. You will never be able to—and I immediately try to make a liar out of you. It gets the juices moving. Let's just say she was a woman of her word! So why did I continue to the very end? She did two things. She wrote about something that I care about: How class defines our lives which she helped me to see in a new way, and (2) I saw for the first time why meetings of Alcoholics Anonymous begin the way that they do.

Ms. Oluo wrote the following about class and race:

> "We people of color, of course, are not the only people who have gotten less. Even without the invention of race, class would still exist even in homogenous countries. And our class system is oppressive and harms a lot of people of all races. It should be addressed. It should be torn down. But the same hammer won't tear all of the walls. What keeps a poor child in Appalachia poor is not what keeps a child in Chicago poor—even from a distance the outcomes look the same …Even in our class and labor movement, the promise that you will get more because others exist to get less calls to people... The promise that keeps racism alive tells you that you will benefit most and others will eventually benefit … a little. It has you believing in trickle down justice" (Oluo, p. 13–14).

My take on this is for those of us who have gone from nothing to something, unfortunately, we are not thinking about who is losing out. To use the phrase, we have our eyes on the prize—whatever form that takes.

Second, is that statement before a person in an AA meeting speaks, he or she says, "I am _____, and I am an alcoholic." Why is that necessary? It seems sort of trite. I could keep reading the book with all of its uncomfortable stuff because the author doesn't divorce herself from the topic of "privilege." She states that she is a racist, an elitist, and so forth. We all think of racism as what one individual says or does to another. That is very important, but she is concerned, as well, with the systems that are in place to foster any injustice. She communicates that she is just like you and me, no better no worse. I am Ijeoma, and I am a _____.

Jesse Jackson shares an interesting perspective on bias. He stated, "There is nothing more painful to me at this stage in my life than to walk down the street and hear footsteps, then turn around and see somebody white and feel relieved." Somehow, I can see Ms. Oluo saying something very similar to Jesse Jackson. Just like the personal introduction during an AA meeting, "I am _____ and I am an alcoholic," is something very important that sets the stage for the feeling that we are all in this struggle together.

Post 44. Spoiled

As I was giving Sadie a piece of pretzel while we were watching TV, Vicki declared, "You spoil Sadie!" My quick retort was, "I try to spoil you, the family, and people with whom I am in contact!" Sadie is sixty-six pounds of entertainment and provides me with free therapy. As an aside, I love the YouTube videos about "Stella the Yellow Lab."

Spoil can have two meanings, one positive and one negative. The positive side of it is that it is other-directed. Vicki and I have stayed at the Ritz. The people who work there always go the extra mile, and they do it naturally as if it is no big deal. Whole Foods is the same way. Ask a clerk where an item is, and they walk with you to its location. Most other stores direct you to the aisle and which side it is on. This is followed by, "Have a nice day."

Jesus said, "If someone asks for your shirt, give them your coat as well. We are at our best when we are living this out in daily life. During COVID-19, people who wear their masks are in this category. We benefit, but it is for those we encounter, as well, to protect them. At one level, we are spoiling them by going the extra mile that is no big deal.

Some don't wear the mask. They cry out, "You are infringing on my personal freedom. This is a pandemic. It is a conspiracy. It's just the regular flu." Studies suggest that men wear masks less than women because men are more afraid of being seen as weak. Yep, another gender issue.

We need to infuse our culture more with the Golden Rule. "Do unto others what you would want them to do for you." You and I are at our best when we are guided by this wisdom. You can have your freedom as long as it is coupled with a responsibility like wearing a mask, honoring social distancing, and washing your hands. I would suggest that people who don't wear a mask are spoiled in a negative sense like the awful smell of your milk that has gone bad. They are all about concern for self and not for others.

We need to think about our choice—mask or no mask. Being spoiled in a positive way is the perfect example of being part of the solution and not part of the problem. There is an impressive word that you can use to wow your friends which they can use with their friends. Wearing masks, the Ritz, giving your shirt and coat as well, are examples of people and places who perform acts of supererogation. It means to go above and the call of duty. Say to them, "I am wearing my mask today because it is a deed of supererogation." When I give that pretzel to Sadie, her eyes say that word clearly, *supererogation,* and a smile comes across my face.

Post 45. Stat and Story

Arthur C. Brooks is an interesting conservative thinker who joined the faculty of the Harvard Kennedy School and Harvard Business School in 2019. He has been the president of various foundations and was a classical musician in the United States and Barcelona. His book, *Love Your Enemies*, is about bringing people together. One of his fundamental beliefs is that stories are more important than stats. Michelle Obama had the same theme in her autobiography, *Becoming*.

He is a provocative thinker who writes, "Here's a practical tip to start telling your story; write it down in twelve words or less (I have done it and you should try it.). Sounds impossible, right? There is a legend that the great novelist Ernest Hemingway once made a bet with a friend that he could craft an entire story in six words. His friend took the bet, because he knew that no one could write a story in six words that would have an emotional impact or importance at all. Hemingway pulled out a piece of paper and wrote down these six words: 'For sale: baby shoes, never worn.'"

Stories touch, Stats not so much. A bit of both is the balance.

I have noticed as we move forward through the pandemic and the Black Lives Matter movement that the print press and visual press have shifted from stats to stories. In the local newspaper, we certainly are given stats, but they are balancing that with stories of those who have died from COVID-19 and those who have beaten it. The Black Lives Matter movement has been covering more with stories from the beginning. I believe that is what has kept the movement moving forward.

Stats inform our head while stories inform our hearts. We tend to remember more of how something makes us feel, and that is what stories help us to do. Who could not be moved by the story of John Lewis whose life was the historical narrative of the history of a quest for civil rights? He will be remembered.

Brooks stated, "Imagine Jesus telling his followers, 'According to the latest surveys, priests and Levites are 42.3 percent less likely than Samaritans to help travelers on the road from Jerusalem to Jericho—on which, violent crime has increased significantly in the last decade. (This would have occurred shortly after he finished his PH.D. at Galilee University)."

I have not seen any stats on the fact that most putting-children-to-bed moments include from a request from a child, "Tell me a story ... again ... and again."

Post 46.   The Power of a Movie

Years ago, I attended an ethics program in Washington, DC, sponsored by the Center for Spiritual and Ethical Education. The program was about the importance of sharing stories of ethical people to serve as a model for doing the right thing. The premise was that a powerful way to teach ethics is to have a class read about what ethical people look like in action. I also had in mind that what worked for me in teaching ethics was doing this but also including videos of ethical behavior. While at the seminar, we did not discuss ethical theories but focused on ethical action from different books and videos where theory could be seen. Many of us learn by reading the printed word. Others learn by seeing examples of ethical action on the silver screen.

I found that students were, at times, more engaged by the visual than the written word. Sometimes we would view a film such as *Before and After* starring Liam Nelson and Meryl Streep, that was filled with legal ethics, the importance of telling the truth, and the ramifications for decisions that we make with unattended consequences of our choices. We also viewed a film such as *Gattica* that is regarded by the Penn Center of Bioethics to be a great source of material that could generate a discussion of bioethics. This approach worked well as students didn't want to leave class when there was a cliffhanger moment that left them wanting more. Most TV series have this approach, so you would tune to the next episode.

The students understood that the movie was a vehicle to discuss the ethical issues and theory involved that we had covered in class. Combining head and heart turned out to be a winning strategy. They also were asked for examples of books to read or videos to see that would emphasize ethical problems. For example, Jodi Picoult's books are based on an ethical dilemma.

What books or movies would you choose and why?

During this time of Black Lives Matter, there are many opportunities for ethical discussion. Recently I viewed the documentary, *Good Trouble: The Life of John Lewis*. He was born on a sharecropper's farm and rose to be a senator in Congress. His story is really the history of the civil rights movement that focuses on the privilege and power of voting. You are drawn in to see what people went through to have the right and responsibility to vote. I can't imagine someone seeing this movie, *Good Trouble*, and failing to vote. Voting is an ethical action for it is an important choice. If a picture is worth a thousand words, this documentary would get many more to the voting booth.

The printed word provides us with the academic nature of ethics. It is not about what you "feel" is right. It is a matter for the intellect or head. The visual actions provide us with an experience that helps us to see what ethical behavior looks like. Whether it be the written word or the visual action, they both help us to integrate the hard right over the easy wrong because "you can't be what you can't see."

Post 47. The Right Stuff

It was big news! Lori Loughlin and Massimo Giannulli are going to jail. That is important, but what is more important is what Judge Gorton said, "You led a fairytale life yet you stand before me a convicted felon. And for what? For the inexplicable desire to grasp even more." Gorton hit on that human trait that is the downfall of many "to give a little and want a lot." We hate to admit it, but it is in each and every one of us. That is why people with the right stuff stand out as an antidote to this dis-eased state of being.

This description of people first appeared with the novel by Thomas Wolf in 1979 with the title *The Right Stuff*. His novel was about Project Mercury and the astronauts whose courage made that flight possible. In the novel, he gives a portrait of people with the right stuff by using the astronauts as his vehicle. They didn't like to talk about their accomplishments. Their desire focused not on themselves but on doing something to advance humankind.

We like to be around people who have the right stuff. I believe that Jesus embodied this characteristic in living and dying for others. This characteristic reflects the very best in the Judeo-Christian tradition. You never hear a person say, "I have the right stuff!" If they do, you know that they don't! People who have it possess the attributes of living for others, being grateful, and having respect for all of humankind, being humble, and being empathetic.

I believe that Joe Biden has the right stuff. The following story illustrates why. Joe is not transactional. He doesn't do things and expect something in return. This story only appeared in the Jewish press and went no further.

Rabbi Beals was new to Delaware and he performed the Mourner's Kadish for Mrs. Greenhouse. During the service, Joe Biden entered the laundry room, which was the only room big enough to hold people in this apartment complex. He entered with his head bowed. After the service, Beals introduced himself to Biden and then asked why he was there. "Listen, back in 1972, when I first ran for Senate, Mrs. Greenhouse gave $18 to my first campaign because that is what she could afford. And every six years, when I would run for reelection, she'd give another $18. She did it her whole life. I'm here to show my respect and gratitude."

Joe is a flawed human being who too often suffers from foot-in-mouth disease, saying the wrong thing at the wrong time. I invited him to speak at the Episcopal Academy. He made you feel as though you had his full attention. He has total focus on the people he meets.

The right stuff. As part of his divine nature, Jesus had it! A black man, Mr. Williamson, who taught me the ways of the world when I worked in a steel mill had it. It is why I listened intently to him. You don't have to be an astronaut to have the right stuff! You just have to know what Loughlin and Gianelli did not.

Post 48.   A TikTok and Snapchat Culture

I didn't know what TikTok and Snapchat were, so I asked my sons. Most of you know that they are fifteen- to thirty-second sound bites of personal experiences. Hugh Evans, Co-founder and CEO of Global Citizen wrote that "The nature of consumption has changed. You are not going to sit and watch a Saturday night movie. You are going to consume content all day long."

It sounds as though, back in the day, that Andy Warhol may have been onto something when he said that "Everybody gets fifteen minutes of fame." We have become a culture of small bites of experience, whether it be visual or experiential. We know that TV commercials are brief with a catchy point and that political campaign propaganda adheres to this central truth. The developmental psychologists argue that this is why students can't receive information that is not given in small pieces. They can't focus for long. People don't read books. They purchase summaries, usually online. This is our world now, and it no longer requires patience.

Along comes the culture's nightmare, the Black Lives Matter movement and the pandemic, both requiring us to deal with the paradox of patience. Patience in receiving justice is neither tolerable nor should it be and patience with using the guidelines to rid us of the pandemic don't do things that quickly. We are relegated to our homes and our phones. You do not become fluent in the art of conversation, and it is an art if you are always checking your phone for TikTok, Snapchat, and what you need to know quickly online.

You don't have to have ever used one of the social media platforms to see how it has shaped us as part of our culture. It is a tacit influence. It is hidden in our daily lives. If you don't use a muscle, it will weaken. If you don't use conversation and tasks that require patience, then those will not be available to you when you need them. If you don't get off your phones, you will never be able to be alone with yourself. The Black Lives Matter movement has a paradoxical relationship with patience. They are part of our thirty-second or fifteen-second culture, so it is difficult to do when you realize that you have been patient long enough. John Lewis captured the dilemma of patience working for and against us when he said in his March on Washington Address that "To those who have said, 'Be patient and wait. We must say that it is a dirty and nasty word.'" Patience will only come when it is married to action to overcome institutional racism. It will come when words on placards become words in our hearts.

If Evans is correct that "you are not going to sit and watch a Saturday night movie; you are going to consume content all day long," then that mindset creates impatience within us. How are we expected to achieve living free of disease and get justice from enduring the disease of racism? The culture needs a long overdue shift!

Post 49.   Parents Make the Difference

There are many great things about teaching high school students ethics for thirty-eight years. I learned so much about decision-making, the nature of human beings, and how to live a good moral life from them. The students referred to it as full-contact ethics, for once you entered the room, you were going to learn about the various systems of ethical thought and how they apply to everyday life. I can't think of an issue that we didn't cover, and I am pleased to say that once the classroom was made safe for sharing their thoughts, they were amazed at how much they agreed and disagreed with one another. It is my job to create this safety by emphasizing civil discourse where you could not attack the person, but you could disagree with their perspective.

Since ethics doesn't happen in a vacuum, we had to talk about relationships and values. I have literally taught thousands of students. I discovered some fundamental truths. There were two things that most of the students agreed on that may or may not surprise you.

First, students are under constant evaluation in terms of appearance, what is cool at the time, and popularity to name a few. Their day is a constant evaluation. There were three feelings that they agreed that they would do anything to avoid. They are guilt, rejection, and vulnerability. They were quick to add that so much of their energy, for the most part, was to set up their life so that they would avoid embarrassment. Think about how much of these ingredients are part of your and my life, for students are an ethical microcosm of us. This helped me to understand a lot of their and my behavior.

Second, students say that they receive their values first from their parents or parental figures, such as a grandfather, a sibling, or a teacher. I met with older siblings of students who were taking care of all aspects of them. Some students also point out that they don't want to live like their parents. Notice the parent is still the reference point. Those character traits of who shaped our values and things that they would avoid reside in all of us as "our inner child of the past." How do they affect me today? How do they affect you today? Would you agree with these students' observations?

Post 50.   If You Don't Want Me to Hurt Him, You Are in the Wrong Place

Whether you are a Republican or Democrat, you have to recognize the tough road for women seeking political office. I have had the opportunity to work with strong women and have learned that the comfort level that I have with powerful women was modeled by a tough-as-nails mother who could care less if you liked her or not.

I had a parent come to see me because she was having a difficult time dealing with a verbally abusive husband during a messy divorce. She had an attorney but wanted another lawyer who may be able to help her more, but she didn't know what that "more" should be. I guess her lawyer was not as assertive as she felt necessary. We sat down across from a lawyer friend of mine, and she poured out her heart to him. Suffice it to say that this woman would be the opposite of my mother. Finally, my friend the lawyer said, "Listen, if you don't want me to hurt him, you are in the wrong place." I personally believe as was true for my lawyer friend that love and empathy are stronger forces than "hurting" another. However, certain circumstances, such as running for office, requires a real toughness as measured by the masses. "You have to be perceived as "tough as a man" but not too much for "you need to be liked." What a classic double bind that men don't have to navigate.

I have been studying gender issues for some time. I particularly have found the work of Deborah Tannen, a linguistic professor at Georgetown University, to be most helpful to me. I have read everything that she has written, starting with her important work described in *You Just Don't Understand: Women and Men in Conversation*. Women like to be liked much more than men. Men don't want conversation, which is the way that women develop intimacy. Men want closure with "a let's just get it done attitude" which is interpreted as decisive. These are culturally formed characteristics. You could find another culture where the reverse is true. They are not biological in nature.

Keep in mind the following during the Republican and Democratic Conventions and throughout the final stretch of this campaign. Here is what gender studies and social psychology tell us. Simply people will vote for a woman if they *first* like her, and then they will look at her leadership skills, political positions, and what she believes. They must like her *first*.

People will vote for a man if they agree with his political positions, leadership skills, and what he believes. That is *first*! They don't need to like him at all.

It was stated frequently that Hilary Clinton was the "most qualified person" to be president in the history of the presidency. It was also known in post-election interviews that people did not like her. People gave little regard for her history (I know that it was stated that she didn't get elected because of her views and a need for change. Deborah Tannen and I would not buy that.).

Donald Trump was not liked by many. Everyone thought that his locker room talk recorded by Billy Bush would be his end. He even thought that it was over, and post-election interviews reflected that he didn't think he would be elected at all. The people who voted for him overlooked his flaws and likability and voted for the *change* that they thought was necessary.

No one has noticed that gender issues and social psychology may determine the election more than we want to acknowledge. "If you don't want me to hurt him, you are in the wrong place." Watch how likeability issues expressed as weakness get carefully balanced with raw power in the days and months ahead. The males only have to win one half of the deal based on the issues. Kamala will have to pass both the issues and the likability test. Doesn't seem fair, does it? It never has been!

Post 51.   The Good Samaritan at Yale

Peter Salovey, president of Yale University, had a copy of his address to the class of 2020 in the recent *Yale Alumni Magazine*. What caught my eye was its focus on who would stop to help someone in need. He cites one of the classic studies from the field of social psychology done in 1970. The study is based on the familiar story of the Good Samaritan. It is a story of just who will care for someone who has fallen on hard times. A man is attacked by robbers and left by the side of the road. The first two people of high standing pass by, and they ignore him. The third man is a social outcast, puts him on a donkey, and takes him to an innkeeper, and says that he will pay for whatever the man needs. This story was the jumping off point of the study. But there was a different take on this parable about the busy nature of our lives. Who would stop if they were running late for a meeting, had some time to help, or had a lot of time to help?

The conclusion was that "the two who didn't help were not bad people. They just had busier schedules." Only ten percent of the groups stopped to help. Ninety percent who did not help didn't feel that they had the time to be of assistance. The study raises the question for the reader, "Are we too busy to help our neighbor, no matter what form the neighbor took?"

For me, there is another important point to this study. How willing are we to inconvenience ourselves to help another person? If you want to have a significant relationship with another person, you have to inconvenience yourselves for them. It's key. When I think of this attribute, I think of the marathon runner who is near the finish line and sees victory in view, and stops to help an injured runner, knowing it will cause him or her to not win the race.

When I was the head chaplain at EA, I tried to get to all the sporting events and performances that the students were in. I enjoyed watching them as I did my own children. The students knew that I had a demanding schedule, so it meant a great deal to them that I would use my time in that way.

Just when I thought that I went unnoticed, the students the next day after a game or match would thank me for coming to the game, match, or performance. They told me that the clerical collar meant that they could easily pick me out of a crowd, although some days I would be one of the few.

I am the same way. If someone goes out of their way for me, I am their friend for life. The relationship becomes cyclic. The military discovered this quickly through training and war. Remember that expression "leave no man behind," no matter how easy it would be to leave them there. You could listen as well to one of our nurses, doctors, first responders, and other essential workers during this pandemic. Their lives are about inconveniencing themselves for others. If we think about it, that is one reason why they are heroes. They stop by that person in need, even if it is an inconvenience, like any good Samaritan would do!

Post 52. Observational Bias: It Isn't Where You Think It Is

There is an observational bias that occurs when people only search for something where it is easiest to look. I would add—where prejudice takes them to their first thoughts. This looking for where it is the easiest place to go to is found in a joke, sometimes called the drunkard's search:

"A policeman sees a drunk man searching for something under a streetlight and asks what the drunk lost. He says he lost his keys, and they both look under the streetlight together. After a few minutes, the policeman asks if he is sure he lost them here, and the drunk replies that he lost them in the park. The policeman asks why he is searching here, and the drunk replies, 'This is where the light is.'"

I think that joke applies to us and how we see others and our own observational biases when we look at the pandemic and Black Lives Matter.

During the pandemic, people looked for the easier way to the simple solution. That is where the light of the easier solution is focused on many easier approaches—no masks, no social distancing, with lots of parties on the beach as well are closed areas. That is where the light is for them. They also have the quick fix of a magical pill. "Back in the park" where the real search needs to be done masks, social distancing, and hand washing will eventually lead our search to find what we are looking for: a reduction in cases and deaths from this deadly virus." It is easy to do as science shines on our solution.

Police think that a black person has a gun when he really has something, such as a camera. Malcolm Gladwell in this book *Blink* does an exhaustive study of observational biases, based on our preconceived notions of others. In fact, his book begins with police shooting someone who is unarmed and not a drug dealer, but as he stands talking with someone on his front porch, they think a drug deal is in process. Perception of people and their actions is a huge responsibility.

If you are a protester or aligned with their goals, you see the police as power hungry violent people. If you are a police officer or aligned with their approach, you see the protesters as people who are disrespectful, violent, and out of control. Observational biases are resolved by conversations and meaningful dialogue. Do I dare say the word, love, is the key? That is the ultimate light where we will find what we want. Think John Lewis. It is a place where religion may be a way to achieve this goal and to break down barriers. Certainly, John Lewis felt this way.

We all have observational biases. We are formed by each and every person we have met, and hence, they become part of who we are.

Jesse Jackson shares an interesting perspective on bias. He stated, "There is nothing more painful to me at this stage in my life than to walk down the street and hear footsteps, then turn around and see somebody white, and feel relieved.

Let's search for finding a cure for the COVID-19 virus or search for better community relations by looking in the right place in the right light.

Post 53. Gaslighting Is About Something Dark

We have heard the term *gaslighting* used frequently by the news media. When I first heard it, I didn't check out its meaning until it became such a daily reference in reporting. It is based on a movie, *Gaslight*, where a husband convinces his wife that she is really crazy. It occurs when the husband reduces the gaslight in the apartment and convinces his wife that she is imagining this reduction of light. His wife becomes a victim as he lies about the gas light dimming and claims that she is imagining things, causing her to question her sanity. The goal is to have the victim lose self-esteem and a grasp on reality. Today it most often refers to lies that are told repeatedly to the point that the victim doesn't know what is true or false.

This phenomenon gave birth to President Trump's calling everything he didn't agree with fake news. He lies repeatedly about his behavior and constructs his own reality.

I had never heard of the term *gaslighting*, but in my training in counseling, I was introduced to the "classic double bind" which can cause people to become unhinged. Double binds are when we are given two contradicting statements that cannot both be true. It was introduced in psychology by Gregory Bateson in the 1950s as a cause of deep distress. Two examples would be when a parent says to a child, "Sit down and be spontaneous in your writing!" An abusive husband may seriously injure his wife and then quickly hug her and tell her how much he loves her. Both examples demonstrate conflicting messages.

If you are constantly hearing someone say that everything is "fake news," a person can begin not to trust their own beliefs about a person or situation, particularly if this is said over and over again. Double binds depend on creating an environment of control, confusion, and chaos. It is hard to separate truth from fiction, and the perpetrator knows this and is effective in manipulating others.

This is countered in the news media by the creation of the "fact checker." In the words of the old detective series *Dragnet*, Sargent Friday wants one thing. "Give me the facts just the facts."

It is hard to confront double binds in relationships, but one proven way is to talk about it with someone who is objective outside of the relationship, such as a friend or counselor.

I saw this firsthand in working with students who were given double bind communication at home or with friends that caused them to feel that no matter what they did, they were wrong. They felt caught with no way to resolve the situation. They would usually start the conversation with me by saying, "Can I talk with you about a problem that I am having? It's no big deal." They really believed that it was no big deal, but then they would share with me a terrible situation with classic double binds, creating tears and sadness right before me.

My response was, "What you are going through is a big deal. That is a fact. Knowing that is the first step to getting your resolution of the issue. I will help you with that." Their relief would be palpable for they thought that they were losing their mind. Intervention produces results. As we have heard, you are entitled to your opinions, but you are not entitled to the facts of the matter. Facts are truth, and truth can set us free. If you feel someone has you feeling that nothing you do is right, get help. Gaslighting is about creating darkness of the most despicable kind, as it dehumanizes others on purpose.

Post 54. Classism

Barry Switzer, former football coach at Oklahoma, has perhaps the best statement that I have seen regarding classism. "These so-called captains of industry who were born on third base and think they hit a triple." In terms of class, where you start makes a big difference. Forty percent of Americans live paycheck to paycheck, with little or no reserve for rainy day emergencies. Children go to bed hungry in our nation. Children of the top two percent don't. Classism for all Americans makes a bigger impact than anything else in our lives including such things as our health and our safety.

I think that Americans have been sold a bill of goods about an opportunity that isn't fair. Follow your dream. Never stop trying. The problem is that a number of us make it out of the low socio-economic group, and we are held up as the standard bearers for those who still do not share in the American dream. By implication, if you don't "rise up," then you simply did not have the desire or the ability. The problem is that the gap between those with means and those without is now larger than ever. The middle class is a dying phenomenon. That does not bode well for our nation.

Have you ever wondered why the movie, *Rocky*, became such an important narrative for our nation? Our blood begins to stir when we hear the music that is a theme song for the movie. We love to see people make it against all odds. We love to see people have a chance to "rise up." Rocky is a noble journey. Every day people are pulled in spirit to the steps of the Philadelphia Art Museum to run up those steps and jump up and down in victory. I did it!

There is a diversity exercise that graphically points out the reality of how important where you start is to your journey out of poverty and into inclusion and acceptability. Questions are raised to see where your real starting line is located. Picture a runners' track! Do your parents have a college education? Take three steps forward. Are you attending a school system that is highly ranked in your area? Take three more steps forward. Can you go out to dinner any time your family would like? Take another step forward. The questions are questions of privilege. When the last question is asked, and you look where you are related to others, you quickly realize that you have had a head start. Some, however, have not moved off that first starting line.

If we assume that this is a race around a track with people of equal desire and ability, the winner is likely to be that person who started the race way ahead of you. The people who are still back at the beginning have to be more talented and harder working than the people who are ahead. Picture yourself in the starting blocks, for it is difficult for most to win in the end because they are weighed down by the internal messaging that life just isn't fair. It is a weight like no other.

The very first moral statement that a child makes is "It's not fair." That lack of fairness in life can weigh down even the strongest runner. The people in the blocks ahead of us at the starting line will have an advantage that is more than speed. They feel that they will have a chance. Those left behind want just that, a chance to "rise up" even if life is not fair. People need that sense of a chance just as much as they need to be talented and hard working.

What base were you born on? Third or just heading to first? Are you still in the dugout waiting your turn?

Post 55.   Born Again

Mark Twain once said, "The two most important days in your life are the day you were born and the day you find out why."

When I think about someone who was born again, I think of Malcolm Gosling. Malcolm was my sidesman, lay assistant, when I was the priest in charge of St. Paul's, Paget, Bermuda. He was everything that some people would want to be. He owned Gosling Liquor Stores, the largest alcoholic beverage vendor on the island. He lived on a palatial estate, was handsome, and regarded highly by all on the island. But what he wanted to talk about to anyone who would listen was how he was saved at a Billy Graham Crusade at Yankee Stadium. That was all that mattered to him. It gave me pause since my family and I were living in a home on the island with a large flower garden then worth 21 million dollars at the time. We had an honorary membership to the Coral Beach Club, and I had use of a car, which were few and far between then on the island. All of these were perks for being the priest in charge of St. Paul's.

Some would say that I had it made. Fortunately, I had already engaged the "why I was born" on my most important birthday.

I am reminded of a recent quotation by Jim Carey that "everybody should get rich and famous and do everything they ever dreamed of so they can see it is not the answer." As I sat in the garden of the estate, that is what I came to learn anew. When you go from nothing in material wealth to something, it can be like whiplash. Wanting more is the great spiritual head-fake. As a priest, I have had the privilege of being with many people at the moment of their death. At that moment, there is the realization that what endures is the spirit, not anything that relates to our acquisition of things or the world around us that we reach out to grasp for safety and relief. It is the spirit that is the "more."

What about the poor? They are nothing by the world's standards. Yet in their nothingness, they are closer to the reality of the kingdom of God than anyone. "Blessed are the poor in spirit for they shall inherit the kingdom of God" (Matt. 5:3). When your back is against the hardship wall, you can experience the gift of knowing the truth without the baggage of things. Did this biblical character not know his "why birthday?" Could this be what the wealthy man needed to know before he could enter the kingdom of God (Matt. 19:24)? His focus was still on his stuff. He was reluctant to enter the kingdom, keeping his faith in his things that would ultimately disappear.

There is another way of looking at Mark Twain's quotation. After we find out why we were born, for some it takes a daily reminder while for others it does not. The important thing is to know the why before you chase having too much. This does not mean that we give thanks for poverty. It does mean that we strive to change the why, knowing that there must be justice for all and that even God would not stand before a starving person except in the form of food. That, too, is the "more" that will connect us to the spirit of the living God in death and in life. We are called to nothing less.

Post 56. Labor Day

Today is Labor Day, which celebrates the importance of the working class. Every politician wants to be part of it and indicates that they came from a blue-collar background. Candidates for office want to demonstrate that they were true blue working class, doing as much with their hands as they did with their minds. Joe Biden is focusing on his Scranton roots, and Donald Trump is still trying to convince others that he only got a million dollars from his father, and he, too, is a self-made man. It is still a mystery to me that Trump's base can identify with this individual who never spent a moment doing hard physical labor. In addition, when his various building projects were completed and he hadn't paid his workers, he would indicate to all that he will give the workers half of what they earned. Take that! It is better than nothing because I will hold up your money for years with my lawyers. Oh, you don't have a lawyer? Tough! He has produced the ultimate "con" with his base of hard-working people who know sweat and toil.

I have had mixed experience with labor unions that are an essential part of working-class America! My father had a stroke and couldn't work for a year. The Meat Cutters Labor Union literally kept us alive with food on the table. My brother and I worked in a steel mill to put ourselves through college in conditions that were the same as those at the turn of the century. We earned money that guaranteed that we could attend a state college and have some leftover. I worked at the Krylon Paint Factory, loading skids of boxes with gallon paint cans until I couldn't raise my arms at the end of the shift. I worked in a ball bearing plant doing repetitive work at three lathes with people who were doing this boring task every day of their lives for a lifetime. I was a substitute teacher in the Philadelphia School System where I witnessed first-hand the union doing what benefitted the teachers first, with not as much concern for the students.

Like everything in life, unions have a cyclic nature starting with what was needed including important health benefits, and then taking advantage of the situation to line their pockets. The steel mill that was the source of money for my college education eventually closed because of excessive demands by the union. If you worked one hour, you were paid for forty hours, you had full health benefits, and every five years, a worker could take a six months sabbatical leave. The day that the plant closed, the members couldn't understand why the gates were closed and locked. They looked on in total disbelief. They thought that management would provide a never-ending giving tree.

The blue-collar worker is the heart and soul of our nation. Without the working class, there would not be an America. The massive amount of distance between the top two percent and the rest is something that we should fear as, without the blue-collar worker, America will no longer exist. It is difficult to fully assimilate that Jeff Bezos is the first 300 billion dollars man who has amassed his fortune on the backs of his $15 an hour workers.

There is something that Trump and Bezos will never know. They will never experience the feeling of doing something hard with your body and mind and feeling that relief as you sink into your bed at night. They will never experience blue collar grit. They will never experience a job with your hands where you feel that it is well done. They will never experience the shared purpose of slogging away together with others. Most important, they will never experience the kinesthetic intelligence where your body remembers the agony and ecstasy of hard physical labor and can become a reference point for moving forward through difficult times. Your body never forgets.

There is a story that John F. Kennedy was at a rally in Boston where someone from the crowd yelled. "Kennedy, you were born with a silver spoon in your mouth." Another member of the crowd yells, "John Kennedy, you didn't miss a thing." On this Labor Day, I couldn't disagree more that he didn't miss a thing because Labor Day celebrates what he missed and what made our country the greatest country in the world, the American worker!

Post 57. Lottery Winners and Accident Victims: Is Happiness Relative?

The title above is the title of a study done in 1978 by Brickman et al. regarding the steady nature of happiness, regardless of the ups and downs of life. In addition, the researcher, Sonja Lyubomirsky, discovered that every one of us has a "happiness set point" that is based on genetics. It makes up fifty percent of our happiness. In addition, ten percent of our happiness is derived from something outside of ourselves such as where we were born. That means that forty percent of our happiness can be determined by us and makes a key difference in how happy we are in life.

Our Declaration of Independence declares that we should fill our lives with life, liberty, and the pursuit of happiness. There is another aspect of happiness that we need to be aware of to live out the words of our founding fathers. It is called the Hedonic Effect or Hedonic Treadmill for you seem to return to where you began. Researchers have discovered that winners of the lottery have an initial burst of happiness and joy, but after a relatively short period of time, they return to the happiness level that they had before winning. Likewise, people who have had tragic accidents and who are in wheelchairs for life return to the same level of happiness they had before the accident.

This is a result of habituation, where you get used to both the good and bad news. A simple example of habituation is when we eat ice cream. It is the first spoonful of the ice cream that we really taste and enjoy, and the rest becomes like it. Another example is buying a loud ticking clock. You notice the ticking in the beginning, but then after a period of time, you don't notice the sound.

I remember when Joe Flacco, then quarterback of the Baltimore Ravens, signed a contract for 120 million dollars. After the signing, he went and had lunch at the local McDonalds. He was asked why he didn't change much of his life with all the money he received. His response was, "Why do I need a Porsche? I am fine with what

I have." He was interviewed six months after he signed the contract, and he reflected that he had the same level of happiness that he had before he signed. We see teams win a championship, and the players proclaim, "I am going to Disney World." It is nothing exotic. It is something that many people could do.

How do the Hedonic Effect and habituation relate to the pandemic and Black Lives Matter? I would anticipate that when we reach some level of closure on both of these phenomena, there would be a gradual return to our previous state of happiness. It may become like a distant memory or could revert to a form of Post-Traumatic Stress Disorder. We haven't seen anything comparable to either event recently, so there is no way to make a judgment. However, it will be interesting to see what researchers discover when it reaches some level of closure.

We have a level of habituation caused by these two phenomena where, for some, each day feels to be the same as the previous one. It reminds me of the movie, *Groundhog Day*, where Bill Murray's character is a cynical weatherman who goes to Punxsutawney to see if the groundhog sees his shadow. He keeps living February 2nd over and over. Habituation is necessary to move through these times. We know that we have been here before and can make it to the day after today. Alzheimer's disease, which has habituation at its core in the extreme, is a devastating illness. A physician friend whose wife has this disease said to me recently, "I now have to introduce myself to her each day when we awake."

That is why we need some form of closure on the pandemic and Black Lives Matter that dominate our lives. We don't want to relive this nightmare of extreme challenge. We need to be able to live with new hope and reclaim the happiness that so many of us can remember as a distant moment. The Hedonic Effect says that the possibility is there.

Post 58.   An Encounter with the KKK

I recall a time when I couldn't see the forest for the trees. We have a home on the Chesapeake in Cecil County, Maryland. I had heard this area is a center of "Klan Country," but that awareness was not on top of my mind on this particular day. The town nearest our home, North East, is ten miles up the road. The town has a community park with a pavilion where I was reading at one of the picnic tables. The book I had in hand was *Race Matters* by Cornel West. He is an African American scholar who is pictured prominently on the front cover. He appears to be coming right off the book cover. He is an intense guy, and his captivating book is as relevant now as it was during the time that it was written.

I was engrossed in the substance of the book and became aware that there were a number of pickup trucks equipped with gun racks holding guns in the parking lot. I went back to reading until it dawned on me that there were a group of white men staring at me with looks of anger and disbelief. I had stumbled into the middle of a Klan meeting. I think they were as surprised as I was. "That white guy must be crazy!" they likely thought. There were a couple of racial epithets spoken my way. I didn't think it would be a good time to share with them how race should matter in America. I didn't think we could even have had a conversation to agree to disagree. Discretion seemed to be the better point of valor. I quietly made my way to my car with a quick step and was relieved to be driving away. I think they were so dumbfounded that they were relieved as well.

What I have learned is that racism or any of the "isms," for that matter, are both taught and caught.

There is a powerful dynamic that bonds the Klan together. They have a common perceived enemy, so they create strong bonds by pushing others out of who they deem as unacceptable. They have their own immoral code, which makes sense to them but doesn't make sense to anyone outside of the group. They have a shared

87

purpose to promote white supremacy. The group enables them to increase their individual self-esteem while at the same time creating a sense of belonging to something that they believe has a larger purpose. They feel "I may be inferior, but we as a group are magnificent." Their actions make bad-intentioned people worse because of the power of increased numbers.

A quick historical analysis of the rise of Hitler contains the same group dynamics that promote the Klan.

Post 59. A Most Important Word

My dog Sadie, even though she is a canine, causes me to think about human nature. She loves food and people in that order. It's a basic truth for Labradors. There is one short word that gets her attention and causes her to run at warp speed to me. I can say in a loud voice, "Sadie, come here! Sadie, let's go!" and any other biddings. They get no response. However, I can say, "Eat!" in a quiet voice that you could barely hear and woe is the person who is between her and me.

I asked myself If there was a short word that gets my attention with that kind of power? There is. It is the word *no*. Churchill said, "You will never reach your destination if you stop and throw stones at every dog that barks." More recently, Steve Jobs underscored this thought that "innovation is saying 'no' to a thousand things."

No is hard for me and many others to say. *No* probably came into human existence when the first parents had a two-year old. They had to hear that word over and over from their child as the child attempted to separate from them and become their own person.

It is much less stressful to say *yes* than it is to say *no*. We will do anything to avoid the emotions of guilt, rejection, and vulnerability. Those feelings can be potentially generated quickly by *no* statements. Likewise, it is human nature to want to have a sense of belonging, and saying *no* to someone can open the door for us to feel that we may be excluded from being part of someone's life.

We have difficulty saying no to our children and forget at times that "to *no* you is to love you." As we attempt to set boundaries not only for children but also for colleagues and friends who have a request of us that we would rather not fulfill, we need to indicate, "Thank you, but, no, I can't."

No has received a lot of press in the legal world in the realm of sexual harassment and rape. *No* has now gotten some gravitas as a word that means "stop right now." It is the key word in defining consensual and nonconsensual sexual relationships. No means no. It doesn't mean maybe."

Our time is our most valuable possession. We have a limited amount so we must use it wisely with moments that promote growth in ourselves and others. *No* one thing could be a precondition for doing something more valuable. *No* is an absolute. There is nothing ambiguous about it in a world moving more toward everything being relative. *No* doesn't permit "I am not sure." to enter the room with us.

Of course, there is a case for "yes." I think that is an easier one to make!

By the way, Sadie does understand *no*, but *yes* not so much!

Post 60.   It Is What It Is

It is interesting how a phrase such as "It is what it is" enters public discourse. The president has said it regarding the number of deaths from the pandemic. It is usually interpreted as "That is just the way things are. You can't do anything about it now." It is a phrase that locks us into the spoken word in the present and the past. There doesn't seem to be any movement forward when you hear it. The phrase calls us to accept an interpretation of reality.

The problem is that it also removes responsibility from the person who is saying it. It refers to something that is inevitable when we know that a change of circumstances could have taken place if we only had a way to go back to do things a different way.

A perfect example would have been the revelations by Bob Woodward in his recently released book, *Rage*, that President Trump knew as early as January that the pandemic could be "the greatest challenge to his presidency." He chose to not only ignore the reality but also to downplay it. The result has been thousands of more infections and deaths.

"It is what it is" was meant to indicate that a harsh reality could not be avoided, like the fire in California. I haven't heard anyone say, "If only something could have been done earlier regarding the cause of the fire to prevent this tragic occurrence" (Notice that I say start of the fire as many of us believe that the fire continued due to climate change.). We can't control the high winds and dry nature of things in the West. It was a perfect storm of natural events.

But that phrase can be something very important if we hear it and say to ourselves "Could there have been anything that we should have done that could have prevented the fire to start?"

That helps us engage one of the truths that I live by that "Everything in life is to be enjoyed or learned from." If something could have been done, it changes our direction forward, making a difference in the future for the good of humankind. The phrase would have a purpose that can redeem what is happening in the present.

When President Trump said those words with a tough interviewer, I was looking for him to follow with a statement such as "It is what it is, but I have now changed the down-playing of the virus and will be encouraging mask wearing, social distancing, and proper hygiene.

I can only contrast two different messages that came about after the release of Bob Woodward's book. President Trump changed nothing in his response to an approach to the pandemic. His followers still say that the danger of the disease is "fake news." He is still without a mask. He is still making excuses, such as he didn't want to cause a panic. Dr. Fauci, on the other hand, proclaimed loud and clear that we better be aware that the fall and winter could be another very deadly time. He also disagreed with Trump's approach.

The next time you hear those words, "It Is what it is," listen carefully to discover if the person saying it has learned anything that would make our lives better now and in the future. Otherwise, you and I would just be joining the ranks of the irresponsible. Don't let a harsh reality go by without something positive coming from it.

Post 61. The Teleological Suspension of the Ethical

I don't know about you, but I had trouble with Bob Woodward interviewing President Trump in February, 2020 discovering that he knew the gravity of COVID and kept that secret until his book was published. A lot of people were crying foul. If he would have let the American people know then, even though President Trump had no plan to do so,'many people would have not died, our country's economy would not be in ruins, and people would not have had dire hardships to confront. He had it on tape! I also noticed that a good many news people backed Woodward up in his decision under the heading of "you have to check out the reliability of what was said. Checking your sources is the be all and end all." I don't buy it, but I can justify what Woodward did by something that I covered in my ethics course that seems to be at the heart of Woodward and the press' position.

I don't think that they had heard of Soren Kierkegaard (1813–1855), a Danish theologian, who introduced the world to the teleological suspension of the ethical in his book, *Fear and Trembling*. It means an unethical action can be performed for results that lead to a better end. Machiavelli, another philosopher, put it another way that "the ends justify the means." Both theories say that you can do anything along the way as long as it produces a greater-good result.

It is also a catchy phrase that you can throw around at a gathering to impress people, even if you don't know what it means. People, in general, don't like to appear less intelligent than others, so you won't be challenged, just as Woodward, in my opinion, hasn't been challenged enough about why he didn't come forward in a timely fashion.

However, I would argue that *Via Media* would be the proper way to go. That school of thought says that you have to choose the "lesser of two evils." Letting others know without proper checking of sources would certainly be more moral than letting people die, the economy tank, and for Americans to be thrown into economic despair. The *Via Media* approach to ethical decision-making also depends on a guiding phrase, "wrong but necessary." Could anyone debate the necessity of getting that news out earlier?

I wish I had Woodward in my ethics class. My students would never have let him get away with his excuse. I can just imagine one of my former ethics students knocking on the front door of Woodward's house, and saying, "I just want to let you know that I am not buying any of this teleological suspension of the ethical stuff." I did have a high-profile student-athlete introduce the phrase to a reporter who was interviewing him. The reporter was impressed. It appeared in his interview on the sports page! The key difference between my student-athlete and Woodward is that my student knew what the phrase meant and the ethical action required in dealing with the information that President Trump said on tape.

Post 62.   Who Boos Unity?

I watched the first professional football game of the season. Before it was played, there was a marvelous video highlighting Black Lives Matter that was accompanied by what is referred to as the Black National Anthem. It is really the hymn "Lift Every Voice and Sing." We had the National Anthem sung. Everything was going well as the Super Bowl Championship team, The Kansas City Chiefs, and the Texans gathered arm and arm across the entire length of the field as a statement of unity. It was then that the booing started.

There was a real danger of everything before the booing being forgotten until Tony Dungy, former coach of the Indianapolis Colts, spoke as one of the commentators. He is a person with gravitas, whose biography describes as a moral force in the National Football League. He said simply, "We can't get bogged down on who is there and who isn't and all of that. Let's keep the bigger picture in mind. The bigger picture was not about the booing. The bigger picture was about racial justice and Black Lives Matter. The bigger picture, without question, was about patriotism and love of country." The booing that occurred was about the *unity* that was expressed by the actions of the two teams. Yes, people were booing unity.

That bigger picture is a commentary on where our nation is today. We have just finished our 9/11 remembrance a few days ago. People were united in support of the families who lost loved ones on that terrible day. You can't imagine someone booing at one of the public services that were held. I believe that is true because we had a common enemy who did something terrible to our people and our place on our soil.

So why boo the gesture of two teams linked arm and arm on a playing field, graphically depicting a call for unity of all things? There is an old saying that, "We have met the enemy and it is us!" We need to be reminded that the most Americans killed in action was during the Civil War (625,000), not a war with a common enemy outside of our nation. It tore our nation apart. We were able to move forward because of leaders, such as Abraham Lincoln, whose words appealed to our better angels. He and others who followed changed the narrative to a new way of seeing things, a new idea to be underscored as equality for all. One of my guiding truths is that "ideas precede action." On 9/11, we have a unified view of what it means to be a patriot. That idea of love of nation comes first.

I think that we have lost the power of that idea of God, family, and country, except if you were or are part of our military, for that idea of freedom and liberty have exacted the ultimate price from many.

We now have patriotism spread throughout our essential workers fighting another common enemy, the virus, to protect us all.

We have the ideas that lead to patriotic action, The Pledge of Allegiance, The National Anthem, and "Lift Every Voice, and Sing." They are ideas that can be taken for granted. We need to say and sing them but also have them become more a part of us. Don't wait until an athletic contest to read their words. I believe it would be harder to boo a call to national unity if those patriotic ideas were more a part of our hearts and souls.

When I was in my final years of teaching, I shared a homeroom with a wonderful colleague. We said the Pledge of Allegiance at the end of each homeroom before the students left for class. There were times when both of us couldn't be in homeroom, and the students would always rise and say the pledge on their own. It was part of them. I would suggest that if they missed it, they would have felt that something was missing. How do I know this? They were quick to tell me the next morning after we weren't there that they didn't forget to say the pledge. They always remembered it.

We need to learn a lesson from them.

Post 63.   Freedom

I was traveling to a meeting at a college in mid-Pennsylvania when I became unsure if I was going in the right direction. I called a colleague of mine, who was studying in a community nearby to this college, and asked him if he could give me directions. He was from the Midwest, had a Mid-Western accent, and was filled with sayings from living in the heartland. He responded to my request for directions by saying, "Jim, it isn't the end of the world, but you can see it from there."

I reflect on his words differently, as I reach an age where it is certainly not the end of my life, but I can see it clearer from where I am at this time in my life.

I read an article written by Jack Riemer that appeared in the *Houston Chronicle* in 2001, describing the following experience. On November 18, 1995, Itzhak Perlman, the famous violinist, was giving a concert at the Lincoln Center in New York City. Shortly after the concert began, one of his strings broke. The sound of it could be heard throughout the hall. Everyone thought that he would stop, but he signaled the conductor to keep on going as he played the rest of the concert with just three strings instead of four. He did this with great passion. The audience gave him a thunderous applause. He smiled and using a humble voice said to the audience, "You know sometimes it is the artist's task to find out how much more music you can still make with what you have left" (Riemer 2001). That is what I am doing at this stage of my life. I am figuring out how much music I have left.

I wonder about how I sought direction in my own life from the beginning to now and how that has shaped who I have become. Have future considerations had anything to do with where I find myself today? I think of the Machiavellian notion that the "ends justify the means." According to him, it is what is in the future that makes right anything that we are doing in our past or present decision-making.

The question becomes: are we pushed through life by being informed by the past and "watching our time" in the present, or are we pulled into the future by future considerations? I believe we are both pushed and pulled in each moment.

Post 64.   Sports Are a Barometer of Friendship

Sports became the barometer of competition in our community. I was athletic but not as good at sports as some of the other boys in the school. We played sports in one of three places. One was our neighborhood, and another was a new sports facility that was built in our small community, the Fellowship House. It is still there today. When competing for our school, we used a field that was off-site.

The town in which I lived was ingrained with all sports. It really didn't matter how bad or good one was. Sports were a platform for my friends and I to meet. I was aware that I was not as good as some of my peers were at a particular sport, but it didn't bother me. However, the older I got, the more competitive I became.

For me, it was a time of innocence, we played sports for pure fun, something that has changed in our culture. Today parents scream from the sidelines of their son or daughter's little league or grade school soccer games where winning becomes the dominant reason for a game. I later became like many who favor the opportunity to win. To me, competition is an indicator that you have left the garden of Eden, where innocence reigns to being outside the Garden, where it is it is survival of the fittest.

An example of the importance of sports can be found in an exchange that I had with my recently deceased friend, Dr. John Kelly, who became a professor and consultant at Villanova University. The way competitions were arranged in Conshohocken often put the public school students, of which I was one, against our parochial school peers like John. I felt like I competed against him all of my young life, sometimes at the Fellowship House that contained a basketball court where some legendary players have played in various tournaments. There were times when I felt that this location was misnamed as the competitions had nothing to do with fellowship as much as they did with the seriousness of the purpose of going to war. Once we left the court or field, we became good friends again, but not a moment before. I think that must be the way of most communities, whether blue collar or not.

Years ago, when I lost track of John, I was walking down a hallway in a hospital. I saw someone with a beard walking toward me with a smile on his face. It was clear that he knew who I was, but I couldn't put a face with a name until he looked at me and said, "Jim Squire, left-handed jump shot." I immediately recognized John's voice, but I could not think fast enough to reply, "John Kelly, deadly three pointer!" We embraced, caught up with what we were doing in life, discussed our families, talked about the good old days, and were reminded that perhaps sports is a universal language. How did we both remember our signature shots after all those years that we didn't encounter each other?

Post 65. Leaders By Definition Always Work With Others

Leaders never accomplish anything on their own. There are four basic requirements necessary for any group to work effectively. I gleaned these principles from years of work with various leadership groups, most notably our Student Vestry, our elected student spiritual leadership group for Upper School. This group planned our chapel services under the guidance of Topher Row and me.

The first critical component of leadership is that everyone has to look forward to attending working meetings in the same way that a team looks forward to the big game. There has to be a positive mindset regardless of the difficult nature of the problem or endeavor to be discussed. What could be more exciting than going up against a great opponent in sports or tackling the solution to a serious problem?

Second, for a group to be successful, participants have to generally enjoy being in each other's company while working with each other. Civil discourse must be the goal. It is the leader, like a great coach, who makes sure this happens.

Third, there has to be a sense that what the group is doing is very important and will make a difference in other people's lives as well as in their own. I would always underscore for the Student Vestry the life changing potential of their work, as they shaped the moral culture of the school. I measured the success of a meeting by how much or how little I talked. The less I talked, the better. Coaches don't run out on a basketball court and get in the mix, but they enter the action when adjustments need to be made and insights shared. The important people are the students or players.

Fourth, when the meeting ends, the participants, including the leader, must feel that the meeting time was used efficiently. Setting clear goals and outcomes for each meeting and reviewing those at the close of the meeting can be a good way to gauge success.

The above four principles are the basics of effective leadership. I wish that all people would commit to learning the art of leadership from leaders who have done ordinary as well as extraordinary things. This approach has the potential to guide a person to develop a leadership style most congruent with their personality. For example, my neighbor on the Chesapeake was the person who led DuPont's efforts to enter the mainstream of Chinese business. It was a huge undertaking. I asked Bob one day to share with me the most important aspect of leadership that enabled him to have the success he did in China. He indicated that great leadership frames the conversation in a way that manages people's expectations. One of the first things that he did was to introduce his people to the concept of the "dirty thirty." The dirty thirty is as follows: if thirty percent of your day is a difficult challenge and seventy percent is filled with good things, then the day has been good.

One of the most valuable lessons I have learned about leadership and human relationships is something that I also taught in my ethics classes. Leadership can often be made strong during times of conflict and anger. Remember that anger is based on expectations. Think of the last time you were angry and seek to discover the cause of your anger in terms of a missed expectation.

I have read many books on leadership. By far, the best book that spoke to leadership in an engaging, enlightened fashion that made sense to me is Doris Kearns Goodwin's *Leadership In Turbulent Times*. It is an analysis of "the transformative leadership of Abraham Lincoln, the crisis leadership of Theodore Roosevelt, the turnaround leadership of Franklin D. Roosevelt, and the visionary leadership of Lyndon B. Johnson" (Goodwin 2018). Please know that an understanding of leadership cannot be gleaned solely from a book. It must be coupled with a deep understanding of human nature and care for others. Courage and resilience are essential.

The most important thing is to be YOU as a leader. *Esse Quam Videri* means "to be rather than to seem to be." There is a leader in all of us. We need only to discover it. The question is not "Am I a leader?" but "What kind of leader do I want to be?" You don't need a title to be a leader. You just need to see leadership as a valuable part of who you could be. No matter what your station in life, leadership awaits you.

Post 66.   The Need for Listening to Others

The inability to listen is a problem that confronts all communities. Compromise has become a dirty word. Too many people are only interested in winning, not understanding different points of view.

When Joe Biden came to our school to have a debate with Arlen Specter, their discourse emphasized a big problem in Washington. Nobody goes out to dinner together with members of the opposite party. The Republicans and Democrats exist in armed camps. They need to take a lesson from Tip O'Neill and Ronald Reagan, two legends of the American political landscape. They were a combative pair during the day. But after intense debate during the day, they would call each other and ask the question, "Is it five o'clock yet?"—their signal for the cocktail hour even if they weren't planning to have cocktails. It was a signal to leave the business of the day aside and talk as one passionate person to another about anything in life but politics. Any community needs to develop relationships first and then let the business to be dealt with after relationships have formed.

There is a tendency today to demonize others. When will we learn that hate and love reside in all of us? I would call our drive to judge original sin. It is part of our humanity. The more you deny a feeling, the stronger it grows. I believe there is good and evil in the world.

We know it when we see it. But let's not be hasty to make judgments about either side of those two moral descriptions.

Randy Pausch, in his book *Last Lecture*, made an interesting point that changed my thinking regarding listening to others. He states, "that there is good in everyone. Sometimes you have to wait to discover it, but if you hang in there, you will" (Pausch 2008). It has helped me to avoid going to a negative place with others too quickly when we are working to solve a difficult issue.

Post 67. Love Is Greek to Me

Love is a difficult word to wrap our minds around, but we overuse it. We love pizza. We love baseball, and so forth. It is a word that needs to be understood. In my ethics course, I taught the nature and characteristics of love, that love is one of the two pillars that support ethical action. The other pillar is justice. I based my observations on the Greek understanding of the four loves that were explored by C. S. Lewis in his book, *The Four Loves* (Lewis, 1960). I added to his thinking by exploring the Greek words in greater depth with the application of the tenants of psychology, theology, and philosophy. I also incorporated what I learned from students and adults along life's way.

Storge is the Greek word for the love of parents. Parents have shaped us more than anyone else in our lives. When I asked students the question, "Who has determined the most of who you are today?" They answered ninety-nine percent of the time that it was a parent or parenting figure, but I witnessed situations in my thirty-eight years as a school chaplain in which an older brother took on the role of the parent. Sometimes we desire to become exactly the opposite of our experience with our parents. Still, parents are the reference point.

Parents tend to love their children unconditionally. They can see the good in their children when others cannot. They love the ostensibly unlovable. They produce a warm and familiar environment for their children. They also need to say "mine" and be possessive in their approach to their children.

For example, the parent who has always been a great athlete will, at times, want his child to become an extension of his dream. This cannot occur when the child has a more intense interest in playing the violin. Parents can want their children to be an extension of their own selves. They assume that what they find enjoyable is what will also be enjoyable to the child. It may be or may not be. This is natural. Think about when you saw a great movie and one of your friends was not able to attend. The tendency is to encourage them to attend because you enjoyed it. They may see the same movie and think that it is terrible and wonder why you recommended it.

Storge, assumes much! This is an important characteristic. You don't really have to wonder whether your parents are going to let you into the house to have dinner. Parents, on the other hand, don't worry that you won't come home. But something that is assumed can be taken advantage of. Parents can take advantage of children, and children can take advantage of parents. *Storge* is a dynamic in friendship as well. We can assume that a friend will do one thing, and they surprise us and do another.

Philia is a Greek word that means friendship. There are many different levels of friendship. Some friends are people that you hang out with while others may be part of your inner circle where you can discuss issues that are very important to you.

Friendship always begins with a shared purpose. In some way, shape, or form, the friendship is forged by doing something, usually important, together. The troops in Vietnam were very diverse in terms of backgrounds and interests, but once they left the military, they became friendly with one another based on their common experience of war. They choose people who were right there with them because they did not have to explain what the experience was like. Research suggests that their war experience became a glue that bonds them together.

Friends tend to have a moral code or an immoral code. It is not written down, but you know exactly what you can and cannot do. It is a set of covert rules.

Whenever there is a group of friends there is always an in group and an out group. Anytime we say "us," we are implying that there is a "them." Anytime we say "we," we are implying that there is a "they."

Friendship is a powerful emotion. The two emotions that are most essential in our lives are self-esteem and a sense of belonging. These are primary emotional needs. Notice that I say a "sense" of belonging. There are times when we can have a large number of friends but don't sense that we belong, for we harbor thoughts of, *If they only knew what I really believe, they would reject me.*

Think about it. With friends, you get two things at once. It is like that favorite item in a grocery store when we can see that we can buy the item and get a second one free. We give a boost to our self-esteem with friends. We tend to gather with people who make us feel better, not worse. It is one of the main reasons we have friends. They know what it is like to be us. There is also the sense of belonging that we get by being part of the group. We feel surrounded by support, and that can take us out of ourselves. Loyalty to friends is what creates peer pressure. Alone I may not be so great, but together we are magnificent. The power of the group can be seen as a driving force, making well-intentioned people better and bad-intentioned people worse. Think of the power of a cancer support group with the power to do good, and think of the KKK as a group with the power to do bad.

Friendship can be the basis of all "isms" and prejudices. When we find an innocent victim who did nothing to deserve our contempt, friendship is a powerful glue to hold the group dynamic together. At times, the best way to feel included is to push someone out of the group. The most up-to-date analysis of bullies is that they engage in this behavior because they have such low self-esteem that they feel as though they don't belong.

Eros is the Greek word for sexuality. Here I am referring to something that is beyond the sex act itself. I am referring to the chemistry of human sexuality. When passion enters a relationship, reason usually leaves the equation in this kind of love. Adolescence is a time when hormones are raging for both the male and the female. Sometimes their actions have us wondering about their sanity. Again, passion causes reason to step aside. Our behavior makes perfect sense to us while our friends may see our behavior as self-destructive. Why would a happily married man leave his wife and children for another? Why does a public servant lose the respect of his constituency by having an affair with someone else?

Agape is God's love for us, seen by C. S. Lewis as holding the natural or biological loves mentioned above together. Each love is like a magnet wherein both the positive and the negative charges are needed. Sometimes this is expressed as, "Life is a two-edged sword." Everything can work for us or against us. The love of God is the source of all love, and our love is a reflection of God's love as the primary source.

Post 68. Temporary and Permanent Mindsets

Have there been certain ways you thought you should act to be accepted by yourself or by others? How did you handle those behaviors? Do you feel you were successful in incorporating them into who you are today? Did you turn away from those behaviors when you thought they were no longer helpful to you? One negative behavior that comes to mind is the quest to achieve perfection. People who chase perfection never feel that they measure up to this unrealistic standard. The quest for perfectionism tends to go along with the whole human package whether we like it or not. Perfectionism can be deceitful. It can creep up on you when you least expect it. One of my mantras for learning has been "learn to fail or fail to learn."

In the 2018 French Open, Sloane Stephens was defeated by the number one tennis player in the world, Simona Halep. Sloane had high regard for Halep, and following the match, paid her opponent a great tribute. After taking time to reflect on her own performance, Sloane posted an inspiring message, "You win or you learn, but you never lose" (Stephens 2018).

In my years of teaching, I have observed that the students who struggle the most are those who have not had a "positive failing experience" from which they have learned and grown. Carol Dweck has a model that is very helpful in framing one's life in a way to address failure and create a positive experience from it. If you have failed a test (or submit where you think that you have failed) and feel that it is a permanent issue for your life, you find yourself depressed, possessing a negative attitude toward yourself, and the inability to cope with moving forward (Dweck 2006).

If after failing a test, you say to yourself or others, "I am stupid. I will never be able to do well in this course," you lock yourself into that mindset. If, on the other hand, you feel that your poor performance is a temporary condition and that you have identified the issues of why you didn't do well, then you will be able to say to yourself, "I didn't do well on this test, but I know what I need to do to correct things to do well on the next evaluation." This attitude will enable you to see life as a challenge but one that you feel confident in addressing as you move forward.

People who frame life in a temporary way as they address issues take baby steps. That is one of the key tenets of Alcoholic Anonymous, still the preferred treatment platform for alcoholism today. They stress the mantra, "Take one day at a time." That approach can also be applied to most problem solving.

The person who has a negative permanent mindset feels that change is not possible. All of us feel this way from time to time. This mindset destroys hope. Individuals with permanent mindsets that are not positive take a long range view that stifles progress. I once met with a parent who was paralyzed by the thought that her child would not be admitted to Princeton. The child was in first grade. Taking the long-haul perspective is not the way to problem solve.

The work of Edison and Einstein that led to their scientific discoveries illustrates that even for the greatest problem solvers, baby steps and many failures along the way were the reason they achieved so much. There are few overnight successes in life. The people, who seem like overnight successes, usually combined years of practice or work that met with good luck or providence.

Post 69. Never Forget Where You Came From

A Paradox: A Seeming Self-Contradiction

Never forget where you came from. Live in the now. Always remember where you are going. Keep these three balls in the air at the same time like a juggler of life. An analogy that can help you to visualize this paradox is a ride in a car. There are times when you are right in the moment, but at the same time, you have to look through the front windshield to see where you are going, and check the rearview mirror to see where you have been, particularly in the heavy traffic of life.

When I finished writing my memoir, I wanted to touch the roots of where I came from. Vicki and I went back to Conshohocken to locate the Alan Wood Steel Coke Plant where I was employed in the summers to earn money for college. It was a place that provided a formative experience for me. We drove up the Schuylkill River that runs along Conshohocken, the blue-collar town where I was born and raised, and couldn't find the coke plant so we went to the borough hall. No one remembered it. They were all pretty young. They suggested that I walk down the street to a frame shop where the local unofficial historian of the town worked. I asked to talk with him. He was enthusiastic about the history of the town and its surroundings, so I told him that I couldn't find the coke plant. I asked where it was. He pulled out some books that contained pictures of the plant and then said, "It's gone!"

I couldn't believe what I was hearing. I asked, "How could it be gone? It was an iron edifice complete with tunnels, ovens, and conveyor belts that reached to the sky?" It took up miles of space. He said just one word, "Dynamite." The area is now filled with new industries, such as the *Inquirer* newspaper printing plant. He let me know that a professional demolition company destroyed the plant and carried the remains away, earning a great deal of salvage money. It was gone! How funny! It can't be gone because I can remember every inch of the place and the cast of characters who inhabited it. My only regret was that I had wanted Vicki to see it!

We then drove past my family home that was built by my grandfather. He raised a family of twelve children in that tiny home. There is a narrow alley in between my home and our neighbor who introduced me to the world of boxing. The home is where I was born and raised. We lingered in front of the home, remembering times we visited my parents there with Thad and Joanna. We then passed the bar where my father was a too frequent customer when I was young. We continued to A. A. Garthwaite Field, one of the first lighted stadiums in the area. It was Conshohocken's version of *Friday Night Lights*. Everyone came to the games. The air was always electric with excitement!

I remembered everything being much larger than it really is. Perhaps the past looms larger in affecting our lives than I was willing to admit. I should have taken the advice that I have given to so many others, "Don't forget where you came from." I will now repeat that statement with more enthusiasm, intensity, and importance.

I believe that we as human beings are more alike than different, no matter what our life circumstances, race, or creed. I believe that an important question needs to be asked to find your purpose in life. That question is, "How did I get here from there?" The answer rests in you.

Post 70. My Faith in Action

I have experienced God and my Lord in my life in very direct ways. I turn to the very core concept of religion itself and one of its important tenets: relationships are an integral part of religious experience. A central tenet of Judaism and Christianity is the *Shema:* Jesus is asked, "Which commandment is the first of all?" Jesus answered, "The first is 'Hear O Israel: the Lord our God, the Lord is one; you shall love the Lord your God with all your heart, with all your soul, with all your mind, and with all your strength.' The second is this, 'You shall love your neighbor as yourself.' There is no other commandment greater than these" (Mark 12:28–31).

The word *religion* comes from the Latin word, *ligare,* which means "to connect." Religion describes our relationship or connection to God, to others, and to self. This is why there is an emphasis on relationships in this book. This emphasis is noted also because ethical decisions never occur in a vacuum. All decisions affect others in some way, shape, or form.

In the Gospel of John, this central point of the *Shema* is underscored with Jesus' words, "This is my commandment. That you love one another as I have loved you" (John 15:12). I believe our faith in God comes about in at least two ways, the way we treat ourselves and the way we treat others. Many years ago, I was taught that if you want to know the deepest truth about a person, ask them what they would like you to pray for. For me, prayer can occur in the most unusual settings, such as staring out into a sunset over the Chesapeake Bay or having a run where I see the nature of God in ways that I had not experienced before. Prayer is central to corporate worship. This is the first part of the *Shema*, "Love God!" meaning to love God with a sense of gratitude for all aspects of life.

The second part of the *Shema* is very important as well, "Love your neighbor." We experience significant physical pain in the world, such as illness, hunger, and war along with all the many forms of injustice and pain that often seem to be wrought by others on us.

Jean-Paul Sartre, the founder of modern existentialism, in his play, *No Exit*, writes, "Hell is the others!" (Sartre 1955). A lot of our pain is emotional in nature and caused by our relationships with others. But just as relationships can create pain, they can also create a sense of heaven coming into our lives.

I believe healthy relationships are critical to happiness, joy, and the spiritual life. Relationships are contracts we make with others. Since the dynamics of these contracts assist our spirituality—Love God and love your neighbor are also a covenant. Covenants have two parts. You need to be living in *both* parts of the *Shema*, not just one or the other. Loving God and loving others are the central ingredients to Christianity and Judaism.

Post 71.   Gone with the Wind

I have the cure for those who don't believe in institutional racism. Watch *Gone with the Wind*, and discover some of its history. I watched it recently. It is an American romance film set in the Old South, released into theaters on December 15, 1939. With adjusted monetary inflation, it is the highest grossing film in history. It was awarded the Best Picture at the Oscars.

Here is what else you need to know: 300,000 people lined a seven-mile stretch to see the motorcade of actors. Hattie McDaniel, who plays a house slave for a family, won an Oscar for the best supporting actress. She was the first African American to win an Oscar. She was not permitted to attend the premiere as it was shown in a whites-only theater in Atlanta. She had to sit in a separate part of the Ambassador Hotel in LA where the Oscars were held. When she died, she was not permitted to be buried in the Hollywood Cemetery that was restricted to whites only. She experienced racism all of her life, even in her death.

Gone with the Wind is considered one of the "lost cause" movies, which attempted to "erase the brutal nature of slavery and preserve a cherished way of life." The movie is regarded as a direct descendant of D. W. Griffith's, *The Birth of a Nation*, whose heroes are members of the KKK. I found *Gone with the Wind* to be repulsive in its demeaning, dehumanized, and stereotypical images of black people. When it is shown now, it has the disclaimer that "It denies the horrors of slavery." Many would like it to be rated "O" for offensive.

It has been noted that the film should continue to be shown to show the impact of Hollywood on institutional racism, for the town always presents itself as the bastion of liberal causes. We should not forget that this is part of their history as well. Something that people are not aware of is that Hitler loved American movies. He sometimes showed two or three each evening in his screening room. Two of his favorites were Laurel and Hardy and Mickey Mouse, but the movie that was thought by film experts to be his favorite was *Gone With the Wind*. Enough said! I will leave it to your own thoughts to speculate why!

Post 72.   Gratitude Is Where Psychology, Theology, and Ethics Meet

Gratitude is the hallmark and characteristic of people who live to benefit others. Their attitude and actions create true happiness. Gratitude is where theology and psychology meet. A grateful heart is the beginning of a truly religious experience. In my career, I have experienced this phenomenon over and over in connecting to others, young and old alike. The chapel experience at EA is a place where people are reminded of this important aspect of creating meaning, happiness, and purpose in their lives. You will see this as a theme in a sampling of chapel addresses included in my memoir. Gratitude is the source of giving. It is important to recognize this aspect of theology.

Gratitude plays a large role in psychology. Students at Penn, who take the Positive Psychology course, do at least two assignments focusing on gratitude as the central tenet of being happy and creating a sense of purpose and a commitment to something important beyond one's self. The first assignment is the gratitude letter.

Students write a letter to someone who they are grateful for in their life and describe what has created this gratitude. The student must hand deliver the letter to the person and wait as the person reads it. It is an emotional experience for both the giver and the person who is receiving the letter. This is a perfect example of "You only get to keep what you are willing to give away." I always tell people to keep these letters and reread them when they are having a bad day to be reminded of their goodness.

Although it did not take the form of a gratitude letter, I saw this over and over again in the ethics course I taught. At the beginning of the course, the students go through an exercise to identify the core personal value that guides much of their decisions. They also have an assignment to identify the core interpersonal value that reflects what is most important in their relationships with others. Where the personal core value and the interpersonal core value intersect is a powerful force in how they make decisions.

In my ethics course, I indicated that I did not want them to reveal their core personal value. It was just for their eyes. I also indicated that I would be the only one to read their essay on their core interpersonal value. When I graded their essays and returned the papers to them, I made a point to encourage them to guard the privacy of these very personal papers. Certain essays were a powerful statement about the students' parents as a guiding factor. At times, I would include in my comments that they should consider showing the essay to the person who has affected them the most. It was always a suggestion, not a requirement.

An Early Morning Visit

This activity became as moving an experience as the gratitude letter was in the course at Penn. One example will demonstrate this. I arrived at my office one morning and was in the process of unlocking the door when I heard, "Good morning, Reverend Squire," coming from someone in the conference room across from my office. I must have jumped a foot off the ground as I wasn't expecting anyone to be there. The woman was crying. Tears streaked her face. I was contemplating what problem could have put this parent in such a state of despair. I was wrong. She had tears of joy. She was a parent of one of my ethics students. The student had written her essay on how her mother was the greatest influence in her life and how grateful she was for all her mother did for her. She showed me the essay that she had clutched in her hand and proceeded to say, "I felt like dirt under her feet. I never knew how deeply she appreciated me." I learned that daughter and mother embraced and cried together. "Now I feel as though we have a much better relationship. It is the nicest thing that ever happened to me."

I have literally taught thousands of students, and I always asked a question of them in class, requesting they raise their hands to answer in the affirmative. I asked them, "How many of you feel that the greatest influence on shaping your values has been your parents or a parenting figure, such as a grandfather?" Every hand goes up affirming that parents are, for better or worse, the value makers of their children.

I asked another question, resulting in all hands raised, "How many of you spend too much time avoiding the emotions of guilt, vulnerability, and rejection?" All hands went up. Does that surprise you?

The second gratitude exercise practiced in the Penn Positive Psychology course has been documented with scientific research to support its efficacy. The exercise entails writing on paper what you are grateful for that occurred that day and focusing on those things or events before bed. This is seen as an exercise that promotes sleep better than other approaches, including medications. I would add that offering a prayer of thanksgiving for those positive occurrences enhances the exercise.

Post 73.   The Road Less Traveled

There is an underlying dynamic in people that creates this ability to take the road less traveled, to work hard, and to take risks. I learned

111

about this underlying dynamic from Chaim Potok, the author of *The Chosen* and other novels. Chaim Potok authored popular books and was a rabbi in the conservative tradition. All of our students on the Merion Campus were required to read *The Chosen*. Potok was influenced by Evelyn Waugh's book, *Brideshead Revisited*. It is a story about different cultures that coexist on an English estate. All of Potok's novels deal with the confrontation of different cultures and difficult choices that need to be made as a result of encountering different perspectives. I asked Rabbi Potok to come to our campus and to speak about his novels and the values in life that are necessary to confront different cultural values.

As a result of this invitation, we became friends. We certainly represented two different cultures, but we found a lot of common ground. He told me a story that I have passed on to my children and others so that they would know that I understood their effort and passion on the road less traveled. Chaim shared with me that in the conservative Jewish culture, it is frowned upon to become a writer of popular fiction as opposed to scholarly works for academia. In this manner, he experienced his own core cultural confrontation.

He wanted to write novels. His mother discouraged it. Then his popularity took off and he was recognized as a brilliant novelist. His book, *The Chosen*, sold 3,400,000 copies. He still felt his mother's disapproval. Once on a visit with his mother at Miami Beach, Chaim walked down the beach and saw many people with his book in hand. He asked one person if he could see the book. It had an inscription inside which read, "To _____ and signed, the mother of Chaim." She had come around to supporting his passion.

This gave me the perfect opportunity to ask the question that was burning inside me. "Chaim, what empowered you to go up against your culture, and more importantly, your mother, to become a popular novelist?" He looked at me. There was silence. A smile came over his face and he proclaimed, "I wish I had a choice."

In a recent exchange with one of my sons, I told him that I would always support him one hundred percent. I also expressed my worry. His response was, "Don't worry. I am fine!" I told him that it is natural for parents to worry when they watch their children struggle, but it is my job to let them know I am with them. Still, a part of me wishes they chose a more conventional path in life.

Post 74. Logotherapy: The Importance of Future Considerations

Years ago, when I was studying in New Haven, I came across a slim volume of a book concerning the Holocaust, *Man's Search for Meaning,* by Victor Frankl. The book has two basic parts. The first shares what it was like for him to be in a Nazi concentration camp. The second part of the book describes a type of therapy pioneered by Frankl, "Logotherapy." The book seeks to answer the question, "How can people find meaning in their lives under the worst possible conditions?" Frankl quotes Nietzsche, "He who has a why to live can bear almost any how" (Frankl 2006). The book is a vivid account of life in a concentration camp. In this extreme setting, he learned how to survive and thrive in any situation.

There are two ideas at the heart of what Frankl discovered and that form the basis of Logotherapy. The first tenet is the value of love and loving as a key ingredient in one's life. Frankl thought that love was the be-all and end-all of life. In other words, we all desire to love and be loved. Beck Weathers, who was part of an ill-fated climb up Mount Everest, was able to survive when so many others didn't because he constantly thought of his wife and children. He could not imagine life without them. He was driven to this reality as a result of traveling the world over, looking for meaning. Then in his quest for survival on Mount Everest, he was led to discover that meaning had always been in his backyard (Weathers 2015).

The second idea on the basis of logotherapy is that one must have a future goal to look forward to. Mankind is the only species whose life is future-directed. Hope is future oriented and beckons us into our future.

The Importance of a Sense of Future in Slavery

The history of slavery in the United States holds many similar survival stories that reflect Frankl's findings. Enslaved people were often criticized for having an unrealistic view of their situation. Their religious fervor and music focused on the Promised Land, not on the justice they needed more immediately. I believe that it was that future consideration of heaven or a better life in the future that enabled them to survive.

The goal of the Underground Railroad was described as getting to the Promised Land. Any enslaved person dreams of being with loved family members and friends. That was part of their identity and a daily dream. Spirituals that were sung by enslaved people had covert meanings. The codes often related to how to escape to a free part of the country. There are many metaphors of "home," for a home is a safe place where everyone can live free.

The "Gospel Train" includes a direct call to get away.

> The Gospel train's comin',
> I hear it just at hand.
> I hear the car wheels rumblin'
> And rollin' thru the land.
> Get on board little children,
> There is room for many more.
> I hear the train a comin';
> She's loosed all her steam and brakes
> And strainin' ev'ry nerve.
> The fare is cheap and all can go;
> The rich and poor are there.
> No second class aboard this train.
> No difference in the fare.

"Swing Low Sweet Chariot," describes the identity and destiny of an enslaved people. It is filled with hope to connect them to a new future.

Swing low sweet chariot
Coming for to carry me home.
Swing low, sweet chariot
Coming for to carry me home.
I looked over Jordan, what do I see,
Coming for to carry me home.
A band of angels coming after me,
Coming for to carry me home.
Swing low, sweet chariot
Coming for to carry me home.
Swing low, sweet chariot,
Coming for to carry me home (www.negrospirituals.com).

Future Considerations in Judaism and Christianity

The enslaved people in the United States were influenced by the biblical traditions of both Judaism and Christianity. These traditions played very important roles in their spiritual lives. One of the central elements of Jewish scripture is the story of the Hebrews escaping the bondage of Egypt to enter the Promised Land "of milk and honey." This event is celebrated every year as Passover. Foods served for Passover symbolize the event. For example, unleavened bread is used to symbolize the haste with which they had to leave Egypt. They had their sense of a future goal to reach the Promised Land. This story is repeated each year across the world. The service of Passover deals with the central question, "How is this night different from all other nights?"

The Reverend Dr. Martin Luther King, Jr. proclaimed these famous words:

Well, I don't know what will happen now; we've got some difficult days ahead. But it doesn't matter to me now, because I have been to the mountaintop. And I don't mind. Like anybody, I would like to live a long life—longevity has its place. But I am not concerned about that now. I just want to do God's will. And He allowed me to go up to the mountain. And I have looked over, and I have seen the Promised Land. I may not get there with you. But I want you to know tonight, that we, as a people, will get to the Promised Land. So, I am happy tonight; I am not worried about anything; I am not fearing any man. Mine eyes have seen the glory of the coming of the Lord (Delivered on April 3, 1968 in Memphis, Tennessee at Bishop Charles Temple).

The heart of the Christian tradition is the Resurrection. It is the core of the Christian identity. Just as Jesus was resurrected, so those who believe in him now will be resurrected. They will have eternal life, the ability to be alive in the fullest moral sense and to look to a future at a heavenly banquet. The Christian identity is clear, and the future destiny of the kingdom of Heaven is just as clear. In the Gospel of Matthew, we hear, "Do not store up for yourselves treasures on earth where moth and rust consume and where thieves break in and steal; but store up for yourselves treasures in heaven where neither moth nor rust consumes and where thieves do not break in and steal. For where your treasure is, there will your heart be also" (Matt. 6:19–21).

Apocalyptic literature in the Bible says that God will have ultimate control over all future events. In the book of the Revelation of St. John, we see the description of this kingdom which we are drawn to as a future home, "After this I looked and there was a great multitude that no one could count, from every nation, from all tribes, peoples, and languages, standing before the throne, robed in white with palm branches in their hands. They cried out with a loud voice saying, "Salvation belongs to our God, who is seated on the throne of the lamb" (Rev. 7:9–10).

One can see how a future perspective could be envisioned for those who are undergoing hardship, "They will hunger no more and thirst no more; the sun will not strike them, not any scorching heat; for the lamb at the center of the throne will be their shepherd, and he will guide them to springs of the water of life, and God will wipe away every tear from their eyes" (Rev. 7:16–17).

Identity and destiny are essential to surviving and thriving in this life and the life to come.

Post 75. I Don't Know and I Don't Care

We can get a first-hand look at a major challenge that we face in our culture by considering recent news. First, a survey indicated that one out of ten Americans blames Jewish people for the Holocaust. Ten percent don't believe that the Holocaust happened or aren't sure that it took place according to a study from the Conference on Jewish Material Claims Against Germany, while sixty-three percent of the people surveyed in our nation don't know that six million Jews died in the Holocaust. All of this comes under the heading of being misinformed, being a history denier, or just unaware.

A head fake is a sports term for thinking that a person will be running one way and then they change direction. Today, the Big Ten reversed course and will play football this fall in a truncated manner. Of the many reasons given, no one can really figure out why this change of course occurred (full disclosure: I am glad that they are playing).

President Trump spoke at the Constitution Center in Philadelphia and broke a record for the number of lies that he has spoken in the shortest period. I hope that people see the irony here that the Constitution is our written version of the truth for us. He also is on record in an audio recording for playing down the lethal nature of COVID-19, but now says that he never said that.

Climate change is a proven scientific fact. President Trump said, "I don't think the scientists know. It is going to get cooler. Dr. Redfield stated, "Masks are more important than the vaccine to deal with the virus," whereas President Trump said, "Masks don't help." I could go on and on, but you get the picture.

The top communications official for the Department of Health and Human Services is going on medical leave after urging President

Trump's supporters to prepare for an armed insurrection and accusing scientists of his agency of sedition. "When Trump refuses to stand down in January, the shooting will begin."

When the Director of the CDC said that a vaccine will be available in the spring of 2021, Trump indicated to the press that Dr. Robert Redfield was "confused." What and who do we believe? This is merely a short week of news. It is filled with a lack of awareness, threats (sedition by the way is treason and is punishable by death), and lies.

The problem is also that we have gotten so used to this kind of news cycle that it hardly affects us with the anger and response to lies that have been told. We are living that experiment where a frog is placed in water, and the temperature is gradually increased to a boiling point. The frog doesn't jump out, which it would normally do if it were immersed in boiling water at the outset. It is boiled alive by the gradual increase in heat. Any of the above news pieces should give us great pause in "normal" times." We need to look at the context and the individual pieces that leave us wondering about the truth of the matter.

We need to focus on the fact that six million Jews died in the Holocaust. We need to focus on the various incendiary statements that are uttered from the White House and the Constitution Center. It would be helpful to know what informed a decision change in Big 10 football and not a lot of speculation. We need to get specific. When we call people on each head fake, misinformation, incendiary comment, we can have the truth that sets us free. Right now, lack of truth has been normalized to the point that it overwhelms us. This context needs to change.

We need to be reminded on a daily basis of the phrase that will permit lies to dictate how we see the world and how we feel. That destructive phrase is, "I don't know, and I don't care!"

Post 76. Spencer and Hawk

When I developed a friendship with Chaim Potok, author of *The Chosen* (sold 650,000 books), and many other novels that had the theme of core values in confrontation with the culture of the world around the individual, I learned why Potok chose to take on that theme of seeing his books as a merging of different worldviews. He had read Evelyn Waugh's *Brideshead Revisited*, the story of the caste system that existed in a grand home with family and servants. It was very different from the world in which he lived. He was a conservative Jewish rabbi in America. Waugh's novel inspired him and took him into a different world of English nobility and estate living that had some shared cultural impact and values in the lives lived in Waugh's novel. Two very different worlds with a shared experience.

I now find myself doing somewhat the same thing. During the day, I read books that would help me help others. I never read fiction anymore. However, I now found myself reading a chapter or two of one of Robert B. Parker's forty mystery books before bed at night about a detective, Spencer, and his partner, Hawk, who possessed the same character traits.

Most of what I read during the day is "heavy" stuff which helped me help people in very difficult physical, spiritual, or emotional challenges. At bedtime, I pick up a Parker book. I do this because he writes beautifully. He has a PH.D. in English Literature and took me into a world that is different from the one that I usually occupy. His books are about Boston and its environs, for that is where he was raised and went to school.

But there are other reasons why I read the Spencer series. Both he and Hawk are part of a hardscrabble world, which helps me to touch my origins in a blue-collar world. Spencer is white. Hawk is black. Their respect and regard for one another transcends race. Spencer never kicks someone when they are down and thrives on an investigation that has a narrative that is against all odds. His books are filled with diversity, religious and otherwise. Spencer's partner in life is Jewish. I also enjoy the way that they go about solving crimes with a "wait and see how things unfold" manner, reflecting a lot of thinking outside of the box, lateral thinking.

Spencer is a modern-day Sherlock Holmes. The books also have twists and turns, which keep my interest. Like Potok, I see that various narratives in the story are similar to my own interior narrative and values that are important to me. Spencer and Hawk are courageous, honest, direct, and empathetic to those they are trying to help. They are "old school" and "new school" all at the same time.

I never read a book more than once, but I can go back and reread books in this series, and it doesn't bother me. It's a bit like when I would read to my children before they went to bed when they were young. "Read it again!" they would say. "Read it just one more time!" I knew that it wasn't all about the story, but how the story connected to them and turned up in their everyday lives. My oldest son loved *The Little Engine That Could*. He would ask that I read that to him over and over. The engine's mantra, as the little engine attempts to take a heavy load over a mountain, is "I think I can! I think I can!" One day when my son was riding his tricycle up a steep hill with me walking behind him, I saw him struggling and finally rising off his seat to get more power on the pedals, and then I heard it, first softly and then louder, "I think I can! I think I can!"

Maybe there is nonfiction in the fictional mysteries that I read before bed. I always want to be reminded of those key virtues that I want to have moved around in my soul that Spencer and Hawk embody, a reminder of virtues even though from another world of experience.

Post 77.   The Importance of a Duet

Chief Justice Ruth Bader Ginsburg died the day before I wrote this. My heart sank when the news flashed across my TV screen. She is one of the truly great members in the history of the Supreme Court. She was brilliant and known as one of the key people in American life for advancing the rights of women. She has been enormously popular among Americans for her courageous stands, for her keen interpretations of the law, and for her grit! But there is one trait that I hope doesn't get lost in the celebration of her life which is sure to come. She loved the law, and she didn't let ideology get in the way of her relationships with others. This characteristic is the vaccine for the dis-ease of the divisive partisan politics that exists across our "land of free and the home of the brave."

When I invited Joe Biden and Arlen Specter to have a dialogue in our school chapel about different issues, there were those who thought that the "cheese had slipped off the cracker of my mind" for they differed on so many issues. I had a different hidden agenda than talking about issues. I wanted our students to see how these two political giants "respected one another" and understood the importance of civil discourse. They did just that. The key line in their remarks was, "Nobody from either party goes out to dinner together. Issues are important not the relationships that we have as lawmakers."

This attitude of respect for others was true for two other people who had polar opposite views but also a commitment to honor one another. These two were Speaker of the House Tip O'Neill and President Ronald Reagan. They made a point to call one another after the close of congressional business for the day to just talk about anything other than politics. They had strong feelings about their points of view and equally strong feelings about the importance of honor and respect in their relationship with one another.

Ruth Bader Ginsburg, a staunch liberal, and Antonin Scalia, a staunch conservative, were best friends. They would actually help one another in making each of their "opinions" stronger. They loved opera. In 2013, a law school graduate from Maryland set their arguments to music. Justice Ginsburg wrote the following in her tribute to Justice Scalia upon his death: Toward the end of the opera, *Scalia and Ginsburg,* tenor Scalia and soprano Ginsburg sing a duet, "We are different, we are one, different in their interpretation of written texts, one in our reverence for the Constitution and the institution that we serve."

As important as ideology is, things will not change for the better in our nation unless the importance of relationships and compromise become more present in deliberations. Nothing gets done in a partisan way. Right now it is tribalism and ideology that count. Congress has set the tone of uncivil discourse for students and the people in the street. The current model is to demean and deceive to win at any cost. That is what our children are learning. I hope that enough of the relationship between Supreme Court justices Ginsburg and Scalia is celebrated in our honoring of her in the days that follow. It is certainly why I had Biden and Spector speak before our community at EA. In contrast, can you imagine in your wildest dreams seeing Mitch McConnell and Nancy Pelosi break out in a duet together? That needs to be the new model for American politics for the man and woman in the street to follow! That is the legacy that our children deserve to see!

Post 78. Metanoia: Is That All There Is?

The Philadelphia Inquirer, 9/20, had a section in the paper on "Life Interrupted." People from all walks of life were asked to comment on how their lives were changed during the pandemic. A bartender indicated that, "Every once in a while, I check with my co-workers and say: How have you been? You're good? You're trying not to lose your mind?" Talking about that and thinking about that is difficult. It is a cloud over everything."

A sports broadcaster reflected, "I think that the silver lining is that it has given me more opportunities to think about what I want from life."

Never let a good crisis go to waste. Learn and experience something that changes your life. "Is that all there is, my friends, then let us keep on dancing." is the refrain from a song made famous by Peggy Lee. It grows out of a sense that something is missing in our lives that we don't realize until we are challenged by experiencing a life-changing time such as the pandemic. The verse ushers in a moment that is referred to as *metanoia* in Greek, which is a change in one's life as a transformative experience of the heart or spiritual conversion.

The event in Christianity that is often associated with *metanoia* is the conversion of St. Paul on the road to Damascus when he is transformed from being someone who persecutes Christians to someone who takes the Gospel into the world.

Events, such as the pandemic, have caused many people to feel "that there is a cloud over everything" until they see the sun that enlightens them that there is more to life than what they have experienced. They are disappointed at first, but that disappointment propels them into a new way of seeing what really matters. They expect more. The pandemic puts the brakes on just moving through life with each day, feeling like the day before. That is the soil that leads to making a difference in your life and the lives of others in gestures that take you out of yourself and turn it to helping others, such as the bartender began to experience. "How have you been? You're good? You're trying not to lose your mind?"

Metanoia can be dramatic such as the lonesome words of Peggy Lee, saying and singing that haunting melody, or the pivotal conversion of St. Paul. But often *metanoia* comes in more subtle words, such as "What do I want out of life?" Usually, the answer is *more*.

We can see the drama in two of my friends who were corporate lawyers who decided after 9/11 that they wanted more from life than what they were getting in the corporate world. They set that vocation aside and became teachers and coaches of young people. Their *metanoia* is clear for all to see. But there is more subtle *metanoia* like the rise of enrollment in independent faith-based schools after 9/11 where parents wanted to have an environment where their children would be getting a spiritual/ethical context for shaping their lives. They wanted a values-inculcated education to have more of a possibility of their children leading an ethical life as opposed to a "winner take all in any way you can" mentality.

"Is that all there is, my friends, then let's keep dancing." is the soil from which meaning and purpose can grow. Who knows what changes for the good could evolve from something so insidious as COVID-19? Don't be surprised if the pandemic changes people along the way who want more from life by asking and acting on caring questions of others.

Post 79.   Oprah Winfrey and Caste

Oprah has chosen *Caste: The Origins of Our Discontents* by Dr. Isabel Wilkerson as her book club selection. What is unusual is that she indicated that it is the most important book that she has ever read and has sent 500 copies to the nation's governors, CEOs, and college professors. Oprah had many renowned experts on her daytime show that turned up in my ethics course. She was an oft-quoted resource by students, many of whom would tape her show so that they could view it later in the day. I have not seen her show very much, but she gets my attention because of how much she meant to my students as a resource.

A good many of my posts on my blog have to do with faith, understanding Black Lives Matter, what we can learn during the pandemic, and understanding how we can make sense of human nature. I ordered a copy of *Caste*, and I am glad for the recommendation from Oprah herself. I gauge the importance and greatness of a book by the number of times that I say to myself, "I never knew that" and how much I have highlighted the book to go back to key passages. Suffice it to say "I never knew that!" is a thought I have on almost every page. The highlighting is so frequent that the pages look yellow.

One review of the book indicates that "it examines race as a social hierarchy, with African Americans confined to the bottom. The book defines racism in the country as an American caste system, comparing it to social hierarchical systems in India and Nazi Germany." I think that it is important to know how ideas and systems of thought are derived from historical events.

For example, in my ethics class, I taught that bioethics grew out of two historical events. One was the Tuskegee experiments where African Americans underwent experiments that were sanctioned by the US Government to follow the progression of the disease of syphilis. The cure was penicillin that was withheld from the test group to see what would happen if they were not treated. This had horrific results as many men died as a result of the study. Some of their wives and children contracted the disease as well. This led to the formation of consent being needed for any medical procedures. The African American community is well aware of this unethical behavior at Tuskegee, which means that they will be hesitant to accept the vaccine during this pandemic as soon as it is available.

The second historical event that created the field of bioethics was the Nuremberg Trial of Nazi war criminals. Their defense was that they were not responsible for their actions because they were just doing what they were told. That defense was rejected. The result of this rejection is that in a court of law the "Nuremberg Defense" is no longer sufficient to justify that one's actions came from someone else's authority.

In essence, *Caste* shows just how we got to the hatred and division that we are faced with today regarding Black Lives Matter. I believe that we tolerate (not agree with but move forward to solve a problem) when we understand it more fully. *Caste* does just that, and its ideas have the potential to move our nation forward to unity.

Post 80. Lessons Learned in The Ring

I had the skill to move safely in the world of adolescence thanks to a neighbor, Raymond "Mushy" Mushlanka, who set up a boxing club in his garage, complete with a punching bag, speed bag, and weights. However, there were no ropes in his garage. It just had four walls. He would comment that "You are your most dangerous when your opponent has you against the ropes. He won't be expecting a knock-out punch." In our case, it was the walls. Once the fight started, there was no way to get away, which is true of the boxing ring as well.

It was not the legendary Blue Horizon Fight Club in North Philadelphia, but I learned a lot from my neighbor. He was very strong and skilled. When we sparred, he would always win, and I would learn another lesson about boxing and losing. It wasn't pretty. Believe it or not, there is a lot to learn about what seems to be a primitive art form. My neighbor walked with a swagger that he had richly earned. He was that good! No one challenged him.

One of the things from my childhood that I loved was the *Friday Night Fights* on TV, sponsored by Pabst Blue Ribbon Beer. This was a great time with my father. My mother and brother were not interested in the program, so it was something that my dad and I did together. I knew that my father bet on horse races. I am not sure whether he bet on the boxing matches, but he seemed most interested in who was going to win. I could care less who won. I watched the fights because, for me, it was a master class in boxing. I cared about what I could learn by watching. One of my favorites was Carmen Basilio who was a hard-charging boxer, who always took the fight to his opponent.

I didn't know at the time why Basilio was my favorite boxer. I just knew that he was always moving forward, and the action never stopped and, since I was a left hander, it was great to learn that his best punch was a left-hand hook. Later in life, I learned that he was the most offense-oriented boxer of all time. He was nonstop action. He wasn't only brave in the ring, but he fought against the mob who controlled boxing. He would never lose a fight to receive more money. He was regarded as a man of courage.

Unlike Basilio, I didn't measure up! I didn't act on the model he provided quickly enough. I remember being afraid at this point in my life. I was afraid of the bullies in our school and embarrassed that I never took them on. The bullies that I encountered were in school and not in the neighborhood. Their behavior took the form of sitting behind me or one of my friends and hitting us on the head. When I turned around, they would just be smiling. Whenever one of my friends was bullied, I found it easy to retaliate on their behalf.

There have been recent studies that indicate bullies are insecure with low self-esteem. When I think back on bullying in my school days, I realize two things: the bullies never seemed to be involved in a contact sport, such as football, wrestling, or boxing where their behavior could be directly challenged, and they always had someone around them when they were bullying. They needed witnesses to their unkind acts or to come to their aid if they were losing a fight.

There were three important things in working-class culture that carried over for me later in life regarding what was emphasized in boxing and how it translated to real life. You never hit someone when they are down or take advantage of another vulnerable person. It has to be a fair fight, no matter what the fight is. Second, the championship boxers are always proactive and not reactive. They don't wait for the opponent to come to them. Third, you never sucker punch anyone. That is when you hit the person when he least expects it, catching him totally off guard. This can be accomplished by words or with a fist. Usually, this occurs when someone has power over a person. People who break any of the above rules are considered to be lacking integrity.

I am sure these guidelines apply in all cultures but, from my experience, they were considered sacred in the blue-collar world.

To this day I regret not taking on the bullies in my early years. I think subconsciously that is why I got involved in boxing in the first place. Any feeling of cowardice went against my need to feel courageous. That was part of the way I wanted to see myself. Failure to take on a challenge was seen as something very bad by me. It related to the other side of freedom in my life. That was the "freedom" to be in control. We tend to want to control things later in life when aspects of life that are very important to us are out of our control during our younger years.

Later on in life, my development was shaped by this drive to take on the bullies of the world that started in my younger years. By not feeling that I did this enough early on, I overcompensated to make sure that no challenge went unchecked. This could be very draining at times. Some who were in my orbit thought that I looked for confrontations when leaving the situation alone would have been a better choice. Certainly, my family felt that way with people that I encountered outside the home.

When I attended my first and only bullfight in Madrid, I was not as bothered by the blood and gore as I was by the fact that it wasn't a fair fight. The bull was stabbed many times by the picadors and was weakened before the bullfighter entered the ring in a very macho fashion. I was cheering for the bull since cowards look for those who they perceive to be weaker. They pick on people who they feel are at a disadvantage. I have yet to meet a courageous bully. To kick someone who is down is one of the things that still bothers me today. There is great responsibility when you have power over another person. I want to see justice in any action.

Post 81.   Ruth Bader Ginsburg Is a Tzaddik

There has been much said and written about Justice Ginsburg since her death, but not enough, in my opinion, that she is Jewish. She died on Rosh Hashanah, a high holy day in Judaism, that begins the Jewish New Year. It is a time of repentance, asking others for forgiveness, and renewal.

There is a Jewish teaching that those who die just before the end of the Jewish year that God held them back until the last moment because they were needed so much in this world. What an appropriate moment for Justice Ginsburg to leave us. Nina Totenberg, an NPR legal correspondent, tweeted just after midnight on that day, "And so it was that RBG died as the sun was setting last night marking the beginning of Rosh Hashanah." Some were saying that she is a Tzaddik, which is a legendary figure to describe a righteous one to keep the dignity of humankind alive. God, according to the legend, places these people around the world to be a witness to all that is good and right.

A shofar, a ram's horn, that marks the beginning of the year is blown nine times to call in the year. One synagogue chose to blow the shofar with eight short loud blasts and then one soft sound, indicating how speechless it left the world feeling upon her death.

Part of the Jewish ethic requires moderation in all things. Two of RBG's quotations reflect this attribute: "When a thoughtless or unkind word is spoken, best to tune it out. Reacting in anger or annoyance will not advance one's ability to persuade." A corollary to this thought is found in her words at a Harvard luncheon in 2015. "Fight for the things that you care about, but do it in a way that leads others to join."

RBG had a powerful impact on our culture, particularly in the empowerment of women. I think that one letter to an editor that I saw has captured her influence in a particular, special, real way. The letter was written by a mother who was a big fan of Justice Ginsburg. She said that "when my daughter was four or five years old that she saw her first male doctor. She asked me, 'Boys can be doctors too?' I replied, 'Yes kiddo, if they work really, really hard, they too can become doctors.' That perception of not even questioning what is achievable is just one example of the giant legacy that RBG leaves to my girls and countless others. What a champion of all things fair and decent. Such an example of morality, strength, and humanity. May we grieve today and fight tomorrow."

Another powerful example is that the most important things in life are taught and caught. Even though we have been asked to not go trick or treating this Halloween, who is not moved by all the pictures of little girls in their RBG costumes ready to take

Justice Ginsberg's commitment to what is good and right to the next generation.

Post 82. Back Up Those Horses: McConnell's Situation Ethics

There was a letter to the editor in *The Philadelphia Inquirer* on September 23, 2020 with the title "McConnell's Situation Ethics." It says, "Mitch McConnell and his fellow Republican senators enforce their strong moral conviction about choosing a Supreme Court Justice during a run up to an election.

Whoa! Back up those horses! I don't think that there is an ethical system that supports Mitch's actions, even Situation Ethics. What he is doing is not ethical! The only non-ethical system that fits what Mitch has done is the perspective of Friedrich Nietzsche who embodied the theory of Social Darwinism where "might makes right" or sometimes referred to as the "survival of the fittest." Power over others is a central premise in this perspective. The highest value in this system is strength/power, and the greatest evil is weakness.

Before I show why Mitch's decision does not reflect Situation Ethics, I want to reflect briefly on a concern about the moral dimensions of our country. Many feel that we are moving to Situation Ethics as a basis for our decision-making. Many, particularly in the conservative mindset, want to see more absolutes that are always present, no matter what. This view contains actions that are fair and filled with integrity and consistency, what is good for one should be good for all, and what was right in one point of time is right in another if no laws have been changed. The more absolutes we have, the less concern about "all things being relative." It would be hard to argue that McConnell's decision inculcates these absolutes or virtues called "Virtue Ethics." Nietzsche would be proud of the senator's perspective, but it is not Situation Ethics.

You are right that a situation informs a decision in Situation Ethics, but there is a lot more to that ethic than just that. Situation Ethics came into being in 1966 when Dr. Joseph Fletcher, an Episcopal priest who had to help people make difficult ethical decisions in hospitals in the Washington, DC, area. It was never meant to be a public ethic but was conceived to handle difficult situations that were part of the bioethics movement in its infancy. It was meant for individuals' private decisions. Fletcher wrote a book titled *Situation Ethics* that had a huge impact during the 60s. His slim volume is about a half-inch thick. It contained dilemmas, such as if you are a Christian during the Holocaust and a member of the SS knocks on your door and asks if you are hiding any Jews (and you are), is it OK to say "no?" Is that ethical? Situation Ethics says that it is.

Situation Ethics has other guidelines that a decision must have that are beyond the situation that is forcing a decision. They are as follows: The decision must reflect that "you are acting responsibly in love," which raises the questions "What is the most loving thing to do?" and "What is the most responsible thing to do? The words *love* and *justice* should be able to be used interchangeably in your decision, you should be able to indicate that your action "wills the neighbor's good," which means that your intentions are good and not about your own self-interest. The last criterium is the one that most people think is the whole picture with this ethic when it is just a part of it. That is the Machiavellian notion that the "ends justify the means" which is defined as "If the end goal is moral, you can do anything you want to get there."

Sorry, but the folks deciding the next supreme court justice, in my opinion, doesn't fit Situation Ethics. They should read some of the work of RBG to see what moral decisions look like. I wish that one of our absolutes in America was to act on the last words of a dying ethical icon, her "verbal will" as it were. Then they would be sure to be ethical!

Post 83.   Three P's: Pandemic, Law of Parsimony, and Parkinson's Law

As we are living through the pandemic, we need to take into account two laws that relate to everything in our lives.

The Law of Parsimony states that the best answer to a dilemma is to choose a simple approach over the complicated. We can see this a great deal in our personal lives as well as the pandemic. The best solution is to wear a mask, social distance of six feet, and use good hand-washing practice. This is a simple way of addressing the COVID-19 virus. A key phrase that addresses this issue in daily life is to "talk less and do more." It is sometimes stated as "less is more." We are sometimes receiving instructions from someone, and we find ourselves baffled. We go to someone else with the same question, and we find that they are much clearer in their explanation. If we think about those exchanges, we may become aware that the person was clearer because they simplified things by going right to the heart of the matter without any extraneous details. We often in that moment say, "Thank you, you made it simple for me to understand."

Parkinson's Law states that "work expands to fill the available time to complete it." The more time that we dedicate to a task, the longer it will take to complete. In other words, the task will be completed in the available time. This law raises two questions that need to be addressed. How much time do I have to complete it? How much time do I need to complete it?

These questions relate directly to the pandemic and daily life. They are the central questions that have shaped the debate about a vaccine for the virus. President Trump would focus on the first question of "what time do I have" where the scientists are focusing on "how much time do I need." A pre-election boost to the president raises question number 1. A safe vaccine that has credibility with the public raises question number 2.

THIS TOO SHALL PASS

A quick reflection on the tension that is created between the two, is whether the task is political or responsible at the heart of the matter. Those keywords *have* and *need* are important considerations to any task that we need to complete in our daily world.

You can use these same two questions regarding the debate over the naming of a new supreme court justice. "How much time do I have to complete it?" means that there is a pressing political agenda. "How much time do I need to complete it?" speaks to the responsible way of handling the appointment with the assumption that it can wait as it had to wait under the Obama administration.

Before your next task, think in terms of "time you have" and "time you need." You will be better off in your decision-making if you focus on which term should guide how you accomplish the task, for sometimes it will be the one and sometimes the other. Procrastinators need to learn that this is the first question to ask.

Post 84.   From Janitor to Jarvis Fellow: A Journey of Hardship

In my middle school years, I became aware that our family financial resources were severely limited. We had just enough to get by, with no extra frills. There were no travels, no vacations, clothing was bought at the least expensive stores, and a simple bill of fare was served at the dinner table. Every purchase of every kind was carefully considered. I am not totally sure where I was and exactly when I became aware of this because all of my friends and extended family members, except one aunt, were in the same circumstance.

My father and I would have good conversations on our front porch during the summer months. It seemed as though whenever I heard about a new job that a person could do, I would ask him, "Well, how much does that person make?" His reply would take the form of a litany. I would think of a job, never a vocation, and ask the same question. He would give me a rough answer regarding whether the salary paid a lot. We went through countless numbers of jobs! Some I dismissed outright because they didn't pay well. Notice it had nothing to do with the quality of life associated with the work or if it involved helping others. It was all about the money!

Our lack of money made me aware that I felt I had no backup. The feeling had to be strong then, for it is still with me today, no matter what I do to try to resolve it. There is no way to completely get rid of it, so I have accepted it, and the acceptance has taken most of its power away.

Alice Walker in a poem she composed in the mid 1930s, *Sunday School, Circa 1950,* wrote:

> Who made you was
> Always the question. The answer was always God.
> Well, there we stood three feet high heads bowed leaning into bosoms.
> Now I no longer ponder the catechism or brood on the Genesis of Life. No.
> I ponder the exchange itself and salvage most of my leaning. (Walker 1973).

I don't salvage the leaning. I loved to read and loved school and, as you will see later in this post, I excelled at the highest level, but there was no talk of college. My parents had no concept of what happens at college. Only one cousin, who would become my mentor, had gone to college.

My brother, Walt, who was two years older than me, was a source of great support. When I entered his bedroom to get help in the sciences and math, he always put down what he was working on at his desk and gave me his undivided attention. He wanted me to succeed, and I wanted the best for him.

And succeed he did. He majored in physics in college. Then he went to work at the Frankford Arsenal in Philadelphia where he was one of seven scientists who were honored for a cartridge case breakthrough. The award was the Army Research and Development

Award and was presented by Dr. Martin E. Lasser, Chief Scientist, Department of the Army.

Walt received a BS in Physics from West Chester University and an ME in Engineering from Penn State. He also completed a good amount of the coursework for a PH.D. in Engineering from Villanova University and became a senior executive fellow at Harvard University. The last years of his professional life were spent as a senior researcher at the Pentagon with the highest level of security clearance. His division was in a location damaged by the attack on 9/11. He initially did not know of the attack for he was deep in the Pentagon structure, working on a top-secret program at the time.

After my brother's death, I learned of the significant work he had accomplished regarding fluid mechanics and munitions that made a distinct difference in the lives of our troops in battle. He was a patriot. His battlefield was the planning and execution of the use of conventional munitions and anti-armor munitions within the United States Army.

In our home, there was no expectation that either one of us would go to college. College was a foreign world. My father had a six-grades education, and my mother graduated from high school in the secretarial track. I think this is a good time to raise the question of why and how two brothers from a family, community, and school that did not place a significant value on higher education wound up pursuing so much of it. There was no college counselor in our school. They weren't really needed. You were on your own to figure it out! What you do with your hands and not your mind is what is valued in the blue-collar world.

I have no idea about why my brother pursued so much education and what drove him to be such a success in life, for we never talked about such things. I was valedictorian of my high school class and would become the Jarvis Traveling Fellow from Berkeley Divinity School at Yale to Duke. Why did I choose to have so much education, eventually getting advanced degrees at Yale and Duke? My memoir, *The Times of My Life*, provides an answer to that question. So why didn't I begin higher education at a private institution? There is a brief answer: lack of money and backup!

My brother attended West Chester University and had a good learning experience there. I was aware of his favorable experience, so I decided to follow him there. Our choice was also largely based on knowing it was a school we could afford as we would be paying for that education ourselves. The state system of education in all states is a valuable starting place for working-class people. In addition, we have a growing community college option today for people to get their foot in the door of education beyond high school. I wanted to be at Penn (The University of Pennsylvania), but it was beyond what I could afford. I knew that the financial responsibility would be mine. Unlike today, there were no scholarships or financial aid that I was aware of. I never heard anything about grants or work–study options either. I would have seized those opportunities quickly. I read recently that Penn has committed to helping those from underserved communities. The two key student leaders for 2020–2021 in their student government are students who are the first to attend college in their families.

Dr. Richard Oermann was the superintendent of the public schools in our area. His office was based in my school. He asked to see me the week prior to my class' graduation. After congratulating me on a stellar high school career, he asked if I had a summer job. I said that things in the community were tight. My brother had found a job at a tire company, delivering mail throughout the offices. That factory eventually closed a few years later.

Dr. Oermann told me that he had a job for me. He knew about my father's stroke and the challenges it presented. I could be an assistant janitor, working with the full time janitor, Mr. Banks, during that summer. This was Dr. Oermann's way of giving me a "scholarship" to pay for part of my college expenses. I was grateful beyond what words could express. Mr. Banks was a dignified fellow who I knew would be a good worker. The first tool Mr. Banks gave me was a putty knife. It was used to remove gum from the underside of desks and from the walkways. It was always with me. I liked painting and doing carpentry work. I didn't like cleaning the public toilets. Who does? Mr. Banks had standards, and the restrooms had to sparkle.

Mr. Banks taught me one of the important ingredients of leadership. His plan for me was to work with him each day. We would meet outside the office area at 7:30 a.m. I assumed that I would end up cleaning all of the toilets, and he would take the easy jobs like cleaning windows. If you have ever had thoughts of cleaning a public restroom, you know that would not be high on your list of desired things to do, so I wouldn't have blamed Mr. Banks if cleaning all of them was to be my fate. But he surprised me. All the tasks for the assigned area to be cleaned were divided in half. He did half the restrooms in our designated area, and I did the other half. This was true for each task. Leaders communicate a radical sense of fairness to those without any say or power.

Backup is about money, support, and love or respect for another. People in a working-class culture always have money on their minds. The thought of money is never far away. When you have money as a backup, you never have to think about it. It is like the air you breathe. It is life giving, and you have the luxury of never having to think about it for much of the time. It is a given in your life. For working-class people, money is the shadow that follows behind you wherever you go. It is always on your mind, and you never take for granted that it will always be available to you.

Backup or lack thereof and a conviction regarding my beliefs are key drivers in my life.

Please don't ever say to someone who has come from nothing or little that money doesn't matter. It does. But it matters in a very particular way. It gives you choices.

No Matter What Anyone Says, Education is The Way Out of Hardship!

Post 85.   Feel or Do or Both

When doing graduate work in psychology and family systems, I was able to see the psychological issues that were involved in my family dynamics. When counseling people, I sometimes think of two different systems that operate in most families or couples. One system is referred to as emotionalism and the other as functionalism.

Emotionalism is when parents or a partner emphasize emotion in their roles. When you return from school, they would first want to know how your day went and how you were feeling. This system emphasizes empathy and the importance of empowering relationships in life. Nurturing would be at the head of the list of important characteristics to have. As a gender issue, we usually think of this as a mother's or female spouse's role. Functionalism, on the other hand, focuses on the question "What did you do in school today?" It focuses attention on various roles parents or partners play, such as breadwinner, homemaker, or someone who is task oriented.

Today many families try to have the parents or partners share roles so that earning the income isn't left to one while homemaking is the sole domain of the other. In my case, I had confusion since my father was based on both functionalism and emotionalism. He earned the paycheck but also was emotionally available to my brother and me. My mother, on the other hand, focused on functionalism. Her focus was on accomplishing the household duties, with emotionalism playing almost no role in her parenting. For example, if I became injured playing a sport or boxing next door at the fight club, she would more likely ask, "Did you win?" not "How are you?"

There is nothing wrong with any of these arrangements, but it was important for me to figure it out. I wish I had been aware of these insights when I was growing up. Perhaps these insights will be helpful to you, the reader. The ideal would be to have some understanding of the balance of emotionalism and functionalism in the family or in your significant relationships that would lead to a clear understanding of roles. All families have overt rules, a situation that leads to the family members or partners having a clear idea of what can be done or said. All families and significant relationships also have covert rules that are not formalized, resulting in a tacit understanding of what can or cannot be said or done.

Below is a reflection/meditation on the death of my mother that shows her emphasis on functionalism.

Epilogue: The Death of My Mother

I wrote the following meditation after my mother's death. My words demonstrate my mother's emphasis on functionalism:

My mother died on June 14, 1976. I learned much about life, about the Christian message, and myself on June 13, the day before she died. There are occasions in life that demand that I stop and take stock of where I am. This represents one of them. I was called to a nearby Roman Catholic hospital. The caller beckoned me simply with the words, "Come quickly. Your mother is critically ill." I waited in the critical care waiting room. Hanging on the wall opposite my chair and slouched body hung a crucifix, a well-done woodcut with the broken body of Christ nailed on. Beyond the wall was a person with whom I had struggled as a child, adolescent, and adult.

Mothers have important meaning to all of us. A friend wrote me a note composed on a plane shortly after she became aware of my loss. Part of what she said is, "I was in my early fifties when my mother died, but even now I think about her every day. I just recently said it was my mother's birthday today. She was 105 years old. So, mothers are special people in many ways." My friend closed by saying, "My mother was very funny and did her own thing and wore slacks long before fashion indicated."

On the day before my mother died, I walked into the room to see her. She didn't say, "Hello! Glad to see you!" or anything that most of us would interpret as a standard greeting. She looked up

139

at the clock before her, noticed the noon hour, and asked, "Have you had your lunch yet?" I was furious. You don't ask someone as independent as I am if they have had their lunch. I informed her that I hadn't, but that there was a nice coffee shop downstairs. I said that I would get a bite there very soon.

She started to say something, but it began to sound like an apology that she couldn't get lunch for me or that she hadn't had the foresight to have something prepared for me in the Special Care Unit. I cut this exchange off and shifted things back to her. I can think of nothing as terrifying as experiencing that awful emptiness of wondering where, how, and in what form your next breath would come. Her lungs were failing. She was slowly drowning. That was her world.

When I left, I got the number of the doctor's service to talk with him directly. This was out of a concern for my mother's life as well as for my own need to show the world once again how tough, take charge, and in control I really am. I went back to the waiting room, back to that Christ on the cross hanging on the wall. Alone. The cross was not a sign, a symbol, or even an instrument of peace for me. It was a challenge. This time I purposely sat across from the hanging form. Since I was raised in the streets of a mill town, the feeling was a familiar one, like squaring off with an opponent just before we lashed out at each other, no holds barred until a bloody end.

The cross of Christ didn't want to fight. I felt silly. What a contrast. I was sitting on the edge of my seat, ready to take on anything and anyone who came along, feeling angry, lost, and alone. Across from me was a broken man hanging in wood, palms turned toward me, saying, "Come, I'm not going to hurt you." I knew the struggle, only I was used to being on the other side. I was used to being a priest and helper, and not one who easily asks for help. I was playing the game that had been played on me so many times. O. Hobart Mowrer describes this game best when he described my work with others who are struggling.

He said, "It is as though the patient and the therapist have sat down to play a game of cards. The hands are dealt out. The patient holds his cards close to his vest, inspecting them carefully. After some deliberation, he selects a card for his first play. He watches the therapist carefully for a response to this first attempt at a strategy to find out if he has made the right play. Now it is the therapist's turn to play. Much to the patient's amazement, the therapist begins by laying his cards on the table face up, ready to encounter the patient transparently and without guile. It often takes a long while before the patient is willing to do the same" (Kopp 1972).

There was that wooden Christ, palms out, cards on the table, face up. There I was, though, with cards close to my vest, the bruises, and the pain of that part of me that is an urchin who is alone.

The cross began to speak within me. I thought of my wife and my children. I thought of people who I had spent the week before with—battered, broken, and bruised. I thought of a friend who signed a letter—Thank you, good person—which lit a spark that I had snuffed out in my own moments of self-destruction. I prayed to be open to that Spirit that hung before me and began to recall phrases shared by one who came to me when I was in the more familiar position of helper and not one in need.

The phrases came back. First, they were just snatches and forms. I was amazed at how much I could remember from a once-memorized verse. Between the Christ on the wall and the street urchin was Alice Walker's words from her poem, "School" Circa 1950:

Who made you was always
The question
The answer was always God.
Well, there we stood

141

Three feet high
Heads bowed
Leaning into
Bosoms.
Now I no longer recall the catechisms
Or brood on the genesis of life.
No.
I ponder the exchange itself
And Salvage mostly the leaning.'
I ponder the exchange itself and salvage mostly the leaning
(Walker 1973).

I look up through the hanging cross to the person who lay helpless behind the wall. Who made you? Have you had your lunch
yet? were her last words to me.

No, I can take care of myself.

My eyes came back to the cross, at first blurred, as if they had
tried to see too much, and it seemed out of focus at crossing too
much time, too much death. But there was the cross, the broken
person, the outstretched palms, the ultimate vulnerability, and
the words saying, "Come I am not going to hurt you."

I ponder this exchange itself and now salvage mostly my leaning.
The ideal is when you are aware of these two distinctions, to
be and to do, to make them work for you, and perhaps to strike
the right balance in the important relationships in families and
with your significant others.

Post 86.   Life for Me Ain't Been
No Crystal Stair

Some years ago, a friend who knows my story suggested that I read
Hughes' poem, "Life For Me Ain't No Chrystal Stair." Hughes
(1901–1987) was an American poet, social activist, and leader of
the Harlem Renaissance. He had a biracial background, as both

great grandmothers were enslaved and both great grandfathers were white slave owners. His poetry focused on the plight of the black working class.

"Life For Me Ain't No Crystal Stair" was a poem that he wrote after a conversation with his mother where she told him what to expect in life, based on her struggles to success.

> Life for me ain't been no crystal stair
> It had tacks in it and splinters
> And boards torn up
> And places with no carpet on the floor...bare
> Don't you fall now
> For I'se still goin, honey.
> I'se still climbin,
> And life for me ain't been no crystal stair.

I thought about it this poem from time to time in my life.

Langston Hughes wrote a poem long before President Trump's slogan was made famous, "Make America Great Again." It is as follows:

> Let America be America again
> Let it be the dream it used to be
> Let it be the pioneer on the plain
> Seeking a home where he himself is free.
> America was never America to me.

Some of Langston Hughes' convictions and words are timely to what is happening today in the racial strife in our land.

> What happens to a dream deferred?
> Does it dry up like a raisin in the sun?
> Or does it explode."
> "It is such a bore being always poor."
> "Hold fast to dreams
> For when dreams go
> Life is a barren field with snow."
> "I will not take 'but' for an answer."

He captures the soul of those who struggle whether be Black or White which means that he speaks of universal truths.

There is a story about Langston Hughes that may be an urban legend as I have never been able to find its source. As the story goes, he was to give a lecture and a poetry reading, but before doing so, he used the restroom. People knew his poetry, but many had never seen him. A man entered the restroom and was shocked to see Hughes wiping the sink that he had used of excess water. The man asked Langston Hughes why he was doing what he was doing, not knowing that it was the famous poet who was cleaning the sink. He assumed Langston Hughes was one of the janitorial staff. Hughes responded, "I always try to leave every place that I am in better than I found it."

What would our world be like if we all followed that moral mandate?

His cleaning of the sink made even more of an impression on the man who raised the question when he entered the auditorium to see the poet and recognize that the person cleaning the sink was a world-famous poet. The man learned an important lesson. Can we?

Post 87.   Wall Street and Main Street

Fifty-five percent of Americans own stocks. If you follow global stock reports, there is a pattern that goes against the "isolation" policy that we currently have in America. America first has some unexpected consequences. That is a lesson to be learned. America may think that isolation and America first is a good strategy until you realize that our financial life is impacted directly by what is happening in global markets. It isn't possible to go it alone, as we need to always be thinking in global terms, whether it is in the world of finance or climate change.

If you were wondering about the power of the Presidency, all that you have to do is follow the stock reports. This past week President Trump sent out signals that he may not go "peaceably into that good night" if he loses. He then put the nation and the Democrats in a double bind by indicating that he would leave the office peaceably if he thought the election was fair. He went on to say that if he wins, then he knows it would be fair. What? He has not put pressure on Congress to offer those on Main Street more financial relief. He is also rattling his sabers toward China and keeping the financial wizards in suspense regarding another possible trade war. All of this has affected Wall Street and the stock market with increased volatility. Wall Street doesn't like uncertainty.

There is one area that has hurt both Main Street and Wall Street. That is the pandemic and a failure to have a national plan that would include mask wearing, social distancing, and good hand-washing techniques. The president should lead the way on this, but now we don't know when the vaccine will be ready and who will be ready to get it due to presidential pressure on the CDC. Will politics win out over science?

I am not sure what street the president is on. He certainly isn't on Main Street. He seems to possess stock in only his brand and businesses. It still boggles my mind that someone who has never done a hard day's work in his life with his hands is supported by working class people on Main Street. He embodies classism at its worse. The only question after using a private foundation in his name to help children and then using all of that money to help his election is how low will he go. Unlike other possible convictions of his crimes, this one was won by the state of New York. He is the hero to his base because they feel that he "hears" them, and that is an important issue for any of us. Trump put it rather well when he said to the Democrats, "You people got me elected." He is right.

I can't get used to people referring to the market in almost human terms like "the market is having a bad day." But maybe that is a good thing because it reminds us that money directly affects our personal lives, and it is like the air we breathe. Everybody needs it. But Main Street isn't getting enough of it!

We have to get back to the realization that Main Street has made and will continue to make America what it should be, a beacon of light to the world. Wall Street depends on Main Street. We can't survive without the American worker. Let's start listening to those on Main Street, for the pandemic has caused the American worker to lose his or her self-esteem and the reality of their central importance to our country. That is what is needed to solve our national challenge, but remember human beings are very reluctant to give up anything that they have to others, particularly financial resources. That is an unfortunate part of us. But then again, millions of lives are at stake here and around the world.

Like the stock reports, maybe we have to realize that what we do impacts everyone here and afar and vice versa. We are all in this together. We will rise or fall as one world. It is time to own that truth. When we realize that with a global identity, things will change for Main Street and Wall Street. It will also decrease the impact of any president on our financial world when a steady hand at the helm is needed.

Post 88.   Blind Spot

The writer of the Gospel of Saint Matthew states, "You can see the speck in your friend's eye but you don't see the log in your own eye" (Matt. 7:3).

I had a regular appointment with my eye doctor recently when he did a complete eye exam. Part of any complete eye exam is checking for glaucoma by using a test where you look at a screen, focus on the center blinking light, and then click a device to see what blinking lights you can see, particularly on the periphery of the screen.

As he does normally, he showed me the computer printout with the dark area on the periphery. This was my blind spot. No matter what we would do we, as human beings, would never be able to see it. It's part of the biology of the eye.

It is important to keep this in mind when we are in a relationship with others. Most often we would find ourselves saying things like, "Why can't he see that trouble he is causing me?" or "Why doesn't she act on that observation?" Another question that may form is "Why doesn't he ever say, 'I am sorry. Forgive me?'"

The first way to deal with our blind spot is to have someone that we trust, such as a friend, point this out to us to help us grow and be better people in relationships with others. This can be a very frustrating experience. Just as we can't see the blind spot in our eyes, it is very difficult to see our psychological blind spot. However, I trust my eye doctor and science and know that he and the computer program are right.

There are many people frustrated by the actions of President Trump. Recently he knew that there were 200,000 deaths due to the pandemic, but gave himself an A+ for his handling of the virus, even though we had the highest per capita death rate in the world. We also never have heard him apologize for anything, largely because I don't think that he sees the cause and effect of his actions. People have also indicated that they admire his grit in going from one crisis to another. I think that is based on the fact that he doesn't see a crisis the way that the rest of the world does. Nothing seems to bother him. Some see this as grit! His blind spot serves him well!

I know someone with similar characteristics. He has been a nightmare for his company as a good many of his workers couldn't stand him and repeatedly were on strike. His board of trustees finally said, "Enough!" They brought in a very savvy conflict management mediator to discover the problem to give him and them some indication of the disconnect and how to work through it.

The mediator had all of the workers meet in one room with this leader and were told to give him feedback on why they did not like him. The exchanges were absolutely brutal as the workers were very direct and honest! After the exchange, the mediator and the leader went to lunch to review what occurred during the morning. The mediator asked, "How do you feel?" The leader responded, "I feel fine!" The mediator's retort was, "That's the

147

problem. You shouldn't feel fine! The problem with this leader was that his blind spot was not working for him, as he could hear any negative comments and not see the connection with his actions. But what worked for him was putting his workers in a very vulnerable place. This story had a very happy ending as the leader trusted the mediator and his board and knew that they had his best interests at heart.

Trust and knowing that others have our best interests at heart are necessary for all of us to cope with our blind spots so that we don't hurt others. This presupposes that, like the leader and his workers, we have an investment in making a change, and others have the courage to give the necessary feedback.

President Abraham Lincoln knew the importance of this fundamental characteristic of leadership. It is seen clearly in Doris Kearns Goodwin's book, *A Team of Rivals*. Lincoln chose people to be in his administration who wouldn't necessarily agree with him. People were free to speak their minds. Lincoln had a mind of his own, but he would listen carefully to divergent points of view. That is what made him one of the greatest presidents in history.

He was aware of our blind spots and knew that this can create havoc in everyday relationships, which involve relatively few people. He also knew it could be a horrific thing if a president didn't see his blind spot and how it was impacting a nation, if not a world. This could be particularly true if people feared giving honest feedback to their leader.

Saint Matthew seems to have understood the biology of the eye and the psychology of a blind spot.

Post 89.   Finish Line

How you finish matters! One of the things that frustrates me is people who are big talkers on the front end of anything, such as a new job. They will be the best thing to happen to an enterprise. This is on my mind because of the great promises made by various

Philadelphia sports teams when they hire a "superstar" and the reality that has ensued. They pay huge amounts of money to stars, there are press conferences to celebrate their coming to town, and then the usual disappointment at the end. There is an old saying in Philly that if you want to be successful, just leave town. Think Andy Reid who is the coach of the recent Super Bowl Champions, The Kansas City Chiefs.

When I think of the words *finish line*, I think of running a race, but recently I have seen these two words to reveal a characteristic of human nature that is crucial to our well-being. For one thing, it is important to know where the finish line is. When I was running in the ten-mile Broad Street Run years ago, I was heading toward what I believed to be the finish line on South Broad Street in Philadelphia. Runners try to pace themselves so that when they are near the end, they can dig deep and find a fast pace to complete the race. However, when I arrived at what I thought to be the finish line, there was a sign pointing me to a U-turn and a run a half mile through a park to the real finish line. It helped me to know that even when you think that you have nothing left, you really do.

I hope that this is true for the Black Lives Matter movement and our successful completion of the pandemic. The Black Lives Matter movement has had many moments when we thought that this must be the end. We catch our breath, thinking that we have finally achieved justice for black people when another senseless killing of a black person occurs. This is certainly true with the recent decision in the Breonna Taylor decision, which seems to lack transparency. Somebody moved the finish line, and we have to dig deep and keep moving forward to a vision of the right actions seen ahead. This is hard to do. People depend on the movement giving up. It shows that they never ran in a race, for every great runner knows that even when they give it their all, there is still more than they can find deep in their soul.

The same is true for our experience with the pandemic. The finish line has moved more times than I can count, starting with President Trump's magical thinking that "it will just go away." The date of a possible vaccine has moved constantly, with no identified real finish line in sight. We all keep powering forward, pacing ourselves if you will, but this is very hard to do with no finish line in view ahead. I believe that this factor is the single most devastating part of our human nature that is weighing us down. Human beings need finish lines to cope. Even in the worst possible scenarios, such as dealing with a terminal illness, we will ask that question that comes from the depth of our soul, "How much time do I have left?" We ask it, for we need to know our finish line. It is the way that we are built.

This makes Jesus' last words from the cross even more profound in terms of his being both human and divine. He uses the word, *tetelestai* in Greek. It means, "It is finished," another finish line that leads to the Resurrection which is at the heart of the Gospel.

Post 90.   Spoiled or Special

When I read accounts of high school, college, and professional basketball players, they seem to fall into one of two categories. They are spoiled or special. Legendary Temple Basketball Coach John Chaney had strong feelings about these two categories, and he made it rather clear that he didn't want the spoiled ones infecting his teams with hubris and narcissistic tendencies. There is the case of one player who decided, before Christmas break and the beginning of tournament time, that he wasn't sure if he wanted to play basketball at Temple. He went to Coach Chaney and said, "I don't think that I want to be part of this team any-more!" I think the issue was playing time! He asked for time to think about it, and John Chaney told him that he could do just that.

Later he called his coach and said, "I have decided to come back and play for you!" Chaney's response was a classic, "Right now, you are interrupting my Christmas shopping. I don't have time to talk with you!" That was the last conversation that the two had.

That is a story that defines the no-nonsense approach of a coach to a player that Chaney thought was spoiled.

I have had the good fortune to know some excellent college coaches like Jay Wright, coach of Villanova, Bruiser Flint, former coach of Drexel, and Pat Chambers, current coach of Penn State. The title of Jay Wright's book, *Attitude Is Everything*, speaks to the importance of coaching student-athletes who fall into both categories.

That is why when a special player such as Ross Carter, who was shot and killed as he sat on a friend's front steps this past Friday night, was such a blow to read about in the press. Statistics of the killing of black people often do not tell enough of the story of a player like Carter and how special he was. He led Simon Gratz to a city championship. His coach was attempting to figure out the best way to assist Ross in his next step to play at the college level. They were to meet the next day. Carter had all the makings of becoming a great player. He had dramatic dunks! He had a great shot and outstanding moves on the court. He was a defensive and shot blocking specialist. His coach, Lynard Stewart said, "This was a good kid. His smile was amazing. His demeanor was amazing." His positive attitude was infectious.

There is a story that defines how special Ross Carter and his coach were in their support of one another. Carter was late to a series of practices early on last season. No coach should show favoritism to a player. It destroys team morale. His coach asked him what was going on. Carter told him that he had to pick up his sisters after school. He had trouble doing that and getting to practice on time. Clearly, his priority was the safety of his sisters and not his basketball career, but lateness is a problem for both the player and the attitude of the team. Coach Stewart and he resolved the problem. He would pick up his sisters and bring them to practice where they could do their homework in a safe place. His sisters' safety took precedence over his basketball career. That story defines both player and coach.

Ross' mother told Coach Stewart that Ross would be buried in his number 33 Simon Gratz basketball jersey. It is a symbol of the past and an amazing future that has been cut short. It also speaks to the fact that although basketball was very important to him, his sisters' safety was more important. He was a special player, as special players bring an important spirit to a team because attitude is everything. It also demonstrates that he had his priorities straight.

Post 91. Puttin' On the Ritz

In the Gospel of Luke we read, "If someone takes your coat, let him have your shirt as well" (Luke 6:29).

"Thank you for that act of supererogation!" It is a phrase that I hope that you can use often to thank another person. Supererogation means to "go above and beyond the call of duty." When I hear the word, I think first of the military and essential workers helping to take care of people during the pandemic. But supererogation can be a word that reflects that gesture in our everyday lives. We can learn to do things for others that elicit that response. We remember those people who thank us and make us feel special. Helping others above and beyond the call of duty can be contagious, spreading among friends and family.

We know it when we hear phrases like: "I don't know how to thank you," "You always seem to know what I need most at the time," You really go the extra mile, don't you." You have to be intentional about becoming a person who helps others. If I go to a Whole Foods Store and ask a member of their team where an item is, they would more often than not walk with me to the location of the item, rather than just to mention the aisle where the item is located. My son and daughter-in-law have done hiring for Whole Foods, and they reflect that most people can do the work that is required in a grocery store, so they are looking for employees who they sense could be the most helpful to others.

My wife and I have had the opportunity to be guests at the Ritz Hotel where the employees take acts of supererogation to the highest level. They always do a little more than they are asked to do, so I thought I would do some research on why this is so and how people like you and me can learn something from them.

Most organizations have a motto or mission statement. The motto of the Ritz is: "We are ladies and gentlemen serving ladies and gentlemen." There is an equality of helped and helper there, not someone in an inferior position serving others in a superior position. Jim Collins, who wrote the Business Bible, *Good to Great: Why Some Companies Make the Leap and Others Don't.* He indicates that you have to first get the right people on the bus. In the case of the Ritz, they are not looking for good servants, they are looking for employees who will see themselves as ladies and gentlemen.

Every employee from housekeeping to management can spend $2000 per day per quest to resolve a guest's problem *without* seeking permission. Each employee takes 250 hours of development training in social emotional intelligence and leadership every year as well. I highlight the *without* above because the Ritz has an advanced form of leadership. If the CEO of the Ritz were asked who is most important in his organization, he would not say "the customer." He would say, "My employees, for they have the most direct impact on the customer's experience." It is similar to a school president who might be asked the same question. The best answer is not "the students." It would be the faculty who are having direct contact with the students each day. If an athletic director at the school is asked that question, she would not say "the players." She would say, "My coaches, for they have the direct contact with the student-athletes. Coaches don't run onto the field to play in a game. School presidents don't have the most contact with students, and the CEO and managers at the Ritz don't have as much contact with the people who come to the hotel as their employees do. It is an interesting way to think about leadership. Leaders empower others so that the customer, student, or student-athlete has an optimum experience.

This empowers the people who are making the difference to do a great job. Trust must be present for this to occur. That is why *without* is written in italics in the employees' contracts.

You can't pass a person on the Ritz staff, who wouldn't greet you with a genuine "hello" and "how are you" with a welcoming smile, and the key is you don't feel that it is fake. It is an exchange that feels genuine because it comes from a lady or a gentleman to another lady or gentleman.

Post 92. Words Matter: How we talk about the Pandemic

I listened recently to a conversation that Deborah Tannen, Professor of Linguistics at Georgetown University, had with an interviewer. She is my go-to person regarding the importance of words and conversations and culture. Her observations about words and the pandemic are useful. I will share some of her observations with you.

We describe the pandemic in interesting and negative ways. We must *quarantine*, which is a word that grew out of the Spanish Flu Plague in 1918. We use *lockdown* to describe our need to stay inside which implies that we are prisoners and someone has the key to our release. We also say that we must *shelter in place*, which is a phrase that is used when an active shooter is threatening us.

She indicates that there isn't one word to describe what we are going through, but we should pay attention to the words that we are using. We referred to 9/11 first as an inaccurate bombing attack. Later it was called a terrorist attack, which was more accurate. We refer to recommended standing apart as social distancing. It would be more accurate to say physical distancing to get the point across better.

One of the things that struck me in her observations is that we and our children tend to get tired when looking at a computer screen for an extended period of time. It is because the eye is a muscle. The ear is not! When you add an exclamation point after a text, it communicates that you really mean what you say.

"Stay home. Save lives." This phrase was first used by the prime minister of Australia. It communicates a clear concern for others. When we use the greeting, "How are you?" we need to follow that up since we are in a serious time of illness. It can no longer be a casual greeting. "I hope this email finds you well!" is similar as we are sharing a concern about a person's health.

We talk about the economy "roaring back," which was first used during the 1918 Spanish Flu Epidemic, referencing another bleak time in our history. However, the term surfaced again in the 1980s in a positive way, mostly as a description for sports teams that were making a comeback.

It is interesting to see how frequently military terms have entered our conversations, particularly during the pandemic. We are "fighting a war" against the COVID-19 virus. The search for the vaccine is referred to as being done as quickly as possible. The operation is called "Warp Speed."

The use of the word *masks* was unfortunate for it communicates that something illicit is being done or an imposition on our freedom.

The question that is also on people's minds is how do we build trust by communicating with others online. That can work for us as to speaking with someone in their home communicates a certain level of intimacy. We also see people face-to-face, which is a plus even though it is impossible to see body language. Language matters during this pandemic where how we communicate with one another has an even more seriousness of purpose.

Post 93. You Just Don't Understand: Women and Men in Conversation: The Presidential Debate That Wasn't

America needs lessons in Gender Studies, which analyzes, among other things, the communication that occurs between men and women. The person who has been most helpful to me in helping others in counseling is Dr. Deborah Tannen, who is a professor of Linguistic Analysis at Georgetown University. I have read many of her books and viewed her lectures virtually. Hillary and Kamala shouldn't have to worry if they interrupted President Trump for fear of being rude if the nation knew that the research shows that men interrupt women much more.

I knew that Trump interrupted Biden throughout the evening, but I am not sure that I would have guessed that he did this on 128 occasions. Interruptions are overt forms of a desire to dominate. Women-to-women conversations have a connection as the goal. Men-to-men conversations always have status or hierarchy as the goal, even if it is not a debate. A debate just heightened the tendency for this to occur.

Interruptions violate a person's right to speak, which we could see clearly in the debate.

There are two different conversation styles. Tannen refers to these styles as "high considerateness" and "high involvement." It is readily apparent that Joe Biden is the epitome of a gentleman, and Donald Trump is not. Think back to the Democratic Party Primary debates. Whenever the host would indicate that Joe Biden's time was up, he would literally stop mid-sentence and yield his time. His natural conversation style is "high considerateness." Donald Trump's interruptions were over-the-top examples of a "high involvement" style.

Something that was missing at the first Presidential debate was rapport talk where each person was attempting to connect in a relationship. Their conversation was almost exclusively reported talk where both were interested in communicating what they had done and what they would do if elected. The situation required rapport talk. Certainly, that would have helped the situation be more productive.

Often males will change direction in a conversation to manage and control. An example was when Joe Biden was citing the impressive life of his son, Beau, to hear President Trump say, "I don't want to talk about him. I want to talk about Hunter who has earned so much money when he didn't know a thing about gas. He's a drug addict!"

One additional thing that research studies point out is an interesting fact. Keep in mind that there will be other elections this fall where women and men will be on the ballot. Research shows that two things make a person electable. One is personality or likeability, and the second is the policies that they represent. Men are elected based on their policies and not their likeability; however, women are elected on their likability *and* their policies. They have to have both ingredients for a successful election where men need just one. It doesn't seem fair, does it? Given this gender issue, if all things are equal, why not vote for a woman as one way of correcting this cultural bias. Make sense?

Post 94.   You Are the Only One That I Can Tell

When people come to me for counseling, two statements at the outset always lead to an important and profound exchange.

"You are the only one that I can tell. You can't tell anyone else." This is a statement that people make to me when they are seeking help from a painful situation. There is instant relief when an individual can share their deepest pain. The mere sharing is a therapeutic moment. The person no longer feels alone. After hearing the problem stated, they will indicate, "You can't tell anyone else." That is usually followed quickly after that moment of relief. I have used the same response for many years that is always agreeable to the individual. "You have trusted me to hear your dilemma, so trust me to choose the way that I see fit that will help you. I would never contact anyone without telling you first." Their response is, "OK!"

People would often say that my middle name was "on a need-to-know basis" for I believe that the people who should know the need of the individual are people who could enhance the help that the individual needs to move forward, and no one else.

There are always two questions that require notification to others. Is the person a danger to themselves? Are they a danger to others? These two questions, while very important, can actually be detrimental to a person's move forward to a better place. Often because of my inability to answer those two questions in the affirmative, coupled with the age of the person over eighteen, I can't get them the help that they need. There is a vast area of psychological concerns that inhabit the land between the fear of one taking one's life or taking the life of another.

Issues of confidentiality are tricky to get the most help needed to the psychological cry of another. Confidentiality is the bedrock of counseling.

The second statement that always brings me pause when a person seeks help from me is, "This is nothing, but I thought I better tell somebody." What they feel is an insignificant issue is frequently a large issue. They have downplayed it to deal with their challenging situation. This is often done to cope with the overwhelming nature of the concern. One of the important roles of a counselor is to help the person seeking help to see the reality of their challenge and to gain the strength and reassurance to help overcome it.

Frequently people are overwhelmed when they see a situation as permanent and not temporary and something that they can manage. At other times they may feel overwhelmed because they are not taking the possible solution one step at a time.

If the Black Lives Matter movement or the pandemic were a person coming for help, they would be stating opposite statements, "Not just you but everyone needs to know about our plight. Hear me and get the news out to any and all. This is a big deal and we need your help! Everyone needs to know about racism and this horrific illness. Some may not be transparent, but we will always seek the facts of those black lives killed or the facts of the pandemic when a vaccine may be available."

Post 95. Trust When You Need It

I am writing this at a time when President Trump is a patient at Walter Reed Hospital after being diagnosed with COVID-19. He is in our prayers. I watched the briefing that his medical team gave to the public after he was admitted. The doctors seemed to imply that there were two possible times when he was infected. The media pounced on this and other details as conflicting information. They are concerned again by a lack of transparency on the part of the Trump administration.

Even though the news cycle seems to change frequently, people don't forget! When there is an ongoing lack of honesty, they don't forgive either. It has been downhill for trust in the president since, most recently, the revelation that he downplayed the severity of the pandemic when it was originally known. One of my neighbors has a sign on her lawn that reads as follows: "I am a Republican, but I am not a fool. Vote Biden." You have to be trustworthy, for people may need to trust you someday.

I think that the media doesn't necessarily need to know the president's exact blood pressure, but there is something crucial that is at the heart of the matter of peoples' concern. When did he actually contact the disease, because it appears that he knew earlier than indicated as a growing number of people seem to be affected by the COVID-19 Virus who have attended functions with him?

There is a critical lesson here, which middle and upper school students know. I did a survey of middle school students regarding the most important thing in their relationships with others. They said clearly that it was the ability to trust another. I repeated the same question to thousands of students in my ethics classes, and trust was seen there, as well, as the most important ingredient in their relationships.

I have written about the importance of honor codes in schools. You learn to be honest early on in life. Honor codes began in service academies for you needed to be able to trust your colleagues in arms in times of war. There would be no time for second guessing, as lives could be on the line. The president is seen as a liar by a good many people. A lie seems to be told each day and sometimes in each statement. As I mentioned, you don't grow up and suddenly start to lie. He has been seen as a con man for most of his life. He didn't learn the lesson that young people know about the importance of trust.

I saw a very graphic example of the importance of trust which I have shared with ethics students over the years. I held up a piece of paper and indicated that this is what trust looks like. I then crumpled the paper into a ball and stated that this is what breaking a trust looks like. I then did my best to flatten the paper out by laying it flat on a table, attempting to make it look wrinkle-free. The wrinkles remained. I held it up for them to see. I then told them that this is what your credibility looks like after you break trust with someone. I watched them nod in agreement, for with young people, you get a first-hand look at the importance of trust in its purest form.

A picture is worth a thousand words. The visual example of the wrinkled paper is worth a thousand words too. That is what my ethics students told me! They remembered that lesson. It is too bad that the president never was taught or caught that critical lesson as more lives are now at stake. His actions to date regarding the pandemic and his failure to keep Americans safe result in a lack of faith in anything that is said by him or his administration. People who were possibly infected by him need to know. There are two ethical questions seem in order. What did he know? When did he know it?

Post 96.   You Shall Reap What You Sow

President Trump had been infected by the COVID-19 Virus. This is an example of the biblical truth that "you shall reap what you sow" (Galatians 6:7). The president had downplayed the virus' seriousness since it was discovered here in our country. There is something else happening here that also needs to be addressed, and we can do so through the ethical system of Utilitarianism. The guiding principle for this system is "the greatest good for the greatest number in my group."

This means that you must first identify your group. If either the Democrats or Republicans see their political party as their primary group and not the nation, then they will make decisions that are in keeping with their political party and not with what is best for the nation. It is not just the greatest number. It is the greatest number in your identified group. Of course, either political party would argue that what they are doing in their party is the best thing for the nation. Party first. Nation second.

President Trump's primary group, in my opinion, is his base! Something extraordinary happened yesterday when he required two secret service agents to drive him around to communicate that he was strong. He would say that he did this to keep people from panicking. The car was not only bulletproof but also protected the riders from outside chemical attacks. It was sealed. The agents had their masks on, but all the air had to be circulated within the car, putting them in danger. They had no other protection. His base thought it was terrific, but doctors and other secret service agents thought that it was a horrible PR piece, like holding the Bible up in front of a church a few weeks ago. He infected many at the Rose Garden announcement of his supreme court nominee. No one wore masks, including the president of Notre Dame, who contracted the disease and apologized for his lack of discretion at the event. What kind of modeling was that for his students at that great university! He also possibly infected the group of financial supporters at his New Jersey golf club.

There has been double talk about when he was infected. The "drive-through" was so reckless for those two agents and people they possibly will infect. The White House has no tracing ability as that would be a contradiction to Trump's message, downplaying the virus. Even the governor of Ohio who was with Trump was not contacted. He didn't seem happy about that! The PR event leads to one horrific truth. President Trump is a group of one. What matters is what matters to him which has been an often-mentioned point. But there was something about that day and those secret service agents put in harm's way on purpose that has put a period at the end of the sentence of who he values.

It is said that the difference between a politician and a patriot is that a politician only cares about himself and his or her party while a patriot always puts the national interest first. We had better get back to sending patriots to Washington. It strikes me that the politicians are destroying our nation that was built by patriots. What does patriotism look like today? It looks like people wearing masks, social distancing, and employing good hand-washing techniques. Those actions which protects others from us are the very definition of a patriotic act! No wonder President Trump didn't want to wear a mask and claimed it was just being politically correct.

There is another biblical statement that introduces "You shall reap what you sow." We can't leave it out. "Do not deceive. God is not mocked." Deception and mocking others! Do those two words remind you of anyone?

Post 97.   Questions and Answers

I read an article that included this story about Johnny Majors who coached the Pitt Panthers Football Team in the 1970s and 80s. He went to meet with the press after Virginia Tech soundly defeated his team. He was not having a very good season but he did as he always did and went to meet the press at his press conference. He asked the reporters, "Do you have any questions?" No one responded immediately. You can tell that this was not a Philadelphia press conference as every sportswriter knows exactly what is wrong about every team, even when they weren't playing during the pandemic. When no one was responding, he asked, "Do you have any answers?"

During difficult times, we always want to get both the questions and the answers right. One of the quotations from the German poet and novelist, Maria Ranier Rilke, has been one of the guiding principles for me in my life. He wrote in 1934 in his book, *Letters to a Young Man*, "Be patient toward all that is unsolved in your heart. And try to love the questions themselves. Do not seek the answers that cannot be given you because you would not be able to live them. And the point is to live everything. Live the questions now. Perhaps you will then gradually, without noticing it, live along some distant day into the answer."

I taught Ethics for thirty-eight years so getting the questions right was as important as the answers. Rilke's insight implies that there is a right time to raise a particular question so that you would be able to experience it. We have a "readiness" factor in learning. You may wish that a ten-year-old child should learn calculus, but that will not happen for the vast majority of children. They just aren't ready to take that subject on.

As a priest who has spent a good deal of time with people who are dying, I can tell you some of the most important questions in life and death are raised by the person who is dying, their family, or their close friends. Daryl Sifford, an *Inquirer* columnist at the time, said that "Nobody who is dying says that they should have spent more time at the office." The essential questions are raised and spoken or thought in those final hours and minutes.

Gertrude Stein found herself in this position in the final moments of her life. She was an American playwright, poet, and novelist who moved to France until her death influencing people, such as Hemingway and Picasso. It is reported that on her deathbed as she pondered the meaning of her life, she asked, "What is the answer' (then silence)? In that case, what is the question?" All of us may have questions that go to the depth of our souls. Sometimes they are vague notions that become concrete and real as we experience the ups and downs in life.

I want to suggest an exercise that may help you reach deeper into who you are, what you have always been, and who you will always be. These are the eternal questions. Some occur in our last days. Some occur all the days of our lives. Assuming that you believe in God for this exercise, what are the three questions that you want to ask Him/Her? Of the three, which is the most important? I have my three. What are yours? These are the eternal questions that can help us live a fuller life because they just may lead to helpful action for you, me, and others as we live. They are like the light that can lead us through a darkened room.

Post 98.   Gossip: The Snake That Hisses

Regarding human nature, I have often said that a significant percentage of my problems as head chaplain of a school could be solved quickly if it weren't for gossip. It is rumor that caused most of my problems in a large community, for rumor has no basis in fact. Talk can have a basis in fact. However, it does venture over into the land of gossip from time to time. Deborah Tannen, a linguists' teacher at Georgetown, has a lot to say about the function of gossip in society. "Gossip is said to be generally done by women as it is a way that can lead to a sense of involvement which is personal. Men generally choose to talk about events such as a team, sporting events, politics, or something that is the news."

Recall from another blog piece that, generally speaking, women are interested in rapport speech while men are more interested in report speech. Women are interested in communication, for the most part, which leads to a sense of involvement, and men are interested in status.

Two well-known journalists, Jimmy Breslin and Russell Baker, helped me to understand why I enjoy the works of the mystery writer, Robert B. Parker, which are my bedtime reading. Breslin and Baker discovered that if you provide details about the story you are telling, this will cause the reader to feel more involved with the narrative. When a person in one of Parker's novels enters a room, he describes the room, the weather, what the people are wearing, and what they look like. Thanks go to Deborah Tannen for that insight that details create involvement.

The Black Lives Matter and the pandemic have been affected by gossip and rumor. When information is not forthcoming from the White House, particularly about the COVID-19 virus, both men and women feel cut off and not involved in something that is literally a matter of life and death for them. A lack of transparency is an ongoing complaint. When you don't feel as though you are involved in the facts and details of the matter, rumor is quick to become the basis of conversation.

When the President keeps referring to news he doesn't like as fake news, it makes it even more difficult to discern facts from rumors and for people to feel connected to the truth. We have been introduced to the fact checker after political statements are made by both political parties. Fact checkers are the new searchers after truth.

There will always be a conversation that is gossip and rumor. It is human nature. Separating it out can be tricky! If you want to expend less energy on all of that talk, use what I use: talking about issues only what I need to know to be helpful. It is not easy for me or others to do, but it is the most helpful approach to take in the long run. For example, recently in terms of the president's illness with COVID-19 and the possibility of his infecting others, two questions will do that you would need to know. What did he know? When did he know it?

Post 99. Audrey

One of the questions that were asked in ethics classes is: if you had to give up your sight, your hearing, or your ability to walk, which would you choose and why? Different people choose different things, and the answers can reveal a great deal about what people value and why. As I write this, Audrey, a dear friend of our family, who is our neighbor on the Chesapeake, is in her final moments of life on earth. She is an artist who works in oil and watercolor.

I have listened to Audrey over the years talk about color, shadows, landscapes, portraits of people, still life(s), and many other aspects that inhabit the world of what artists need to know about. She always sent out sketches at Christmas of various homes and places that had special meaning to her family.

We have in our home two of her paintings. One painting is of my daughter, Joanna, who died in 1978 of leukemia, which Audrey painted from a favorite picture of ours. The painting is perfect. Audrey also managed to capture Joanna's outgoing spirit. The other painting that she did for us is of our home of over thirty years on the Episcopal Academy campus in Merion. Some may remember that the home had an enclosed front porch with many panes of class. Audrey painted every detail including the panes of glass. She must have used a brush with few bristles to accomplish that feat.

A special experience was to walk through the Philadelphia Museum of Art with Audrey and have her comment on aspects of the paintings. She would analyze a painting and would point out things that I didn't have the artist's eye to see. There is no doubt in my mind that the one sense she would not choose to lose is her vision. Audrey became blind about a decade ago. The universe is not forgiving. It sometimes takes what we value most. Two of my former students who were great athletes are now in wheelchairs.

One of the things that could not be taken from Audrey was her spirit, seen in her paintings but, more importantly, in her life. I never heard a single word of complaint from her about her plight and the hand that she was dealt. Especially difficult to comprehend is that two of her grandchildren preceded her in death. I regret that I never raised the question of how she was making her way through life with her blindness, her other medical challenges, and the loss of her grandchildren.

I think that during the recent phone calls Vicki and I made to her, I found the answer. She had suffered several mini-strokes in the last week but always asked how we were doing even with garbled speech. She asked how our children were doing as well. She would reluctantly give us the medical report but would quickly add, "How are you?" If anyone deserved to voice a complaint or to have the focus be on herself at that moment, it would be then, for she knew the end was near and was in hospice.

But there it was. The secret for Audrey. It was always "we," never "me!"

Maybe there is truth in that statement that "Art imitates life." For Audrey, her life imitated the spirit of her art.

Post 100. A Mother's Dilemma

I would normally begin my ethics classes by raising a question or describing something in the news so that the students could see how what we were studying could be applied to real life. These would turn out to be a lively way to begin a class.

One of the questions that I posed was, "What would you do if you pulled into a parking lot, opened your door, and by accident scratched a Porsche that was parked next to you. There was usually a flurry of issues raised by the students. How big is the scratch? Did anyone see you do it? If a person could afford a Porsche, they should be able to pay for it on their own body work. Eventually, the key question would be raised. Should you leave a note with an apology and your telephone number to be reached to pay for the repair? Their answers were all over the place regarding what they would do and why.

They indicated that it would depend on whether their car was ever scratched like that, as that would involve your being empathetic. If you had someone leave a note on your car, then you would be more empathetic and more inclined to leave a note. Would you feel guilty if you didn't? Has that kind of thing ever happened to you, and what did you do? Did you have a reference point of your action available to you?

I added to the discussion when they had finished their exchanges with one another about a situation that happened to me. The situation pointed to how context shapes decisions. I went to see our student-athletes play in a game at a nearby school. I had to park on the street, which was legal to do. If I had parked illegally, that would have changed the shape of the discussion. When I came back to my car, the electric rearview mirror on the driver's side was hanging off the car by its wiring. I was angry. However, there was a note under my windshield wiper with an apology, name, and a phone number to call. I must say that I was surprised!

I made the call. The woman who tore off the rearview apologized and directed me to go to my body shop, have it repaired, and send her the bill. She had no idea who I was. I told her that I was the chaplain of my school and asked her permission to share this great ethical action on her part without naming her. Then there was silence. She then indicated that, in that case, she should tell me the whole story to be totally honest. Her two school-aged children were in the back seat, watching the accident occur. She then said that she would probably not have left a note, but she did because she wanted to be a positive role model for her children. In ethics, you need to know what additional information you need to know to make the most ethical decision. Being a role model for her children was key.

When the class and I returned to our discussion about the scratched Porsche, most but not all, stated that their parents would have done the same thing for the same reason. For the most part, they felt that they would do the same thing as the woman and their parents after seeing a real-life example of how leaving the note was the right thing to do.

During the Black Lives Matter movement and the national response to the pandemic, we should keep in mind what kind of modeling we are doing for our children. That would change a lot of the shape of our decisions. Keep in mind that Kamala Harris' parents, one an economist and one a researcher, put her in a baby carriage so that her mother and father could continue to protest against injustice in a march. She remembered those times vividly. Could that behavior by her parents even back then set her on the path that would lead to Congress where correcting injustice should be the job of every politician? That would make them something even better than politicians. They could become patriots!

Post 101. Notre Dame Scandal

Notre Dame has an ongoing scandal, and it's not about one of their athletic teams. I am a big Notre Dame fan. Many of my students and friends attended that university. Our school motto at the Episcopal Academy in Merion, Pennsylvania, is *Esse Quam Videri*. It means "to be" and *not* "to seem to be." I am sure that one of the reasons that we chose it long ago is that doing what you say you will do and expect others to do the same is a big deal with young people. You have heard of bounty hunters. Students are integrity hunters. If you say you should do something to students and don't do it yourself, watch out!

According to an "Inside Higher Education article" on 10/9/20, The Reverend John Jenkins, president of Notre Dame University, attended the White House Rose Garden announcement of soon-to-be Supreme Court Justice Barrett who went to Notre Dame Law School and became a gifted teacher there. President Jenkins attended the event, along with several Notre Dame faculty and administration. Everything was fine except for the fact that Father Jenkins came down with the COVID-19 virus.

I think that things would still be OK for him except that he chose not to wear a mask, social distance, and refrain from hugging and shaking hands with others who attended the Rose Garden event. All of this was caught on camera. Strike one. Still, you might say, so what, he is just human. That doesn't go over well with students, knowing that he was one of the college presidents who pushed hard for opening on time on his college campus. He also laid down some heavy penalties for students if they failed to honor the CDC guidelines. Students could be sent home for an offense. OK, but it was just a one-time thing. Well, it wasn't. He broke his rules in August and had to apologize then for taking photos with students, breaking social distancing rules. Strike Two.

In case you didn't see something coming, you don't know the integrity hunters who gave him a pass on the August event.

Two quotations from the student government are as follows: "Students and faculty and staff have been asked to refrain from unnecessary travel yet Fr. Jenkins travelled across the country to participate in a large gathering," the resolution said. "A professor's nomination to the U.S. Supreme Court is significant and could be framed as necessary travel, but Fr. Jenkins could have fully participated in the event while following COVID-19 guidelines ... Fr. Jenkins public displays of disregard for public health directly contradicted his commitment to the Notre Dame community, directly endanger the safety of students, faculty and staff," The resolution went on to read, "He can no longer, in good conscience, call the student body, faculty, and staff to adhere to the safety protocol that he ignores."

The faculty had a vote on all of this too. They weren't pleased either. The resolution that came from the students didn't pass, but the student senators are open to more resolutions on the matter in the future as they thought "his behavior was an embarrassment." The integrity hunters, better known as students, will usually give someone a second chance, but he is on thin ice because my experience working with students says, "Three strikes and you are out!" Students, in terms of integrity, don't listen to what you say, they watch what you do even more so than those in the adult world. They "listen" by watching your actions.

One of my great memories when I was at Episcopal as chaplain was inviting, on behalf of the school and the Murphy family, The Reverend Monk Malloy, then president of Notre Dame, to give a lecture on moral issues of concern for young people. The Murphy family, who are very close friends, set up an endowed lecture on moral issues in memory of their daughter, Maura. Dr. Brien Murphy, Maura's father, had attended Notre Dame. Monk Malloy was a great athlete, stayed with the students in a dorm, and was known to play a fair share of pick-up basketball with them. He knew kids. The students loved his personal anecdotes on the moral life that he spoke about in his lecture. Monk made a hit with my integrity hunters. He talked the talk and walked the walk. Bottom line, that is what students *listen to*.

I will be rooting for the Notre Dame Football Team this weekend.

Post 102. Patience

There is plenty of evidence that patience is a virtue. St. Paul indicates in his letter to the Romans that "if we hope for what we do not see, we wait for it with patience." Tolstoy wrote that patience is a warrior. For Aristotle, patience is first bitter and then sweet. For Lao Tzu, it was a great treasure, along with compassion and simplicity. If it is such a virtue, why can't we human beings have more of it? Even my Labrador, the Wonder Dog Sadie, knows that she is fed first thing in the morning, at noon, and 5pm. She has an internal clock that one can set their watch to that her food should arrive at that time. If it doesn't, she sits in front of me and just stares.

There was a classic study that was done at Stanford during the 60s and 70s where a researcher gave little children a marshmallow and told them that if they could wait fifteen minutes while he left the room that he would give them twice as much when he returned. They followed the children in a longitudinal study and found that the children who could wait did much better in life. When people have less time to live, such as those with a terminal illness, they can be the most patient of all. They don't rush things. They value their time in a different way than the rest of the world.

REVEREND JAMES R. SQUIRE

There are two kinds of patience. One is when you know when you are going to get something that you will like, for kids, when Christmas will arrive. The other is when you don't know when something will arrive. Hence the cry from the backseat of a car, with little children asking minutes after we leave if we are there yet. It is the second kind that has shaped us during these times of Black Lives Matter and the pandemic. It is hard to be patient when you don't know when these two very important issues that are part of our daily lives will conclude. The likelihood is that we will know about the end of the pandemic before we have a full resolution of equal justice for all people. I heard from disease experts that COVID-19 may be with us forever, like cancer or the flu. We, however, will be able to reduce its impact, which is what a flu shot does for us now.

I learned recently that patience is something that you can learn. Jennifer Roberts at Harvard University did a study in which she took people who had a problem with patience to an art museum where they had to sit and look at a painting for three hours. She chose that length of time so that the experience would sink in. What occurred was when the people were able to sit in front of a painting for that long, they saw so many different things and dimensions that they had not seen at first glance. They began to enjoy the experience and, according to Roberts, it got translated to their feelings so that they could be more patient.

I don't think that would work for Sadie the Wonder Dog, but if you are growing impatient day by day during this trying time, you might give it a try, and maybe, like the Stanford Study of Children, you may have a better life going forward.

Post 103. Young People Are Not Our Future

Young people are not our future. When I saw this title of an opinion article, I had to stop and see what this heretical statement meant. It certainly got my attention. I have been in education for thirty-eight years and am a drum major for honoring the power of young people. The point of the article was to celebrate all that young people are doing right now to make the world a better place. They are acting now. They are being spokespeople for the most important causes, such as climate change, regulation of guns, civil rights, and other challenges that we face as a society. They do this despite being dismissed too much by the adult world.

Young people, however, are also not our future when they fail to wear masks, social distance, and don't obey the COVID-19 guidelines. Quite frankly, this is one thing that I don't just understand. The young people that I have been with over the years tended to be the most polite and responsible people that I know. What happened? Most young people's bad behavior has been associated with college students on vacation or partying in large groups on campus. When interviewed, they would too often say, "I'm going to party! I am not worried about the virus."

When you think about it, we don't see working-class kids not in college highlighted much at all.

The same is true for the underserved young. I am sure that they have broken some of the guidelines, so why no press on them? It could be that their sense of entitlement is not like those in this generation of college students. Have you noticed that, or is it just me? The economy is tight. The people who feel it the most first are working class and underserved families who need to stay well to keep their jobs. There is little time for risk-taking activities compared to those on the college scene.

Over forty percent of Americans don't have much back up in their savings accounts. It is what it is. I saw a student from one of my alma maters being interviewed about what struck him most about college life going to a high-level private university from an underserved background. It sounds a bit crazy, but he said, "Second homes!" (Full disclosure: I have a second home). It never dawned on this student that people could have two homes when it was hard enough for his parents to have one. That's what we call a "where the rubber hits the road" observation.

We get the daily statistics on how many people are affected by the virus. I would want to know the percentage of middle-class young people compared to the underserved and overserved young people who have the COVID-19 virus. Which group is spreading the virus the most? Can we focus attention on the answer?

Young people are not our future reflects a fundamental truth that I saw recently. "The best math you can learn is how to calculate the future costs of current decisions." That statement will, in fact, decide if our young people will be the future and not just the inheritors of present bad decisions. The obvious decisions that need to be made now to ensure a future for the young is climate change. Let's make the right decisions now so that our young people have an opportunity to shape the future. I think that is a more accurate statement or young people will not be our future.

Post 104. Blink: Other Considerations of Black Lives Matter

Black Lives Matter is a movement that seeks justice. But there is something else going on that I am surprised hasn't come up at all. Malcolm Gladwell, author of *Blink,* researched what is happening when the killing of black men occurs along with racism. Gladwell's book begins with Amadou Diallo, a black man who had been shot forty-one times by New York policemen in 1999.

If the police were biased and assumed that black men carry guns, that was the start of their reactions. Diallo was not armed and was holding a wallet, not a gun. Gladwell studied the case and came up with ways to avoid this injustice. He asked, "What was going on in these officers' minds to commit this horrible crime?" The police were hyped up with adrenalin, which causes the thinking centers of the brain to shut down. It is counterintuitive, but one policeman approaching a situation will be more cautious than those in a group. They have tried this in Dade County, Florida, and it works.

Scientists have discovered something called "thin slicing" which means that we evaluated people in the first seconds of our experience of them. We have all heard that first impressions are very important. As it turns out, they are. When the police officers were attempting to arrest Diallo, they were trying to hurt him as they lost touch with their other emotional reservoirs of taking care of the suspect. There was also a good bit of "surrogate threat" in their feelings. The police have preconceived notions of what and who black men are.

There is a video where Denzel Washington arrives at the same time when police are attempting to arrest a person who is resisting arrest. This was real life and not a movie and occurred during the Black Lives Matter protests. Washington communicates in many different ways that he wants to help the person and the police back off enough to let him intervene. Washington's care for this black man is palpable. The black man responds and becomes cooperative and calm. This raises another important question that is raised by the black community. Why is a black person apprehended in the first place? A broken taillight has led to more than one black person man losing his life. Parents of black children are now educating them on the "ways of the current world."

At that time, President Trump had outlawed and refused to fund any diversity training in any public organizations. That is where people learn implicit bias, including black people about black people and black people about white people. No one is immune.

There is one other issue that Gladwell addresses in *Blink* that needs to be mentioned. We are used to seeing a shootout by police and criminals or even in dramas set in the Wild West in the movies or on TV. They present a fictional account, regarding how people are affected by shooting another human being. Most people think that police officers are used to firing their guns at a human being. They aren't. Most police never shoot a person in their entire career. It is an immensely stressful experience, particularly when you think that the person has a gun to shoot at you. Police are often trauma- tized as a result of firing their gun.

Some questions for your consideration. How many deaths of a black man occur when there is just one officer? How many deaths of a black man occur when the black man feels that the police officer has the best interest at heart and communicates that he cares about him? I believe that, in all the complexity of this issue, that answering those two questions with "not very often" would take us a long way toward social justice. Recall when a black man is stopped for a bad taillight. What if the officer knocked on his window and said, "I am stopping you to let you know that you could get in an accident with the taillight out!" would change the context from, "Show me your license. Keep your hands where I can see them?"

A person when using a gun against a person is different from shooting a target. Researchers suggest that people "lose their minds" and their ability to think rationally when firing a gun. The cops and robbers movies on the silver screen are good for movies, but they are not descriptive of real life.

Post 105. What's on the Pad?

The Supreme Court nomination of Amy Coney Barrett has brought out the best and the worst in people. You can choose which side you are on. I want to focus on the candidate herself. I have watched some of the deliberations in her confirmation process and listened to some on NPR. She is impressive. She has been referred to as the finest law student to ever attend Notre Dame Law School and has the distinction of being Teacher of the Year there as well. Constitutional law is her special area of expertise. I wrote a blog earlier where I indicated that there is no correlation between a per- son's intelligence and ethical behavior. Robert Coles, a professor at Harvard, made this case when he discovered one of his brightest students was treating a housekeeper terribly.

Barrett was nominated by President Trump, which raises red flags, and she is being confirmed before an election when the Republican leaders showed their true colors as hypocritical in the extreme. It is ironic that she is the very model of the anti-hypocrite, as she is a person of integrity. She lives out EA's school motto, *Esse Quam Videri,* to be rather than to seem to be. In common language what you see is what you get.

I am one of those people who believe in Malcolm Gladwell's assumption in his book, *Blink,* that I can reach my impressions of her in less than fifteen seconds. Researchers call this "thin slicing." She has seven children and one husband. One of the children has Down Syndrome, and two are black, adopted from Haiti. I think that Ibram X. Kendi, author of *How To Be An Anti-Racist*, is brilliant, but I thought his comments that Ms. Barrett was a "colonizer" for adopting black children were inappropriate and unhelpful. I must admit that I, and others, don't know how she is doing everything that she is doing, but she is!

Sometimes small gestures tell you everything that you need to know about an individual. First, that question from a senator, "What's on that pad in front of you?" He was leaning over his notebooks and binders spread out before him. She said, "The title of the United States Senate." It was a pad from the Senate. That's it. Two things occurred to me. One is a sense of humility. The second was that she is self-confident and didn't think she would need assistance in answering their questions. As it turns out, she didn't.

The other thing that I noticed was the respect that she paid to each questioner. No other nominee in the confirmation process, including beloved LBG, would succumb to a litmus test on some of the most important issues to come before the court. Game changers are words that quickly come to mind. When she was asked what she thinks about when she makes a ruling, she indicated that she sees each person affected like one of her children. When I indicated that same attitude in a faculty meeting, it was met with criticism. "You can't possibly be objective," was the retort I received. Yet for me it was true. I believe that for her, it is true. When you relate to people in that way, our better angels kick in so that we can balance objectivity and empathy. She was taught a way to think and consider others in law school as I was taught a way to think and consider others in my university graduate school training.

A commentator from CNN, the bastion of everything liberal, said it best, "If this were a different time, both Republicans and Democrats alike would be voting for her." Count me in on that proclamation. I was struck when the camera moved away and showed the whole room, she was alone at the table on national television with half the senators asking difficult questions. What courage! We have significant issues coming up before the Supreme Court that will shape the future for millions of people. I am not sure how she will vote. It may be in a way that angers me, but I will know that her vote came from a deep place as Frederick Buechner put it, "the place that God calls you is the place where your deep gladness and the world's deep hunger meet."

I hope that people know that at the heart of the Roman Catholic ethic is a view of the world that faces the headwinds of difficult challenges. She knows, as Rabbi Howard Kushner, said, "Tragedy doesn't have a ticket into our lives. It has a box seat." I am convinced that Amy Comey Barrett knows that.

Don't think for a moment that this leopard has changed his spots. Not that I would, but if President Trump was invited to my home for dinner, I would still insist on counting the silverware before he left.

Post 106 Wave or Ocean

We have a beachfront home that is on the Chesapeake Bay. The views of the sunset are astounding. One of the reasons that Vicki Squire and I love being that close to the water is that we can hear the crashing of the waves against our bulkhead. Of course, it depends on the tide, for it fluctuates a great deal on the Bay. You can hear the wave just before it crashes as a crescendo of sound builds. It is like someone knocking on our front door. Then the sound of the water hitting the beach and bulkhead makes itself known as the visitors enter. It is very soothing and connects us to nature in a direct way. Waves have a way of drawing you in, particularly when there is silence in the home. You find yourself listening to the rhythm of their coming and going.

There is a danger to just focus on the waves for you may forget something else that is essential. It was described best by Mitch Album in his book, *Tuesdays with Morrie.*

"There was once a wave. Bobbing along in the ocean, having a grand old time. All was well and the wave was enjoying himself. He was just enjoying the wind and the ride until one day he noticed what was happening to other waves in front of him. They were crashing against the shore. 'My God, this is terrible,' the wave said. 'Look what's going to happen to me!' Then another wave came along who asked, 'Why do you look so sad?' The first wave says, 'You don't understand! We'll all going to crash. All of us waves are going to be nothing! Isn't it terrible?' The other wave's response: 'No, you don't understand. You're not a wave, you're part of the ocean."

You are not just a black man. You are not just a protester. You are part of a movement to bring social justice to all. You are not just a statistic. You are not just a single number. You are part of humanity that is struggling and moving forward attempting to bring this Pandemic to an end. The Black Lives Matter movement and the pandemic reflect that old axiom, "We will either rise as one or fall together."

I am afraid that our politicians in Washington have watched and listened to our challenges, seeing themselves as isolated waves being part of partisan politics, and have forgotten that their role requires them to be part of what is best for our nation as a whole, the ocean.

Post 107. Gender and Manhood

I never saw anything regarding gender issues and manhood until I came across an opinion article, "Gender is the Undercurrent in Trumpism and Fracking" by Zach Rearick in the *Inquirer* (October 19, 2020). One of the assumptions of the article is that men need to "work with their hands" and need to "get dirty" to keep their self-esteem and identity. There are complex competing psychological strands that I experienced first-hand that underscores the accuracy of Rearick's point of view.

I cover the issues in my memoir, *The Times of My Life*. What separates the blue-collar worker from the rest of the world is that working-class people work with their hands more so than their minds. That was a primary piece of my identity when I was old enough to get into a factory to earn money to help support the family and to assure that I would be able to go to college. My father had a sixth grades education, and my mother graduated from high school in the secretarial track. Dad worked hard as a butcher, and my mother was a stay-at-home mom.

Real men worked in factories, such as I did. I loaded skids in a paint factory, was a laborer in a steel mill (one of the best examples of manhood), and was a lathe worker in a ball-bearing plant. When I finished a day's work at the paint factory, I couldn't lift my arms from loading heavy boxes of gallons of paint. When I finished a day at the steel mill where I worked primarily in the coke plant that converted coal to coke to fuel the open-hearth furnaces, I had muscles that ached and a body that was black with coal dust. When I worked at the ball-bearing company, I was bored to death at the end of a shift, creating those little small steel balls. But all of these jobs produced a psychological swagger, if you will, producing high self-esteem based on a working-with-your-hands mentality. That was my idea of what a blue-collar man should be. When people asked me what I did, I could identify my various jobs with great pride.

There was just one very large problem. I didn't want to spend the rest of my life doing any of that kind of work, even though that is where my self-esteem was based. I wanted out! At the same time, I was hedging my bet by doing very well in school, so off I went to college where you worked with your mind. That produced fake self-esteem as it is difficult to change self-esteem centers in one's psyche and soul.

Having a better life through technology and working with your mind can be threatening to your manhood. Real men don't do that, particularly when you live in a family, go to a school, and live in a community that doesn't value that stuff. "Why do you want to go to college again?"

This is what is scaring male voters today when they hear about changes to the workplace from "hands work" to "head work." They think *Will I be as good at this "head work" as I was with "hands work?"* A promise of a better life is not just about money, it is about gender where your manhood rests, and what a source of your self-esteem is. Fear of failure in this "brave new work world," is at the heart of why Trump gets his working-class votes. He works against the "nothing ventured, nothing gained" mindset. The promise of better jobs for more money by working with your mind can be threatening. Keep in mind that we will always need the "hands work" people in the workplace.

Lucky for me, I loved to learn new things and was quite good at school, studying at some of the best universities in the nation, and eventually having a mind and soul job. I also had a risk/benefit/ analysis attitude to the precarious nature of my identity and self-esteem that shaped my manhood. The risk/cost/benefit analysis seemed worth a try. But you never really forget where you came from. For me and others, I took the middle-class work ethic with me. That is a way of keeping the best of the blue-collar world.

We need to reimagine what constitutes manhood with a soul. Otherwise, there will be no identity as manly, no self-esteem, and no moving up to the "mind class" so men have a real choice about taking that direction. Let's keep in mind that some men actually *choose* to work with their hands. They love it and wouldn't trade it! Let's not forget that this is an issue for women as well, or why would Trump use the term "suburban housewives." It was very 50s of him! It drove women crazy to hear it!

Post 108. Fake News: How to Remove Bandages

I am an alumnus of several universities, but no one can compete with contacting me more than the average of three emails I get a week from Duke. In a recent email, they pictured new faculty and tenured professors who had written new books. I had seen Dan Ariely's picture before, but it grabbed my attention once again, announcing his newest book, *Amazing Decisions*. I have used his thinking in an ethics class that I taught, as he makes decisions with lateral thinking, meaning thinking outside the box of conventional approaches. He has a PH.D. in Business Administration and a PH.D. in Cognitive Psychology. He teaches Behavior Economics at Duke, which is a new field that brings a new lens to decision-making that is the heart of ethics.

Ariely was burned over seventy percent of his body with third-degree burns when he was a teenager. Half of his face was burned in such a way that facial hair doesn't grow there. He literally has a half beard. He spent three years in a hospital and thought about how people make decisions. His first observation started him out in this new field of Behavior Economics. It was part of his daily routine that he had his bandages removed and replaced. Most of us operate from the truth that the faster you pull them off, the better it is in terms of pain management. I still do that today with Band-Aids. He proved that to be wrong. What he learned was that it is more manageable to remove the bandages slowly over a short period of time. He changed the field of pain management when the experts discovered that most people prefer the duration of pain relief over the intensity of pain all at once for long-term, painful injuries. This is counterintuitive and was an uphill climb for some to adopt this technique. It is the standard of care in burn centers today!

He makes important points about decision-making and the pandemic. Most of our systems and our behaviors are based on efficiency. We depend on the trains running on time. We value getting a plane into the airport, unloaded, cleaned, and then to board food and new passengers in the shortest possible time. The more time a plane is in the air, the more money an airline will make. The quicker a race car driver can have maintenance on his car in the pit during a race, the better shot he has of winning.

Think about how much of our life is governed by efficiency. What is the quickest way to do anything or get to any location? Our GPS controls list both the mileage and the time it will take by using various routes. We can decide! We depend on hospitals and hotels to have full occupancy to bring the most profits. It is ironic that the only thing that is efficient about the COVID-19 virus is its ability to kill. It has been the very embodiment of what has been inconvenient to say the least for us all. It requires resilience.

The dilemma with this efficiency approach in most of our lives is that we have few resilient approaches to life, which contain flexibility in how we handle a crisis. We make certain that we know the best way to leave our home in a fire, but not much more. The one system that has built in resiliency is the military, with different approaches to different changes that are needed.

During this pandemic, we have juxtaposed fear over fragility. We look at the daily cases and deaths, but after a period of time, fear reaches a point of diminishing return. Fear doesn't last when you don't know when something is going to end. We have fear fatigue. Going out to dinner once during a spike in cases makes going out a second and third time easier to do. We are built that way, even with constant reminders of how bad things are.

If there is a silver lining in the pandemic, it is that we now have a much greater global understanding that we are all in this together—literally around the whole world. That sense of global awareness and responsibility is dependent on a key issue, trust, which is in high demand with not enough of this commodity to go around.

Running counter to this need for trust is a president who no longer sees us as part of a world community and someone who has created a lack of trust in every place that he goes. The same is true of other autocratic-leaning leaders throughout our world. Without global trust, a vaccine will do little good over the long haul. It will take time to build our relationships with everyone on the planet. We will rise or fall as one whether it be climate change, the pandemic, or Black Lives Matter. This lesson has to be learned. There is no time to spare.

Post 109. It's Business! It's Not Personal!

Leave it to Dr. Fauci to summarize the partisan dilemma on both sides of the aisle. President Trump recently attacked Dr. Fauci on his incorrect predictions and assistance with curbing the COVID-19 virus. I suppose that when someone calls you an "idiot," you have to make a response. Fauci channeled words from the *Godfather* movie, "It's business! It's not personal!" meaning that it is not about you and me. It is about the issue at hand. In this case, it is about the pandemic!

In ethical language, Trump's approach has been to attack the person with whom he disagrees. It is referred to as *Ad Hominem* attacks, which means against a person. He demonizes them with such statements including words, such as low life, scum, and terrible. His comments don't have much to do with the issues. Joe Biden fell into this pattern at the first debate calling Trump a clown and liar. It is very easy to require a defense to what a bully says. Notice how *Time Magazine*'s Man of The Year and the recipient of a leadership award by a scientific infectious disease society responded to Trump's accusations. "It's business! It's not personal!" No one could have made a better response identifying the issue for what it was, a matter of science and not a personal attack.

The problem is not fake news. It is blood news. We are all to blame. A story about polite behavior doesn't sell. What does sell is attack and counterattack. The media may regret that they get what they pray for, namely to get rid of Trump. He has been the best thing ever for the news media. Each day there is something outrageous to write about him. The president rarely disappoints! The problem is that is all that our children are seeing to the point that it has become the new normal. They assume that this is the way everyone acts.

A political contest will make my point. Have you seen anything on the news about Democrat Darren Parry of Providence, Utah, and Republican Blake Moore of Salt Lake City, Utah? They are in a race to replace outgoing US Rep. Bob Bishop in Congress. Both Parry and Moore have pledged to run a positive, issue-oriented campaign. The two candidates are very different in their backgrounds and their policies. Parry has been active in Utah politics for years. Moore is a business consultant, who is a novice in the world of politics. Both have stated that discussion of the issues in their campaigns should build bridges. Moore stated, "I think that there is more that binds us together than divides us." Moore went on to say, "If I am successful in winning the seat in Congress, I hope to be able to stay in touch with Darren and solicit ideas from him."

The comments that they make about each other are uplifting. I am reminded of the reason we shake hands before an athletic contest. It is to thank your opponent for the opportunity to compete. Without them, there would be no game. One candidate calls the other "very cordial." The other says, "He is a great guy. I like him a lot." What if this election in Utah was part of a news cycle so that our kids could see first-hand what an ethical approach looks like? They would have something to contrast to the verbal bloodbath in the national arena.

After a Town Hall Meeting with Biden, Trump and his public relations person said, "It looked like *Mr. Roger's Neighborhood*." I think that we have had enough of might makes right. Let me give you a personal example. When I was a parish priest in Swarthmore, Pennsylvania, I had parishioners from the faculty of Swarthmore College, one of the top small colleges in the nation.

One of those faculty members was Dr. Lin Urban who was chair of the Religion Department. His father, Dr. Percy Urban, had taught me at the Berkeley Divinity School at Yale. Lin and I would debate issues. Debate is what you did in Swarthmore, as it was like a "swing through an intellectual jungle gym." When one of us would be struggling to make a point, the other would say, "Have you thought about this? It strengthens your point of view." We were on different sides of several issues. But this approach of getting the best idea on both our parts strengthened our debate, leading to a better conclusion. (Full disclosure alert: He helped me more than I helped him.).

Accusing a Town Hall was like *Mr. Roger's Neighborhood* was meant as a criticism. However, maybe it's the very definition of "civil discourse." It is what is needed.

The Utah race for a congressional seat doesn't get much attention compared to "attack politics," but it is exactly what our kids and the nation need to see. Forget the ratings or the number of subscriptions that your newspaper or online news has. Tom Friedman, a writer from the *New York Times*, said this election is about "America being on the ballot." It is. But how to conduct our public business is on the ballot as well. We don't want our children growing up seeing what passes for political discourse in Washington. They deserve better.

Post 110. An Eagles' Game and a Possible Solution to the Pandemic

The final debate between Joe Biden and Donald Trump was a few days ago. I watched that and taped the Eagles and Giants football game. As we know the debate and after debate commentary kept

THIS TOO SHALL PASS

us up later than usual. I checked my phone before bed and saw that the Eagles had won. When I am taping the Eagles during a Sunday afternoon game during a normal season, I always go to great lengths to make sure that I didn't have a glimpse of the score. I was watching the taped version on the same day, not knowing what the final score would be.

If I taped the game and didn't have an opportunity to see it but knew the score, I would never watch it after the fact. I was not interested in seeing "old news" about the game. But something different happened with the Eagles and Giants game that was on at the same time as the debate. I knew the final score and enjoyed watching the taped version the day after. As I sat there, I thought that this was crazy. What was different?

What was different is it was during the pandemic. My soul has yearned for closure, for knowing an end date to the virus and the illness and death score count. I wanted to watch the whole game to see how it would end, even knowing the final score. I wanted to see it end in "real" taped time. Closure dominates not only my psyche and soul. It also dominates the lives of most of the world.

I came up with an idea of how to get closure on the pandemic as a result of this desire for closure. The pressure now is on the first responders, essential workers, health care workers, and business owners. They are under enormous misplaced pressure caused by the people who are not following the CDC guidelines. This could be a lack of awareness of the true deadly nature of the disease, a desire for their personal freedom, or just an immature or irresponsible way to go through the pandemic with no pressure on them.

One of the things that I learned in teaching ethics and working with kids for thirty-eight years is that young people believe that "peer pressure" is the best two words in the English language in dealing with their parents when they get into trouble. If they get drunk or do something wrong, the first two words out of their mouths are "peer pressure made me do it." I would be quick to add that some parents will repeat the words to authorities, such as the police or school administrators, in their defense. Kids will go on to say, "Nobody pressures us. We drink because we want to."

I am talking about a different kind of "peer pressure" where there is much more on the line. That different peer pressure is saving 150,000 lives by following the CDC guidelines. The Administration claims that there is nothing that they can do to enforce "mask wearing." What if there was a national law that everyone had to wear a mask, socially distance, only gather in small groups, and commit to good hand washing? The mask wearing and social distancing and small groups are the ones that could be monitored or controlled. Hand washing, not so much! In exchange for doing this, we would open everything up. We will still have the "my freedom or my death" complaints, but If I wanted to finally be let out, albeit, with some limits, that would be a deal that I might take. You have to know kids to agree with this. They may say that peer pressure doesn't affect them, but quid pro quo and transactional relationships do, as well as being seen as cool.

A national plan will not work. The issue of accountability overwhelms people because of the large numbers. A national plan to not have a national plan but a local community plan would work. The plan needs to be broken down into smaller entities. Joe Biden alluded to this when he was asked about accountability with his national plan. He indicated that he would involve governors, mayors, or other local authorities in obeying the law. Not wearing a mask would be equal to having a "loser" label placed on the forehead of a person. The pressure would be placed on those who won't obey the law infringing on others' freedom. "That wouldn't work," you say. "You are right!" An additional thing is needed!

Malcolm Gladwell in his book, *The Tipping Point*, makes the point that you need a critical mass of people thinking the same way and feeling the pressure to be a part of right thinking. It is how group dynamics work. He uses many examples to explain this. We can look at the fashion industry and how styles change from not cool to cool where everyone wants a particular style. Remember the Care

Bears Christmas toy? It was very hard to find when kids were clamoring for them. The bears became cool. During the Harry Potter series, people stood in line to get a book. Fashion styles come back because they move to a tipping point of being cool again. Think of Converse high-top sneakers that I wore as a kid. They are back! When I was a faculty chaperone at a school dance, I watched almost every girl who entered wearing a black dress. That was in!

Word of mouth is the compelling approach to reach a tipping point for anything. We would depend on that to empower the new law.

We haven't reached a tipping point for the CDC guidelines. That is at the heart of the issue.

I am also depending on a human being's desire to give a little and get a lot. Give a little, such as obeying CDC guidelines, and you will get a lot such as the freedom you want, plus opening the economy. But everybody has to be in. One or two could ruin it for the rest. Appealing to the better angels of folks to reduce the number of cases of those ill with the virus or dead from the virus hasn't worked. I wish it did, but it hasn't. Let's do something different because it better reflects how human nature works. I am also hoping that the desire or pressure for closure kicks in as well. I want those who won't adhere to the new approach to suffer from overwhelming virus fatigue to move to adhere to the guidelines because of another piece of human nature. We choose pleasure over pain in whatever form it takes. For better or worse, it is how we are!

Post 111. The Biology of Racism

Another black man was shot by police officers. This time it was in Philadelphia. The victim's mother had called for assistance regarding a domestic incident. His mother made it clear that her son, Walter Wallace, age twenty-seven, was mentally ill and taking medication for his illness. Walter had a knife in his hand and was making his way toward the officers. His mother and bystanders were pleading with the police to put their guns down. They tried to deescalate the situation.

Fourteen shots were fired, seven from each police officer. Ten shots entered his chest. Given everything that is happening in our country with the Black Lives Matter movement, you would have thought that common sense would have prevailed. The officers didn't have tasers with them because of a shortage of funds, but he could have been saved with his mother and bystanders willing to intervene. Why did the officers do what they did, knowing that this would be a cause for the killing to become a national story on the evening news? It doesn't make sense. We can't understand it! It isn't rational, let alone humane. Lack of rationality is the reason for the killing of Mr. Wallace. I believe the shooting was based on emotion and biology.

In an earlier post, I cited research done by Malcolm Gladwell in *Blink*. Firing a gun at another human being produces trauma in the shooter. It's not like it is portrayed in the movies. Officer McNesby, president of the Fraternal Order of Police Lodge 5, said that as well when he was interviewed shortly after Walter Wallace died. His officers are traumatized by firing a gun at another person.

What else is going on? You have to pay attention when Oprah selects a book and says it is the best book that she has ever read, and then proceeds to send it to leaders across the land, including CEOs of Fortune 500 Companies, owners of professional sports teams, and anyone else that she can think of.

The book that she chose was *Caste: The Origins Of Our Discontents* by Isabel Wilkerson. If you are only going to read one book on racial issues, this should be it. Wilkerson offers a view that makes sense of the origins of racism. It is about caste, not class. She alludes to a possible solution for all of this killing of black people as well. The solution is understanding the biology of racial interactions and interracial encounters with a shared purpose.

Wilkerson states in her book, *Caste*:

> People perceive people of a different ethnicity as a threat, even in a safe laboratory setting. The threat they perceived as a result of their prejudice produced automatic physical responses as would occur if they were in combat or confronting an oncoming car — restricted blood flow to the heart, the flooding of the muscles with glucose as the body releases cortisol, the hormone useful in the rare moment when one might need to escape danger, but damaging to the body regularly

> Even the briefest exposure is all it takes to activate the body's response. Among whites, the sight of a black person, even in faded yearbook photographs, can trigger the amygdala of the brain to perceive a threat and arm itself for vigilance within thirty milliseconds of exposure, the blink of an eye, researchers have found. When whites have a bit more time for the conscious mind to override the automatic feeling of threat, the amygdala activity switches to inhibition mode. When whites are prompted to think of the black person as an individual, imagine their personal characteristics, the threat level falls (*Caste*, pp.304–305).

Wilkerson goes on to say that there are two interracial groups that don't experience this "biology of fear." They are sports teams and the military. Different races spend time together with a shared purpose. That is the answer. We need more opportunities for races to mix with a shared goal. This is what occurs in diversity training. That is the thought behind police and community interactions to get to know one another. We know it works with sports teams and the military. Yes, it will take a lot of planning. If this sounds too simple, what is the alternative?

I have always subscribed to the thought that once you spend time with someone who is different from you, you will be less likely to disrespect them in any way. That has been more than my thinking. It is my experience.

Right now, biology is running too much of our crisis with racial strife. Unrecognized bias, coupled with biological realities, is a very dangerous combination. Let's get after it. Certainly, Oprah has!

Post 112. Newton Was Right

Sir Isaac Newton's most famous words were "For every action, there is an equal and opposite reaction." During a recent post, I suggested that the best book on race is *Caste: The Origins of Our Discontents* by Isabel Wilkerson. She makes the point that America has a caste system much like Nazi Germany under Hitler and India with its lowest caste, the Dalits. One of her points regarding America as a caste system is that white people must have someone in the lowest caste, so that there is always someone that they feel is inferior to them. That is Wilkerson's reaction to today's racial conflict.

Newton's words ring true in understanding the opposite reaction of the popularity that President Trump has as we move into the final week before the election. It was pointed out that Trump's comment to women that they "should love him for getting their husbands back to work" was certainly offensive to many women, but it was a welcome statement for many white men who feel threatened by anything that further threatens their status in life such as the Black Lives Matter Movement. Institutional racism, according to Wilkerson, is designed so that white people feel that they are better than somebody.

Why, in these final moments of the election campaign, has President Trump continued to have such a strong showing in the polls when he has offended more groups than I can name? Eighty-two percent of Republicans approve of his response to the pandemic. How can that be as he has done nothing to stop it? The answer is that white people in general and white men, in particular, are feeling attacked. If they read *Caste,* they would be frozen in fear and anger as an opposite reaction to Wilkerson's point of view. *The Atlantic Magazine* published an article to address this issue titled "Why Many White Men Love Trump's Coronavirus Response" (10/20) by Olga Khazan. It reflects some of my thinking after reading *Caste* and helped me to see the issue very clearly in terms of why.

Trump is still in the running for another term. Khazan referenced a 1954 study which I went on to read in more detail. The study is about a football game between Princeton and Dartmouth. It was hard fought. Subsequently, students from each school were asked questions about the game. The answers reflected that they saw two different games, depending on which school's side they were on. It documented something that we all know. The study pointed out "my side bias" in such a situation. We see our school team being honorable and the opposition as lacking in honor. This exists with political parties as well. It applies to people who voted for Trump in 2016 and are reluctant to change "team."

But there is something else going on that I wrote about when looking at gender issues. When men have exchanges with other men, these exchanges are generally usually done for "status." When women have exchanges with other women, they are generally about intimacy. Trump understands "status." Everything is the best, greatest, and something "like you have never seen before." It is why Black Lives Matter produces such a negative response from Trump and a great many white men. They need to feel superior to others who they consider are beneath them. Trump becomes their hero to restore white men to a safe position that they have held. Khazan's article is about how Trump feeds the "emotional self-interest" of white people. One aspect of human nature is to feel that if others have a lot means there is not going to be enough for me. The great disparity in wealth in our country only makes this feeling stronger.

In her book, *Strangers in Their Own Land,* Professor Hochschild of UC Berkeley lists the grievances of white men including "women competing for men's jobs," that society "punishes men for just acting like men," and "doesn't affirm that I am proud to be an American again and a manly man." Hochschild goes on to make the point that white men's economic prospects are bad, and American culture tells them their gender is too. They have turned to Trump as a folk hero, one who can restore their sense of former glory. Exposing themselves and others to the coronavirus is part of their heroism."

As one person put it regarding elites, "Trump speaks the way people do at a barbecue, not a dissertation defense." You may say that white men shouldn't feel this way. Remember my axiom for behavior, "How you feel is how you feel. You shouldn't have to justify it."

Many of Trump's followers feel that degrading white men has become an acceptable thing to do. I believe that our answer to our divided nation rests in two words, empathy and trust. That doesn't start with "You shouldn't feel that way." We need to address caste and class in a public forum. We need to understand what it means to be a different race from another whether you are white, black, or brown. We need to address the vast discrepancy between wealth and opportunity. Like a sports team or the military, we need to work toward the shared purpose of understanding people who are different from us.

If this happens, we will have the opportunity of living out *E Pluribus Unum,* one from many. That's who we are. That has not changed. Otherwise, the events in Charlottesville with overt displays of white supremacy will not just be our nightmare. It will be our reality! It will be the extreme opposite reaction to what America should mean for all.

Post 113. The Ikea Effect

Vicki and I have just purchased a treadmill that has taken up residence in our lower level. It has joined a set of weights used by one of my sons. I never realized that treadmills were in short supply because of the pandemic. There were none available in our area, so we went to New Jersey to purchase it. It weighs 300 pounds and does everything but take your blood pressure. However, it does take your pulse. When the salesman asked if we wanted it shipped and put together when it arrived, there wasn't a millisecond that went by when we said, "Yes!" I am an out on the street exercise kind of guy, but with COVID-19 and the danger of going to a gym, this seemed to be the answer with the winter months just around the corner.

My family and I built a house with our own hands, with the help of subcontractors, but we knew that putting the treadmill together would be well above our pay grade. The house required a lot of hard work. Have I become too lazy to attempt the new acquisition? When asked how long a project on the house would take, it always took ten times longer. Did I not have a big enough investment in getting the treadmill set up? These are questions that psychologists, such as Angela Duckworth, a professor of psychology at Penn, wrestle with a phenomenon known as the Ikea Effect.

When friends visit us from afar, some will ask, "Can you take me to the local Ikea because we don't have one in our area?" We have put many Ikea products together and are always happy when there aren't parts leftover. The Ikea effect is when you put something together yourself or do something that requires hard work, you want to show it off. There are times when someone you are talking with doesn't quite see your excitement for your new product. What meant a lot to you may not mean a lot to them. As I have written about in my memoir, there is an axiom that says, "What may not be important to us, may be very important to someone else." We need to tune into that more as people show appreciation to others for what is important to them.

The Ikea Effect also raises the question, "Are we basically lazy?" Given the choice between buying something that needs to be put together as opposed to buying it already made, it seems that six-ty-three percent of people prefer to putting it together themselves. This can be the basis for the popularity of the Ikea stores and the reason that some visitors from a different part of the country want to go there to pick something up when they visit that they can build at home. I am guilty of this phenomenon because anyone who comes to our home on the Chesapeake and hasn't been there before, I never fail to mention, "We built it!"

The Ikea Effect relates to what we are going through during this pandemic and the election. If a candidate has not involved himself or herself in a solution to a problem, you won't hear them bring it up. In fact, they wish that no one would. Likewise, those issues where they have been engaged and involved are the ones that become the focus of any campaign. If engagement, involvement, and hard work are keys to our personal pride, just as it is for the politicians, we should look for ways to get more of that in our daily lives. The Ikea Effect is one of the motivations for the volunteer efforts of many, which is a key part of our gross national product.

In 2018, 63 million volunteers did eight billion hours of work. At $24.69 per hour, they contributed 297.5 billion dollars to the GNP and felt great about their engagement, involvement, and work. As it turns out, the Ikea Effect is a wonderful part of human nature, particularly during difficult times.

Post 114. The Mask of Silence

There have been complaints about masks being a reduction of people's personal freedom, being political, and being politically correct. However, let me tell you what a real mask problem looks like. Not enough people have thought about how masks are a great problem for those who are deaf or hearing impaired. I am not deaf, but I am very hearing impaired. Not all people know this. For many years, I was one of those who constantly asked, "What did you say?" I was vain and didn't want to get hearing aids until I was forced to get a hearing exam and purchase hearing aids. I remember the morning after I got them. I walked outside of our home to get the newspaper, and I heard the birds singing loudly. I stopped and listened, as it was the first time that I had heard that sound in a very long time. I just stood there and listened. I wanted to absorb it fully. When I told Vicki about it, she just smiled.

Since I am hearing impaired, I struggle to hear high women's voices, English accents, and people who don't speak clearly. You learn that when you go to a crowded room, such as a restaurant, you position yourself so that your back is against the wall. I can't hear people who are talking to me from another room. When I take the hearing aids out, I can't hear much at all, so Vicki has to yell at me for me to understand what she is saying. Since Sadie the Wonder Dog is more tuned into the emotions of people than most people, she runs quickly to us to see what is the matter. When you wear a mask and hearing aids, the aids get caught up in the mask when getting it off, so one has to constantly be checking that the aids are not lost. There is one plus to hearing aids. The receivers are in the back of the aid which means I can hear people behind me better than others.

My students still wonder how I could hear their off-the-record conversations behind me. My voice is muffled as well. Pre-mask my students would always say, "We would recognize your voice anywhere. When we hear it, we feel safe."

Now if you add a mask to all of this and you are deaf, there is the additional issue that you can't read facial expressions, or for the deaf, even worse, you can't read lips. They are caught between hearing and safety from COVID-19. They and we have to be more in tune to body language, including looking directly into people's eyes, which does not come naturally. What about the smile? Smiling or not smiling is one of the great ways that we communicate with one another. I know that there are masks with smiles on them, but since we aren't happy all of the time, they can add to the confusion. Who wants to walk around, looking like the movie character, the Joker?

Another way to help those who struggle with hearing is to ask questions that just have a yes or no answer.

I love the tv commercial that simply states, "Wearing a mask says a lot about you." Then the screen goes blank, followed by the comment, "Not wearing a mask says a lot about you as well are examples

If we are sensitive to the above as well as being responsible to our neighbor, we will live out a phrase used by Martin Luther, founder of the Lutheran Church. We would become the *Larva dei* "the mask of God."

Post 115. The Importance of the Ending

We all know that how things turn out, in the end, makes waiting worth the effort—or not. Moving from the mundane to the very important, a few nights ago Vicki and I were watching a British mystery on Netflix and were captivated by the suspense. The drama, narrative, and acting were superb. We couldn't wait for the final episode to see who was really the victim of a crime and who perpetrated it. We watched the ending, looked at one another, and said at the same time, "What? That is a terrible way to end a movie." The ending was so bad that it was anticlimactic compared to the tension beforehand.

After we read novels, we aren't sure of the importance of some works until the very end. I know that some people will read the ending first as they can't wait for closure to occur. Others refuse to know an ending and pay strict attention to "spoiler alert." The theme that holds my memoir together doesn't appear until the last few pages of the book. It surprised some who read it. I know some authors who actually write the ending first and then work the entire novel toward that ending.

I think you know where this post is going after a week of waiting for something very important. Think how badly we wanted to know the result of all of the political elections, particularly the election for the President of the United States. In these days of ending, we need to quickly consider beginnings and pray for the hand of God in the work ahead. In the book of Revelation, we hear the Lord God Almighty say, "I am the alpha and the omega—the beginning and the end" (Rev. 22:13).

We have work to do as a nation as the world watches. President-Elect Biden said "That is not who we are. We are better than that." There are many including the Black community who have said, "No we are not better than that. Racism prevails!" We are a nation divided. That is one of the important lessons that we have shown rather graphically to our global neighbors. We are not that city on a hill that President Reagan said to describe us. We need to climb up! We won't have time to savor this ending, for we have too many challenges in front of us. I am mindful of T. S Eliot's words, "What we call the beginning is often the end. And to make an end is to make a beginning. The end is where we start from." It will take the spirit of the living Lord and God to empower us in our new start toward a greater ending.

Post 116. On Eagles' Wings

Many were struck by President-Elect Biden concluding his address to the American people on Saturday night with words from the hymn, *On Eagles' Wings*. It is a hymn composed by Jan Michael Jones, a Catholic priest, in 1970 and is a favorite to many including me. We hear it often in the Mass of Christian Burial in the Roman Catholic tradition as well as in the Episcopalian tradition. I define a favorite as a hymn or song that stays with me long after I have heard it and find myself humming it throughout the day. Its text is based on the book of the prophet Isaiah with the following refrain, "And he will raise you up on eagles wings, bear you on the breath of dawn, make you shine like the sun, and hold you in the palm of His hand." Those words are based on Isaiah 40:31, "But those who hope in the Lord will renew their strength. They will soar on wings like eagles. They will run and not grow weary; they will walk and not grow faint."

Why are the words of this hymn just right to be said at the end of Joe Biden's remarks? The Biden family chose this hymn to be sung at Beau Biden's Mass of Christian Burial in 2015. We know that the memory of his son walks with him in everything that he does. He may have known that the hymn was one of the favorites of John F. Kennedy. I often taught students that they should remember the Eagles' Wings passage from Isaiah for two other very important reasons. The words were written during the Babylonian captivity when the Jewish people were taken from their land in Judah to Babylon, the capitol of the Empire. It was a different land with different laws. I believe that over half of the American people, particularly people of color, have felt that they have been in exile during their past, and may have felt this more explicitly during the past four years. The Isaiah passage has its roots in the book of Deuteronomy 32:11, "like an eagle that stirs up its nest and hovers over its young that spreads its wings to catch them and carries them aloft."

My family and I are blessed to witness eagles nesting in the trees on our property and see them soar high above the waters of the Chesapeake Bay. There are times that the winds pick up under their wings, spread ready to catch and carry anything aloft. They barely have to flap their wings as they find the right currents of the wind and soar with little effort. They are at one with nature.

One of the interpretations of this passage is that we have to be more than strong; we must also be righteous. The American Eagle was chosen as our national symbol in 1782 because of its strength but also because it represents the ingredients that produce freedom— freedom to soar with integrity and care for those who need care. President-Elect Biden couldn't have chosen a better hymn to point to America's future.

Post 117. Ethics Class to Create Patriots

If you are someone who likes a good moral argument, take an ethics class. My students called our class "full contact ethics." Once you entered the classroom, you were going to be involved in the discussion whether you liked it or not. Not surprisingly, a lot of students chose to take the course as they like to be challenged. It wasn't for the faint of heart. The guideline was also something that we have heard repeatedly recently. "You are entitled to your own opinions but not your own facts." They also must practice "civil discourse," respecting different views and not attacking someone who sees things differently from what they think.

David Callahan wrote an important book in 2004 on social ethics called *The Cheating Culture*. He and I had phone conference calls as I wanted to use the essence of his book in ethics class. Keep in mind that year, 2004. His book was a welcome addition, analyzing the epidemic of cheating in all segments of society. His words have stood the test of time, seeing such things as the following at the heart of the American phenomenon of dishonesty:

- "Tax evasion by the rich is widespread and the average taxpayer has to come up with an extra $3000 a year to cover the shortfall.

- Half of resumes contain lies

- Employee theft totals $600 billion or six percent of the GDP

- Reporters have fabricated stories and major writers have been caught plagiarizing"

Add to this in 2020:

- President Trump's payment of $750 a year for taxes and other ethical issues too numerous to mention that has caused the American people to accept his unethical behavior for it has become such a norm for him.

- Parents have been sent to prison for bribing universities to accept their children based on phony accomplishments. They felt entitled to do so.

- The swamp still exists in Washington with a good many of Trump's administration guilty of multiple felony counts.

If I could summarize Callahan's book and research in one sentence, it would be "given a choice between money and integrity, people will choose money."

Part of what has caused this cheating culture is the phenomenon of the rise of the "winning class." We have to consider that the top one percent of households have more wealth than the entire bottom ninety-nine percent have combined. We have private clubs, gated communities, chartered jets, and exclusive restaurants. President Trump said, "You are going to get tired of winning if I am elected. The one thing I can't stand is a loser." I still remember Leona Helmsley, a New York winner, saying that "Rules are for the little people." The winning class makes up their rules as they go along and don't mind if they are better rules than for the little people. That is what Callahan's research showed then and still continues today.

One of the reviews Frederic and Mary Ann Brussat wrote of his book points to the true north of ethical action that Callahan is suggesting is as good now as it was then:

> Anyone who plays by the rules can get ahead. Everyone has some say in how the rules get made. Everyone who breaks the rules suffers the same penalties. And all of us are in the same boat, living in the same moral community and striving together to build a society that confers respect on people based on a wide variety of accomplishments. He also wants government agencies to enforce these rules of fair play, more work on establishing ethical standards in the business community, more emphasis upon honor codes in schools and universities, and a return to civic-mindedness where individuals sense that we are all in the same boat and can work together to create a better and more just society.

Our elected officials are, for the most part, politicians concerned with party above everything else. They need to change their identity to patriots who have love of their nation first. This will require a familiarity with ethics more so than getting what they want to benefit their party. John McCain proved this could be done.

I know that many of my former students who know the ethical language and ethical systems and how they apply to daily life could be called to Washington to engage these folks in what it means to be an ethical person. They would be far more successful than another adult in that role, for students don't suffer fools gladly, would not put up with spin, and can spot hypocrisy and inauthenticity a mile away. All of their filters lean in that direction as a result of their growth as human beings. Trust me. They would get the job done!

Post 118. Nudge Theory and Lever Therapy

An innovation from the world of psychology and economics has provided an approach to helping people in their decision-making as well as in the process to help an individual become a more whole person. Over time I developed an approach that could be used by anyone who wants to help another person. My desire was to take the mystery out of the counseling process, based on my experience of how effective faculty could be in helping others. I call this simple approach "Lever Therapy." I believe it is a tool that can be used with the other modalities of counseling. In counseling, we deal with the ultimate challenge facing people who are struggling with barriers in their lives. If the person comes to know the right thing to do, why don't they act on that insight and do it? Or in the words of Saint Paul, "The good that I want to do, I don't. That which I don't want to do, I do" (Rom. 7:19).

This is the important question that led me to identify Lever Therapy to raise and seek to answer. There are three ingredients in Lever Therapy. One is to identify the strengths of a person, and the second is to nudge them to seek help and move in the direction they have identified as their desired goal. Between these two aspects is a consideration of how past, present, and future considerations inform the development or lack thereof of the person seeking help. Issues such as self-esteem, a sense of belonging, as well as their experience with avoiding the emotions of rejection, embarrassment, and vulnerability are also part of the mix.

When a person comes to me for help, I initially listen carefully to their concerns, but I also identify their strengths and positive personality traits. These are not always evident at first, but if you stay with the person or situation long enough, you will find something to work with. Everyone has strengths. I build on that strength to establish a positive foundation for self-actualization and action. Once I know what strengths and personality traits, I have to work with, I bring "Nudge Theory" into the process. Nudge Theory is a system of thought with practical implications. The theory was developed by Richard Thaler, professor of Behavioral Economics and Finance at the University of Chicago, and Cass Sunstein, professor at Harvard Law School, and director of the Center for Behavior Economics and Public Policy. They worked for five years on this theory and articulated it through the publication of their book simply titled *Nudge* (Sunstein and Thaler 2008).

Their theory relates to every aspect of life, from getting people to slow down on a highway, to collecting taxes from people who don't want to pay them, to the latest approach to effective fundraising. On October 12, 2017, Richard Thaler won the Nobel Prize for his work on Nudge Theory. I think their theory can be applied to creating forward movement in the counseling process.

A typical example of Nudge Theory at work is the flashing speed signs placed along highways. When I am driving too fast and see one of these flashing signs, I am "nudged" to slow down to the legal speed limit. There are various ways in which counseling can nudge a person in need of help to begin to go in the positive direction that they have identified. Alcoholics Anonymous employs Nudge

Theory by simply having their members gather in groups to nudge each other in the right direction to attain sobriety.

As clients are responding to nudges to move toward healing, I employ the integration of how a person's past, present, and future work together, as well as the issues mentioned earlier. I have used this approach with many people in crisis and feel it moves the client toward healing in less time a traditional approach does.

Post 119. Parents, Seat Belts, and the Viral Spike

It is the law to wear seatbelts. I sometimes forget to put mine on, and I am grateful that my car reminds me. I notice when watching a movie or TV show that when people get into their cars, they automatically put their seat belts on.

As is true for wearing masks there are certain human behaviors that no one thought that people would accept as a necessary change. There was a great deal of pushback in the 1950s on the suggestion that seatbelts should be worn by everyone. It was the same argument that we hear today about "interfering with a person's individual freedom." President Johnson issued a law in 1966 requiring people to buckle up. Seatbelts now are used by ninety-one percent of Americans. Their ability to save lives has been documented. It is now the norm. People frown when you are in a car with someone who doesn't buckle up. Others in the car speak up, and the fellow passenger buckles up quickly.

In 2005 the Italian government banned smoking in restaurants. Everyone said that it was unenforceable. I have been to Rome where smoking is prevalent in the population, but no one smokes in places where people eat. The Italian people are free spirits. The people park their cars on sidewalks and are known for a relaxed culture. Mark Hall, professor at Wake Forest University, works in the area of health care and public health. He indicates that Italy used hortatory laws which are laws that promote social laws rather than mandating them. The Italian government used such examples as driving at the speed limit as the same thing as not smoking in a restaurant. It is unhealthy and will save your life *and the lives of others*. It will make dining a better experience.

However, we know that persuasion has not worked in our country regarding masks. We know that masks were not accepted during the 1918 influenza either. There was even an anti-mask league. Governor Doug Burgum, of North Dakota, is the newly re-elected Republican governor. He opposes a mandate to wear masks. The Republican governors of our nation recently told the Biden transition team to "not waste their time trying to require masks in their states." As I write this post, we are in another spike of the virus which has been referred to now as a humanitarian crisis.

What is the answer? Joanne Silberner, a health and medical researcher, offers part of what is needed. She writes, "In the end what worked for seatbelts were efforts by public health advocates, financial incentives, state-level mandates, enforcement, solid research, effective health messaging—all activities that are possible with masks." But something else needs to be addressed to have masks as a norm. It is confronting that major ethical issue of taking away someone's freedom when you require that they wear a mask. We are already doing that. We take away your freedom to drink and drive as well. That is now an accepted norm for freedom is linked to a person's need to be responsible. The general public is appalled by people who drink and drive because it may affect other lives beyond their own.

But there is something else that is very much needed. It is the third ingredient to freedom and responsibility. It is accountability, which no one talks about—except recently, I saw a doctor in the Midwest make the following statement (I will paraphrase), "You may not wear a mask because it infringes on your personal freedom. Your freedom is the most important thing to you. Helping others may not be. But let me give you another fact. If you come to our hospital when you have the COVID-19 virus and there is no more room for us to treat COVID-19 patients, you will have to go to another state."

You can also listen to people who have had the virus, such as Chris Christie, former governor of New Jersey and friend of President Trump. He spent a week in intensive care after prepping the president for a debate. You know the governor to be direct and pull no punches, "It's terrible. Wear a mask, damn it! Just wear a mask!"

One's freedom stops when it crosses the boundary of affecting another negatively. We need more ethical talk on this issue and accountability as well. Our medical providers are burning out on this recent spike. They are overwhelmed.

If we can stop smoking in public places, require seat belts for all, punish drivers who drink, we can get people to wear masks. In the words of Senator Elizabeth Warren, "I have a plan for that!" That's what the Biden administration will give us.

Post 120. What's Next? Who's Next?

Vicki and I have started watching *The Crown*, which is a continuation of the Netflix series tracing events in the history of the British monarchy. It is certainly not a thriller or a mystery, although the history that I didn't know is part of the narrative. At the end of each episode, as the viewer, I have a strong impulse that I want to see what's next. Authors of books and TV series seemed geared to produce this feeling in us.

I remember as a child going to the Saturday movies with friends. There was always a serial that went along with the designated movie. The classic example would be that we saw most often was of a woman tied to the train tracks with the locomotive coming down the tracks at high speed. Just at the moment when we would all be screaming, the serial would stop and a sign would appear on the silver screen with the words, "To Be Continued."

"What's next?" drives a great deal of human nature, particularly as we continue our way through the desert of the pandemic. As I write this, the virus is spiking, deaths have reached new records, people are refusing to obey the guidelines set out by the CDC, and our health care workers and other essential workers are overwhelmed, as well as businesses and families.

All the questions in our hearts and minds seem to be geared to what's next? The news about vaccines seems to have reduced our fear of what's next? We are in a place in politics where we are on the uncharted ground of a president who won't release vital records and funds to enable a smooth transition of a new administration. Clearly, one of the many downsides of the present administration has been four years of American citizens nervous about "What he was going to do next?" as each day was filled with a new self-manufactured crisis. "What's next?" is an unsettling question to dominate one's life.

When someone has a serious disease, such as cancer, their lives are dominated by this question as well. The only way that I know to deal with this unsettling question is to pray, stay in the moment, and take one day at a time. Psychologists refer to this as compartmentalization. We focus on things that take us out of ourselves. That is key. We have all heard the expression, "If you think you have it bad, just know that there is someone out there struggling more than you." That doesn't help us with our immediate pain, but I think that is an attempt to have us move from concern for ourselves to concern for others.

One of the important stories that addresses this issue is *The Tree of Sorrows*. The story indicates that when we die, we have the opportunity to walk around the Tree of Sorrows and to put our sorrows on it. The catch is that we have to take someone else's sorrows off and claim them as our own. As the story continues as we leave the Tree, people put their acquired sorrow back on the tree and choose their source of pain.

I think that there is a paradox here, whether handling the epidemic or any other challenge. Take it one day or even one hour at a time, but learn something from the world of sports. It is "next man up."

When one player is injured and unable to play, they say "Next man up." They are not thinking about the next man during seasonal play. He or she is not their focus. They are focusing on each game and each play, but he or she is there and ready in the wings. How do you and I use that approach? Name your greatest fear. Then ask yourself, "What is my greatest hope?" Think about how you would address that fear so that you would have some control over your life if that fear arrived. Then put that hope in the bullpen of your life, knowing it is there when you need it. The goal would be not "What is your greatest fear?" but "What is your greatest hope?" That would move your question from "What's next? to "Who's next?" Hope will be waiting there as your answer. Hope could always be "your next man up!"

Post 121. Wisdom at the Rodeo

No one talks about the value of wisdom anymore. Perhaps interest in it has waned with the ascent of our technological culture. You can get what you need to know by going to Google and punching in a concern or a question, such as a medical diagnosis about which you want more information. It doesn't take much trouble for you to get instant answers. It used to be that we valued more highly people who had a lot of experience in a matter or someone who was older. We no longer look to people with personal experience from a lot of failures matched with a lot of success in life. Wisdom comes to someone willing to put in the effort to be in the mix of things in life and not to sit on the proverbial sidelines. Wisdom does not play it safe. It is involved in the fabric of our lives whether we like it or not.

When someone is in the middle of solving a challenging problem, wisdom wants to hear someone say, "Don't worry, he's been to this rodeo many times. He will do what needs to be done." Wisdom is "expertise plus" and is usually given to those who have been "around the block." Some call it having the X factor or having the right stuff.

Wisdom is different from expertise. Malcolm Gladwell in his research on successful people demonstrated that it takes 10,000 hours to reach a level of excellence in any given field. A standard joke is, "How do I get to Carnegie Hall" in New York City? The answer is "practice, practice, practice!" A concert pianist may not be someone that you would think has wisdom, so choose your top athlete in any given sport and you may not label him or her wise.

You may know gifted teachers, but you may not say that they are people with wisdom. Education doesn't seem to guarantee it as we hear people say about a grandmother "that she didn't have much education but she had great wisdom."

What makes wisdom a unique gift? There is a key in the rodeo metaphor. I have attended several rodeos in Colorado where close friends live. Everyone should take in a rodeo to see why that word is used to describe someone with that intangible extra, something that we call wisdom that is experience plus. Once the bull rider or rope wrangler takes off into the arena, the crowd cheers, even when he is thrown and hops up dusty and bruised. The audience may see him get back on another horse later in the competition. Wise people are people who know victory and defeat. They know success and failure. They have experienced the agony and ecstasy of life. They are seasoned. Your age does not matter! It can happen at any time.

Teddy Roosevelt used the image of an arena to describe this rodeo creating wisdom. He gave his famous address, "Citizen in a Republic," at the Sorbonne in Paris, France, on April 23, 1920. He describes how someone gains wisdom in life:

It is not the critic who counts; not the man who points out how the strong man stumbles, or where the doer of deed could have done better. The credit belongs to the man who is actually in the arena, whose face is marred by dust and sweat and blood; who strives valiantly; who errs, who comes up short again and again, because there is no effort without error and shortcoming; but who does actually strive to do the deeds; who knows great enthusiasms, the great devotions; who spends himself in a worthy cause; who at the best knows in the end the triumph of high achievement, and who at the worst, if he fails, at least fails while daring greatly; his place shall never be with those cold and timid souls who neither know victory nor defeat (Roosevelt 2014).

One of the people that I knew who had wisdom was a former student of mine, Alex Bilotti, EA 12. She was a small person in stature but a giant in the world of wisdom and courage. I still wear an orange rubber bracelet inscribed with her initials AVB and Courage to remember her and her message of the need for all of us to live from a deeper spot. She gave a chapel address when she was a senior at our school. She said in her concluding remarks:

But I do know this. Because cancer chose me and because of what I've gone through I've been given a rare glimpse of death. If I would like to leave you with anything, it would be to think of one of those servants whispering to the emperor *Memento mori,* remember death. Don't dwell on it, don't get lost in it, just remember it and live your life accordingly. And though I think each person is entitled to figuring out what that means for themselves, for me at least, it has meant to live from a deeper spot. Not to do more, but to appreciate more. Not to always be happy but to figure out why I'm sad. To carve into this stuff called life because I know that at some point, I and those around me will no longer be here to do so. Thank you.

I can't count the number of times that I have used her words "to live from a deeper spot."

If you want to see and hear what wisdom looks like and sounds like take note of Alex's Chapel Address in 2012 during her senior year at the Episcopal Academy. Directions to view are below. The text of her chapel address is found as well in my memoir on pages 239–246. She died from Ewing's Sarcoma in her junior year at the University of Pennsylvania. Alex had been to many rodeos over her years of agony and ecstasy, and many people learned wisdom from her words and life. People who didn't know her but knew of her attended her Mass of Christian Burial along with 1,000 of her friends and family. They knew there was something about her that was different. That something, among many other gifts, was the gift of wisdom.

The video of Alex's Chapel Address when she was a senior at the Episcopal Academy, March 16, 2012, can be found on my blog on website under the title, "Wisdom at the Rodeo."

Post 122. Joy and Self-Reflection

The following are themes covered in my book, *The Times of My Life*. They may help you redeem your time during this period when we are in isolation because of COVID-19.

GRIT: Pat Chambers is mentioned in the book. He is a graduate of the Episcopal Academy where I was head chaplain. Pat is the coach of the Penn State basketball team. His team was to be part of March Madness. Pat is quoted in the press as saying, "It's a great reminder that nothing is guaranteed, not tomorrow, not an hour from now, not the NCAA Tournament, not the selection show. But there are so many lessons to be learned here." Then referring to a 2002 incident in center city Philadelphia, he added, "Look I was stabbed and I think I could have been dead, and I was given a second chance. So, there are blessings, there are rebirths from tragedies and setbacks."

Pat and I remember the period after he was assaulted like it was yesterday. The Chambers family, the school community, his basketball mentors, Jay Wright, Dan Dougherty, and Herb McGee supported him. He is now one of ten semifinalists for the Naismith Coach of the Year award. We have stayed in touch even as recently as today.

POSITIVE PSYCHOLOGY: College professors at Harvard and Yale have taught courses on this topic. These courses have the largest class enrollments in the history of those schools. I taught that subject in my ethics course at EA. Why did these colleges have a record number of students sign up for this course? You can find out why if you go online to coursera.org and register for a free course, *The Science of Well-Being*, being offered through Yale University.

OUR FOXHOLE: Our relationship with God involves the same kind of communication that we have with family and friends. Consider an adage, "There are no atheists in foxholes." We are in one right now. Prayer is communication with God. Talk to them more. Practice mindfulness and meditation. Read scripture.

A MOVIE: Watch *A Beautiful Day in the Neighborhood*. Discover how someone becomes a hero.

Post 123. The News Cycle

Since Ted Turner founded CNN in the advent of cable news in June of 1980, we have been introduced to the phenomenon of the news cycle. It broadcasts twenty-four hours a day and became more a part of the culture with CNN's coverage of the Gulf War. CNN made you feel that you were right in the mix of the action. The average cable news coverage of an event is forty-one seconds. Experts even feel that is too much to keep the viewer involved. The worst time to release a story is 5:00 p.m. on a Friday as the news staff is reduced at that time.

The newspapers have a twenty-four-hour news cycle where some are feeling is too long to wait. Hence, one of the reasons for the growth of cable news is impatience. I am amazed at how quickly a news story will leave the headlines while another perceived as more exciting and relevant takes over. It seems, at times, that it is more like entertainment than the news as it strives to get the attention of the viewer. I watch CNN and have learned that if you stay on for twenty minutes, you will get all you need to know before the next reminder of what is in the cycle. The cable networks feed on our short-term memories that we will forget quickly about the story that was so important a day ago.

Let me introduce a cycle that is more important to produce meaning and happiness than today's news cycle. It is the biblical book of Ecclesiastes with its news cycle and is fitting for our days of the pandemic and Black Lives Matter. The author of the book is Kohelet. Others feel that it was written around 1000 BC by Solomon who God gave the gift of a lifetime, wisdom. It contains in 3:1–8 those oft-heard words, "For everything there is a season and a time to every purpose under heaven, a time to be born and a time to die, a time to plant, and a time to pluck up what is planted, a time to kill and a time to heal," and it continues by reflecting that "life is a two-edged sword" where everything has an opposite issue. It reminds me of Tevye in *Fiddler on the Roof* when he says on the "one hand this and on the other hand that."

The book reflects the limits of human power, something that folks in Washington need to consider. We can describe our current dilemma of 2020 that we are in the midst of an unpredictable world. Even so, Solomon presses us to try to find enjoyment and meaning despite what we are experiencing. In this biblical news feed, Solomon addresses the all-too-usual paths that we take to achieve happiness. He takes us through a series of things that we do to be happy. Keep in mind that this book was written around 1000 BC. What was true then of our search for happiness is still true today, particularly during the 2020 times of challenge and heartache. Solomon's cycle has us seeking happiness through education, pleasure, work, wealth, winning, and women and men who seek the pleasures of sex (Solomon had hundreds of wives and concubines). Solomon knew all of these avenues that he and we pursue. Each one of these is seen in the book as a news feed that comes and goes as we move through these choices until we reach the Big Breaking News that God must be the center of our lives for any of these choices to have any effect on our happiness.

During 2020, confronted with disease and injustice for black people, many find themselves throwing up their hands proclaiming "What good does it do? What will really change? What's it all about?" These questions lead to a sense of meaninglessness. A central bias of Solomon's words is his slant on things, not conservative or liberal, but something else. Simply the book of Ecclesiastes proclaims there is joy in connecting to God. This biblical news feed interprets the Hebrew word for meaningless "as walking through a fog."

What brings clarity is to consider another news feed in Ecclesiastes. "Vanity is vanity. All is vanity." These are also words included in this book. They are a reference to those who have a sense of arrogance and lack humility. We have heard the word *narcissistic* many times this year. It means to love yourself to the point that it destroys you. It is based on the Myth of Narcissus who fell in love with his reflection in a pool, tried to embrace the image, and died.

The words of Ecclesiastes were written eons ago yet are so apt to what we are going through now and how in the end we achieve true happiness with our relationship and connection to the living loving Lord and God. That is the big story. It shouldn't leave us in a news cycle, for it will be what brings us to a better today and tomorrow and each twenty-four-hour period that follows. CNN gives us the facts over and over. The words in Ecclesiastes are the real breaking news, which have been there down through the ages. I think even Wolf Blitzer would tell you that truth quickly after he proclaims, "Breaking News. Stay with us. It is coming up after the next break."

Post 124. Gratitude in the Year 2020

Thanksgiving is here. It is the moment in the year that draws us in to consider our feelings of gratitude. Gratitude should be a verb, not a noun. It sits in the center of the Christian faith, for it is nourished by the call to action by Jesus himself. We hear it clearly in his message about His identity. In the Gospel of Matthew, we hear him talk about who He is. He is not just a stationary figure but is also embodied in action. We shouldn't miss the message or messenger when He says, "Then the righteous will answer him, 'Lord, when did we see you hungry and feed you, or thirsty and give you something to drink? When did we see you a stranger and invite you in, or needing clothes and clothe you? When did we see you sick and took care of you, and when were you in prison and visited you?' And the King will answer them, 'Truly I tell you, as you did it to one of the least of these who are members of my family, you did it to me'" (Matt. 25:35–40).

What a profound question. When did we see you, Lord? Consider 2020 and the people who have given us a glimpse of what unselfish love looks like? The essential workers, doctors, and nurses who have demonstrated courage beyond human understanding but not beyond God's understanding come first to mind. Who have you reached out to help with no thought of getting anything in return or who has reached out as well to you expecting nothing in return? Just think! You will discover them.

The Matthew passage allows us to see who Jesus is, and what we could be as we are the *imago dei,* created in the image of God. Matthew's words focus on an action where one will feel gratitude in the give-and-take of life reflected in someone's need that has been addressed, usually without fanfare. The passage seems to be saying regarding the Christ that we should look to exchange with another. We need to look for Him where you might not expect to see Him. Remember the question, "When did we see you? They were baffled? They were looking for a human form, and He was looking for responsive and responsible action. They didn't see it because they didn't expect it. You can't be what you can't see.

Gratitude should be a verb, not a noun. Gandhi put it this way, "Even the Lord himself would not stand before a starving man except in the form of food." It resonates with Matthew's question, "When did we see you, Lord?"

If gratitude is to become a verb and not a noun, we need to see it in action. If you want a profound learning experience, teach young people for thirty-eight years, for they turned out to be my best teachers. They don't pay attention to what some adults are attuned to, like the policeman at the airport arrival area who sees my collar and directs me to "just park right there, Father." Students didn't care if I had a collar on or not. They didn't care what schools I attended.

They didn't care about where I was from. They cared about what I did. They are not impressed by all the things that adults, at times, focus on. They must have all been descended from someone in Missouri for their watchwords were the frequently heard words in the midwestern proclamation, "Show me!" That is what Jesus is saying in the book of Matthew in answer to the question, "When did we see you, Lord?"

I have always been a fan of an expression that is a central lesson in that passage in Matthew for, when you think about it, it is really a passage about gratitude. You saw me when you *did* it for the least of these. That favorite expression of mine is "Preach the Gospel. Use words if necessary!"

Gratitude should be a verb, not a noun. Be thankful for when you did something for someone in need and for someone who did something as well for you when you were in need. Those people exist, but you may have to look in a new way, as the disciples did, with that question in need of an answer, "On this Thanksgiving 2020, when did we see you, Lord?" We need to see with a new vision. Jesus shows up in the strangest of places and with people that you wouldn't expect. He could be wearing a mask, keeping social distance from others, and observing good hand washing.

Happy Thanksgiving!

Post 125. The Last Shall Be First

Questions loom over us now that the approval of vaccines is on the horizon. We are confronted by a significant bioethical question that matches the difficulty of discovering the vaccines in the first place. Who gets the vaccine first? How is that decided? The Advisory Committee on Immunizations for the CDC set forth a process to answer that question. Ethics has taken a central role in their decision-making and contains two ingredients that I have taught my ethics students over the years. First, we tolerate (not necessarily agree with) that which we understand. Hence, a good deal of the

ACIP's reasoning had to make sense to the rest of us. Two, the people that are most affected by the pandemic or any other bioethical issue should have the most to say in the decision. The ACIP's decision was to give voice to those people.

The words of Jesus in Matthew 19:29–30, "The last shall be first," is at the core of this bioethics decision. "The last" here refers to those who have been the most vulnerable to the disease. Wealth in our country usually has dictated access, and access is a key in bioethics decision-making. "Who has access to what we all need and when will we get it?" is the important driver of the discussion regarding the distribution of the vaccine.

Currently, we are in the final approval stages with AstraZeneca, which has the greatest flexibility to be transported, and with Moderna and Pfizer. ACIP has employed the ethical system of Utilitarian belief in their process. The central guiding principle of that system is the greatest good for the greatest number of people in each group in line for the vaccine as opposed initially to the group being the entire United States.

Currently, their phases of ranking are as follows for various groups: The first group to receive the vaccine are the doctors and nurses on the front lines because they are the most vulnerable as well as minorities and those with lower income. Long-term care residents would be part of this first wave. The next group would be firefighters, police, educators, food service people, and those who work in the area of energy. This group is placed there because, among the issue of their value, they cannot do their jobs at home. The next would be those with underlying health issues and people who are over the age of sixty-five and those in congregate settings, such as jails and homeless shelters. Research shows that young adults tend to be the super spreaders so they would follow. Middle-aged people in self-contained working situations would be next. The remaining people would follow these categories.

It is important to note how bioethics is based on situation ethics as well, meaning the situation dictates the approach taken. The ethical language applied to the above groups is the Machiavellian notion of the "ends justifies the means." The ends in the pandemic decision-making for groups are based on vulnerability and value to the whole nation. The nation becomes the final group as the greatest good for the greatest number in our entire country. "The last defined as those most vulnerable shall be first."

This is a very different bioethics decision-making process than what occurred at Memorial Hospital in New Orleans during Hurricane Katrina. Keeping in mind Situation Ethics and how the situation dictates decision making, the process at Memorial Hospital divided people into two basic groups with the knowledge that they couldn't get everyone out of the hospital alive in terms of time and resources. They chose the patients who they thought had the best chance of surviving to be taken out first. They were the group identified as the most likely chance of surviving. The others came next in a group.

I write this post as we are in the midst of another spike of the virus. Already we are seeing hospitals that can't take all of the patients. Some of the patients could be taken to other facilities, but the fear is that we will run out of space and medical personnel to care for the need. How do you determine who is treated and who is not? That is the kind of question bioethicists have to address. Do you do first come, first served; do you look for a precedent that is like this or something else? I took a group of twenty-four faculty from EA to the Penn Center for Bioethics for a two-week intensive course on bioethical decision-making taught by Drs. Caplan and Sisti. After two weeks, I asked the teachers how they felt. Their response was "depressed and stressed" as this kind of decision-making is tough. The title of one book, *Come Let Us Play God!* captures the tension.

We are not done here yet. There are other important issues to address. We know who will have access to the vaccines, but we also know that not everyone will risk taking a vaccine. One group feels that vaccines have been politicized and therefore rushed and inaccurate. Black people are already suspicious of government-funded projects because of the Tuskegee experiment. This was a study of untreated syphilis in African American males sponsored by the US Public Health Service between 1932 to 1972 to observe the terrible consequences of untreated syphilis. They were told they were getting free health care from the government. As a result of this travesty, laws were introduced where consent had to be given for any further medical treatments or surgeries in our country. That trial is still in the cultural psyche of black people in our country. In addition, we have anti-vaccine groups who are opposed to all vaccines of any kind.

There is one other serious ethical decision that must be made. I have been privileged to travel to many different foreign countries. One thing that you learn as an American is that the United States is not the center of the universe. I have talked about utilitarian theory and identifying your group first in the decision-making process. We share one planet. We are one global community. We are one global group. What countries should get the vaccine and in what order? What we will do when that question is raised if we follow bioethics guidelines is to look at other global health crises like AIDS, malaria, polio, and others. I am of a certain age where I remember getting the polio vaccine in a sugar cube at my elementary school. Precedents should be examined regarding ethical approaches used in the past to address pandemics in the same way that judges and lawyers look at precedents in law cases to make a decision.

In my opinion that would be the best way to start, but we need an ethical guideline for those conversations. I would suggest for consideration the words of the Gospel of Luke, "To whom much is given, much is expected." That verse is one of the two core values of the Gates Foundation. I would put it simply as, "Those who have much have a moral obligation to those who don't." That is what makes human beings different, the ability to be forward looking with moral guidelines to address global challenges. Other primates can't do that.

Post 126. No Coincidences from Wednesday Evening to Thanksgiving Morning

On the Wednesday evening before Thanksgiving, we forgot the sage for the parsley, sage, rosemary, and thyme combination which are needed for the filling. All the stores were now out of it. I asked, "Do we really need it?" The response was, "Yes." Our oldest son had some at his home, and we were saved. I asked why is that sage herb so important? No one knew the answer, so I checked because every time that I hear Simon and Garfunkel's song, "Scarborough Fair," which refers to those four herbs, I am immediately transported back in time to a wonderful summer before Vicki and I were married.

She lived in Raleigh, and I was at Duke Medical Center in Durham taking a three-month program in counseling before returning for my final year at the Berkeley Divinity School at Yale. When I was not on call at the hospital, I was in Raleigh with Vicki. That was the summer that "Scarborough Fair" became so popular with those words, "Parsley, Sage, Rosemary, and Thyme." It is actually a new version of an old song, a ballad composed in 1620 meant to be a secret to the "true love of mine." There was a Scarborough Fair in England where people brought their herbs and vegetables to sell. Chefs will tell you that the four herbs mentioned in the song are a great combination of nutritional foods. Parsley at the time the song was originally written was symbolic of comfort, sage of strength, rosemary of love, and thyme of courage.

That summer, although it was a rigorous program at Duke, was the time that forged our relationship in the "smithy of our souls" (James Joyce) as we were married the following December. Music does that to us. We hear a song or an expression, and we are transported quickly to good and bad times. I wouldn't have remembered that without the "missing sage." I didn't even know what to call the phenomenon of being transported in such a wonderful way by

221

just hearing the names of four herbs or words from another. What a coincidence that produced great feelings.

I awoke on Thanksgiving morning to see a Thanksgiving greeting from a good friend, Richardson Merriman. Attached to his email was a video called "No Coincidences." It deeply moved me, and I hope that it does the same for you. I now know what to call those unexpected times that help us to recall wonderful moments in the past as they still nourish us in the present. They are shoulder taps.

The video "No Coincidences" regarding shoulder taps can be found on my blog on my website under the title "No Coincidences".

Post 127. Not Good Enough

The story told by Secretary of State designate Anthony Blinkin says it all about how we will now want to be perceived by the world. His late stepfather, Samuel Pisar, after surviving four years in a concentration camp, made a break from a death march to encounter an American tank. The hatch of the tank opened, and an African American man looked down on him. Pisar said the only words in English that he knew, taught to him by his mother before the war, "God bless America." "That is who we are," said Blinken. "That is what America represents to the world, however imperfectly."

There is more to this anecdote than meets the eye. The first group to liberate concentration camps was a segregated Engineers Combat Battalion. Dr. Leon Bass, who was a friend of mine, was part of that troop that Blinken is referring to in his remark. Dr. Bass was an educator and a first-hand witness to the liberation of Buchenwald. He came to speak at the Episcopal Academy at the Chapel services. He continued to honor my request to come and address the community about his life experiences long after he retired from public speaking. He died on March 31, 2015. When I heard of his death, I stopped, thought about our friendship, his experiences, and was silent in prayer to honor his Quaker tradition.

He describes his "not being good enough" from the time that he volunteered for service in the United States Army in 1943 through his days following the war. He fought racism and all the "isms" his entire life. His words are powerful. It puts Blinken's comment in a bigger context. There once was a statement in our culture, "Be like Mike," meaning to be like Michael Jordan as a standard of excellence. We need as well to "Be like Leon" as he is faith in action. After that horrible event at Charlottesville, Leon's words make an even bigger impact. White supremacy couldn't happen here in this country, could it? Leon would say, "Yes, if you don't keep being vigilant." He, like President Obama, thought that America was the Promised Land.

After college, Leon was chosen to be the principal of one of the most challenging, violent high schools in Philadelphia. He told others that he was going to turn that school around with love. People just laughed. Leon was present for the Reverend Dr. Martin Luther King's "I Have a Dream" speech in Washington and was influenced greatly by it. His experience at that speech and his witness of the liberation of Buchenwald were moments that changed his life forever. He was a practicing Quaker, not a Quaker in name only. He made the school into one of the very best in the city. He filled those students with a sense of the promise of what their lives could be like.

He had some hard truths to tell our school community that I thought should be heard in the many times he came to speak. At the end of his address, he would say (I paraphrase), "You think that what happened in Germany could never occur again. It can and it does. Injustice occurs in our nation. It occurs in this school as well. It happens when you bully someone, when you know what is right and don't stand up for that right or another person being treated badly, and when groups are targeted because of their race, religion, or sexual orientation. It happens when you keep silent with the noise of wrongdoing sounding in your ears. It happens when you choose the easy wrong rather than the harder right."

The students and faculty always gave him a standing ovation after hearing some very challenging words of what our nation and school should be, a place of liberty and justice. They did it because they always chose authenticity over easy wrongs that could be done. After all the school motto is *"Esse Quam Videri,"* to be, rather than to seem to be. There was always *being*, not *seeming*, in the life of Dr. Bass. I like that Anthony Blinkin set the tone for his leadership with that story. Leon lived exactly what Anthony Blinkin was urging us to consider as our future together.

The video of Dr. Bass' address can be found on my blog on my website under the title, "Not Good Enough."

Post 128. Fierce

Alexis de Tocqueville, in his book on American democracy published in 1835, reflected that at America's core is a belief that a person's fate lies in each individual's hands. It is why American's love stories of achievement against all odds. Think Rocky! Amy Gutman, President of Penn, announced with great excitement that one of Penn's students, MacKenzie Fierceton, '21 received a Rhodes Scholarship. But she wasn't any regular achiever. According to the "Penn News Release" and an article in the *Inquirer*, November 24, 2020, by Joe Holleman, "She was like no other. She was among the first in her family to go to college as a low-income student. She was queer. She bounced from one foster home to another throughout her life." During her junior year in high school, she was in a toxic foster home where she had to live on friends' couches for weeks at a time. Only two percent of foster children graduate from a four-year college. So how did she not only graduate from college but achieve one of the highest awards given? I believe that the answer is found in a statement she made after receiving the Rhodes Scholarship. "I would have traded all of this to have been adopted and have a family and have had that experience and that never happened. I have healed from all of that, and I can carry it with me now in a way that feels very empowering." She was fiercely passionate in her pursuit of knowledge. It is where she found joy! Teachers and schools were her families. She will give back to her community as she seeks a PH.D. in Social Policy from Oxford University.

She made it because she was "fierce." She couldn't have a better last name to coincide with her passion for reading, learning, and knowledge. I am not using the word *fierce* as "ferocious aggressiveness" but as it is sometimes defined as "a heartfelt and powerful intensity." I would call it "passion plus for learning" in Ms. MacKenzie's life. For me, learning is the way out and up from the conditions in which we were born. It is the great equalizer, which is why I worry about students who don't have the opportunity to participate in learning during this pandemic for lack of resources. That must be addressed if we will keep the dream alive.

Being first in your family to attend college is a big deal, for as Frank Molina, '21, University of California San Francisco, a first-generation student put it, "Oftentimes, being a first-gen student is cast in a negative light, as if we are missing something because we are the first to go to college. Instead, I think that first-gen students have so much to offer. They have much resourcefulness and tenacity from having to do so much on their own." As someone who was one of those first generations in a family to attend college, I can underscore the importance of what Ms. Fierceton has done and what Mr. Molina has said.

I don't know how religion plays any role in the life of first-generation students, but for me, it did in a curious way! When I was in high school, I had a portrait of "Christ Our Pilot" hung over my desk. I looked at it every time I sat down to work, even when I could hear friends outside playing ball, and part of me wanted very much to join them. It pictured a muscled youth with his hands gripping a wheel on a ship in a storm. Behind him with a hand on his shoulder and the other pointing forward was the image of Jesus. There were times when I would drift off while studying to look at the painting.

During this pandemic when we are asking so many questions about a vaccine, we should be asking with fierce intensity what we can do to give young people another life-giving dose of an ingredient for their future, excitement about learning. I am concerned for those first-generation, low-income students who could potentially be bound for more learning when they leave the home. It is their way out and up. Not enough has been said nationally about MacKenzie Fierceton, Rhodes Scholar, who was a product of the enormous challenges of foster care. She could inspire. Who could forget what is needed for that kind of achievement with a name like Fierceton? I can hear that Rocky music playing in the background.

I first met Amy Gutman when she was teaching at Princeton's Ethical Center which she founded. I was attempting to form a relationship with her program and one that would occur at Episcopal Academy. She had another event, however, come into her life at that time as she became president of Penn in 2004. She has always been an incredible leader. The first thing that she did at Penn was to start a program for first-generation, lower-income college students. When she arrived, one out of twenty students was part of that initiative. Today one out of eight are part of that program.

By the way, Amy Gutman is a first-generation college student as well, who went to Radcliffe College at Harvard on a scholarship. Go figure!

A Portrait of the painting, "Christ Our Pilot," can be found on my blog on my website under the title, "Fierce."

Post 129. Day One

Walter Isaacson has written about the lives of some great people, such as DaVinci, Benjamin Franklin, Ada Lovelace, Steve Jobs, Alfred Einstein, and most recently, Jeff Bezos, founder of Amazon. Isaacson wrote the introduction to the collected essays of Bezos. Bezos is in the same league with some creative, artistic talent. There are some key characteristics that these people have to warrant Isaacson's interest. "They must be passionately curious, love to connect arts and sciences, must think differently, and have a childlike sense of wonder." Bezos' book, *Invent and Wonder*, gives us insight beyond how to become the richest man in the world but, more importantly, some observations about how to go from nothing to something, which is a message for how to live in a post-2020 world.

First, Bezos is always "obsessed with the customer" and not the competition or what the shareholders want. Bezos is most concerned that people benefit from what he is doing. This is something more than "The customer comes first" or "The customer is always right." He will do whatever it takes to make us happy. Can you imagine a nation where all that the leaders cared about was the well-being of "We the People?"

I am always interested in a leader's decision-making process. He used the same process building Amazon as he did when taking the risk that no one thought would work to begin Amazon. He left a great job because of a question, "Would I regret not doing this (starting Amazon), when I reached old age?" That question powered his enterprise, and when you think about it, it was a question behind the risk required in the founding of our nation. If caught, our forefathers would have been hung. They had no regrets.

Bezos has three criteria for people who are hired. "Will you admire this person? Will this person raise the effectiveness of the group he or she is entering? Along what dimension might this person be a superstar?" These questions are being answered each day of this pandemic by the actions of our medical personnel, other first responders, and essential workers with a resounding "Yes." They are "We the People" centered. Bezos' memo to the newly hired is, "You can work long, hard, and smart, but at Amazon, you can't choose two out of three." What an apt description of those tireless workers who keep us alive and well during this pandemic. They do all three for "We the People."

At the core of Bezos' success is the expression "Today is Day One." He always wants others to remember the core values of when they first began, those values that put people first and everything else second, those questions that he raised for those who would be hired, and finally the characteristics of recognizing hard work when you see it.

In my memoir, I identified Day One for me, "Never forget where you came from," and ask that question that can empower us, "How did I get here from there?" Unlike politicians who operate from Day One of "What have you done for me lately?" we need to embrace the patriots of our land going forward, like John McCain whose Day One mentality was his integrity and courage in his life to "Never leave anyone left behind." including those in prison camp with him. Find your Day One core values and questions that result in action. You will need them as we move forward as a nation into 2021.

On July 29 of 2020, Jeff Bezos testified to a house hearing along with the CEOs of Facebook, Google, and Apple. In his testimony, Bezos framed the challenges the nation faced, "We are in the middle of a much-needed race reckoning. We also face the challenges of climate change and income inequality, and we're stumbling through the crisis of a global pandemic." And then he shifted his tone to that of an innovator, "Still, with all our faults and problems, the rest of the world would love even the tiniest sip of the elixir we have here in the US. It's still Day One for this country."

Day One for President-Elect Biden is "Build Back Better. Unite and Heal." The least we can do for the new breed of patriots that we find caring for others in a hospital, including hospital workers who keep the premises clean, first responders, grocery store workers, and teachers, and so forth is to put on a mask. To do that makes us a patriot. To not do it makes us people who only ask, "What have you done for me lately?" And lately, just may be too late!

Post 130. Gotcha

When I picked up the *Inquirer Sunday Edition* (December 6, 2020), I was looking for what was happening in our world during these troubling times. What I saw first was at the bottom of the front page. It was a story about a women's basketball coach who was accused of allegedly being insensitive to her college players and abusive to them by putting them down during practice and requiring them to play when they were injured. The story was important, but did it belong on the front page when people are dying in Africa from famine and tribal and political warfare? We are in the midst of food insecurity and a rising COVID-19 rates and an ongoing political nightmare with inaccurate comments being made about the election of President-Elect Biden threatening the core of our democracy. I could have responded to the story about the coach better if it was in the sports section. Was the story necessary for me to be an informed citizen? I read the article, and the first thought that I had was how does the team, school, coach, and parents make something positive come out of this negative experience? The coach has not been fired but she is now "toast."

The press is essential to our democracy by printing the facts, but what about "the greater good?" In this case, a team, coach, parents, and school are trying to make something positive happen with this dilemma and possible lessons learned by everyone, including the coach. We have lost something in our news coverage. The story gives credence to a former editor of the *Inquirer* who told me and a group of students that he got the biggest response to a story he wrote about municipal incompetence. He said, "The response is what counts. It doesn't matter if it is bad or good." This is the attitude that fosters "gotcha" news.

The press complains constantly about President Trump, and he complains bitterly about them. Where would he be without the press, even though he refers to them as fake news? Where would the press be without him? They are a marriage made in heaven or, perhaps I should say, in hell. He makes for outrageous gotcha news with fact checkers highlighting his lies, and the press is right there to capture every one of his many mistakes. President-Elect Biden has been putting together his new team. I was struck by how many people in the media are already saying that he and his appointees are boring. They go on to say that they love boring after four years of chaos. Do they really? The readers may relish "boring," but I don't believe that the press will.

A "gotcha" mentality could be the ruin of us and folks like the local basketball team that needs to figure out if there is a way to move forward. Let me suggest two people who could serve as models for moving forward with responsible reporting. I was struck by what Fareed Zakaria, an American journalist, wrote recently about President Obama. Zakaria said that Obama is different. He doesn't ask questions that he knows the answers to. He genuinely wants to know the answer to his question. He went on to say that other politicians know the answers to questions they ask. Politicians wait for the other person to respond so they can then say what they think with a voice of authority that leaves no doubt that they are right. I can honestly not remember President Obama asking someone a "gotcha" question. He respects others in his response even those who disagree with him. His children don't ask him questions at the dinner table, for he gives them an answer that is worthy of someone's time. They also don't like their dinner interrupted by long responses.

Second, one of my favorite news journalists is Michael Smerconish, now a talking head on CNN. He is a former parent to three guys who attended the Episcopal Academy. First and foremost, you can't put him in a nice tidy box with a label such as liberal or conservative. He is his own person. He is a registered Independent. He and I would exchange occasional emails with one another after I read his *Inquirer* column that he used to write. He was also a great parent at our school and someone who cares deeply about people. (Full disclosure: I am biased for I know how helpful he was behind the scenes to a family that is close friends of mine.).

If you watch him on CNN now, he is mostly giving commentary on an issue. However, he interviewed President Obama on six different occasions. Why would President Obama consent to six interviews with a person? Mike was the first radio broadcaster invited to conduct a presidential interview inside the White House after Obama's election. Mike is asking questions that he genuinely wants to know the answers to. Second, he treated President Obama with great respect. In fact, I can't imagine Mike interviewing a homeless person any differently.

A commentary on those interviews that Mike did with President Obama said it all. The commentary read, "They were civil and substantive." That is the kind of news that is newsworthy! That should be what we see on the front page of our newspaper, so a team and a coach have an opportunity to move forward. There is that expression to remind us what we should be hearing and reading "all the news that is fit to print."

Post 131. A Catholic in the White House

Former Philadelphia Archbishop Charles J. Chaput has recently said in the *Inquirer* (December 8, 2020) that President-Elect Joe Biden should not be given the sacrament of Holy Eucharist because he is a Catholic who supports abortion. Chaput goes on to say that Biden is not in full communion with the Catholic faith. Biden is the second Catholic president in the nation's history. John F. Kennedy was the first. People may have forgotten the anti-Catholic bias that has existed in our nation and was evident when Kennedy was running against Richard Nixon in the 60s. The fear expressed overtly was that the Pope would be running the nation. Nixon said that he would not make religion part of his campaign but secretly encouraged Norman Vincent Peale, a prominent Protestant clergyman who authored *The Power of Positive Thinking*, to make religion an issue in the campaign. Peale stated, "Our American culture is at stake. I don't say it won't survive, but it won't be what was." He was quickly joined in this effort by Billy Graham and the evangelical Christian community.

It was the harassment of Baptists in Virginia that led Jefferson to include the language for a separation of Church and State as he laid the foundation for our government. This was one of Kennedy's points when he addressed the Greater Houston Ministerial Association where he made the now-famous statement that "I am not the Catholic candidate for president. I am the Democratic Party's candidate for president who happens to also be Catholic." He went on to use the "slippery slope" ethical argument that if there is prejudice against his Catholicism, this could be opening a door to prejudice against such candidates who were Baptists, Quakers, Jews, and other faiths.

Let's take a look at this issue through an ethical lens rather than a political one. What Chaput is doing is taking a "single-issue ethical approach." He is not alone in taking this view as many conservative Christians have stated a similar view. For example, what if all of Chaput's leadership of his archdiocese was judged on his complete failure and coverup of the sexual abuse scandal of his clergy? There were other aspects of his ministry that were noteworthy that should be part of his legacy.

Conservative Christians have supported President Trump, focusing as well on his position against abortion, which was not always his view but recently was politically expedient. They ignore one of the core doctrines of Christianity that is "When did we see you, Lord?" The answer is, "When you have done service to the least of these, you have done it to me" found in Matthew's Gospel. I don't think that anyone can justify President Trump's abrasive nature, bad language, constant assaults on others (particularly women), and moral lapses too numerous to mention. We have to look at the whole picture of anyone who is running for the Office of President. Most of the analysis of why Trump lost to Biden was not only his policies but more so his behavior.

There is a cultural ethical issue here as well. Seventy-six percent of Catholics today feel that abortion should be a choice. I grew up in a working-class town where we had three Catholic churches, one for the Irish, one for the Polish, and one for the Italians. I was in a unique position then and now to look at this issue of a Catholic president, for half of my family was Protestant and the other half Catholic. The only time that religion came into play, however, was when on Thanksgiving Day, the public school where I attended played football against the parochial school where some of my relatives attended. The tension wasn't really about religion as much as it was about bragging rights at the dinner table that followed the game.

My neighborhood was mostly Roman Catholic, and therefore, so were my friends. I was Episcopalian, so my Catholic friends would refer to me as a "second stringer." When a hard-fought basketball game was being played on a late Saturday afternoon, there was a time-out so that the Catholic guys could go to confession. I don't know what good the confession did as they returned with even sharper elbows.

Some things are bigger than religion for kids, like a common intense football game. Later in life when I was asked to be on the altar for the burial office of the father of one of my students, the five Catholic priests present wouldn't talk to me when I arrived until they learned that I was on the same football field as the leader of the group for that Thanksgiving Football Game. We became instant great friends.

When you have an intense shared experience with someone, other things go by the wayside. The American people shared in the president-elect's experience from his upbringing, compassion, soulfulness, loss of his son, and that he would be an American president, not a Democratic president.

Abortion is a critical ethical issue in America. There are different positions. Catholicism has a system that believes in natural law, which is for a natural continuum. There can be no abortion, no contraception, no mercy killing, and no capital punishment. Do nothing that interferes with the natural flow. Sanctity of life includes the sanctity of providing for a child once they are born. We can't forget that second part.

There is an ethical position referred to as *Via Media,* the middle way, which states that abortion is "wrong but necessary." The women's choice position is based on the theory of John Locke and "his primacy of property" ethical position where the woman's body is her primary property, and she should have the right to decide about anything related to her body. The Jewish ethical view is based on the "Law of the Pursuer" where the fetus is seen as a possible threat to the psychological or physical health of the mother. I think that everyone should know these above-mentioned ethical positions and *why* people adhere to certain ideas about abortion. Many of the essential ethical issues are focused on the issue of abortion, which is at the heart of much ethical debate. That is why there are such intense feelings about it.

Since I started with Archbishop Chaput's statement, I would like to close with words from the present Philadelphia Archbishop, Nelson Perez. He did not immediately respond to requests for comment about Biden and communion. He previously told the *Inquirer* in a statement, "I pray God may grant President-Elect Biden the wisdom necessary to govern in a manner that promotes liberty and justice for all as well as respect for the dignity and sacredness of life."

Referring back to Archbishop Chaput's comment, there is a great irony here. Joe Biden could be an example of what it means to be a "practicing Catholic." He is regular in his church attendance. He sometimes carries with him the rosary beads of his son, Beau, who died in 2015. I doubt that there are very many politicians who do the same.

Post 132. Parable of the Mask

Jesus must have been a lateral thinker for he used parables to get his points across. A parable is a simple story to make a deeper moral point. Instead of saying the kingdom of God starts small and grows into something large, He refers to a mustard seed as a small thing that grows into a large tree. For each of his messages, He helps people to see what He is talking about differently. Lateral thinking is solving a problem or addressing a situation by an indirect and creative approach. It is typically done through viewing the problem or situation in a new and unusual light. This was the foundation of His teachings.

Lateral thinking can be taught. It can be done through various exercises that I gleaned from a textbook used at Penn in my ethics classes. The text is *Pumping Ions* by Tom Wujec. It helped the students in their moral thinking in approaching different problems. Students loved using lateral thinking skills to solve dilemmas in the same way that others love to solve riddles. Below are some examples of lateral thinking.

We now take for granted that every time we turn around during the pandemic that we have hand sanitizer available to us. Atul Gawande, a surgeon and author, was confronted with a high rate of infections years ago in the hospital in which he was working. He installed hand sanitizer pumps outside of each hospital room with signs instructing everyone to use them before entering the room. The infection rate in the hospital dropped remarkably. Nobody had thought that something so simple could reduce the infection rate so dramatically, and now hand sanitizers are commonplace.

One of the most profitable items in the 3M company is their Post-It notes. Everyone just assumes that they were made to perform the function that they have today to be stuck in places to help us remember things. As it turns out the Post-It notes were discovered by accident. One of the researchers at 3M was attempting to create a super-strong adhesive that would stick two things together so that it would form a strong bond. The glue that he made, however, was a low-tack, reusable, pressure-sensitive adhesive that would hold only just enough to keep a piece of paper in place but could be removed easily as well. One of the researchers involved sang in a choir and used small pieces of paper with this newly formed substance to hold his place in his hymnal. He could remove it from his hymnal after the service and then could reuse them over and over again. It is currently one of 3M's best sellers.

One of my pet peeves is waiting for a slow elevator particularly now when only a few people at a time can enter them because of social distance rules. The answer that would first come to mind would be to find a faster motor. Right? Not necessarily. Maybe that is not the real problem. Let's look at it another way. Maybe the problem is that I am bored while waiting for the elevator. The answer was to put a mirror near the elevator doors to draw peoples' attention. Another way of addressing the issue of waiting once inside was through music. Have you ever wondered why "elevator music" was installed? It helped to pass the time once you got in the elevator.

We have been living and dying in the year 2020 with the ravages of a pandemic that has made us sick, killed us, forced us inside, caused great fatigue, destroyed our economy, and made us as afraid as we could be. One of the reasons that this has been difficult is that, even though a vaccine has been found, we just don't know when all of this will end. The goalposts are always moving on us.

We have been told to wear masks, but some say they are not doing any good. The time to wear the masks, however, has been too open-ended. We can do anything if we know the answer to the important question. How long do I have to wear it? What if it isn't about the masks even though mask wearing has become political. What if it is really about the duration of the time to wear them, not forever but for a definite time. Joe Biden tells all of us to wear the masks for 100 days when he begins his presidency. He is helping us to see it differently. I bet this will get more, not all, to put them on. I bet that people see the difference that this will make. That difference will change our thinking about mask wearing. He is a problem solver. He used lateral thinking. We could create a simple story that points to a more responsible moral action. We may even want to call it the Parable of the Mask.

Post 133. Lying in Politics

One of the astute ethicists that you have never heard of who has greatly influenced me is Sissela Bok. Most have never heard of her, but the last name may ring a bell as her husband was once President of Harvard. Her seminal work was *Moral Choice in Public and Private Life*. Her expertise is on why people lie. She has helped me to understand why people lie, why Trump's base is so devoted to him, and why our politics are so partisan in nature. So, here is some of the "gospel" according to Sissela Bok, integrated into my thinking.

Why do people lie? The tendency to lie appears in childhood. When children lie and get away with it, it gives them their first sense of power. Once the power is felt, it is easy to develop a pattern, as power becomes an enjoyable feeling. It is the first way that a child learns to protect himself from threats. Overt and covert threats can hurt children as well as the rest of us. One reporter commented that "President Trump's bark is worse than his bite. He just wants to be petted." He craves kindness and acceptance. Most children are successful in unlearning lying, and there are ways of unlearning this behavior later in life, as questions could be considered. What would happen if my lie was on the front page of the paper? What would a group of reasonable people say about my lie?

When I lie, I have to remember what I said. Lying is often the "gateway" experience to other immoral behavior. It is the bedrock of bad behavior, as lying breaks trust in personal and social exchanges. Trust, on the other hand, is the foundation of a civil society, whereas lying erodes any society from family to nation to international relations.

In ethics class, I taught the "Ticking Time Bomb of Decision-Making." If something horrible is about to happen, people will lie for the greater good. Therefore, any action can be seen as good, even lying. This behavior was the heart of the *24* TV series where there was no time for certain honest actions to take place. A bomb seemed always ready to be set off in the espionage thriller.

Why is Trump's base so loyal to him? How could they identify with his "raised with a silver spoon in his mouth" lifestyle? That can't be it. He has nothing in common with them. As I write this, Congress is still debating a stimulus bill that every economist think is necessary. What is it like for many in his base who are worried about their rent, their next meal, their lost benefits, and their children's schooling? Many refer to his base as a cult, and in many ways it is. Ethics is part of every group dynamic. I have always taught that groups have various characteristics. His followers are no different. Groups can make bad-intentioned people worse and good-intentioned people better. They have their own moral or immoral code that makes sense to the group but not to others outside of it. Being part of a group helps you to have the important emotions of self-esteem and belonging. The last of the dynamics, which is big for Trumps' followers, is "I may be inferior, but we as a group are magnificent." This is a powerful feeling to have when you feel that Washington is not responding to your needs. This is the replacement of your identity for another's. In this case, it is being at one with Trump's identity. If he loses, you lose.

From the perspective of Trump's followers, they see themselves struggling (although some people of means). They look at Washington politicians "playing with the lives of those in need," going home for a nice Christmas vacation, living without seeming to have a care in the world, free medical care, and a lifelong pension, and his supporters are "mad as hell and aren't going to take it anymore." He is against the elites. Listen to what his followers say. He has our back. He cares about us. He's standing up against all those politicians who have ignored us forever. It baffles people as to why they believe this when it isn't true, but that is how they feel, and they are *passionate* about him. Feelings and passion for him trump (pun intended) reason. Reason doesn't motivate more than feelings and passion do. Some say Trump is crazy. His childhood has made him "crazy like a fox." His behavior worked when he was seven. He believes it will work when he is seventy-four.

Every group thinks in us-versus-them terms. He has on his side those who believe as he does, as the "us." The "them" are the elites. The elites were soon seen as that "smartest boy in the class who thinks he knows it all with his hand up." It was easy to dislike them. We are a nation of the poor and working-class, becoming more so every day. He has numbers on his side.

Partisan politics is not a Republican or Democratic thing. Partisan politics is about party loyalty that makes us blind to reality. Your identity, once again, is lost in your identity with the party. Recall the group dynamics that I mentioned. Let's take a moment to look at two revered politicians, Reagan and Johnson, and lying.

Lyndon Johnson was the Democratic president during the 60s. He passed more legislation to help Americans than any other president, including the Civil Rights Act to Medicare. He lied about the number of Americans killed in the Vietnam War. He was told lies by members of his administration, which made the war longer. He also lied about the war because he couldn't face losing, all in the context of the outstanding social programs he was instituting. He would often use a phrase to cover his lying. He would say that "There is no escalation of the war happening (at this time)." During the 60s, the war was seen as a war of the Democrats, with famous protests occurring at their convention. The lies eventually split the party. It was the reason that Johnson would not seek a second term. That was the consequence of lying.

President Reagan did wonderful things and was one of the most popular presidents of all time. He reduced taxes and spending. He created many jobs through his Recovery Tax Act of 1981. He rolled back communism and won the Cold War. He was, however, also involved in the Iran-Contra Affair, which allegedly involved selling arms for hostages and supporting rebel troops in Nicaragua fighting against communism. These actions were done by bypassing Congress and then lying about it. This was revealed and Reagan's great popularity dropped. He was, however, the Great Communicator. The truth shall set you free. He went on TV and indicated that he was not honest with everyone about what occurred during the Iran-Contra Affair (some say this was not as clearly stated as it should have been). Following that broadcast, his popularity soared as the nation could trust him again. Telling the truth after a lie can do that for any individual. You may choose to watch his four-minute video of his address to the American people, admitting his mistake.

Sissela Bok recommended several things that we needed to do as a nation following this ethical lapse during the Reagan years. I believe that they are the same actions we must do now to make things better in our divided nation to address the pandemic and Black Lives Matter. First, we should renew our commitment to our core values as a nation. Second, ethical action starts with us and people seeing goodness in each of us. The axiom for me is a Christian goal, "They will know that we are Christians by our love." (You can insert your religious or secular belief system for mine). Second, we should not tolerate any "breaches of law." Third, we should not tolerate any "breaches of promises." Fourth, we should have transparency in government deliberations. Truth and trust are at the heart of all successful relationships for people and for the government that we hold dear. That is the Alpha and Omega of a good society.

Reagan's Address on Iran Contra Findings can be found on my blog on my website under the title of "Lying in Politics."

Post 134. Seeing When Blind

Andrea Bocelli live-streamed a concert called "Believe in Christmas." Bocelli is a blind singer who has merged opera and pop music since Luciano Pavarotti discovered him. Bocelli was born almost blind from birth and then became totally blind after a soccer accident when he was twelve. His mother was encouraged to perform an abortion since the doctors knew the infant would be blind. His mother refused. This is one of the pro-life arguments against abortion, as the point is that you risk killing a Beethoven or a Bocelli.

The life of Bocelli can tell us a great deal. He started out singing in bars until he was discovered by Pavarotti for the once-in-a-lifetime talent that he possesses to become one of the greatest vocalists of all time. He is a devout Catholic and views a high point of his career singing for Pope Francis. He was reminded of St. Augustine's words that, "singing is an extraordinary form of prayer." Celine Dion commented, "That if God has a voice, it must be that of Bocelli." He has sung for millions across the world. His foundation has raised funds most recently to combat COVID-19 in his beloved country of Italy. Hearing him sing in his "Believe in Christmas" concert sent chills down my spine. It was a spiritual experience for me, and I am sure, for those millions across the world who heard it.

One of my personal beliefs is that all of life is to be enjoyed or learned from. What can we learn from this extraordinary life and voice? As I mentioned he is a devout Catholic. I am sure that the title of the concert is one that came straight from his heart. He was addressing the Christian community and all who watched with three little words that go to the heart of our faith. He didn't name it "Sorta Believe," "Kinda Believe," "If You Get Around to It, Believe." It is "Believe in Christmas." His voice and song were as prayerful as any prayers one would ever hear. He proves St. Augustine right.

Some of the concert was in Italian. Although I couldn't understand the words, that didn't seem to matter. They transcended the moment. I was very moved when he sang "Amazing Grace" and got to that phrase "once I was blind, but now I can see" because of the new meaning that it brought to me.

The concert begins with his eight-year-old daughter, Virginia, leading him by the hand to his place on the empty opera house stage. It was not a reach for me to think of those words from Isaiah that "a little child shall lead them" (Isa. 11:6). Strangely, it didn't seem as though he was relying on her as he made his way forward. He walked with confidence. As noted in an article by Ciara Dwyer in *The Independent* (July 15, 2001), "His other senses have developed as a result of his blindness. He can click his fingers and can tell where a wall is. There was a movie made of his life, *The Music of Silence,* "where he didn't want the person playing him trying to act like he was blind because I spend so much of my life trying to pretend that I can see."

How does he see? He told a reporter his attitude toward life. "One morning, raising my eyes to the sky toward the sun whose warmth I felt on my face, I realized I could no longer see it. From that moment on, I tried to get used to the idea, as one learns to live with sadness and pain." That is an important lesson for us all.

Bocelli doesn't move around the world or the stage that he is on with his eyes open and does not like his blindness mentioned in interviews. As Ciara Dwyer mentioned in her article, "As I was about to get up and go, he opened his eyes and gave me a look with his beautiful light blue misted eyes. He was making fun of the taboo subject. It was a beautifully bizarre moment."

In the Gospel of Mark, we hear the words from Jesus, "Do you have eyes but fail to see and ears and fail to hear, and don't you remember (what I have done)?" (Mark 8:18). Bocelli remembers!

"Once I was blind, but now I see." Believe in Christmas.

Post 135. Questions of the Heart

I sometimes ask four questions when being very impressed by someone. The first two questions drive my children crazy. They don't think that people are interested in them, but I have spent a lifetime in the education business. Where did you go to college? I don't care where you went to college as some people do. I want to know about your experience there so that I could recommend it or not to others. What was your major? I want to know what people are interested in and whether their major impacted their life. I also want to know two other questions. Where did you get your courage? What are the skills that have made you a great leader? I would hope that I could judge their character and empathy before asking any of these questions.

Regarding leadership, my neighbor on the Chesapeake was responsible for taking DuPont into China and making that company a great success there. Most people know how difficult it is to do business in China with their repressive government. He lived there for five years. I asked him the leadership question. He replied, "I told those who worked at the company that they should keep in mind the dirty thirty. That means that if on any given day, you are winning seventy percent of your challenges and losing thirty percent, that is a good day." In essence, keep your expectations realistic in leadership and life.

I wondered where Georgia election official, Gabriel Sterling, got the courage to confront President Trump bluntly about his accusations of fraud in the Georgia election telling lies and conspiracy theories. What Trump is doing is undermining our democracy. Sterling is one of the few Republicans who have had the courage to do that. Sterling stands out! If you want to see what courage looks like, see the video of his speech on my blog.

I got my answer in an article in the *Los Angeles Times* (December 14, 2020) by Del Quentin Wilber and Jennie Jarvie. The article confirmed what I had come to believe, which is why teaching young people ethics is so important. Sterling is a life-long Republican who voted for Trump. As a result of his courage, he has received death threats and was told to sleep with his eyes open. People have encouraged him to commit suicide. He is on a website that lists Trump's enemies with his face shown in gun crosshairs. Now he is looking into an election in January for a Senate runoff and facing the same kind of potential backlash, but he keeps moving forward.

How?

Pay attention to what made him speak out. Sterling got a call from an upset manager at Dominion that produced the voting machines. One of the company's technicians got a message accusing him of wrongdoing. Next to the man's name was a photograph of a noose. Sterling reflects my long-held belief that courage develops when someone is young. All of his life, he has taken on bullies. He always has felt responsible for other people. He couldn't abide that the election worker from Dominion had to go through what he and others had to do as he was a technician, not an election official, who was the face of the election. The guy was just doing his job.

What would it be like to be Sterling's father whose son was going through all of these threats? His dad was not surprised by his son's taking on Trump. He said, "Ever since you were a little boy you have been focused on what is right and wrong."

Courage is shaped when a boy or girl sees someone bullying another and stands up for the person bullied. Courage is shaped every time a boy or girl does the hard right and not the easy wrong. They are not born this way. Courage reveals itself and can be accessed in the face of any wrongdoing. Courageous people can do no other. I have been blessed to know many young people who are like Sterling.

One of my students who died after he graduated from college due to a heart issue was such a person. Ricky Whalen was a standout person and athlete at the Episcopal Academy and at Brown University where he won the Unsung Hero Award on his lacrosse team. After his death, the award was renamed The Richard Q. Whalen Unsung Hero Award. Ricky had a great impact on others. A thousand people attended his memorial service in our school chapel. Buses filled with lacrosse teams arrived from various parts of the East Coast. Sometime after the service, his brothers, Dennis and Reid, had a tattoo put on their inner arms with the initials RQW. I saw a close friend of Ricky later in life. He had initials tattooed on his inner arm. It is an "R." I asked him, "Why?" He looked at me and said, "I want to see his initial every day so that I remember what goodness and integrity look like in a person." That close friend with the tattoo on his arm is James Biden, nephew of the President-Elect.

The video of "Sterling Addresses Threats Regarding the Election" can be found on my blog on my website under the title of "Questions of the Heart."

Post 136. They Have Lost Their Minds

Do you remember when you first fell in love? Love can make you crazy. I have worked with young people for many years. On occasion, there were times when they exhibited crazy behavior that their parents, friends, and teachers couldn't understand. I heard the statements "They have turned into someone else," "They are not operating in the real world," and "I just don't get it." It is a description of a normal person gone wrong. I found out an interesting correlation after I was living in the world of adolescents for a long time. On many occasions, they had lost their minds. Parents, friends, and teachers worried about them. I found that in many cases they were "in love."

The faculty referred these "crazies on the deck of life" to me. I always let the students guide the conversation so that I was getting their real views and not my projections. They didn't bring it up at first, but then I would hear, "I have met this guy or girl." Their relationship with that person then dominated what they wanted to discuss. I couldn't have changed the subject if I tried. I couldn't make a new route to get to the heart of where they were at the time. I also discovered that those who call adolescent love "puppy love" have not been around enough kids to know that their feelings of love for another are the same as the ones that I and others have as adults.

I also had a student who was a great athlete but not a great student. He fell in love with one of the smartest, hard-working girls in our school. They broke up in August before their senior year. He entered my office one August day in a rage. He was angry. He got to the source of his anger, and it wasn't the breakup. When he was dating his girlfriend, he had to do as she did, which meant that they spent a lot of time together studying. This guy became a rather fine student in the process. His complaint was, "I can't go back to my former ways. I like academic success." When he asked, "What should I do?" I said, "Love does that. It does things that we aren't use to, some good and some bad. Let's go with the good here." He did. Today he is a very successful hard-working businessman, married to someone else, with a great family. He has been to see me with pictures of his wife and kids.

When counseling others, the counselor needs to have a great deal of empathy for the situation. Fortunately, I could identify with what the students were going through in their "crazy" world. I met my wife, Vicki, at the worst possible time. It was in June. I was in Philadelphia, but she lived in Raleigh. I was leaving for school in New Haven in late August. I didn't think it was a big deal to leave work on a Friday afternoon, drive to Raleigh, spend the weekend with her, and drive back to Philly on Sunday night. It is a seven hour drive each way. My friends thought I had lost my mind. They were right.

What has this got to do with the followers of Trump who have not only refused to wear masks because it has infringed on their freedom when we "know" it is about protecting others from the virus. As bad as that is, public health officials, particularly in rural areas, have been threatened by others regularly and have resigned from their positions. The public health officials are where the "rubber hits the road" to reduce the cases of the virus. They are as essential as anyone to stop the pandemic.

The "crazies" in our nation have many motives for their actions, but I want to underscore one thing that is causing this behavior. It is love manifest as passion. C. S. Lewis, a Christian apologist and author, has helped me to understand my students' behavior, my behavior, and a good bit of the behavior of the anti-maskers and those supporting Trump in his attempt to overthrow the election. Lewis' ideas about the dynamics of love are found, among other places, in his book, *The Four Loves*. I taught his thinking integrated with my own about psychology and philosophy in my ethics class.

I have been over the four loves in other posts. In Greek, they are *storge*, a parent's love; *philia*, a love of friends; *eros*, the chemistry of love and passion; and *agape*, God's love. Today I want to focus on *eros*, which is most often associated with sexuality hence the use of the word, *erotic*. It has another emphasis as well, and that is passion. Keep in mind the following aspect of *eros* that when passion enters our lives, reason leaves.

We see this vividly when we consider why a business person leaves his or her spouse and family that makes no sense to others. Passion has brought down the powerful. When those with power are named, we often raise the question, "What were they thinking?" Why do that when you lose so much?" The general feeling is always, it is not reasonable. These incidents occur because the feelings of passion can sideline any notions of reason. Think of another passion that you have. It may be painting, playing a musical instrument, or a sport. Passion is at the heart of many creative geniuses, such as Beethoven, Picasso, or even Elon Musk, who lose themselves in their work and creative processes. A passion is what drives them.

Passion is a sense of purpose on steroids. We all need something to get us up in the morning, but passion takes purpose to a new level as it may preoccupy the waking life of an individual.

I am not saying that it is right for a person to run off with another, but I think that we need to understand what is happening there. Look at the crazy stuff that we have been experiencing with masks, election fraud, or in its extreme, a cult. People who exhibit crazy behavior are experiencing "purpose plus." I have read some articles on the relationship between Giuliani and Trump. The relationship doesn't make sense. Trump is in unreality, and Giuliani has fallen far from his perch as one of the most respected people in our nation. His actions have fed *Saturday Night Live* with ample material, wacky witnesses, lack of evidence, and hair dye dripping down his face. When Trump fires people at will, people ask why Rudy is still a devoted friend. Then you hear those words, "It doesn't make sense." The answer, I believe, is that they feed the passion/ purpose-driven parts of each other. Giuliani recently said that he got great care when diagnosed with COVID-19 because he was a "celebrity." That is the word that he used. Remember the name of Trump's reality show. It was *Celebrity Apprentice*. A deal for celebrity status and power is what drives them. It is their common bond. Any time you find yourself saying, "It's not reasonable," look around and see if *eros,* passion, is nearby ready to highjack reason. You may be surprised by how often it is present.

Post 137. Where Was Bob Dylan When We Needed Him?

During the recent election and follow-up challenges by Trump, where are the composers and singers of protest songs to awaken the American people and proclaim the pain of the pandemic and the Black Lives Matter movement? Trump has used some of the music that fit his need during his campaign but never asked for permission to do so and has been sued by the musicians each time that he has done that.

I am a product of the sixties and still remember being moved by the anthems for freedom. I could not be part of the Flower Power Movement as it was not a working-class phenomenon. The move- ment touched deeply into our psyches and souls, however, because of the sounds of the voices who shared with others the rhythm of war and unrest. They moved the hearts of people and became more important than many addresses that were spoken, with the excep- tion of Dr. Martin Luther King's "I Have a Dream" speech.

Why no song for 2020 about our struggle? Recall a few of the 60s classics: "Give Peace A Chance" by John Lennon, "Respect" by Aretha Franklin, and the anthem of the 60s, "We Shall Overcome" by Pete Seeger. Perhaps the most songs were created by Bob Dylan such as "The Times They Are A-Changin," and "Blowin' in the Wind."

So where is our Bob Dylan for 2020, the worst year that Americans have experienced in some time? I have a nomination for the anthem of 2020. It is "Big Yellow Taxi" sung by Joni Mitchell that included the phrase, "You don't know what you got 'til it's gone." We recall as well that poignant line from "Amazing Grace," that "Once I was lost but now am found." If there is one word that describes our lives during this challenging year, it is the word *loss*. If there is anything positive that could come of this year, it is that we have appreciated more who and what we have in our lives. This has been true for the increasing numbers of deaths due to the pandemic and the deaths that have spurred others on to fight racism in all of its forms in the Black Lives Matter movement.

Those are the big losses, but there have been other losses that have been part of our daily lives that have taught us to appreciate more the things that are now missing, such as a loss of security regarding the jobs that we had, the food that we had, the place where we were living, and the health that we took for granted. It included the schools we attended and the open spaces outside as well.

If there is a gift to us from 2020, it is the realization to never take anything for granted, including the day that we have before us and the loved ones in our lives. We will never take for granted the courage of all who helped us move forward through the pandemic. We will never take for granted those who spoke the words and did the deeds to never take for granted the struggle of people who may be different from us regardless of race, religion, class, or sexual orientation. We took our democracy for granted until it was put in jeopardy by others who refused to acknowledge our election of a new administration.

Judith Viorst wrote a book, *Necessary Losses*, which helped me to see life as a series of gains and losses. Perhaps this is the way that we need to frame our lives moving forward. Viorst wrote, "I have learned in the course of our life that we leave and are left and let go of much that we love. Losing is the price we pay for living. It is also the source of much of our growth and gain. There is plenty that we have to give up to grow. For we cannot deeply love anything without becoming vulnerable to loss."

The Christian faith is based on loss, as well, when we hear the words "Anyone who finds his life will lose it, anyone who loses his life because of Me will find it" (Matt. 10:39).

We cannot lose, whether it be a big or small loss, without a sense of grief. We grieve for that which we leave behind. As we leave the pain of 2020, we must let that grief transform into a gain from everything that we lost. I have not seen a better description of all grief, big or small, than that by Dr. Colin Murray Parks:

> Grief never ends, but it changes
> It is a passage. Not a place to stay
> Grief is not a sign of weakness, nor
> a lack of faith.
> It is the price of love.

2020 by James Squire

What was your loss?
What was your gain?
What caused you pain?
Where was the love that you found in between?

Post 138. Pareto Principle

The Biden family is part of the EA family. I was, therefore, able to invite Senator Biden to have a debate with Senator Arlen Specter, a friend of Joe Biden, to represent the Republican side of an issue. The debate was in our school chapel, and the topic was political morality and the failure of both parties to be able to work in more harmony on behalf of the American people. They both agreed on the problem and the solution. It still was a great moment of articulating the problem and solution for those gathered to hear these two seasoned politicians.

Both said, "Nobody goes out to dinner together anymore in Washington." The social norm had changed. Even years ago, there was great difficulty, dealing with people across the aisle. It is very difficult to work with people when you are only seeing one another in the context of partisan politics. It seems that everything is seen in an opposite way when it is stated by either party. If the sun is out and this was noticed by the Democratic Party, the Republican Party would say it is raining. No matter what the issue, both parties gear up for a fight. That perspective needs to change if issues, such as social justice and the Black Lives Matter movement, have a chance of leveling the playing field. The Pennsylvania Republican legislators are still sitting on the floor of the State Senate without wearing any masks. No wonder the American people are confused about the issue of mask wearing during the pandemic.

There is an answer. I was reminded of it in an article written by George Will in the December 21, 2020, opinion Page of the *Inquirer*. It is precisely what Biden and Specter were addressing some years ago in the EA chapel. Will writes:

Senator Lamar Alexander says fifteen or twenty Senators must set the tone for more collegial behavior within the Senate's permission rules. Note the number 20, and the Pareto principle are germane to the Senate. The Italian polymath—economist, sociologist, engineer, political scientist, and philosopher—Vilfredo Pareto (1848–1923) showed that eighty percent of the land in Italy was owned by twenty percent of Italians. Soon the 80/20 ratio was being discerned here and there. Twenty percent of patients use eighty percent of healthcare resources. Twenty percent of the criminals commit eighty percent of the crimes. Twenty percent of the beer drinkers drink eight percent of the beer. Probably twenty percent of the legislators account for eighty percent of the legislature's accomplishments. The Pareto principle is also called the "law of the vital few."

The vital few are what is needed to shape things in the Senate and the House. I have been mistaken by an observation that I used to state. I would say that God so loved the world that he didn't send a committee. Perhaps I need to modify my thinking as the first thing that Jesus did before starting his earthly ministry was to assemble twelve disciples who changed the world more than Washington politicos have. They were the vital few.

The Pareto Principle is also applied to business as you get twenty percent from eighty percent of your clients. It is also applied by psychologists who believe that in a healthy relationship, you only get eighty percent of what you want. The other twenty percent, you need to provide for yourself.

Post 139. Play the Hand That You Are Dealt

I had hand surgery on my left hand which is my dominant hand on December 24, 2020 and will have a secondhand surgery on January 14. It is painful and took away so many things that I have taken for granted. I now can type clumsily with a lot of effort. I know that the next surgery will take that ability away again for, I hope, a short time. I always use the four R(s) in moments like this: Reading, Reflection, Ritin', and Religion, defined as our connection to self, others, and God.

Since one of my guiding principles is that life is to be enjoyed or learned from, what have I learned that may help you? Remember what we learned in biology class that our development as humans was advanced because we evolved to the point of having the opposing thumb/finger connection. Without that ability to utilize that function, life is difficult. Tape your thumb to the next finger and see and experience what you can't do.

The most basic tasks become a chore. Religion—I thought of faith that can be a powerful tool in these moments. I have not found myself bargaining with God during all of this, but I have come close. Reading—I am making my way through the second book by Isabel Wilkerson, the author of *Caste*. Her second book, *The Warmth of Other Suns*, is the story of the great migration of black people from slavery in the South to places in the Northeast, West, and Central areas like Chicago in our nation. I came to an awful realization when reading about the Jim Crow period in the South and all that the people went through in their history as slaves and during the reconstruction period. Her book is much better researched than anything before it. I realized that the number of lynchings was far more than I thought. Black people could be lynched for the smallest perceived infraction of the white code of behavior. Lynchings were public events where children were in attendance to watch the lynchings, followed by the barbaric practice of burning the bodies as they hung in the air with the children present encouraged to applaud.

I co-taught a course on Diversity Issues with a colleague, Courtney Portlock, who was an expert on the use of the "N" word and why it is such a terrible word to use. There were times when the "N" word would be the last word that a black person would hear before they were hung. Women and children were lynched as well, not just men.

Growing up in a working-class community, I was completely unaware of the injustices that black people were still experiencing in abundance through the 60s and 70s. Racism was still an integral part of American life then and remains so today even after the Civil Rights Act. I was not aware of the extent of the injustices because I had teammates and classmates who were black, and I worked in places with black people that were integrated, quite frankly, because the work was so tough. I was always at the bottom of the pecking order in various mills. I was very much aware that Dr. King had been assassinated because I was taking a graduate course at Temple University the evening after he died where riots were occurring, literally as I was trying to make my way to my car in North Philadelphia and had to ask people what happened. Fires were being set. Anger was the fuel.

My wife and I have purchased a copy of President Obama's memoir. There is one negative thing about his election. A conclusion was reached by some that his election was the end of racism in America. It is not. Trump did not cause the bitter sores of racism. He permitted people to reveal racism overtly. The Black Lives Matter movement has work to do that cannot be accomplished in a short period of time. It means we will have to work even harder to make our nation a place where all are equal. One of the central premises of the two books authored by Isabel Wilkerson is that racism is present because everyone needs someone to look down upon.

Relationships and Reflection—There have been many people who have inspired me during this temporary time being handicapped, pun intended. I could not make it through all of this without the private duty nurse who is my spouse. I also reflect on the life of one of my heroes, John W. Frommer, Esq. John lost both of his arms in an accident when he was a teenager. He attended Swarthmore College and graduated Phi Beta Kappa. He went on to receive his law degree from Yale. He never let his life be limited by his loss of limbs. He and his wife, Dorie, were the first people Vicki and I met when we arrived in Swarthmore to join the staff of one of the most progressive parishes in the Diocese. We had dinner together. I marveled at how John did things. He could fold the newspaper in such a way to read it as he took the train to his center-city law firm. He was a champion of civil rights. He was undaunted.

His wife and he lived an exemplary life. We have a picture of them seated on the beach together at the Jersey Shore, happy and at peace. John was diagnosed with cancer in his forties. He underwent rigorous chemotherapy treatment. Like his loss of his arms, he treated cancer as a new part of his life and made his way forward. He died a few years after his diagnosis in his late forties. His death broke many hearts. His death raised that cry to God in the book of Job. Why do bad things happen to good people?

The word *handicapped* is derived from a game of chance called "Hand in Cap" where the participants have an equal chance of winning or losing. Later, the word was applied to putting stones around a fast horse's neck in a race to slow the horse down. The term is still used today in horse racing and betting.

The word *hand* is found in one of the great truths of life. You have to play the hand that you are dealt. I am reminded of that now every day.

Post 140. The Girl Without Hands

I received an email from the Reverend Dr. Alexander (Sandy) McCurdy after I posted, "Play the Hand That You Are Dealt." He is a close friend, who is an Episcopal priest and analyst. I was the advisor of his son, Gregory, during his time at EA. He is the only student I have ever encountered who read most of the *New York Times* before he arrived at school. Sandy indicated that he always asks his fourth-year psychiatric residents at Jefferson University Medical Center Hospital, where he is a member of the faculty in the Department of Psychiatry, to read Grimm's Fairy Tale, *The Girl Without Hands*. He did this at the beginning of his time with them. Sandy is a brilliant and caring priest/therapist, so I always look forward to his feedback.

I talked with Sandy after I received his email, to discuss with him his reason for doing this. He responded that he did have them read this fairy tale "to loosen them up" to appreciate the rich nature of their inner selves. So much of a psychiatrist's training focuses on the objective with a keen interest in the facts, but there is much more to us as human beings, particularly if you are interested in treating the whole person. He shared with me, as well, that a friend of his, who is head of the Emergency Department at Jefferson, did a similar thing with his students. He would take his students out of the ER once a month for half a day to the Philadelphia Museum of Art. `No matter what you do in life, everyone needs to develop imagination and empathy in relating to others. Procedures and hard facts are not enough in caring for others. Knowledge of our rich interior life is essential.

I have provided a link to a summary of the story of *The Girl Without Hands*. You will see the rich symbolism in the story and an analysis of the themes. Piety, faith, and devotion are mentioned as the values that we should hold.

It is interesting to me that in my own training as a therapist that *The Uses of Enchantment: The Meaning and Importance of Fairy Tales* by Bruno Bettleheim was a recommended read for me. Bettleheim makes a strong case that fairy tales provide a unique way for children to come to terms with the dilemmas in their inner lives. What many of us consider to be children's literature turns out to be a window into the soul/psyche of children, a tool to assist in helping them move through the challenges and hopes and fears that they find in their daily lives.

An Article About "The Girl Without Hands" can be found on my blog on my website under the title "The Girl Without Hands."

Post 141. Woke

I had the privilege of being the chaplain of the Episcopal Academy for thirty-eight years. During that time, I experienced the agony and ecstasy of what it means to be the spiritual leader of a large community. There were occasions when I went to bed in the evening and had a nightmare, only to awake the next morning to learn that it was not something in a dream state but a reality that I needed to address and act on.

I am writing this the day after the insurrection at the Capitol incited by President Trump. As was true in the past, when I went to bed last night to sleep, I was fooled in my sleep to think that the events of yesterday were a nightmare from which I would awake. However, it was a *real* nightmare for our nation. As I lay there this morning, I thought of other tragedies that were part of my life. I thought as well of some of the nightmares that our school community experienced, and I thought of my former students who made their way to our service academies or directly to our armed forces to guarantee that our democracy would be a light to other nations. I thought of one of my former students who emailed me as he was landing in a violent city in the Middle East as a soldier not in uniform, who was scared because there was a high probability that he would not return from his secret work. All were working to preserve our freedom and liberty. All were working to support our democracy.

I thought about how our school community always remembered 9/11, Memorial Day, and Veterans Day during chapel services. I then remembered the images of what occurred on January 6, 2021. Then I thought of Trump, his smirk, his bone spurs, his cowardice, his lies, and his failure as a leader. There has been much commentary on television and in the press. I have been reflecting as well on how we arrived at this day of infamy.

I wondered why 70 million Americans voted for him. That fact has been one of the arguments of his enablers. Recall an earlier post where I wrote about choices people make when they must choose between integrity and economic security. They will often choose economic security over issues of integrity. In a recent exit poll, people were asked why they voted for Trump. They stated that they didn't like his behavior but thought that he would be the best person to help the economy.

Yesterday, the enablers in the House and Senate said that their constituents did not believe the election was fair. Recall that months earlier, Trump was sowing the seed of this reaction by stating that "If I lost, the election must be rigged." I wrote a post about lying. I used the thinking of Sissela Bok who is an ethicist and expert on lying. She conducted a study where she concluded that the frequency of lying has been seen in action in our nation since the election on November 3, 2020. If you repeat a lie often enough, people will come to believe it and be certain that it is the truth. The repetition of the lie and conspiracy theories causes people to think that there must be something to it. Instead of the enablers focusing on their constant lies made to people, they have focused on the fact their constituents have concerns about an election. Their lies are the origin of the concerns. They should be ashamed. I am glad that Simon and Schuster has refused to publish Hawley's book.

The question has been raised about inadequate police protection of the Capitol compared to the police presence at the Black Lives Matter protests when Trump took his walk to the church for his photoshoot holding the Bible upside down. There was a more advanced notice that January 6 would be violent, online, and otherwise. Why no protection? The answer is racism. Black people pillage and riot, white people do not. That has been a message back to Jim Crow America. Wrong. It was difficult to watch the police take selfies with the mob and to watch them hold the doors for the rioters as they entered the Capitol. Trump added to this surreal event by finally saying, "Go home." Those were the two wrong words. What about his favorite line to "Lock them up!" The proof is in the numbers. Few of the white people in the riot were arrested compared to the hundreds during the Black Lives Matter protest.

I have learned in my training in family therapy that the same dysfunctional dynamic in families occurred on January 6 in the insurrection. I have been involved in many situations where parents will ask for help with their incorrigible child. The bad behavior can include violence perpetrated by the child. I do meet with the young person, but the parents are usually surprised that I want to meet with them and talk about their relationship with each other and the other family members.

They want to focus on the bad behavior of the child. The child/ adolescent becomes the "identified patient." So far there has been a lot of focus on the domestic terrorists who stormed the Capitol and security lapses. Let's punish those who we can identify for their bad behavior. But they are like the identified patient. The real problem is the parent or parental interactions in this case that includes people different from a father and mother. In the case of January 6, 2021, we need to include different parental influences. It is Trump, his family members, Giuliani, and politicians interested in running for office with Trump's base behind them, fundraising for their future, as well as various media who have empowered him and others and perpetuated his lies and bad behavior. We need to welcome these bad actors into the real world of moral response and responsibility.

The only way to "fix" this identified patient of the mob is to curtail the dysfunction of Trump and his enablers. Their legacies are now fixed by history. I hope that this becomes a cautionary tale for others. Look carefully for those who are partisans and only want a way to continue in office. Think Lindsey Graham. Look for the patriots who put nation over all considerations including their own political future. Think of John Lewis and John McCain.

Our country needs to awake or woke, which means to alert to injustice in society, especially racism. Woke sounds like awake. It is the only way to prevent this kind of nightmare.

Post 142. A Brokenness in His Soul

An angry Republican, Senator Ben Sasse, said that Donald Trump had a "brokenness in his soul" and was "addicted to division." Let's look at the horrific events of the insurrection at the Capitol through the lens of considerations of the soul. What were the spiritual issues at play on that day, and what do those issues have to do with our daily lives?

A few years ago, I had a meeting with an Episcopalian clergyman who I had not met before. I always pay attention to the first impressions that I have of others as often, according to Malcolm Gladwell in his book *Blink*, they tell us a great deal about an individual. Remember when a mentor or parent said that "first impressions count." This clergyman was unaware of his statement's impact on another when he said, "You know, Jim, I am an evangelical!" That is fine to say, but in the context of first meeting with someone, I felt that he was saying, "I am this, and I know that you and I don't share the same expression of religious belief." We have to watch out for black-and-white thinking that may drive others from a relationship with us. At the insurrection, the souls of the mob implied "I am right and you are wrong."

I always tried to have a variety of speakers in our chapel services at the Episcopal Academy who represented a wide range of interpretations of faith. I had one caveat. The speaker can say what he or she believes, but they cannot say, "I am right, and you must believe what I believe or else." That statement that "I am right. You must believe as I do or else" reflects the thinking of the interior life of the mob. Many people stood up to this threat, including most recently Michael Pence.

I had been asked by a family in our school community to have a speaker, who headed a prominent religiously conservative organization, address chapel. The family had given a large amount of money to our school. The speaker and I met before the service. I didn't feel comfortable with what he wanted to say to my very religiously diverse people in the chapel. He said, "They need to view their salvation as I do or else." I answered by saying that I couldn't permit him to speak. He got a smile on his face and said, "You know that family who wants me to speak has given a large amount of money to your school." He was still smiling.

I do not do well with threats, so I responded, "You can say how important your faith is to you, but if you impugn the integrity of my students and faculty with an "or else," I will stop you in mid-sentence and remove you from the pulpit." He stopped smiling and did exactly as I instructed him to do. After the service, the family thanked me for having him speak in chapel. He did not. I think that this is what Michael Pence did. It was a straw to break the camel's back after years of licking the boots of this president. Trump certainly said the "or else" to him on many occasions, both explicitly and implicitly.

It is important to know that the soul is filled with the black, white, gray, and "or else" of life. It is also important to know that life is a two-edged sword and the way to hell is paved with good or grandiose intentions.

Trump lacked a moral center. What we need to do is make sure that we have found ours. I believe that the Gospel guides my life. That is an absolute for me. "Preach the Gospel. Use words if necessary. They will know that we are Christians by our love." It is black and white. I also recognize that much of the world that I live in can be less clear and colored gray. One lesson that is critical to learn after the failed insurrection is to appreciate the gray in your soul but find the absolutes by not listening to just one perspective or TV station. Make sure that the "or else(s)" that come into your life are supporting your faith, your values such as no violence, and is something that you would be proud to see on a front page of your local press. Almost every front page of mainstream newspapers in the nation has denounced Trump. In black-and-white terms, Trump and his followers were wrong.

Let me offer up another Republican senator as someone who has had a whole soul of healing, balancing all of those ingredients of black, white, gray, "or else." It is a retired Republican Senator from Missouri who is an Episcopal priest, John Danforth. He served as well as an attorney general and US Ambassador to the United Nations. A recent book that he wrote is *The Relevance of Religion: How Faithful People Can Change Politics*.

Michael Gerson, a columnist at the *Washington Post*, wrote the following about his book and his life. John Danforth does this country another public service after many.

> His book is both a serious critique of politicized religion and a strong defense of religion's indispensable role in our common life. He talks of faith as an antidote to egotism, as a force of reconciliation, and as a source of public virtue. His case is illustrated through autobiography, in an honest, winsome, and self-critical tone. Danforth speaks for civility, collegiality, and useful compromise—and is compelling because he has demonstrated all those commitments himself over decades.

Danforth was a mentor to Josh Hawley, one of the Republican senators who actually asked the recount to continue after the insurrection was put in check. Danforth helped him with his political career. A few days ago, when Danforth was asked about his support of Hawley, he simply said, "It is the worst mistake that I have made in my life." That is what a whole soul sounds like to the brokenness of another soul.

Post 143. The Larva Dei

We are a few days away from the insurrection at our Capitol, the people's house. Most of the response by media has been focused on Trump, his enablers, those who were injured and died, and what our political leaders will do to hold him accountable. There were pics as well of black people cleaning up the capital and the mess created by this assault on our democracy. That could be a metaphor for racism in America. Once again black people were cleaning up the mess of white people.

But some have been forgotten. What about the families of those who disagreed with their family members being part of this day that will live in infamy or who were simply unaware of their extreme views? There is the family of the retired Air Force officer from Texas, who was seen marching through the aisles of the Senate floor. He was a patriot who had flown missions over Afghanistan. His family watched him descend more and more into the depths of belief in Trump and various conspiracy theories. They were helpless to change this mind.

I watched as the FBI arrested a man involved in the insurrection. As he was led to the car that would take him away, his grandmother followed closely behind. She put her face directly into the camera and with great bitterness and anger said, "Thank you, President Trump, for inviting my grandson to a riot, and now he is being taken away."

The story that hit me the hardest was that of a teenage girl who knew that her mother and aunt would be gone for days and told the young girl that they were just spending time together. The teenage girl watched in horror as her mother and aunt appeared on the footage of those who were taking over the Capitol. There is a cruel irony here! When the girl returned from a Black Lives Matter rally, her mother forbade her to go to any other rallies with the words, "You know those people are violent!" The teenage girl turned her mother and aunt into the authorities.

Here is the question: what would I do if I saw one of my sons in that footage? It might destroy my soul! What if it was one of your family members who appeared on the screen attacking the Capitol, and you had to watch helplessly of disagreement with their extreme political views?

It was Martin Luther who described family life as the *larva dei,* the mask of God, where God reveals himself in sacred relationships with one another. When we are praying for our nation, all of those affected by the insurrection, and our political leaders, say a prayer for those families that were not complicit in this but were helpless to change the heart of a family member who participated in it or simply didn't know of their plan. Pray for God's peace that passes human understanding. As you think of the mother and aunt who stormed the Capitol, think quickly of the teenage girl who had no say in the matter and watched in horror.

Post 144. Word from England

Vicki and I Facetimed this morning with Roger and Margaret Harwood, dear friends in England. Margaret is a retired school teacher, and Roger is the retired chief architect of the Church of England. They live in Aylesbury, which is outside of Oxford. We met them as we exchanged houses and cars with them some years ago and have kept in touch.

The US has a very important bioethics decision to make soon. Should we vaccinate as many as possible now and worry about the second shot later, or should we stay the course as it is presently stated in our vaccine policy to save the vaccine for the second shot later?

We can learn some important lessons from what is occurring in England regarding vaccine distribution and the negative consequences of the insurrection for stability in the rest of the world.

The authorities in England have decided to get as many people vaccinated as possible now, for they have a greater threat than we have at the moment. Their decision makes sense to them. One of their daughters is an administrator at a hospital in Oxford, who points out that some of these vaccines have a shelf life. Use it or lose it. Their decisions are also based on the fact that their leader, Boris Johnson, almost died from the COVID-19 virus. That has shaped a lot of his thinking. He knows the risk firsthand. Their decision is based on risk/cost/benefit analysis. There is a bioethics model that emphasizes short-term decisions weighed against long-term ones and the consequences of each. England has chosen the short-term consequences as weighing more than long-term considerations. England is also developing a plan to get the vaccine into the arms of Third World nations.

Our decision should be based on the UK risk model that weighs the risk now or the risk of not getting the vaccine later. We shall see what our leaders decide and why. I have not seen anything addressing this yet from two of my mentors, Dr. Dom Sisti at the Penn Center for Bioethics or Dr. Arthur Caplan, once at Penn but now the head of the New York University Center for Bioethics.

Our friends indicated that there are consequences in addition to what will happen in our nation as we move forward. They and others like them in England and the EU are scared of Trump's actions for he has emboldened others of the political right across Europe. He has permitted others to follow. The US has always been the model for democracy. I believe, for that reason, he should be removed from office as soon as possible. He is not only a threat to our nation but people across the globe.

Post 145. Mistakes Were Made but Not by Me

The title of this blog is the title of a book by Carol Tavris and Elliot Aronson. I used several different theories in my ethics class to help students understand why people do unethical things. They should have each politician read the work of Tavris and Aronson as they are deliberating on actions to hold the president and his enablers responsible for the insurrection. Better yet, call on my ethics students to come down and lead the way.

I will share some of the thinking of Tavris and Aronson and my thoughts to help you understand why Trump and his enablers have not backed down from their acts of sedition. It is all there in the research about why people can't admit their mistakes. Watch the actions of Hawley and Cruz in particular.

The inability to say I made a mistake is based on self-justification and cognitive dissonance. Cognitive dissonance is when you are forced to consider two things that don't go together like a fair election and the fact that this is true and my desire to say that it isn't to advance my political career. If new information is consonant with our belief, we say, "That is what I always said." But if the information is dissonant, we consider it wrong or biased. Research shows that when people become more certain they are right about something they did, they just can't undo it. We live in a culture that equates mistakes with stupidity. Hawley and Cruz are smart. They cannot accept a stupid action as something they would do.

When most people are confronted by evidence that they are wrong, they double down on their point of view. Think of the actions of Cruz, Hawley, and others, which allow people to convince themselves that they did the best thing that they could have done. *In fact, come to think of it, it was the right thing.* This is why self-justification is more insidious than a lie. It allows people to vigorously convince others that they were right as well. What happens is that cognitive dissonance, such as the election was a fraud but all evidence says that it is not, causes people to attempt to try to resolve the two things that just don't go together until they find a way to reduce their inner tension. Doubling down is often their strategy."

Think of the last time that you or I made a mistake and how hard it may have been for us to admit it. Believe it or not, we can learn something from all of this unethical behavior. I don't think that any of the enablers should escape consequences as that will not hold us in good stead with the global community. I agree with George Will, a conservative Republican, who wrote that Hawley and Cruz (and others) should walk around with an "S" on their chests. It doesn't stand for Superman or Superwoman. It stands for Seditionist.

Post 146. Free Speech Isn't Free

The home of free speech in recent American history is based on protests at the University of California at Berkeley in the 60s. I begin with a humorous story at my expense. When I arrived at Berkeley years after the 60s protest, I landed late at night. My dorm was at the top of the Holy Hill where several different seminaries and institutions for graduate study were found. I was there for graduate study beyond the programs that I took at Berkeley at Yale and Duke.

Since it was late and I was hungry, I walked down the hill on Euclid Avenue that is lined with restaurants. I stood in line outside of one. I was still dressed in my khaki pants, a blue blazer, and a buttoned-down collared shirt. All the patrons chatting away in line ahead of me and behind me were scantily clad, had many piercings and tattoos, sandals, and long hair. The person in front of me, turned, and asked in a loud voice, "Hey dude! What planet are you from?" I responded, "Philadelphia!" He replied, "That explains it!" Everyone laughed. I had to chuckle myself. I stood out!

Various Republican politicians are now crying foul that Trump and their social media platforms have silenced him and them. I want to offer the same proclamation that the person in line in front of me raised to them. Hey dude, what planet are you guys from? We teach in ethics that your right to free speech stops when it infringes on someone else's rights or could put them in danger. The classic guiding principle is that you can't cry "Fire!" in a crowded theater. But it is also part of our basic human rights granted by the First Amendment.

The tricky thing is to define moments of free speech being suppressed. It is like the oft-mentioned definition of pornography. It is hard to define it, but you know it when you see it. Free speech is not free because it could produce a cost for a certain person or group of people. This is why we have hate speech laws to handle these exceptions.

Some of the things that you cannot say under the guiding principles of free speech are the following: libel, slander, obscenity, pornography, sedition, fighting words, incitement, classified information, copyright violation, trade secrets, and food labeling. All these examples have been tested in the courts. But notice three on this list. They are sedition, fighting words, and incitement. In the words of my aunt Nellie, "Bingo!" Our Republican colleagues and Trump enablers need to check out these guiding principles. Trump's enablers say that his voice has been cut off. Really? What about the White House Briefing Room? Who has one of those in his house? He can speak from there. Oh! I forgot. That would take courage, something which he has in small supply. Keep in mind that this applies to Democrats and Independents as well. The strongest argument on the Republican side of the hall is that you are slandering our group. The insurrection, the sedition, fighting words, and incitement would probably carry the day in the free speech court against the accusation of slander.

One day, I took a walk around the Berkeley campus. There is an entrance that is directly across from the street where one of the beginning camps of "hippies" stood their ground. It was common for me to see men, women, and children who were locked in a time warp of the 60s. I could smell the pot haze coming from various stores and encampments. As I made my way back to the entrance that I just mentioned, there was a metal circle in the pavement that was the size of a manhole cover. The Free Speech Movement began at Berkeley. The metal circle states this fact. It also indicates that anyone can step into that circle and say anything they want at the top of their lungs. The caveat is that it is located in such a way that people don't have to hear it or be hurt by it. You can always walk away. I wish we had such a circle in Washington, DC.

Post 147. Oleaginous

I love words and reading. Ever since I was too young to get a library card, I began using my older brother's card. I would go to our public library to read a whole series of books about American heroes. I will never forget the books' orange covers. I was blessed to have a Latin teacher in a public high school, Ms. Higgins, who treated me and others as serious students when the blue-collar community in which I was raised did not have a priority of pushing education for its young people. Few went to college. I think that Ms. Higgins thought she was teaching at Yale. She didn't care about what others thought or did. She had the highest standards and pushed all of us every day to achieve our best. She was demanding!

I loved Latin for two reasons. Since the ending of Latin words determines parts of speech, Latin gives you a solid grounding in grammar. Second, a vast number of our English words are derived from a Latin root. Even after rigorous football practice when I was tired, I still tried to do extra translations and math problems when doing my homework. I also began a process in middle school that I still do today. If I don't know what a word means when I am reading, I look it up. I then use it myself. That is the true way to develop a vocabulary. You don't do it through SAT courses.

George Will, a conservative author and columnist, loves words as well. In a recent editorial, he found the right word for describing

Hawley, Cruz, and the president and his enablers to resonate with how I felt about these seditionists. He described them as *oleaginous*, a word that means oily or slick. Its root in Latin is oleaginous meaning "of an olive tree." That word would make Ms. Higgins proud. What a great word to describe the Trump family.

I was introduced to the importance of words differently by one of my ethics students who came into my ethics classroom and proclaimed, "Rev, you have given me uninterrupted dinners." He was a running back on our football team and would come home after practice, ready to eat anything in sight. The family always ate dinner together. His father was a terrific guy, but he had one fault. He could never admit that he didn't know something.

Just as my student would be ready to pounce on his dinner, his father would always ask that dreaded question that is asked of students. "What did you learn in school today?" He also wanted to engage in discussion after his question landed, just as my student was ready to dig in. Then it happened. He asked my student what he learned in school. My student responded by saying, "Existentialism in ethics!" Then there was silence. My student looked over, and there was no response except, "Go ahead. Eat your dinner!" Dad had no idea what my student was talking about.

Then for an entire term, his dad would raise the question again and again. Each of my student's responses contained theory or words that his father wasn't in a position to discuss. "Today we learned about the slippery slope argument in bioethics." My student received one term of responses of, "Go ahead and eat your dinner."

What Ms. Higgins passed down to me was to treat each and every student as though they could learn anything, the value of their learning, and that they could do anything that they had as a goal. She was a single lady who always enthusiastically clapped her hands when a struggling student would get a question right. I can't remember any time where she played "gotcha," catching any of us repeatedly answering something wrong. I had some tough customers in my class. She was a little lady. One got the distinct impression that she cared deeply about Latin but cared even more about us. Everyone showed her the utmost respect. I would even say she was revered.

Regarding the unethical behavior of Trump and his enablers since November 3, 2020, I wonder how things would have played out if he and they focused on the truth of the election results and not their lies. What would have happened if they celebrated the election as the core of our democracy and didn't spend their time playing "gotcha," focusing on their lies and wrong answers to benefit their selfish desires?

Too bad that they didn't have Ms. Higgins for Latin. They would have gained the same kind of respect that she received from my Latin class. They are left instead with the adjective that describes them best. They are "oleaginous!"

Post 148. The Vice President-Elect and Vogue

I write this blog, admitting that I have never written about women's fashion at any point in my life. Notice I'm afraid of backlash. Our country is still like an open wound after the insurrection, and I just read about the furor over what Kamala Harris was wearing that appeared on the print version of *Vogue* and its digital version. I gather that she approved the digital version but controversy is swirling over whether she approved the cover for the print version. Women pounced on what they saw. The only salvific notion was that a black person was the photographer.

I have no fashion sense. Since I am a clergy person, I wear black shirts and sometimes dark suits. I was approached by a fashionable EA parent who informed me a few years ago that, "This is your year, Jim! Black is in!" When people admire what I am wearing, I comment on the long period of time it took me to pick it out! They know that I am kidding! I usually put on the first thing I see in the closet.

From what I could gather from the article, the controversy is over the print version where Ms. Harris is wearing a black jacket, perhaps leather, white blouse, black slacks, and sneakers. The digital version pictures her in a light blue blazer, a white blouse, and blue slacks. I learned that *Vogue* is the fashion Bible. I couldn't believe the conflicting points of women's responses. One woman indicated that "she looked like she forgot to do her homework" in the print version. The article stated that Michelle Obama appeared on the cover, and all was fine.

Clearly, the tension rests on the Vice President–Elect's handlers who let the offending picture get by them.

But here is the point! I didn't see Joe Biden on the cover of GQ. Who thought that this was a good idea? Focus on what she has done. Don't focus on her attire! This has a gender issue written all over it! Kamala Harris is a savvy lady.

Quite frankly I never knew that there was so much to learn about what constitutes good fashion. It reminds me of being at the Metropolitan Museum of Art in New York City. What is art to some looks like sticks thrown in a corner to me,

I am tempted to mention the importance of the "eye of the beholder" in ethics where what counts is not what you say that is important as much as how a person receives it. I would bet that the Vice President-Elect is OK with it. She is the embodiment of grit and toughness.

Forgive this post, but I needed some levity in a week that has been so heavy. I will remind all the folks who are commenting on Kamala Harris' attire to remember the biblical phrase, "Consider the lilies of the field, how they grow; they toil not, neither do they spin: yet I say unto you, that even Solomon in all his glory was not arrayed like one of these" (Matt. 6:28–29). That has always been good enough for me!

Post 149. Dr. King's Words Transform a Holiday into a Holy Day

The Reverend Dr. Martin Luther King's holiday reminds us of the legacy of important words that he has left to shape our way forward as a country to ethical conduct, harmony, peace, and justice. Recall holiday sounds like a holy day. Dr. King said the following, "Cowardice asks the question, 'Is it safe?' expediency asks the question, 'Is it politic?' vanity asks the question, 'Is it popular?' Conscience asks the question, 'Is it right?' There comes a time when someone must take a position that is not safe, political, or popular. One must take it because one's conscience tells one that it is right." I believe that this moral code articulated by Dr. King was meant for the moment in which we find ourselves today. It succinctly defines the ethical view that is needed now.

I would suggest that we should open our eyes to see the cowardice, expediency, vanity, quest for popularity, and yielding power with the knowledge that what Trump, the insurrectionists, and his enablers did was wrong. It is beyond what can be justified by any legal maneuvers or rationalizing. We will certainly see some attempting to make what is wrong into right, denying any wrongdoing. Consequences must come before healing can occur.

But we have heart work to do to keep our hope and faith alive. I would suggest an exercise on this Martin Luther King Day. We should read Dr. King's words written above repeatedly a few times and then shut our eyes to see a deeper vision that is offered by our faith in God and one another. Why? Denzel Washington's words point the way, "Why do we close our eyes when we pray, cry, kiss, or dream? Because the most beautiful things in life are not seen but felt by the heart."

Our homework on this day should be our heart work. That will make our holiday a holy day. That is what has always moved people to the Promised Land.

Post 150. Pay Me Now or Pay Me Later

In the mid-1970s, the Fram Oil Filter Company introduced its legendary slogan, "Pay Me Now or Pay Me Later." Make a small payment now for one of our oil filters, and it will save you lots of money later. It was the key statement for their brand. It is also a key statement on how to live a good moral life. We are a culture of sound bites. Companies focus on the short attention span of people. The Fram sound bite is right up there with "Plop Plop Fizz Fizz! O What a Relief It Is!" the sound bite for Alka Seltzer, another iconic sound bite in market popularity.

How is "Pay Me Now Or Pay Me Later" an iconic sound bite for the moral life as well? Present choices will determine how we will live into our future. I have written in a previous post about Judith Viorst's book, *Necessary Losses*. She reflected that every action causes us to lose something as we move forward. Life exacts a price! We need to assess in our daily lives what that price means to us. Dietrich Bonhoeffer, a theologian, wrote a book called the *Cost of Discipleship*. Bonhoeffer stood up to Hitler and paid the ultimate price. He was imprisoned for his views and hung the week before the Allied Forces defeated Hitler. He based his decision to stand up against injustice on his understanding of the Gospel of Jesus. He knew the price that he would pay in attempting to save others. He was paying the price of love. In a World Religions and Christianity course, this is the question that counts. "Is my action preparing me to love?"

We should consider how our choices affect future considerations. We saw this graphically in the insurrection incited by Trump and his enablers. Many people depend on the news cycle. I can do what I want to do, regardless of the consequences, as people will forget about what I have done and move on to the next newsworthy topic. There is an interesting result of thinking that out of sight is out of mind. We are seeing the consequences of the Republicans' actions and others who supported Trump's fiction. *Forbes Magazine* wants businesses to refuse to hire any people associated with Trump because they would not bring truth to their organization. Businesses are withdrawing support from his enablers. The lifeblood of his brand is tarnished beyond repair. It has been speculated that in the future, parents will tell their children that they shouldn't lie or they will wind up like Trump. Trump will sit beside McCarthy as his name will reflect the worst form of behavior. He will be known as the antithesis of our first president's folk tale that "He never told a lie."

There is some credence to people's view of the news cycle to just wait out bad news and keep our heads down. This is less likely to occur with women. Deborah Tannen, one of the leading voices in gender studies, makes the point that "women never forget" for they create intimacy by communication and resolution whereas "men want closure on an issue, forget about it in the interest of moving forward." It is interesting to me that when I was teaching this aspect of gender issues in my ethics class that every girl and boy in the class nodded their heads in agreement.

You have to look at relationships if you are going to study ethics, for ethical issues don't occur in a vacuum. One girl summed it up when she volunteered, "I remember what one girl did to me in first grade." Forgive maybe, but not forget. Deborah Tannen was in search, not of who we should be, but of how we are. Gender is shaped by culture. Another culture may find men and women acting in the opposite way.

As we move through life, what is the consequence of what I am doing now that may exact a price for me in the future? We refer to this as cost/risk/benefit analysis. There is a system of ethical thought that is literally called consequentialism. "Pay Me Now or Pay Me later" would perhaps be expressed in today's culture as good and bad Karma. What you do can come back to you as an approval or put a stamp of disapproval on you. People in a moral culture know that their past deeds eventually catch up to us. That is Trump's cautionary tale.

Post 151. Brandenburg Test

The Brandenburg Test is a political ethical occurrence that is not known to many, as it occurred in 1969. It relates to free speech. Like many ethical issues, it placed future legal cases in a gray area where a good bit of ethics finds itself. Most of us are clear about right and wrong. Those categories are certainly central to ethical thinking, but ethics also finds itself frequently in areas that are not black and white, but gray. The Brandenburg Test as a legal precedent is one of those. It attempts to interpret what speech is OK and what speech incites others to commit crimes. It took the place of the "clear and present danger" test established in the 1919 Supreme Court Case *Schenck v. United States*.

We need to keep in mind the Brandenburg Test as we move to step 2 of the impeachment process, for the test contains the same issue that now confronts Trump. Trump will be seeking a way that makes uncertain if his actions incited the insurrection on the Capitol.

Let's look at the context for the Brandenburg Test. In this case, Clarence Brandenburg, a rural leader of the KKK in Ohio, was appealing a $1,000 fine and prison sentence. He was charged with advocating violence to achieve a political goal. He was also charged with *assembling* a group of people to perform violence. He complained to TV cameras and the press that the white race was being suppressed. He was not armed, but his fellow Klansmen were. His words used the "N" word to describe black people who he said should return to Africa.

The Supreme Court voted in favor of Brandenburg because his words did not cause *imminent* action against the group of people who would attend an Independence Day March in Washington, DC. Despite the vile language that he spoke, this case is often referred to as "an unfortunate price of freedom."

The gray ethical area of the Brandenburg Test rests on two words which I have italicized: *assembling* and *imminent*.

One has to show that a person brought the crowd together and that his or her words were the direct cause of criminal consequences. Regarding the insurrection at the Capitol, look for people to question what Trump was bringing the people together to do. Second, is what he said a direct, imminent effect on creating the ensuing violence?

I already heard Donald Trump Jr., not a paragon of ethical information or action, question the direct connection between his father's words and what followed. Someone must have told him about the Brandenburg Test. I can't believe he learned it in an ethics class. It must have been a "Loophole 101 seminar."

Post 152. Mar-a-Logo and the Horned Man

Many seditionists stand out as we view the footage of the insurrection at our Capitol. We have the man carrying the confederate flag, a person sitting in Nancy Pelosi's chair with his feet propped up on her desk, the woman who is in a rage because someone sprayed her in her eyes, and many more. The one who captures the most attention by me is the "horned man" who is seen in frequent shots. He is covered with an animal skin and has his face covered with red, white, and blue paint. He looks like someone from a different age when the wheel was invented.

As I was watching the cast of characters taking over the Capitol, I thought that none of those people would be seen at an event at Mar-a-Lago. It was the epitome of cognitive dissonance when two things just don't go together. It points out that a good many of those domestic terrorists had nothing in common with Trump except the sharing of the same lie that the election was stolen. We did have people who were senators and professional athletes who Trump did feel were good enough to be at Mar-a-Lago. Most of the terrorists seemed to be working-class individuals, which is a group that Trump stiffed in the building of his structures. He would declare to those blue-collar workers that they should take fifty percent of what he owed them, or they would get nothing because his lawyers would tie them up in court for a long time. A good many of those small businesses went bankrupt. There were some 3000 lawsuits filed against him by such workers. Why didn't that reality filter down to his working-class supporters?

Trump used his supporters in the same way that he used the contractors for his buildings. This is what most news reports state. But this was a marriage made in hell, for the radical fringe of his supporters like Bannon and Miller were using him. The radical fringe in his group knew that he was a narcissist and played to his ego and manipulated him, as he manipulated others.

Let's shine the light of ethics on this scenario! When you start treating people as an "It" and not a "Thou," you do the worst thing that you can do to another person. You dehumanize them. The Jewish theologian, Martin Buber, was the first to coin the phrases, "I/It" and "I/Thou" as categories of relationships. The "I/It" relationships are transactional ones, focusing on what I can get from another person. The "I/Thou" relationships see the other person as a whole to be honored, respected, and seen as a child of God. You can recognize "I/It" relationships for they contain that mindset of "What have you done for me lately?" We see this graphically in his relationship with Vice President Pence. Pence supported Trump in every way until he didn't. It was then that Trump turned on him because he wouldn't do the President's bidding.

Trump did not have a moral center. It was replaced by "Tell me how great I am." Some see the bookends of Trump's presidency as the expletive word, pu—y. He was caught saying that he could do anything to women because he was a celebrity, including grabbing them by their genitalia. This was heard for all to hear in his interview in the trailer with Billy Bush. He used the same expletive when he called Pence by this word at the end of his presidency. "You can be a person of courage or a pu—y. We see his treatment of women as "I/It" in the many women who have come forward to call him a sexual predator.

This also points to a corollary that he is misogynistic. When he is talking about "Make America Great Again," he is really saying is, "Make America great again for white men." He had little regard for women, as he was locked in the 1950s mindset referring to "suburban housewives," and "I am the only thing keeping low-income housing from taking over your suburbs." He was fearful of strong women. His worst nightmare came to fruition in the form of Nancy Pelosi.

I am looking forward to the day when I see the horned man and Lindsey Graham play a round of golf with Trump at Mar-a-Lago. Cognitive dissonance. I won't be holding my breath in anticipation of that day coming. Hell would have to freeze over first.

Post 153. If I Can Help You in Any Way, Give Me a Call

The Biden and Harris inauguration was a high point in our country's history after four years of a constant series of low points under Donald Trump. I am biased in many ways about today's transition to a new way forward for our country.

I have witnessed many inaugurations, but I cannot think of any that were more faith centered than this one, based on President Biden's strong faith. It began last night with prayers, silent and spoken, as we looked over the flags on the mall, honoring the 400,000 victims of the COVID-19 disease. A prayer was said and "Amazing Grace" sung. This is the first time that the nation came together in prayer about those who died in the pandemic.

Four hundred lights shined in the darkness. There was no complaint about crowd size, as we had at the inauguration of Donald Trump. It began a period lasting through today where the emphasis was on "we." "We the People" was very much front and center throughout these last twenty-four hours.

Today at the inauguration, we began with a prayer and concluded with one that touched on our hope and faith in God as we move to a new tomorrow. The patriotic music moved us to tears. President Biden's address was perfect because, among other things, it was authentic. All the issues and pain were covered, the path ahead was laid out as hard, and hope and faith were proclaimed to assist us all in moving forward. The word *united* was found throughout. The young poet laureate's words were stirring.

Episcopal Academy connections were present today. One of our alumni, Fran Person, worked with Joe Biden for years as an aid. Joe Biden's brother, Jim, is an EA past parent. I called Jim the morning that Beau Biden died. I asked him to communicate the prayers of our school to Joe and his family, which he assured me he would do. Jim's children, Caroline and Jamie, are graduates of our school.

Joe Biden never changes in the places you don't want him to change. He welcomes change in areas where we do have a fervent desire for change. I asked him and Republican Senator Arlen Specter to speak in chapel years ago about what was needed in Washington to improve communication and avoid never-ending gridlock. Both responded by the need to work together and to be united in causes that would lead our country forward on the moral course of social justice and peace. Senator Biden said, "It may sound simple, but nobody goes out to dinner together anymore. We see each other as politicians and not as people." That will be the change that we will look forward to seeing in the next four years.

I got a glimpse of Jamie leaving the inauguration stage with the rest of the family. Jamie Biden and I spoke a few weeks ago by phone. When we finished talking about the business at hand, he concluded the call by saying something to me that I always say to my former students, but he beat me to the proverbial punch, so to speak. He said, "Reverend Squire, if I can help you in any way, give me a call."

I think those words, "If I can help you in any way, give me a call," may be the very heartbeat of his uncle, now president of the United States.

Post 154. Truth, Consequence, or Courage

"Truth or Consequence" is more than a name of a game show. It is what confronts our elected officials who will vote on Part 2 of Donald Trump's second impeachment. A few days after we celebrated the Reverend Dr. Martin Luther King Day, his words should also be the theme for what lies ahead for our elected officials who claim that voting against Trump will further divide the country. Along with truth or consequence, we hear the words of Dr. King, "True peace is not the absence of tension, it is the presence of justice." We must keep our eyes fixed on Trump's enablers who were interested in keeping the big lie alive and well as they sought profit and power.

There is something else that must be part of our prayer life during this forthcoming trial and literally in our four years ahead under the Biden administration. Pray for courage for our elected officials. I remember as a young man reading John F. Kennedy's, *Profiles in Courage*, where he wrote about people who stood up for truth when it was the risky and unpopular thing to do. They did what was right and not what yielded power or profit.

There is another book that is not as familiar to most people that speaks as well about the importance of courage. Like Kennedy's book, John McCain's reflections on courage in *Why Courage Matters* is a thin volume of 209 pages of inspiration. I have reread my dog-eared copy many times.

If you have read my memoir or posts, you know that I feel that John McCain has "walked the walk" with courage. Here is some of his thinking as it relates to what is needed in our days ahead. It was Eleanor Roosevelt, who made one of McCain's key points, when she said, "It is more important to need to have courage than to want to have it. Needing courage won't guarantee it, but putting ourselves in situations that demand our courage will more likely stir it than day dreaming about it."

McCain makes the point that when he lacked courage when a prisoner during the Vietnam War, it was because he was concerned about his own dignity. It wasn't until he had a communal understanding of courage where his brave soldiers insisted on a community code of honor that his courage reappeared. That change in attitude brought about shared responsibility for honor among all the prisoners. There was no "I." There was just "We."

Each member of my family has inspired me by demonstrating their courage. They have given me a high standard to live up to, particularly my wife, Vicki!

There is no courage without fear first. I think of a woman student who fought cancer for most of her life and taught me and others "to live life from a deeper spot," before she died. I think of a former EA parent who lives each day with serious cancer but moves through each day with the support of his family, friends, and teammates from his playing days. He asks the hard questions of his doctors, knowing that he will get the hardest answers in response.

I think of that student who entered my office when he was in tenth grade. His first words were, "I am afraid." I received an email from him as he was about to land in Islamabad on a dangerous mission for the army. He wrote that he was facing the most dangerous thing that he had ever done, but he was ready.

Perhaps the courage of Mitt Romney and John McCain will rub off on our elected officials during this trial. Courage involves fear and people at a crossroads where they must choose the easy wrong or the hard right.

They may have to look to Russia, of all places, for an example in Aleksei Navalny who is the loyal opposition to Putin. He was at death's door after a poison attack ordered by Putin. He has returned to Russia, knowing that he would be imprisoned and possibly killed, but he will not be silenced against a government whose leaders seek power and profit. He has inspired his followers and the nongovernment press to do the same.

Our elected officials need to know that America does not have a corner on the courage market. We are about to become part of the global community again where, like McCain, we will be inspired by the local and global community effort to raise us up to seek the right thing to do in all things. Truth, consequence, and courage have always been the fertile ground of a moral life on this earth, our fragile island home.

Post 155. Bioethics and Vaccine Distribution

My first opportunity to do bioethics at an institution was when I was invited to join others to vet the controversial Body World Exhibit that was coming to the Franklin Institute in Philadelphia. We were to offer recommendations after thoroughly going over the exhibit. The exhibit was touring the United States. Its creators used the process of plastination to show the inner workings of the human body. You could see the nervous system and other systems that were difficult to see as a whole. The medical schools in the Philadelphia area took their anatomy classes there. They could see first-hand the systems in the human body.

Our recommendations included having the exhibit of the fetuses that was part of the exhibit placed in a room off the central pathway through the exhibit to be sensitive to the Roman Catholic population and other pro-life groups who would be attending the exhibit. They could choose not to view that part of the exhibit. We made sure that there was tracing for the consent that must be given to all the people who donated their bodies to this exhibit. We also asked that the gift shop not contain plastic kidney key chains and other items of that nature. The Institute and administration of the Body World exhibit accepted all our recommendations, except what would be sold in the gift shop. Vicki and I attended an opening night gala and reception for the Body World Exhibit at the Franklin Institute. I was criticized by several people who attended for approving the exhibit in the first place. This bioethics vetting was easy compared to who should get the vaccine and when.

Bioethical thinking is a lot like law school. You follow precedents for your decision-making. There were no precedents for this pandemic. You couldn't even look at how the Spanish flu epidemic was handled because of the different historical context.

Let me touch on some themes that have made vaccine distribution very difficult in terms of who should have priority to receive it. There is no national recommended policy on who should get the vaccine and when. States are making those decisions. There is an overarching reality that has produced part of the vaccine controversy. Vaccine distribution is a zero-sum game meaning one person's gain getting the vaccine is another person's loss.

There is the Mickey Mantle Factor in bioethics. Mickey Mantle, a famous baseball player, was an alcoholic who received a liver transplant after a short waiting period over people who were just as needy. That event created a formula for how you get a transplant. In essence, fame shouldn't matter. The same is true for the order of who should get the vaccine. Sports teams have been criticized because they can get testing on a daily basis when others can't. The ethical principle here is "what you do for one, you should do for all."

The vaccine priorities that seem to be a part of most conversations are smokers and obese people are higher up the list as they have a choice to change their lifestyle. The bioethical debate is the question, "Are they life choices or underlying conditions?" My vote would be for life choices.

Nursing home patients are at the top of the list because forty percent of the deaths in our nation are found in nursing homes. The argument against vaccinations for the elderly is that they don't prevent the spread of the disease. My vote would still be for giving them the vaccine because it feels fair and right. Our elders should be honored.

283

I have saved the most controversial to last. Should prisoners be given the vaccine before others do? This gets the blood boiling. States like Colorado are totally against this. The argument for giving the vaccine to prisoners is that you are putting the prisoners in harm's way. The idea in the Hippocratic Oath has been used here where "you should first do no harm." The argument against is the zero-sum game that other people need it more. One of the categories of bioethics is justice versus mercy. I would vote for mercy here for the prisoners. The gray area is determining how to relate to poor communities as well where people have to live in close quarters. This has still not been addressed. Ranking people is ultimately about access to the vaccine. For example, in Texas, most of the vaccination sites are in the white affluent areas, but more than half of the fatalities in Texas are found in the Hispanic community and almost ten percent have been in the black community. These areas are not affluent. This is racist!

Remember the first ethical statement that we human beings say. "It's not fair!" This too is the subjective guideline for a discipline that has to operate frequently in the gray area. The people who are responsible for the ranking consider this. They are also looking at the driving force of the theory of the Utilitarian view of the "greatest good for the greatest number in a particular group."

I mentioned in an earlier post that England is getting all of their vaccine out because of the significant, fast transmission of the disease. They are risking that the second shot will not be available, but their formula is for short-term gain over long-term consequences, which makes perfect sense to them in their situation. They have used cost/risk/benefit analysis, which is a decision-making process that we will be seeing more of in the days to come in the US as well.

The "Body World Exhibit" can be found on my blog on my website under the heading of "Bioethics and Vaccine Distribution."

Post 156. Red-Handed

State Republican Senator Jeff Pyle from Western Pennsylvania is facing calls on social media to resign and being censured by colleagues for mocking the appearance of a transgender woman, Dr. Rachel Levine, who served as health secretary in Pennsylvania and now will serve in the Biden administration. Pyle's description was offensive. He stated as, per the January 24, 2021, *Inquirer* that "I had no idea it would be received so poorly as it was. Tens of thousands of heated emails assured me it was." He went on to say that he did not come up with the offensive post on his own. He merely shared it. He offered a humble apology. Notice it was not an apology for the content of the post as much as it was an apology for getting caught. Otherwise, we would not have heard from him.

Growing up in my working-class community there was an expression that was used frequently that someone such as Pyle was "caught red-handed." The origin of this phrase goes back to fifteenth-century Scotland and meant that someone had "blood on their hands" for murder or poaching. It emerged over the years to mean an obvious serious breach of ethical action.

Recently Kevin McCarthy reversed course and said that Trump did not incite the insurrection. It was everybody's fault. Previously, he had said that Trump was responsible. I can't wait to see the logic behind that reversal when all of his statements have been caught on news videos. He has been caught "red-handed," a serious breach of trust that violates a code of moral behavior.

There have been more incidents like "I never said or did that" (referring to something related to telling the "Big Lie" about the election). I wouldn't know where to begin to list them. They have been as numerous as the sands on a beach, which is why a segment of the American public came to believe that the election was illegal and stolen in the first place. They didn't come up with that notion on their own. One of the more outrageous examples was the Texas

Lt. Governor Dan Patrick, who is offering up to a $1 million reward for examples of voter fraud if whistleblowers and tipsters could find any. Texans were angry because Patrick never demonstrated how they would get the reward if they found any fraud. Regarding those caught during the insurrection, there have been multiple excuses, but the one that I like best is that the seditionist who went into the Capitol to see the artwork in the hallways.

Focus on your favorite people who have blood on their hands such as Hawley, Cruz, and Lindsey Graham. Focus on them because these people do literally have blood on their hands, which was the result of the insurrection.

I believe that we need to start using that "caught red-handed" phrase as we go into the impeachment trial, Part 2, for it graphically reflects the serious nature of the crime and the literal result for some who were bloody. Can you picture Kevin McCarthy saying, "Trump doesn't have blood on his hands?" That is a stronger irrefutable visual that could enhance the accusation of his inciting the crime. I found that the more visual examples that I could provide to my ethics students, the more long-term memory of them and good choices would occur.

Years later, after students took the course, I had students call me and say, "I almost lied about something I did wrong, but I thought of that movie, *Before and After,* that we saw, and I didn't do it. Others would list a host of unethical acts that they almost committed but remembered that visual or video that they saw in the ethics class and chose the right thing to do. I remember visuals as well.

Yes, "caught red-handed" is much better than any other phrase to capture the seriousness of the issue and the murderous attempt that we now know would have happened if the insurrectionists weren't stopped. We can't forget that blood was shed. Neither should those at the trial.

Post 157. The Big Lie and the Laramie Project

One of the things that I have learned through various decision-making models is that if you want to understand what is happening currently, go to a previous event that had similar characteristics. You should learn from precedents. That is the heart of law school as well.

In trying to understand the "Big Lie" that the election was stolen I went back to a personal experience that I had in the early 2000s. It was decided that our theater department would present *The Laramie Project* as the fall play. *The Laramie Project* is about the events that surrounded the murder in 1998 of Matthew Shepard who was a gay University of Wyoming student in Laramie, Wyoming. *The Laramie Project* was drawn from 200 interviews conducted by Artistic Director Moises Kaufman and is still studied in schools as a method of teaching prejudice and tolerance. The play dealt with prejudice specifically against gay people.

There was one problem, however, as our school had not done much then to address the issue of prejudice against gay people. A courageous gay faculty member met with me in my office and volunteered to address chapel as a way of introducing the whole subject of respect for others different from us, which is found in *The Laramie Project*. Most of his speech was about respect. A small amount was about his sexual orientation. After chapel, I went to my office, and the phone was already ringing about how I supported someone for "coming out" in chapel. This was true of phone calls to other administrators as well. There was nothing said about "respecting others who are different." The "coming out" issue dominated the community conversation. Since our school has alumni who are in this country and abroad, I was hearing criticism from all over the world.

The "Big Lie" here was that the intention was not on revealing the faculty member's sexual orientation but on respect for differences as we got ready for the fall play. That was the context for the address. The way to hell is paved with good intentions, and I and others found ourselves very much in a hellish situation.

I want to mention one conversation with a caller to make a point that is similar to what happened in the "Big Lie" that the election was stolen. He did not tell me who he was but wanted me to know that he represented a large group of parents who were angry about my promotion of a "gay agenda." He berated me with disrespectful statements that I will spare you from reading. I volunteered to meet with him and his large group at a time and place of his choosing to discuss the matter. I never heard back from him again.

The story of the chapel address on respect became fixed in the culture of our school as a "coming out story." Years later I received a call from one of our development officers who was meeting in Florida with alumni who were potential donors. She said, "Jim, people here are still angry that you let a faculty member come out in chapel." The video of the address was available then, so I asked if any of the people were familiar with the content of the address. They were not, but they *heard* about it. As is true about the stolen election, their view supported what they wanted to believe, and to make the situation more complex, a good many of these folks were friends of mine. There was little looking at the facts or content.

I am pleased that now EA is a school that has moved forward to a much better place. People now feel safe to talk about the issue, some agree to disagree, and some have spoken about this in chapel with great support and little community conversation.

I made some mistakes along the way. The chapel experience was then and remains now the safest and most important place on campus for what is said and done there. I had Brian Sims, one of the Pennsylvania state legislators, address the issue of respect for those with a different sexual orientation in chapel as well as others. Criticism was made about the chapel not being a place for these addresses. I had a few students who requested to speak about this.

I had them speak in the theater in place of the chapel because the place became the lightning rod for criticism. I thought I was protecting the students, but this was a mistake on my part as I should have had all those student addresses done in chapel as a statement of social justice, which is at the heart of the Gospel.

I learned something very important a few years ago, when I was asked if a transgender alumnus could address chapel. She would be the first transgender person to speak in chapel. She was the recommendation from our fiftieth reunion class and would kick off Alumni Weekend. The class was all male. Their recommendation was a woman transgender classmate. They all voted for her to be the speaker. They did this for two reasons. She was their top student and became an award-winning attorney in Colorado. But more importantly, they knew her and respected her. When she finished her chapel address, she received a five-minute standing ovation. I still had people who were angry with me, but Vicki and I had dinner with the fiftieth reunion class that night. The speaker's tears of gratitude, having been moved by the community response, made it all worthwhile.

I had just finished co-teaching a course on diversity issues when I got the request. Their request underscored what I was teaching. If you take the time to get to know someone no matter what the isms, you will more than likely gain respect for "the other."

For the "Big Lie" of the steal, not enough people went beyond what they heard to examine the facts. At times, we look for self-confirming data of what we want. Like the man who berated me on the phone, who represented a large group of people, that sounds familiar as the words of our elected officials and Trump whose cowardice hid behind the "mythical they" and "mythical facts."

By the way, *The Laramie Project* was well received and generated great discussion in our school community after it was performed.

Post 158. Occam's Razor

Occam's razor is not something that you use to shave. It is sometimes referred to as the Law of Parsimony. Occam's razor states that of all the facts, the simple one is usually correct. It has a wide range of applications in the disciplines of religion, physics, and medicine. It is also critical to know about this phenomenon as we go into the impeachment trial of Donald Trump, Part 2. The Articles of Impeachment have been delivered to the Senate. Occam's razor is central to living a moral life and is very important to the ethical conduct of this trial.

Occam's razor is a principle that was developed by William of Ockham, a logician and Franciscan friar who lived in the fourteenth century. He once said that "God's existence cannot be deduced by reason alone." That statement makes sense to me, but it got him into trouble with the Pope at the time.

The truth of this principle set forth by this fourteenth-century monk has proven to be true for our daily lives as well. There is a colloquialism that is a brief summary of Occam's belief. It is KISS, meaning *keep it simple, stupid*. That will make you smart.

A good many of the members of Congress are lawyers, who are politicians. My lawyer friends will reflect with me on the trait that lawyers like to hear themselves talk. They have the "gift for gab." The same is true for clergy.

I have a now-deceased friend who was a lawyer who became fabulously wealthy by winning workmen's compensation cases. That was his specialty, so one day I asked him the secret to his success. More to the point, I asked him what course in law school helped him the most in his practice. He was quick to say that it wasn't a course in law school. It was theater courses that he took as an undergraduate. I exclaimed, "What!" He indicated that he learned about using words to create a character that would influence the jury. He made his complaints come alive. He went on to counter

Occam's razor by saying the more words the better. It is easy to confuse the jury that way.

I watch CNN. I love to see a follower of Trump be interviewed by any of the anchors. The enablers of Trump ramble on. The anchor waits and then says simply, "That's not true!" The person interviewed will again use a lot of words to describe his or her case, and the anchor would simply say, "That is false!" What is remembered is what the anchor says. Not the enabler.

This is why the filibuster is the very example of a never-ending speech to have a questionable goal. I checked and the longest filibuster is twenty-four hours and eighteen minutes by South Carolina's Strom Thurmond. Its goal was to not approve the Civil Rights Act. Trump's wordy enablers come up with alternative facts to address the short responses of the CNN anchors. I also read conservative journalists, such as George Will and others, but not Fox News. They have recently reduced their news time and added opinion time which means more words without meaning except to make their point in a long-winded fashion with no short, "That's not true!" welcomed into the room.

Keep in mind the spider who elaborately weaves his web. It is an insect that depends on a lot of webbing to trap its food supply. It can't exist without the formation of an elaborate web and not a single thread. The spider would make a good mascot for the politicians. I know that some of you are thinking about another animal for a mascot that has a white stripe on their back and uses a spray of many bad smells to protect themselves. I don't want to go there.

One of the most valuable examples of how Occam's Razor operates in real life was given to me by a member of our staff at EA when he retired. He knew that I was having trouble with a particular person, as this individual could talk their way out of anything that the individual said that was not true.

I asked this person who retired what he learned that I should know to improve my leadership skills. He looked at me and said, "You know_____. The faster that person talks, the more you should worry!" It turned out to be a valuable lesson to learn.

As you watch the upcoming trial. Follow the guidance of Occam's Razor and my retired friend and successful lawyer buddy. "The more a person talks, the more we should worry!"

Post 159. The Wave

Today, January 27, 2021, is International Holocaust Remembrance Day. We can learn much from Holocaust studies on why Trump became a cult-like figure to have millions of people following him, including many enablers along the way. I am not suggesting that Trump is another Hitler or Trump's millions of followers are like the German people who followed him and approved of Hitler's policies, but I want you to understand why and how the insurrection happened.

I have attended Holocaust studies workshops which have helped me to understand why we are where we are today with Trump's followers and enablers still in his grasp and control. I want to raise the most difficult question. Why did so many normal people allow Hitler do what he did? Why have so many normal Americans who supported Trump through their votes during the election and continue to support him during the upcoming impeachment trial? Let's put aside group dynamics, lack of courage, and a quest for power and profit, and look at a phenomenon that has not come up.

There was a 1967 classroom experiment that proved how easy it was for Americans to become Nazis. I am indebted to Nina Renata Aron in *Timeline* for the details of what occurred in this experiment. I will give you a truncated version of the experiment known as the "wave."

A high school teacher, Ron Jones, in Palo Alto, California, wanted to teach his social studies students how normal people can be easily

led to follow a fearsome leader. He became very stern and introduced a new set of rules. It was fun at first. The students had to
stand to ask questions and were required to give the Nazi salute.
They adopted a slogan, "Strength Through Discipline."

Those who went along with the experiment would get an "A."
Those who refused to participate would get an "F." The experiment rules extended beyond the classroom. If someone saw you not
obeying them, they could turn you in. You never knew who would
do this to you. Rumors spread among rumors.

Jones realized after a few days that the experiment got out of hand.
He had created a monster. He announced to the students that they
should meet in the auditorium the next day as a presidential candidate would be announced. When his students arrived the next day
in the auditorium, they saw in front of them a movie screen with
nothing but static on it. He revealed to the students that they were
part of an experiment to demonstrate how fascism occurs. He then
showed them a film on the rise of Nazism in Germany.

The students expressed relief. Parents and other faculty thought
that what Jones did was terrible. Two years later his contract was
not renewed. A movie version of *The Wave* was made in 1981 for
an after-school special.

Aron states, "But as a simulation of the normalization of fascism—
the pleasure of membership, the creeping thrill of exclusion, and the
comfort of discipline and rules—the experiment was unquestionably
a success. It vividly illustrated the chilling conclusion theorist
Hannah Arendt came to at the trial of the Nazi war criminal Adolf
Eichmann, 'that most members of the SS were neither perverted
nor sadistic, but rather, terribly and terrifyingly normal.'"

That certainly couldn't happen to me, or could it? During one
Holocaust workshop that I attended, one of the workshop leaders
entered the classroom where my group was seated. She told us to
move to another room. We did. She told us when we arrived at
another room to move again to a better room. About five moves

later, someone in our group said, "What's this about? You have us moving all over the place." The leader proclaimed with a smile on her face, "Welcome to Germany!"

I wish that the movie, *The Wave,* could be shown before the impeachment trial, Part 2, begins. I am an optimist. I think we might get those seventeen votes needed if the politicians were aware of why they are doing what they are doing. This would be icing on the cake, explaining their quest for power and personal profit under an authority figure articulating the "Big Lie."

Post 160. On a Need-to-Know Basis

Gossip, rumor, and the "Big Lie" depend on telling people what they want to hear. I was part of a large school community. I said that ninety percent of my problems as the spiritual leader would go away if we could just do away with rumor and gossip. Rumor and gossip have the same dynamic of the "Big Lie." We have been focusing on who shares the rumor, gossips, or those who spread the "Big Lie" that the election was stolen. We have not been focused on those who listen.

I noticed that certain people in our school community loved to hear a juicy piece of rumor or gossip. Others would discourage people from spreading gossip or rumor to them. People knew who these people were. One of the phrases that I used in talking to or listening to others was simply, "I only want to know what can be helpful to another." Nothing else. I expressed this by indicating to as many who would listen that we should be having conversations "on a need to know basis." I said it so much that people referred to "on a need to know basis" as my middle name. I have found that this is a difficult guideline for people in any community to adhere to. I frequently said that gossip was the snake that hisses because of those two (s) in the name.

People forget that someone who shares gossip with you has declared part of their identity, meaning they would someday share gossip about you. There is a saying, author unknown, that "Don't tell me what they said about me. Tell me what you did to make them think it was OK to say it in your presence."

Women students transferring from a single-sex school to my school, which is coeducational, seemed to have a common complaint. Girls are tough on girls, in terms of listening to the lies found in rumors. This was not as evident in the Trump insurrection because of the undercurrent of "Make America Great Again for White Men." However, we do have a significant female presence supporting him.

Trump and other authoritarian leaders are not necessarily smart, so why do people listen to them in their telling of lies? Trump and others of his ilk are "dumb like a fox," meaning they have PH.D. (s) in changing a lie to truth. Most are narcissistic in nature, but people listen to Trump because it helps them to be part of something bigger than themselves. Recall that passion trumps (yes, I meant to use that word) reason. The stronger the passion, the more unreal or surreal life becomes for the listener and those outside of the manipulative orbit. I was struck by a comment of one of the women insurrectionists who proclaimed, "This is the best day of my life, along with the birth of my three children." Her children were an afterthought.

Listening to rumors or the "Big Lie" helps people sense that they belong and builds their self-esteem. These are two vital parts of our psyche and soul. We see this graphically with young people's strong connection to their cell phones. It is called FOMO or fear of missing out. It is like going to the grocery store and coming upon that item that is two for the price of one. You get self-esteem and a sense of belonging from one action of listening to rumors.

But there is another issue that Trump tapped in a brilliant toxic way. At our basic instinctual nature, we are people of the narrative. There is an old story that "God loved people so much that He created stories."

After the insurrection, the seditionists told stories of their best day and their heroics. They fist-bumped and had cocktail parties, which uplifted them all. They flooded their social media with statements, pictures, and videos that reflected the joy of their actions. Notice that, initially, they didn't think that they did anything wrong. It was like a day at the beach. When it became clear to them that what they did was wrong and there would be consequences, they removed their posts and went into hiding. The Trump narrative of "Stop the Steal" was powerful. It is heady stuff to be a revolutionary.

I saw this first-hand in the 60s when I was a student at the Berkeley Divinity School at Yale, where many of my classmates who were from affluent backgrounds took to the streets in protest, having been assured of backup money from their parents. I couldn't identify with their narrative. I was a working-class kid who knew work, study, eat, sleep, and being on my own.

One of the best examples of connecting to an underlying narrative is found in the novels of Stephen King. When asked by an interviewer why his books were so incredibly popular, he had an interesting response. "People who buy my books are the same people who slow down when passing an accident on a highway. Everybody likes to get a glimpse of blood and the scary." It strikes me that Trump and the seditionists had the same impulse.

Post 161. Rain Dog

There is the old reminder for dog lovers that 'God' spelled backwards is 'dog.' Therefore, let me begin with my Wonder Dog Sadie to unpack some reflections on the afterlife. Sadie loves to eat. At precisely 5:00 PM if I am home, she comes and finds me and sits in front of me and gives me that "haven't you forgotten something look" with her big brown eyes fixed in a stare. She doesn't arrive at 4:59 or 5:01. She arrives at 5:00. How does she know it is 5:00? I don't know any humans that can do that. I must admit that she has been slipping lately coming in earlier. One of my sons refers to her as the Rain Dog after the movie of some years ago,

Rain Man. You may recall that was a movie starring Tom Cruise as Charlie and Dustin Hoffman as Raymond, his brother who is a savant, someone who has a special brilliance. The savant's special ability was, among other things, immediately knowing the number of toothpicks that fall on the floor or computing square roots in a flash. This ability is beyond a reasonable explanation. The movie is about limitations. After many adventures on a road trip to California, Charlie finally accepts Raymond unconditionally which results in his all-abiding love for Raymond. Theories of brain research cannot completely understand the phenomenon of the special things that a savant can do.

It is beyond understanding to explain how savants do what they do because it may involve a dimension that we can't access with reason. I pointed out in an earlier post the importance of a consideration of the reality of another dimension in Abbot's book, *Flatland*, published in 1884. The book describes the transformation of a square to a cube and a circle to a sphere. We are the square and the circle before we can experience life or the afterlife as a cube or a sphere and see the world in an enhanced dimension. According to the modern theory of dimensionality called String Theory, there are at least ten dimensions. We only experience height, width, depth, and time. Six are beyond us.

This brings us to a consideration of another world, the world of heaven. What if Sartre was right in his play, *No Exit*, which was a description of hell not as a fiery place but as a room where three people created hell for one another by not meeting each other's needs. Sartre's classic line was "Hell is the others." He meant that we can make another person's life hellish here on earth.

Last evening Vicki and I watched a documentary on the life of Audrey Hepburn. I didn't know much about her. I had never seen her break out movies of *Breakfast at Tiffany's* or *Roman Holiday*. She achieved much in her life by the world's standards of fame and fortune. She lived a life that most would envy, but she was missing one thing. She desired to love and be loved after an unhappy child-hood and abandonment by her father.

What gave her the closest thing to "love" was to stop making movies and eventually move to a place in Switzerland where she could rid herself of fame and concentrate on her children. Through a chance occurrence, she was asked to be an Ambassador for UNICEF, the organization that is devoted to feeding starving children around the world. She used her fame to raise funds to feed hungry children and held them close during her many trips to the places where children were most in need. Her quiet life with no travel was transformed by helping the hungry. Recall Jesus' words regarding those in need, "When you help those in need, you have helped me." The documen-tary makes real what I believe to be the goal of each of us, some-times known and sometimes not, to be able "to love and be loved." That is what Hepburn wanted all of her life as well.

If Sartre has a point, and I think he does, that "Hell is the others." so it must be true that "Heaven must be the others." as well. Heaven or hell is right now on earth, but what about the Rain Dog. What about that dimension beyond this life and this world that we hav-en't yet experienced, curiously referred to as the afterlife or life after what we can know now?

The documentary ends in a way that caused me to think about the Rain Dog. Audrey Hepburn is on her death bed as she has stomach cancer. Her beloved son has kept a vigil. He is in a chair next to her bed. Before she dies, he said she spoke something that astounded him. She said, "There are people in the room that are waiting for me." Her son looked around. There was no one that he could see.

What is the key to open that door to leave our room of this life? I believe for me and other Christians it would be Jesus. For Jews, it would be Yahweh. For Muslims, it would be Mohammed. For the Buddhists, the Buddha. For the Hindu, the soul is reincarnated in another form. Like so many things important in life, reason can only take us so far. We have our limitations. Where reason cannot go, faith leads the way.

I don't think that God would be offended by the analogy that connects the afterlife to Hepburn or Sadie the Rain Dog. How could one not love her as Sadie is a living example of loving unconditionally as God does? It is called grace. Unlike Sadie, it took Hepburn a lifetime to find it, to love and be loved. Unlike us humans, Sadie has known it all along.

Post 162. Sports Is the Game of Lovers

January 26, 2021 was the anniversary of the death of Kobe Bryant and his daughter, Gianna, a budding basketball player who was coached by her dad. Kobe's high school was ten minutes from where my family lived on the campus of the Episcopal Academy. Kobe was highly regarded, and no one doubted that he would be a player in professional basketball. What no one knew then was that he would become one of the greatest of all time. I knew that our students would talk about him, but I cannot ever remember seeing him play. We had a "one for the ages" basketball team ourselves at our school that included Gerald Henderson and Wayne Ellington, who went on to Duke and North Carolina respectively and then to the pros. Wayne received the Most Valuable Player Award when his team won the national championship. Our team was highly ranked in the nation. Those were heady basketball times.

Our school shared many connections to Big Five Basketball at the time. Bruiser Flint, an alumnus, was the coach at Drexel. Dan Leibovitz, an alumnus, was the assistant coach at Temple. EA parents Jay Wright was at Villanova, and Fran Dunphy was at Temple, and Phil Martelli was at the Jesuit school, St. Joseph's University, right across the street from us.

However, today I want to write more about another legend, John Chaney, who died January 29, 2021 at the age of eighty-nine. Chaney is one of the most highly regarded coaches in basketball and earned the right to be called a legend. Chaney is known for what he did on the court, but there is much more to his legendary status because of who he was.

Chaney was "old school." He believed in virtues that some of our modern college athletes and coaches have forgotten. If you look at his entire life in basketball, there is an underlying theme that what he enjoyed most in life was lifting up those athletes who were in need. He had little time for spoiled players who did not put the importance of the team first and wanted to be pampered. There was a story in the press that if you were late to one of his practices that were held between 5 and 8 a.m., you would spend the entire practice running. My favorite story about him is not found in any publication, for it was told to me by our legendary basketball coach at our school, Dan Dougherty. All of these local coaches knew one another well.

As the story goes, as it was told to me, one of Chaney's heavily recruited players came to him on an early December day and said that he wasn't sure if he wanted to continue playing for Temple anymore. He wanted to skip the Christmas tournaments to think about it again. The athlete called Chaney later on in December before Christmas and indicated that he decided to come back to play at Temple. Chaney reportedly said, "I'm busy doing my Christmas shopping. Call me later." He never played for Temple again.

Dan Leibovitz knows something about basketball. Dan is now the associate commissioner of the Southeastern Conference. Remember my earlier post on Occam's razor that the simple approach will be the best. Here is another example. Dan talked about innovations in basketball. Princeton gets the award for the most innovative offense. Temple gets the award for the most innovative defense under Chaney. Dan said that Chaney was a genius. "People think of the complexity of the zone. But in basketball his genius was simplicity. We were great because of the simple things and they were non-negotiable. They were the same from the first practice to the last game."

Each one of the coaches that I have named in this post have one thing in common. They didn't coach basketball first. They first coached a player to be a better human being. The development of the character of their players was primary. Basketball was secondary. I have many stories about them, but I want to focus on Phil Martelli, who was fired in 2019 after twenty-four years as coach of the St. Joseph University's Basketball Team. He was fired after "an extensive, long-term view of the success of the team." That translates to the issue that he wasn't winning recently. He had taken the team to seven NCAA Tournaments. People at the college were shocked. Basketball communities across the nation were shocked as well. Coach K at Duke was the first to call Phil. The accolades poured in from all over the country to this one-time Coach of the Year. He was sixty-five when he was fired and is now the assistant coach of the Michigan Wolverines.

Martelli said, "I lost my way of life when I lost my job because it never was a job." He was the kind of guy "who would play you as hard as he could play in a game of one on one. He is also the kind of guy that would give you the shirt off his back."

The 2003–2004 basketball season was one for the record books. During week 16, his team was ranked No. 1 in the nation. His team made it to the Elite 8 in the NCAA Tournament. This was heady stuff for this small Roman Catholic College. It was big news in Philly. He was hounded with requests for interviews. I had a strong relationship with the Jesuit community that founded the school and was still part of the administration and faculty. That season was a David-and-Goliath story.

I don't remember which important game it was. It was probably a game related to the NCAA Tournament. I called Phil and left a message of congratulations after a game. I received a call early the next morning from Coach Martelli who had just arrived at the Philadelphia Airport with his team. He called to thank me for the call and asked if he could do anything for me. I indicated, "If you can find time in your schedule, could you come and talk to our faculty and kids in chapel about character? I will never forget his response, "What time is Chapel?" I told him. I will be stopping there on the way back from the airport. He had not been asleep at all during that night.

He talked to our school gathering in chapel about how what you do now will affect the rest of your life, whether it is sports or in your daily life. Make ethical choices now so that you can live an ethical life later. I could bring the Archbishop of Canterbury in, which I have done, but he would not get the rousing, standing ovation that Martelli got as I told the community he came to speak to them right from the airport.

Nelson Mandala said, "Sports have the power to change the world. It has the power to inspire, the power to unite people in a way that little else does. It speaks to youth in a language they understand. Sports can create hope, where there was once despair. It is more powerful than governments in breaking down racial barriers. It laughs in the face of all types of discrimination. Sports is the game of lovers." People are fooled that sports are just about a player dribbling a ball or a coach teaching his team in a huddle. Phil Martelli, John Chaney, Kobe Bryant, and other players and coaches prove it is so much more.

Post 163. Just War and Insurrection

Can we justify the behavior of Trump's followers in attempting to storm the Capitol? We have heard and seen shouts by the insurrectionists that "They are taking back their country after the steal," "Kill Nancy Pelosi and hang Michael Pence," and "Death to the members of Congress." Perhaps Trump's new lawyers will not go down that dead end street of justification. They will probably argue that the impeachment trial is unconstitutional. Trump lost his first team of lawyers because he wanted them to argue the case that the election was stolen. They refused to do so, as that would have jeopardized their lives as lawyers in the future. You can't argue something that has been proven to not be true. Trump still argues that the election is stolen. He argues this point either because it helps him to justify what happened in his mind, or he is completely delusional and irrational.

The Just War approach is the very embodiment of reason and actually could make the case for those who are prosecuting him. If anything, the Just War clause is the embodiment of reason and is a key example of an expression of Natural Law. Natural Law is the philosophical underpinning for the Roman Catholic ethic. It is a complex theory based on consistency and action. You can't choose just some parts of Natural Law to make your case and exclude other parts that don't fit your needs. Let me describe it simply.

Natural Law states that you cannot interrupt the natural continuum of life. Contraception, abortion, genetic manipulation, mercy killing, and capital punishment are components of Natural Law and the reason that the Roman Catholic Church is against *all* of these issues.

John Locke adds to this idea by saying that Natural Law is an argument against abortion, but his view is complemented by his other basic belief of the importance of "property" in our lives. It was a paradox for him. The woman's most basic property is her body. She should therefore determine what she does with it. This is the primary argument of the pro-choice advocates. When Congress was questioning Clarence Thomas about his philosophy when he was being interviewed for a position on the Supreme Court, he indicated that he was a follower of Natural Law. The interviewers were caught short because he would not indicate if he followed the Roman Catholic version or that version held by Locke with his view of the woman's body being her primary property. They couldn't push him for an answer, but they wanted to do a litmus test to see if he was a conservative (Roman Catholic view) or a liberal (Locke's view).

The same contradiction can be seen in the Just War clause. It is a matter of interpretation, but here is how it works. It is based on reason, something that our former president has in short supply. If you have taken geometry in school, it is like a geometric proof.

You start with a general principle that "Thou shall not kill." But at the end of your reasoning, you find that you must go to war and kill people. How will you justify these contradictory positions? There has to be an interim step or a "justification" for going to war that is just. Drum roll, please. Enter the Just War clause. It has many steps, but I will focus on just two ingredients that are needed to justify going to war. First, the war has to be in self-defense. Second, it has to be fought conventionally. Think of a football, basketball, or field hockey game where everyone has an equal chance of winning by might and skill, as opposed to a sneak attack or someone stealing the other team's plays. When you think of self-defense honoring the war, you have to think of World War II and not the Vietnam War with guerilla warfare and agent orange.

Was the insurrection a just war? Did it follow the guidelines of Natural Law? Trump is inconsistent. I don't know his views on some of the issues, he is definitely against abortion, but he is for capital punishment. You can't have your way on one issue and not be consistent with another. It reminds me of the inconsistent positions of McConnell, McCarthy, Hawley, and Cruz. "We are trying to respond to our people regarding the validity of the election." versus "What we really want is profit and power."

Regarding the justification of the insurrection, were the seditionists acting in self-defense? According to them, they were. They had no other way to "stop the steal." Most reasonable people wouldn't agree with that position, but some would. They also wouldn't agree that it was a level playing field for war. The Capitol police were unprepared, and the members of Congress were unarmed. Nobody likes sneak attacks. Just war doesn't sanction them. The antithesis of the Just War Clause would be the attack on Pearl Harbor and the terrorist attack on 9/11.

Was the insurrection fought conventionally? Certainly not. It was a mob against quasi-prepared police and totally unprepared people in Congress and their staff. If anything, odds were on the seditionists' side to do better than they actually did. But did they have the element of surprise? This is still up for discussion.

Come to think of it. This would make a great argument for the prosecution. No one has emphasized the cowardice of Trump and his "I will be right with you!" No one has emphasized the pure cowardice of the seditionists who somehow knew this "war" would be easy pickings. There was a no show of adequate defense. It was like "shooting fish in a barrel." That is an entirely different ethical issue! Cowardice is the one truth that describes both Trump and the rioters.

Post 164. What's in a Name?

I slightly cringed when the first Latina member of the Supreme Court, Justice Sonia Sotomayor, mispronounced Kamala Harris' name at the inauguration. Then I forgot all about it, but it was understandable that people from India probably did not. David Perdue, former Republican Senator from Georgia, repeatedly mispronounced her name like a schoolyard bully. He made fun of her. Then Tucker Carlson, who spends a great deal of time playing the victim, complained about all the focus there was about getting the pronunciation of her name correct when others should just move on to more important things. "Sticks and stones will break my bones, but names will never hurt me." is an expression to silence a name caller. It was something that I heard on the playground when I was growing up.

What's in a name? For one thing, my name is very important to me when receiving a call from certain telemarketers who ask for Mr. Squirrel. It is difficult for them to double back on that mistake. But, on a serious note, there is a great deal of importance to one's name.

We use names to show affection or a special familiarity, hence the use of a nickname, which goes back to early in the fourteenth century. It meant "an additional name." Nicknames can uplift, demean, or point to an interpretation of a name. It would be demeaning to call someone Fatty. It would be uplifting to refer to someone as Fearless Leader. We refer to our dog, Sadie, as Bubba.

Words meant much more in biblical times. For example, when one of the patriarchs of the Jewish people changed from an ordinary citizen to someone, such as the first patriarch, Abram changed his name to Abraham, which means "Father of a Nation" in Hebrew. Abraham's wife changed her name as well from Sarai to Sarah. The change of name here symbolized a change in vocation. We see this change in Saul, a persecutor of Christians, who became Paul when he changed to become an evangelist for Jesus. Israel is a name that means "he who runs with God." In some Christian baptisms, a child is named into the Christian community at the time of pouring water over a child's head and using chrism to make the sign of the cross on his or her forehead.

If names weren't so important, parents wouldn't spend so much time, and perhaps arguments, in coming up with just the right one. Perhaps it is a name handed down from generation to generation. A name becomes an inheritance of sorts.

A name can be a call as well to the moral life. I am always impressed when Joe Biden references various sayings that he quotes from his father that made a big impact on him. My father didn't speak as many sayings as President Biden's dad did. However, there is one saying that all of us can use as central to us as a guiding ethical principle. When seated on the front porch feeling the heat on a summer night, I remember him saying, "Remember that at the end of the day, your name is all that you have. Never do anything to tarnish it." For my father, that should be our ethical brand.

It is no wonder that the people in New York, and perhaps elsewhere, are trying to remove the name *Trump* from all of their buildings. His brand has been what was most important to his family for business reasons. Now the name reminds us of a legacy for corrupt behavior that they now have earned. Perhaps in the future instead of asking, "Did you lie about that?" People may be saying, "Did you Trump that, or is it true? Your name is really what people remember or forget at the end of the day. As my dad said, "Don't do anything to tarnish it.

Post 165. "Big Lie" and Big Violence

Most of us have heard the country music song "Looking for Love in All the Wrong Places." I think that Congress needs to look in all the right places in the history of totalitarian governments and dictatorships to get the right answers that they seek in the impeachment trial, Part 2.

One can measure where many in the country are in their thinking by looking at the books that Amazon has had to restock after the inauguration. One was George Orwell's *Nineteen Eighty-Four* and another was *The Origins of Totalitarianism* by Hannah Arendt. Arendt isn't a household name, although I did reference her on the post title, *The Wave*. Arendt writes in her book, *On Violence*, published in 1970, "When institutions, particularly those of government, start to break down and lose their legitimacy, they lose their power over every day conduct of citizens. So, what they do as a response to the loss of power is to incite violence. Violence floods into the loss of power rather than being an expression of it." Can you think of a better description of what went on during the insurrection on January 6? One can argue issues of constitutionality and intent until the cows come home, but history is about patterns of facts.

Arendt's theory can be summarized by the phrase, "the bigger the lie, the bigger the violence." Can you think of a bigger lie ever told to the American people than that the election was stolen? The lie is frequently mentioned, but why not ask the questions, "Is there any bigger lie ever been told to American citizens? Has there been any other insurrection as violent as that at the Capitol in history that was linked to a president losing an election? That is where looking for the love of justice is.

"The bigger the lie, the bigger the violence" is on my mind because of a television series that I am watching on Showtime. It is the story of a judge's son, Adam, who kills a teenager who is riding a motorcycle. Adam leaves the scene of the accident, making it a hit and run. He tells his father who is a judge. They intend on telling the police until they discover that the person killed is the son of a notorious crime boss. They decide to cover up the crime, because they fear retribution from the mob. They commit the big lie.

An innocent man is accused. The series, *Your Honor*, is about what happens after their big lie. Innocent people die all through the narrative, such an innocent victim's family is blown up and the innocent victim himself is brutally murdered. Extreme violence follows their big lie. There are many twists and turns. It is a gripping cautionary tale. I used movies in my ethics class that were cautionary tales. I know that if someone watched *Your Honor*, they would think twice about leaving the scene of an accident.

From an ethical perspective, the impeachment trial, Part 2, is a cautionary tale. If we see it as a "Big Lie" and "big violence," we are more likely to see it for what it is, as a call for justice. But keep another distinction in mind. It is a political trial, not a criminal trial. That is an important distinction. I am not holding my breath that justice will be served unless the Senate sees that this trial of someone who has told this "Big Lie/big violence" is an important part of history. Just think of any dictator or totalitarian regime that you have studied. Think Putin, Navalny, and Russia. Justice and love are the two pillars that hold up ethical choices. Let's look for justice in all the right places of history and ethics. I hope that Congress does.

Post 166. Shaking Hands Is an Important Ritual

The Super Bowl is this Sunday. There will be a lot of hype before, during, and after the game. There is something that should be highlighted more. It is what comes before and after the game. Before the game after the coin toss, the designated captains of the teams will shake hands with one another. After the game, the winners and losers will mill around each other on the field with embraces and shaking hands once again.

The shaking of hands is an important ritual. The history of it is something more than just sportsmanship. I have always been taught that you are thanking the other team for the *opportunity* to compete and to play the game. We have lost this primary moral action in our culture. At least some have, but perhaps not all.

Another thing that has been lost is the shaking of hands between the Democrats and the Republicans. Both are needed to have a democracy. We need a strong Democratic Party and a strong Republican Party in order to have a strong democracy. Perhaps after taking the British version of their court system as a good model for our own, we should take that phrase the "loyal opposition" from them to describe our political parties with an emphasis on the ethical value of "loyal." Here I mean the dictionary definition of *loyal*, which is "giving or showing firm and constant support or allegiance to a person or institution." This means support and allegiance of a two-party system.

We need a return to the virtue of *loyalty* and *support* for the opposition and not just our political party. Democracy implies that you need two in a two-party system. Can you imagine if either political party thought that they should thank the opposing party for the *opportunity* to have a democracy like ours where checks and balances are just as important as majority rule?

I know that Trump has attempted to buy the Buffalo Bills and the New England Patriots football teams. He would be a terrible owner.

Can you imagine him adhering to that moral maxim of Grantland Rice, the American sportswriter, that "It's not whether you win or lose, it is how you play the game?"

He has said a lot about winning in his presidential campaign. The statement that sums up his declarations about winning is "You are going to be winning so much that you can't believe it." I don't believe, from what I know about his cheating in golf, he would adopt the value of sportsmanship, which is one of the key virtues of EA. It is one of our stripes of character. Trump is confused about what winning really means. His definition of winning is "domination and humiliation." He has proven that over and over during his four years as president.

I am afraid that his attitude has rubbed off on too many coaches. I think first of Nick Saban and the Alabama football team. He beats a lot of teams by a whole lot to a very little. I have been in some games where that has happened to me when I have been on the "very little" side of the score. My team and I didn't have the feeling of losing as much as we felt humiliated and certainly dominated by our opponent who had a lot. I would like to see a return to the days when a team was ahead by enough that you know that they would win. Then they would put in anyone who had a uniform on. It gave the third stringers an opportunity to play. If you were on the winning team, you could celebrate your winning, and if you were on the losing team, you could celebrate that your loss was an opportunity to learn from what transpired on the court or field. You would feel bad that you lost, but you never felt humiliated or dominated by the opponent.

Other presidents who lost an election didn't feel humiliated or dominated, although certainly, the loss hurt. Could it be that Trump could not bear the thought of shaking President Biden's hand, which would mean saying thank you for the opportunity to run against you? His world is inhabited by enemies, not opponents. Why else would he prefer domination and humiliation?

I wish we had a little less hype before the Super Bowl and a lot more explanation for why the players would shake hands. Can you imagine how that would affect people, particularly the young people in our country, and what it means to be the "loyal opposition?" Both teams are needed or there will be no *opportunity* to play the game.

Post 167. What Would Jesus Do?

What would Jesus do? was often a phrase abbreviated to WWJD. It was particularly popular here in the United States in the late 1800s after a widely read book by Charles Sheldon entitled, *In His Steps: What Would Jesus Do* was published. It regained popularity in the '90s when people could be seen wearing bracelets inscribed with WWJD. It has fallen by the wayside. I think that it should be brought back into our culture to help Christians and others make better-informed choices.

The rubber bracelets with WWJD on them were obviously placed on people's wrists as a reminder of how Jesus would make difficult decisions that folks had to make now. This phenomenon could have an important place in our culture as getting two things for the price of one. No one can turn down "a buy one, get one free" offer in the grocery store. The bracelet would (1) remind us of Jesus' teachings or get familiar with them, and (2) would help us to employ some important research done at the University of Michigan.

A new study has been published in the *Clinical Psychological Science Journal* on an effective strategy in making good choices and helping the person maintain a calm state of mind. We wouldn't say to ourselves, "I wonder what I should do?" We would say "I wonder what Jim should do?" or "I wonder what you (meaning me) should do?" The researchers, Celia Furman, Ethan Kross, and Ashley Gearhardt, have found "distanced self-talk" to be a successful strategy in making good choices, even when it comes to choosing healthy food over junk food.

This confirms what many have been doing since the dawn of making choices. "I wonder what my dad would do with this problem?" "I wonder what my grandmother would do in this situation?" Raise the choice question in any of these ways, and avoid ever saying, "I wonder what I should do?" A simple way to express how self-distancing works is when you do something wrong, instead of saying to yourself, "Why did *I* do that?" say "Why did *you* do that?"

According to the researchers when you say "you," it is more calming and results in better decisions. Angela Duckworth who is the author of the best seller *Grit* and professor of Positive Psychology at Penn, is an advocate of this approach. Angela is a national leader in the science of psychology. I trust her advocacy of ideas. I attended a meeting with her and a dozen others at Penn on strategies for teaching grit to school students which resulted in a benefit to students who needed more resilience. What is as old as the origins of mankind has now been proven as the cutting-edge research in making good/ethical choices. Who would have thought?

There isn't research on the benefits of WWJD, but I would like to suggest that question could be an even better way for those in the Christian community to make some of our choices. The question would be, regarding this hard choice that I have to make, "What would Jesus do?" It is an ideal way to act on our faith. It removes our ego from the decision, through "distanced self-talk." It also allows our belief in Jesus to guide the answer in the same way that we asked, "What would my grandmother do?"

I remembered an image from words I read by Robert Jastrow in his book, *God and the Astronomers*. In a statement that concludes the book, he describes this relationship between science and religion best. "For the scientist the story ends like a bad dream. He has scaled the mountains of ignorance; he is about to conquer the highest peak; as he pulls himself over the final rock, he is greeted by a band of theologians who have been sitting there for centuries."

"Distanced self-talk," the cutting-edge scientific research on making good choices and WWJD. Who would have thought?

Post 168. It's A Small World After All

Have you ever wondered about how once you have experienced something or made a purchase, and you begin seeing those experiences or purchases all around you when you hadn't seen them before? They were always there, but now you are noticing them. They are on the landscape of our mind, psyche, and soul.

There are some obvious examples. One of the moments of embarrassment for women is when they attend a function, such as a gala, and another woman arrives in the same dress. You buy a car and suddenly you begin seeing that same kind of car being driven in many different places. You have a medical diagnosis. You discover that others have the same medical problem. Is this an example of great minds think alike? No, I think that it is the power of what is already there in our lives to be discovered through a desire to connect to one another. We are all aware that the world seems to get smaller and smaller through our contacts. The tune of "It's a Small World After All!" is heard deep within our being. We use the term *global village* to describe the world.

We meet someone and may experience that surprising notion that "We both know the same person" when there doesn't seem to be any reason that would be so. Perhaps the greatest example of this is found in the cultural phenomenon of the game, "Six Degrees of Separation" from Kevin Bacon. This phenomenon was started by a group of Albright College students who were watching *Footloose* in their dorm room. This game's theory was that only six or fewer connections existed between Kevin Bacon to linking anyone in Hollywood to this actor by their roles in six film titles or less. It became a game in popular culture.

This idea that started as a college game in a dorm room at Albright College was picked up by scientists to see if there were these six-degree connections among regular people with one another. In a 1969 study, Stanley Milgram and Jeffrey Travers asked a few hundred people in Nebraska and Boston to send a letter through acquaintances to a Boston stockbroker. Sixty-four letters reached the stockbroker. Of those letters that were received as letter chains that were complete, the average number of degrees of separation was 6.2.

Gardner Morse supported this conclusion in an article entitled, "The Science Behind Six Degrees," in *The Harvard Business Review* originally published in *Time Magazine* in 2003.

If this small-world hypothesis is correct, it has important implications for the nature of social networks. But Milgram's actual results were far less conclusive than most people realize. So, my colleagues and I are conducting an internet experiment to try to settle the matter. We now have over 50,000 message chains originating in 163 countries in search of eighteen targets around the world. The preliminary picture is more complicated than Milgram realized, but it looks like his main finding of six degrees is in the ballpark. Until recently, it's been hard to study this small world issue because we lacked computing power.

I don't see it as a problem. I see it as an amazing possibility. The pandemic has pointed this possibility out in a graphic manner in terms of our responsibility of caring for those in Third World countries. We have a moral, small-world mandate to assist those countries. We have a pragmatic mandate as well that if one person in one Third World country has the COVID-19 disease, we all can possibly get it. That is the reality that we learned during the AIDS crisis. We rise or fall as one.

I trust that the Biden administration will rise to acknowledge that we are one, whether it be climate change, the pandemic, or the return to the world political stage. It is a small world, and we are brothers and sisters in it. We need to start acting like that.

What about the small world that includes other races? One of the truths is that race is a social construct. Our racial differences are determined by 0.1 percent of our genetic make-up as discovered in research on the human genome. We have made the racial differences. God didn't make them when He made us.

In the *Daedalus Journal,* James Franklin Crow wrote an article entitled "Unequal by nature: a geneticist's perspective on human differences." "In February of 2001, Craig Ventnor, president of Celera Genomics, commenting on the near completion of the of the human genome project, said that 'we are all essentially identical twins.' Based on an examination of our DNA, any two human beings are 99.9 percent identical. The genetic differences between different groups of human beings are similarly minute."

When we feel that sense of that strong connection to all others and realize just how small our world is, we will call it another name. We will call it the Promised Land. Those connections are always there. We just need to see them better, like we see that new car we purchased just like the ones we see when we take our new car out for a drive. We see the ones we didn't see before because we are now "tuned in." Let's get tuned in at the global level.

Post 169. Ethics and the Impeachment Decision

It was a foregone conclusion that Trump would not be found guilty of the insurrection even before the trial began. The great underpinnings of ethics are justice and love. Justice is defined as a decision that contains truth and shows genuine concern and respect for people. Love is not the sentimental emotion with which it is often confused. It is "willing the neighbors good." It is that action that brings about putting others before yourself. It does not contain self-interest over the interest of the greater good of others.

"Let justice roll down like waters in a mighty stream" are the words of the prophet Amos. It is a good image to keep in mind.

Let's look at the key ingredients of the impeachment trial, Part 2, which made the acquittal possible by locking the door, not permitting justice and love into the Senate Chamber.

First and foremost, how many trials have the accomplices to the crime be the jurors? I noticed that this was a conclusion that Hillary Clinton highlighted as well. Keep in mind that this was not a civil or criminal crime. The prosecution of those crimes of Trump will hopefully come later. It was a political trial. If this was a criminal trial, none of these jurors would have been added to the jury list. Anyone who has served on jury duty knows that they would be rejected from serving. How could they find Trump guilty if they themselves were part of the "Big Lie?" Recall in political ethics that certain questions were moving around in the Senate Chamber that led to this miscarriage of justice. Who has the power? How do I get it? How does power get distributed throughout government in a way that benefits *both* the minority and the majority? The last question got locked out of the Senate Chamber as well.

If Trump was innocent, why did his Republican colleagues call him and indicate that he was the only person who could stop the insurrection?

How many people bring the wood and a noose to construct a structure to hang someone if this was a peaceful protest and shout, "Hang Mike Pence?"

The lawyers themselves were channeling Trump. Both Philadelphia lawyers are regarded as the Ted Cruz of the legal profession. No one likes them. We could see why in the trial. They are big on show and small on substance. Castor tried to charm his way by rambling on and saying nothing in the hope of confusing the senators. Recall he refused to prosecute Bill Cosby. I am sure that, after his opening comments, that senators were looking right and left, seeking an answer to the question, "What did he say?" Michael Vanderveen is really a "slip and fall" personal injury lawyer who uses his bullying ways to win cases where bullying and lying are the preferred methodologies. Some of their comments were cringeworthy. But there was a very important dangerous entity that was let into the Chamber. That was not Mr. President. It was Mr. Precedent.

Ethics pays a great deal of attention to precedents as law school does. What happens in the present sets a bar for making future decisions? Who could be impeached in the future after this impeachment trial? But even more dangerous are the words of Mitch McConnell. After the whole Senate voted to disregard any jurisdictional issues regarding whether the trial could proceed, he went ahead and stated that the trial was not constitutional because Trump was out of office. He completely ignored the vote of the entire Senate. Everyone in the room knew that he would not bring the Senate back from their recess to have the trial while Trump was still in office. That delay was on him. There is no neutral ground in ethics. Not to act is to act. But he added injustice to injury by claiming that his failure to bring the Senate back was the very reason that he would acquit.

Going forward means that the vote of the whole Senate is meaningless because of that precedent-setting statement. His final remarks saying Trump was guilty but couldn't be impeached are not consistent. Inconsistency in the application of the law is the greatest ethical enemy of justice. How many times did we hear, "The president is not above the law. He is like everyone else?"

There was another ethical person who was locked out of the room. It is Mr. Reasonable Person Standard. Interview twelve people who are not Democrats or Republicans, and give them the evidence. Ask them if Trump was guilty. We heard references to Thomas Paine's book, *Common Sense*. We know what their vote would be. It would be common sense. It would have been interesting to see the Senate use a secret ballot. I would bet a hefty amount that Trump would be found guilty.

The last political, ethical person locked out of the Chamber was perhaps the most important. That person is our future. We need a strong Democratic Party and a strong Republican Party without Trump to have a strong democracy. Only time will tell if future damage has been done. We now know how fragile democracy is, which is why so few make it as long as we have.

Post 170. Ash Wednesday During the Pandemic

The pandemic has not stopped churches from figuring out creative ways to give our faith communities ashes that are usually given with the sign of the cross on a person's forehead. There will be fewer services where ashes are placed on peoples' heads, but churches have figured out creative ways to honor this tradition.

Some are placing the ashes on the forehead with a cotton ball, and others are sprinkling the ashes on the heads of people. You can get ashes as "take out" at a train station. I have seen where ashes can be done by Zoom as well. Some churches are delivering ashes to those who are homebound by sending them in an envelope by mail. Others are sending a Lenten daily reminder, which includes scripture and prayers.

The Ash Wednesday service was a big deal in the school where I served as head chaplain. Students, faculty, and members of the school community could also come by the offices of the chaplains throughout the day to receive the ashes. Hundreds would stop by.

Why does it seem even more important this year than it mattered before? Remember that Ash Wednesday 2020 was one of the last moments of public expressions of our faith in our parishes or faith-based schools. It was a few weeks later that the COVID-19 virus took hold and started our time of trial in a different wilderness. This year, Ash Wednesday will help us feel a bit more normal in our daily religious deliberations, and "normal" is a desired feeling by all. This year is filled with hope for our future life. Our world has become too aware of the possibility of death that has surrounded us each and every day. We, as a world, know mortality as we have heard those Ash Wednesday words said with the administration of the ashes on foreheads as our daily mantra in our hearts and souls, "Remember that you are dust, and to dust you shall return."

Ash Wednesday and Lent are days to remember our mortality, but it is also a day and season to remember how to live. The following is a sermon that I gave to the EA community during my last Ash Wednesday service as chaplain of the school before retiring:

The season of Lent begins today on Ash Wednesday. It starts forty days of preparation for Jesus in the wilderness before He begins his earthly ministry. It is a day where we hear the words, "Remember that you are dust, and to dust you shall return," reminding us of our mortality.

It is a time marked with hardship in the wilderness experienced by Jesus and the necessity for change before He begins his earthly ministry.

One of the movies that I used in ethics class is *Before and After*, which has, as one of its themes, that your life can turn on a dime, and you never know when it is coming. You are one way one day and in a very different place on another, not necessarily bad but different.

During any change, we lose something, and we gain something else. That's the way it is. This Lent will take on new meaning for me as I go about losing my formal role as your chaplain and gaining a new chapter in my life still to be determined, but certainly, there will be more time with family. Loss and gain are the ebb and flow of life. It is the ebb and flow of Lent.

I have been doing the hard job of packing and sorting through boxes of memorabilia to get ready to move. I was surprised by some of the things that I encountered. I was slowed down by reading notes to me and reliving times in my own life and in the lives of others that changed drastically and not for the best. Yes, they were balanced out by those letters that caused me to smile and to remember sharing in the pure joy of someone's most joyous moment in life.

Lent is also a time when Jesus was constantly surprised by challenges, to be given power, to be given food and drink, all things to make his life easier.

When I was going through the boxes, I was surprised at the things that I forgot. I forgot the way that I was as a young person and not remembering that person but knowing that time empowered me. Jesus is in the wilderness in hardship but propelled forward by it.

I was going through one box when my identification badge from the steel mill where I worked as a laborer to pay for college fell out of a group of notes. My picture was encased in a one-inch by two-inch steel badge with only the words Alan Wood Steel Company, the name of the steel mill. Stamped on it was the number 368, not a name just a number. It was very much like how they identify you in prisons. What stared back at me was a kid with black frame glasses who was doing his best to communicate that he was a tough guy, flexed neck, and eyes that said, "I am not afraid of anything."

What it didn't show was a kid who was scared to death that he wouldn't be able to do the difficult jobs in conditions that would be outlawed today in the steel industry and knowing that this was the only way that I would get what I wanted—college. In ethics class, we learn, "Walls are there to show us how much we want something."

After the first ten-hour day, my father picked me up at the mill. He took one look at me and was in shock. I was black from head to toe with coal dust. I was working in the plant where they turn coal into coke to be the fuel used in the open-hearth ovens to create the steel. I just responded with "It's OK. Forget about it!"

I think that what it has taken me a lifetime to properly learn existentially (that means experience right in the moment) is that you must embrace it all—the good times and the bad—not like it all but embrace it all. Both are necessary to lose and to gain and to change.

I heard someone recently say that when you die, you will know that you have died because the faces on the angels who greet you will be those of your family members who have gone before us. That will be true for me—my mother, my father, my brother, my daughter, and so many from my EA family. That was true for Jesus. In His case, it is the face of His God and Father.

Lent for me is an existential experience to embrace it all and live it all right now. I don't think the Jesus that I know was thinking about what happened the day before or what He was going to be facing the next day. When you read the scripture, you feel that He concentrates on what is occurring right in that moment.

I recently read the faith paper of an eighth-grade student who also gave her faith paper at a middle school chapel address a few weeks back. I have her permission to share one of her thoughts with you. She knows something of joy and sorrow as she lost her mother to cancer just a few years ago. She said the following:

> I hope to live each day as if it is my last and seize the moment. Anything that we can do or say that makes us or someone else feel great, do it. We never know what is waiting around the corner. The Dalai Lama said, "There are only two days in the year that nothing can be done. One is called yesterday, and the other is called tomorrow, so today is the right

day to love, believe, do, and mostly live." My faith
has guided me so that I can move on.

She is an eighth-grade student who has embraced it all—
wise beyond her years. She lives from a deeper spot,
experiencing more than most experience in a lifetime. She
is what some would call an "old soul." I hope that we can all
move through Lent with her wisdom attached to our souls.

Because "Remember, you are dust, and to dust you
shall return."

Post 171. Does Peer Pressure Exist?

One of the things that I told my ethics classes on the first day of the
course was that they would be working on two important questions.
One question is, "Why do I do what I do?" There is a corollary to
that question that we examine as well, "Why do people in groups
do what they do?" Understanding relationships is critical to understanding behavior. Ethical and unethical decisions do not occur in
a vacuum. Not to decide to do something is to make an ethical or
unethical decision. If you decide to walk by a fellow student who
is in obvious need, you have made an important unethical choice.

As I noted in an earlier post, it is important to understand the power
of *philia* or behavior among friends, and the importance of the "buy
one, get one free" deal with friends where you get two important
aspects of relationships at the same time. The result of *philia* or
the power of group dynamics is that you get two emotional foods
that human nature yearns for: self-esteem and a sense of belonging.

When we apply group dynamics or philia to the insurrection, we
can see these dynamics in action. What you can't do on your own,
you can do in a group, sharing the same concern. Life is a two-
edged sword. Recall *philia* makes good-intentioned people better
and bad-intentioned people worse. There is power in numbers.

Would the insurrection have occurred with just a few people? I doubt it. But like all things having two sides, the other side of *philia* is the basis of such enterprises as AA and cancer support groups. "Alone, I may feel I am not worthy, but in a group, I feel I am magnificent." It is the same dynamic that when your favorite sports team loses; you feel the loss to be very personal and vice versa when your team wins. Your identity is merged with the team. Just listen to Philadelphia Eagles talk radio after a game to have this observation confirmed.

All groups have a moral or immoral code. It is a value judgment, but any reasonable person would say that the insurrection was coming from an immoral place. The flip side of that aspect is that the seditionists thought they were being patriotic, following the bidding of their president. They believed what they were doing was patriotic and therefore good.

They certainly felt that their self-esteem was up as a result of their self-perceived moral action, and it certainly was a powerful feeling to be part of a group with a stated moral goal, "Stop the Steal." Why else would a woman who was interviewed say, "This is the best day of my life, along with when my children were born." They felt empowered as well by pushing anyone who disagreed with them "out" so that they could feel "in." That dynamic is the glue that holds groups together and is the root of most "isms."

Philia always says, "We," so that anyone else becomes "They." Negative *storge* or behavior seeks scapegoats. In the case of the insurrection, it was the Democrats and Michael Pence. For the KKK, it is black people.

But there is one aspect of all of this that needs to be addressed. One of the great things about teaching ethics to young people is that they are brutally honest. My job was to create a classroom environment where they felt safe to do so. When teaching *philia* or group dynamics to classes, I would look at them and see some puzzled looks on their faces. They agreed that all of the above is true, but they had another observation. One student volunteered the dilemma, adding a new twist to be addressed. He said, "Rev., peer pressure are the two best words in the English language. If we get caught drinking or any other behavior that our parents see as wrong, we just say, 'Peer pressure, Mom! I wouldn't have done it otherwise." They all nod in agreement. The hard question is, "Did peer pressure counter my idea of the dynamics of groups?"

I don't think so! When students use that expression, "peer pressure," they are quick to indicate that they knew what they were doing was wrong. The seditionists didn't think what they were doing was wrong. They operated in the light of day. The students agreed with this "wrongful action" point of view. Their drinking or wrongful acts were always done in secret. In ethics, we refer to that as the private domain as opposed to the public domain of the location of the insurrection for all to see.

There is one other aspect of the insurrection that has not been addressed by anything that I have seen in the media. Clearly, our media types have not worked closely with kids who are a clear microcosm of adult behavior. This goes to the issue of I/It relationships based on what you can get from another in a transaction and I/Thou relationships where you respect the other person for who they are. I/It relationships have a quid pro quo. I/Thou relationships don't.

The dominant attitude in the media is that Trump, being the great transactional guy that he is, used these people to advance his personal agenda. That is true! But life is a two-edged sword. The organized seditionists that were present such as the Proud Boys, Oath Keepers, and QAnon were also using him. It was an I/It relationship made in hell. Trump was a dream. All that one had to do was to "love" him bringing all of his narcissism out to influence his actions, and they got exactly what they wanted. It was a marriage made in hell. He was the perfect, maybe the only, guy who could bring about their agenda. Their dream and his dream became our nightmare.

I think that I should recommend my former ethics students to this newly formed Commission on the Insurrection. One of the great things about kids is that they can spot a phony a mile away, and they would make the best debaters there are, as they are quick to see the weakness and strength in any argument. My only hesitation is there is nothing political about them. They tell you straight out how they see things. If the Commission accepted this quality, they could get to any truth.

Post 172. Justice, Kindness, and Humility

Each year, our school would gather ideas from everyone in the school community regarding a theme for the next academic year. The key question that was behind someone choosing their nomination for the theme was to answer the question, "What does our community need to have as a focus for conversation and chapel addresses during the next academic year?" The theme offered guidelines for our community-wide discussions. It was student run. The process ended with a meeting of the lower school, middle school, and upper school student spiritual leaders gathering together to come up with the final theme recommendation. All the student leaders were involved in this decision, and they never failed to provide one that was taken to heart by the school community.

One year, our theme was from the book of Micah 6:8, "He has told you, O man, what is good and what does the Lord require of you, to do justice and love kindness and walk humbly with your God?"

We live in hyper-partisan days where this central guideline of Micah has been forgotten by most. These are the elements of justice, kindness, and humility. We all witnessed the case presentation of the house managers and Castor, Vanderveen, and Schoen for the defense. I read a recent statement of what was going on with Trump's team behind the scenes. There was jockeying for power among the three, strong disagreements where people quit only to come back to the defense team and a president who threw in ideas of how he wanted them to proceed. It struck me that there were bruised egos all around. When Castor and Vanderveen returned to Philly, they were not welcomed back as they thought they might be. Protestors and threats were what they received. Vanderveen had to hire a security firm. Schoen wrote a letter of apology to the people of Philadelphia for things that he said. Trump declared victory with a less-than-humble declaration of being acquitted of another witch hunt.

Vanderveen concluded his thoughts with a statement that "I never want to be involved in the politics of this country again as perverted as it has become." I think that Gandhi may have made a stronger statement when he said, "An eye for an eye makes the whole world blind."

There were a lot of complaints and not a lot of compromises after the trial. When I was head chaplain at EA, some of my colleagues referred to me as the complaint department. Someone would call when they felt that another avenue had closed. My agenda was to get them back to that avenue where they felt cut off. One parent called and complained that another parent had a "strong personality." I responded quickly that "all my parents have strong personalities." The woman who called broke into laughter. The same can be said about the strong personalities of politicians.

You can have a strong personality as we saw in the impeachment trial, Part 2, but still seek justice and be kind and humble. If our Philly lawyers had a similar reaction to how badly they were treated, we need to have politics "as unusual" to take the place of conflict. Unfortunately, a campaign for governor of Utah didn't get enough notice in the national bipartisan attacks. Fourteen days before the election, Republican Spencer Cox and Democrat Chris Peterson, candidates for the office of governor, decided on campaigning in an "unusual" way. They did joint campaign ads. "We can debate without degrading each other," Peterson said. "We can disagree without hating each other," said Cox. "Win or lose, we will work together. Let's show the country there is a better way," said Peterson. These two showed that it can be done. I would like to think that they read Micah 6:8, for their whole approach was based on justice, kindness, and humility.

When I began my ethics course each term, I indicated to the students that there would be no *ad hominem* (against the person) attacks. They could fiercely debate a topic but never attack the person who was making a point. If someone else was talking, no one else could interrupt. I told them that this would be "civil discourse." Our national culture of conflict made this difficult for the first few days, but once they felt safe which was part of my job, they quickly got into this "Micah pattern." They called the course "full-contact ethics." Once you entered the classroom, you couldn't sit back and not voice an opinion. The class goal was to have every person speak at least once during each class in these usually large, diverse classes. Mentioning anyone by name in or outside the class was forbidden unless they were a public figure.

They sought justice in the issues, were kind to one another, and were humble in their approach to some difficult topics. When they evaluated me and the course at the end of the term, it was not unusual for me to read, "I never knew that so many people could have so many different views where we could talk about our own opinions, feeling safe to do so."

Kids love to argue. If they can walk the path with Micah and the Utah candidates, maybe Washington can do the same. Politicians need to channel Micah and change their ways. Both candidates for the governor of Utah said, "It's time to reforge a national commitment to decency and our democratic Republic." Seventy-four percent of Americans said they want a return to civility.

Post 173. Racism and the Chain

As my oldest son put it on an occasion. "My dad has run when he is well and when he is sick. He runs when it is bad weather or good weather, including when it is too hot or too cold." That is true. Everybody is paying a price. Is It worth it? For me, I love to run.

If you read my book, *The Times of My Life*, it would be clear why running is important to me. Over the years I have injured many body parts from the top of my head to my feet.

I have a terrific physical therapist, Michael Quintans, who has helped me recover after two spine surgeries and two total knee replacements and other running challenges. I saw him recently, and I was reminded of something that is a truth in physical therapy. The injury is often not where the pain is, but it is the pain that drives people into his practice. He talks about the chain. If you think you have injured your hamstring, it may be based on the lower back and not the hamstring. You have to find the source of the pain and work from there.

I think this is true for racism and the current protests. We see the pain that has led to the marches. We must go down the chain to identify those parts that have led us to this moment. It starts with the evil of slavery and blends into a myriad of causes such as overt situations of inequality, such as funding for urban schools, being in the back of the bus, bathrooms for colored and separate ones for white, and the various micro-aggressions where black people feel the burden for speaking not only for themselves but their race. There are so many examples that I wouldn't know where to end.

Although less than 0.10 percent of our genetic material determines skin color, the color of one's skin has been ninety-nine percent–plus painful for people with black skin. Although it is difficult for white people to acknowledge this truth, as we move up and down the chain, let us listen to our black brothers and sisters' stories of what it is like to be them. Those of us who have good intentions need to be reminded that "the way to hell is paved with good intentions" or a phrase in diversity work referred to as the "eye of the beholder." It doesn't matter what we intend. What is important is how it is received.

Post 174. Move and Waco

Vicki and I finished watching the Netflix series, *Waco*, at the end of last week. It is a recounting of the conflict and showdown between the Branch Davidian religious sect led by David Koresh living in a compound in Waco, Texas, and the government. The movie details the confrontation between the ATF (alcohol, tobacco, and firearms) and the FBI and the Branch Davidians. Blame was placed on the FBI and ATF for the deaths of children and adults in the attack. The press is ambiguous regarding who started the confrontation. People on both sides of the conflict died.

It is ironic that today is the thirty-fifth anniversary of the conflict between first responders, including police and firefighters, and MOVE, a Black Liberation sect that refused to come out of their compound on Osage Avenue in Philadelphia. Law enforcement acted in response to complaints by neighbors that MOVE was "disturbing the peace" in various ways. People on both sides of the conflict died, including five children. Mayor Wilson Goode, the first African American to hold that office in Philadelphia, gave the order for the police to use force to remove MOVE members from the home. Later he would shoulder the responsibility for the outcome, but he indicated that he was not aware of exactly how that decision would be carried out. He expected one thing and got another. He has publicly apologized for the deaths and neighborhood devastation that ensued. Houses on the block went up in flames after a helicopter dropped a bomb on the home of the MOVE members.

Since Osage Avenue is near the Merion Campus of the Episcopal Academy where we lived at the time, we saw flames and smoke reaching the sky for several days after sixty-one homes burned to the ground.

We felt this terrible event was "in our faces." A piece of irony was that Wilson Goode spoke to the EA students and faculty in chapel the week before the MOVE event occurred. Wilson, at that time, was highly regarded and was being encouraged to consider running for a higher office. There was talk of a possible presidential candidacy.

I remember his address as if it was yesterday. He had a few "handlers" who accompanied him to chapel. He was born into a family of tenant farmers in Seaboard, North Carolina. He spoke about the hard road he traveled before becoming mayor of the city. Then he hit his theme, "The way up is hard and difficult. The way down could be the result of one bad decision." The MOVE event was just one week later. His political fortunes changed, but he continued his road up in a different way. He became a minister, a professor at Eastern University, and started a program to help children of convicts. We were together socially years after the MOVE event. He remembered me, and I remembered his powerful words to our school community, important words for all to remember a cautionary tale. Waco and MOVE contain similar themes clouded with ambiguity.

Post 175. Rocky, Downton Abby, The West Wing, and You

What do stories seen in movies and on television such as Rocky, Downton Abbey, and *The West Wing* have in common? The answer can be found in research done by Bob Waxler, English professor at the University of Massachusetts-Dartmouth. He designed a program called Changing Lives that involved recruiting hardened convicts to join reading groups.

After reading various stories, such as Hemingway's *The Old Man and the Sea*, the prisoners met in groups for discussion. Then insights began to surface. *The Old Man and the Sea* is the story about a fisherman, Santiago, who perseveres after returning home empty-handed from three months of fishing. A prisoner said, "This story is really my story." Similar insights were repeated over and over by these hardened criminals who read different books. They saw themselves in the literature. For many people, this approach is working. Changing lives this way costs $500 per person. Jail time costs $30,000 per convict per year. Changing lives causes greater empathy for others and respect for human beings. This approach also revealed that underneath everyone is a flawed person who still deserves dignity (Jamil Zaki, *The War for Kindness*).

The movies and television shows mentioned above are stories in which we see ourselves. Comeback kid movies, such as *Rocky,* get us in touch in a deep way with our own comeback stories, no matter how large or small. *Downton Abbey* describes a way of life that few of us could connect to, yet it is a story of a common aspect of humanity, that money doesn't buy happiness. In *The West Wing*, we can reflect on the hard decisions that we have made as we experience the daily decisions of a president and his staff. We see as well the intrigue in our own lives in the moment-by-moment intrigue of Washington politics.

Christians and Jews look for their story in the biblical record while Muslims look to the Koran. "This story is really my story."

Pick your favorite story or movie/TV show, and I will bet that somewhere within it is a situation or person who reflects your personal story. It touches you at a personal level that empowers you because a connection is made.

I have gotten a lot of feedback from my memoir, *The Times of My Life*. In two recent phone calls, both people said the same thing. "Jim, I can see myself in your book!" My response to both was, "Great because the book really isn't about me. It is about you."

Post 176. For Whom the Bell Tolls

Britannia Insula, which translates to "Britain is an Island," is the very first phrase that I learned in Latin class many years ago. John Donne, the English poet, wrote the familiar words in 1624 in his *Devotions*, "No man is an island entire of itself. Every man is a piece of the continent, a part of the main." Most people are familiar with this statement, but few know how his words continue after those. "If a clod be washed away to the sea, Europe is less, as well as if a promontory were, as well as if a manor of thy friend's or of thine own were, any man's death diminishes me, because I am involved in mankind, and therefore never send to know for whom the bell tolls; it tolls for thee."

That last phrase, "For whom the bell tolls; it tolls for thee," could be a theme for Ash Wednesday and Lent. The tolling bell is a reference to the tolling of a church bell, announcing the death of someone. Recall that we began the Lenten season with the reminder of our mortality. Donne's phrase could be a substitute for, "You are dust, and to dust you shall return." The passage is also meant to underscore the connectedness of all people. When one of us dies, we each feel a bit of ourselves dying as well. Violence will never cease until all of us commit ourselves to a nonviolent world.

Ernest Hemingway chose the phrase "For Whom the Bell Tolls" as the title to one of his most poignant and popular books that was published in 1940 about the Spanish Civil War. He wanted those phrases, "For whom the bell tolls," and "No man is an island," as themes that he hoped would become rather commonplace. He wanted to establish solidarity with the allies who were fighting the fascists. Donne is really working on answering the biblical question, "Who is my neighbor?" His answer is that all humankind is our neighbor.

What does the above have to do with the power catastrophe in Texas where people have been without electricity, water, food, and warmth? As they examine what happened, they may want to channel some of the thoughts of John Donne and leave their island mentality. On top of this, they received power bills for thousands of dollars amid this crisis. The political officials asked the federal government for assistance. The Biden administration has provided all sorts of aid in response to their request, even though the governor tried to blame the whole thing on renewable energy.

But hey, it's Texas. The great state that has given us the most hated man in Congress, Ted Cruz, who fled town to Mexico and threw his children under the bus, blaming them for wanting a trip to the warmth of Mexico. He returned to Texas when he was caught. His children's school had written all parents, telling them not to travel because of the pandemic. He broke that rule, as well, along with shirking his responsibility to be on the ground with his people. The school will be requiring his children to quarantine for seven to ten days. The parents in the school have applied pressure to make sure that happens. Cruz was only thinking about himself. That's a lesson for all the Texans to learn who acted like Cruz.

The ethical lesson here is rather obvious. It is a cautionary tale. I have many friends in Texas who don't buy into the supersized ego of how things are bigger and better than in any other state. We have all heard the jokes and seen the T-shirts with maps of the USA with Texas taking up most of the country with the rest of us pushed to an insignificant corner.

Let's go back to the very beginning of the Texas power system, ERCOT. Texas decided not to get involved with the rest of the nation because they didn't want any of the national regulations. ERCOT guaranteed that they would always have power and lower electric bills. Boy, that decision has come back to haunt the residents. You don't hear much about the root cause on the news. In essence, they weren't ready for low temperatures.

I am aware of a businessman who worked for a year to set up a program in Texas, with the condition that it would be part of a national enterprise. After a year's work on the ground, the board of directors of the Texas part of the company indicated they didn't want to contribute to a national initiative. They only wanted to just serve the people of Texas.

We all need to have pride in our state, but this cautionary tale of the loss of power in Texas reminds us all that we live and die as one nation. That tolling bell during Lent reminds us of what should be commonplace in our souls that we share a common mortality, as well as a common humanity connected to one another. That is the real power! It's also our hope to curtail climate change.

Post 177. Consent with a Twist

Al Vernacchio, a sex education teacher at the Friends Central School outside of Philadelphia, has gotten a good deal of press regarding a $250,000 grant from the Ford Foundation. He and the school received the funds to develop a sex education program around the ethical issue of consent. One of the articles that I read about his proposal stated, "Vernacchio believes the notion of consent is something that's required whenever we interact with another person's property, body, or reputation, and that by normalizing the idea of gaining permission, it'll feel familiar when students discuss its role regarding sexual interaction." He is doing the opposite of the dictum, "It is easier to ask for forgiveness than it is for permission." In essence, he wants consent based on the normal social fabric of polite society in which asking for permission has fallen by the wayside. Our parents and grandparents would say we need better manners.

When I first met Vicki Squire, I was impressed by the cultural norms that she had received as a daughter of the South. Please, thank you, yes ma'am, no ma'am, yes sir, no sir, and excuse me were quite natural in her everyday exchanges. She had learned this approach from friends, family, and school. Somehow, her thick southern accent added to the proper nature of her conversation.

Culture shapes honorable conversation. You hear the same kind of respect coming from those in the military as well. Honor codes in schools have made cheating less likely later on in a student's life.

I think that Mr. Vernacchio is onto something important. When I think of consent, I think of the necessity for consent before medical procedures after the horrible misuses of lack of consent in various medical experimentation that was done without patients knowing the possible side effects. Think of the Tuskegee Project where black men were infected with syphilis and then watched how they progressed through the disease process. That was sponsored by the federal government.

Vernacchio's proposal for the grant was a brilliant piece of thinking. As a sex educator, he was thinking about sexual permission by one of the partners is essential. But he took it a step further. Consent and permission at the sexual level need to have the cultural backing of asking consent and permission in other areas that are not as emotionally laden. We live in a culture where we do not ask for permission enough in everyday life so how can we believe that consent and permission would work in the heat of the moment in sexual relationships. How many times do we begin a question with, "May I ...?

We "borrow" things from people with little thought of asking. Gone are the days when that last piece of pie was secured by anyone saying, "May I have that piece, or does someone else want it?" Where a lack of permission is moving into the legal domain are issues related to social media. We are in the age of the retweet, and too often, permission to do so is not raised. Facebook has taken seriously this need for consent or permission to send posts forward by having a share option on its public domain but not on its private domain.

Consent became a very important part of my life as a priest and counselor. I indicated to people who came to see me for help that I would always ask their consent to share the content of our exchanges with others before I would do so. In most situations, this was key to developing trust in our relationship. If we had this standard in our everyday lives, it would go a long way to stop the rumor mill and gossip. Consent and permission as part of our everyday exchanges would make our world a better place.

Just as honor codes created the environment for trust in high-stakes military operations, asking consent more as a cultural norm will assist in making sexual relationships more responsible as well. You don't want to be uncomfortable with issues of consent and permission in a potential sexual experience if you have not had consent in your daily experience. "Yes" or "No" shouldn't be your first experience of giving or receiving consent from another person that you care about for sex is a high-stakes emotional act.

Post 178. The Ethics and Social Nature of the Phone Call

Please listen carefully, as our menu options have changed. Your call is important to us. This call is being recorded for quality and training purposes.

I had to choose a surgeon for a procedure a few months ago. The surgeon, who was referred to me by a physician who I trust, was highly regarded in her field. Something else entered into my choice. When I called her office, I was put through directly to one of her staff. I chose to use her expertise based on something that never entered my mind at the time. I had direct access to her. That was just as important to me as her medical expertise and skill as a surgeon.

Access is important to me. I have a twenty-four-hour rule. I served in a large school community. If someone emailed me or called, I tried to get back to that individual within twenty-four hours. This was very important to the people who contacted me, so what was important to them became important to me.

One of the things that was an adjustment for me when I retired was that people who didn't know much about me didn't get back to me in a timely fashion. I was use to everyone getting back to me very quickly when I would call or email. I was spoiled. I had to adjust in terms of the reverse of previous access issues. One day when I called a surgeon, as chaplain of a school, I assumed he was in his office. He said that he was just finishing up a surgical procedure and had his resident close. I was shocked. I told him to get back in there. He said the resident is handling it. Then he said, "Rev, everybody knows that you never call about the weather." To this day I am not good about chit chat. I am all business, but I am trying to "learn" to make casual conversation. That sounds strange but true.

Access is still one of the things that still informs a lot of my decisions today. I tell people that I am quirky. Getting back to me in a timely fashion is important. It is now part of my DNA.

The three answering machine responses listed following the title of this post are handled by businesses apart from who you are calling. That is why they all sound the same, but they say something important about conversational style. If you add the word "please" to any request, it is better received by anyone who is on the receiving end of what you want or need. It softens conversation. It also reflects good manners.

They legally can record your phone call if you stay on the line, as the law reads that only one person, in this case you, agrees to be recorded. It is required that banks record your phone call. If you harass a person on the phone, you are in ethical gray land, depending on the nature of the harassment if it is recorded.

The message that describes how important the call is to the company or person receiving the call touches on my issue, which is also universal. One doesn't make a random call. Calls have a purpose or why make them even if it is to have a casual conversation to connect with someone?

Access is tricky. From an ethical perspective, you should be aware of how important it is to you and in what circumstances or with what person. People who take 911 calls are the embodiment of all the good aspects of a call, whether it be recorded, important, or the fact that there may not be time to say "please" because of the urgency of the calls.

There is a gender issue here as well. There are some generalizations about conversational style among men and women. Deborah Tannen, a linguist and conversational style authority, supports the notion that women talk more than men, particularly on the phone. Men talk to get things done. Women talk to make an emotional connection. Men talk to preserve their independence and to gain social status. When I raised these characteristics in ethics class, both the guys and girls agreed wholeheartedly that the above characteristics were true. However, there is a growing number of research articles that disagree with the above premises. They emphasize that these descriptions perpetuate a stereotype. These studies indicated that this generalization is unfortunate because they encourage these behaviors to continue.

Two observations that support and do not support the above generalizations: I knew a football coach, a manly man, who would have half-hour conversations with those dreaded people who make nuisance calls about products that we should want. I also have a woman friend who thinks of things that she is experiencing during her day so that she has topics to bring up at the dinner table with her husband. Otherwise, there would be silence.

When you think about it, those three answering machine statements are about as gender neutral as you could get. It is because men and women both desire easy access to a phone conversation regarding what is important to them.

Post 179. Lex Talionis, Hammurabi's Code, and Justice for Jamal Khashoggi

The Biden administration revealed that an intelligence department report confirmed that Saudi Arabia's Crown Prince Mohammed Bin Salman had approved the operation to kill and mutilate the *Washington Post* reporter, Jamal Khashoggi. President Trump knew of the report for two years but did nothing to act on it. The Biden administration will issue no sanctions against the Crown Prince but will "recalibrate" the Saudi/US relationship. They chose an interesting word, *recalibrate*, to define any actions again the prince. Recalibrate means to "make *small* changes to an instrument so that it measures more accurately." That action does not coincide with Joe Biden's response to a question about justice for Khashoggi's death that he was asked during a debate. He indicated a strong response was necessary to hold the crown prince accountable.

Let's shine the light of ethics on this decision. We need to simply go to two historic codes of law and ethics, one biblical and one based on the high culture of Babylon in 450 BC. *Lex Talionis* appears in Genesis 9:6, "Whoever sheds human blood, by humans shall their blood be shed, for in the image of God has God made mankind." This has sometimes been misinterpreted as an "eye for an eye" or get revenge. Its actual meaning was meant to honor the sanctity of life and that "the punishment should fit the crime," which guarded against too little or too much punishment as descriptive of justice. St. Paul makes clear in Romans 12:19 "Do not pay anyone evil for evil. Do not take revenge." So, the issue here is justice, not revenge.

Woven into this decision to have the punishment fit the crime is the issue of whether the decision will produce a moral outcome. Utilitarianism would say that the decision must be the "greatest good for the greatest number." This could be part of what was guiding both Trump and Biden's decision to do little, as doing more had the possibility of causing harm to the political relationship between the Saudis and the US. But part of Utilitarian theory stresses the importance that choices must have consequences. Hence, this theory is sometimes referred to as Consequentialism.

Hammurabi's Code is one of the first codes of law. He states in its prologue that he wants "to make justice *visible* in the land, to destroy the wicked person and the evildoer, that the *strong may not injure the weak.*"

Let's pretend for the moment that President Biden has read this post to this point. Here are two additional ethical points that nail down the decision to do more with a visible response to the crown prince's action in addition to what is above.

Context is a big shaper of all ethical decisions. Let's change the characters and context. What if the crown prince approved the killing and dismembering of a senator or a vice president? Would our response change? You betcha! Our decision should be based on how highly we value peoples' lives over what power the crown prince may have. This was Hammurabi's point to level the playing field for the weak and the strong. They should play out this decision with a new character inserted in the decision who is thought to be stronger or, dare I say, more important.

We are all paying a price? What price are we paying in this decision? Is it preparing us to love and do justice? A major part of the reason that Biden was elected was his high moral standards. Remember his statement about people who worked for him? One inappropriate comment against a colleague, and you are gone.

In ethics, this brings us to where cost/risk/benefit analysis enters as a final but important thought. Will we "recalibrate" in a small way because of the possible loss in the transactional relationship that we have with the Saudis? Will we get more by leaving this alone as Trump did but add a small gesture in our response? Will we do something that shows that might doesn't make right? Will we show in "big" action that every human life is of great value? Remember Khashoggi was a *Washington Post* journalist. We have spent four years listening to how journalists were an enemy of the people. The prince knew what he was doing with the Trump administration. Journalists weren't worth much in Trump's mind, so killing one wouldn't get much of a response except if he was from *Fox and Friends*. The world is watching. Journalists are watching!

I hope the secretary of state and President Biden know what Hammurabi, *Lex Talionis*, and St. Paul, would advise.

Post 180. The United States vs. Billie Holiday

The United States vs. Billie Holiday is a biopic that was recently released and reviewed on NPR. The movie is a fictionalized version of the real-life story of the FBI pursuing Billie Holiday for drug abuse. Billie Holiday lived during the time of J. Edgar Hoover's leadership of the FBI. Billie Holiday was a drug user. The basis of the story, however, is that the FBI framed Billie Holiday, one of the greatest jazz singers of all time, so that they could stop her singing a controversial song called "Strange Fruit," which is a thinly disguised song that describes lynching.

Billie Holiday was twenty-three at the time she sang "Strange Fruit" for the first time to close her performance at New York's Cafe Society. The song is mournful as it describes the lynching of black people in the Jim Crow South. She created the metaphor that the black bodies of those lynched were like "fruit hanging from the poplar trees."

She sang, "the bulging eyes and twisted mouths slowly." She poured her soul into the lyrics such as, "Scent of magnolias sweet and fresh. Then the sudden smell of burning flesh." "Strange fruit" is the theme that runs through the movie. She was one of the most popular singers of the time. The FBI refused to give her a license to sing in certain places and had a campaign to silence her because she insisted on singing that song that the FBI thought just stirred up trouble. Holiday died at the age of forty-four from liver disease. Holiday's life was rough, and so is the movie, as well, so I would not have children in the room if you choose to watch it.

Like an emotion, the more you suppress it, the more it grows. "Strange Fruit" had a resurgence in popularity during the Civil Rights Movement. *Time Magazine* gave it the distinction of being the "song of the century" in 1999. It was recognized for its importance to history and culture by the Library of Congress.

The movie is a gut punch to racism, but I wasn't prepared for what appeared at the very end of the movie as the credits were rolling. The credits stopped and a statement appeared on the screen, "The Emmett Till Anti-Lynching Act has still not passed in the Senate in the 2020 vote" (Emmett Till was the fourteen-year-old black boy who was tortured and killed in 1955 in Mississippi.).

So far, 3,446 black people and 1,297 white people have been lynched. Isabel Wilkerson in her book, *Caste*, describes the additional damage done to black people because lynching was used to create fear in African Americans. The fear was based on the fact that you could be lynched for the smallest of perceived offenses. It was not unusual for a lynching to be public, to have children brought to them as a public event, and to have bodies burnt in front of the crowd. Lynching caused the Great Migration out of the South to the North and West, which Wilkerson writes about in her book, *The Warmth of Other Suns*.

I couldn't understand why the bill was not passed and how I missed any news about it. I checked. In essence, ironically, the bill was being decided upon during the Black Lives Matter movement this past summer and the accompanying protests. Our nation was also in the midst of the pandemic.

The New York Times headline read "Frustration and Fury as Rand Paul Holds Up Anti-Lynching Bill in Senate." Nicholas Fandos wrote on June 5, 2020, "Mr. Paul argued that the lynching bill was sloppily written and could lead to yet another injustice, excessive sentencing for minor infractions, unless it was revised." The *Times* article concluded with words from Senator Booker. "The frustrating thing for me is that at a time this country hungers for commonsense racial reconciliation, an acknowledgment of our past, and looking forward to a better future, this will be one of the sad days where that possibility was halted." One person held it up. Paul is not my favorite person. He oozes privilege in moments when he went swimming in the congressional swimming pool when he had the COVID-19 virus and how he chose to not wear a mask during the approval vote to elect Joe Biden president. If you are above the law, you think you are privileged!

The Republican Party is now Trump's party. His actions on January 6 changed only a few thousand minds. Millions are still enthusiastic about him. We need a strong two-party system for our democracy to thrive. Regarding the Black Lives Matter movement, how long will Blacks be able to match their enormous amount of grit and resilience with the quality of patience. Make no mistake about it, we are where we are as a nation because we seem to be having a significant increase in white supremacy and now even more bias against Chinese Americans. Think of it. One man, Rand Paul, stopped the anti-lynching bill, and one man, Donald Trump, has divided the Republican Party.

Perhaps it is time to start singing that "Strange Fruit" tune again by someone too popular to stop her voice from proclaiming the truth. Think Beyonce.

Post 181. Say It Isn't So! Seuss and Cuomo Go Down!

Say it isn't so. Today on Dr. Seuss' birthday, six of his books have been discontinued by Seuss Enterprises for their racial insensitivity. They have been recognized for what they are, and the books have been removed from publication. They consulted with educators to come up with this response. It was a functional approach. It didn't strike me that they have a dog in this fight. In fact, it may make their overall sales better. *No excuses.*

As the fates would have it, none of the six books were read to my children, so I was mystified at first when I heard the breaking news. Our staple reading list contained *Green Eggs and Ham, Oh, The Places We Will Go,* and *The Grinch.* Immediately, when this news was released, Amazon noted that the six books were flying off their shelves. Some were getting quite a price for them.

When they were written in the 50s, it was another time and another age. They were not appropriate then and they're not appropriate now. *No excuses.* Of course, Fox News is having a fit and accusing all of the people who subscribe to this view as yet another example of cancel culture.

Understanding that Dr. Seuss wrote the books during another time helps us to "get it," but we are living now in a different culture, and we must make the adjustments that Seuss Enterprises has made. I gather that Dr. Seuss himself made some changes to the texts during our changing culture. This was a business decision. *No excuses.*

Today we heard that a third woman has come forward to accuse Governor Cuomo of sexual harassment. There is a difference between his response and that of Seuss Enterprises.

His excuse was he was misunderstood. I should make it known that I was a big fan of Andrew Cuomo. I thought that he was providing a model of leadership, which was more heightened in my awareness because of the non-response of Donald Trump. I don't think that I was alone in that feeling. I didn't know his history of bullying tactics, but I admired his grit in handling the COVID-19 crisis. I did have some of my more conservative friends even back in the fall, who questioned his ethics regarding his statistics on deaths in nursing homes.

As I write this post, I am not sure of the political outcome of his crisis, but I am sure of the response from his office—excuses. I am also sure that there will be pundits like John Oliver who are thrilled that this has occurred. I want to focus on four things right now since these two stories were important breaking news today. These four things are *excuses, no excuses, functionalism, and emotionalism.* Seuss Enterprises had a *no excuses* response because it was a business decision based on function, what they did or did not do.

We can go to the biblical story of David and Bathsheba to see how things are different for Andrew Cuomo. His decision has *excuses* because it is based on emotion. There is an important dynamic to notice. David initially denies that he had Uriah, Bathsheba's husband, put at the front of the line in the battle to be killed to usher in the coverup of his affair with Bathsheba. But the prophet Nathan tells David a "hypothetical" story that closely resembles David's actions and crime. He then asks David what he would do with that man who sinned. David says that he would kill him. Nathan, the great therapist of self-discovery, replies, "You are the man." David admits his guilt, but it wasn't until it became personal and not a distant act that he moved from a position of *excuses* to *no excuses.* When something becomes personal, like the accusations against Cuomo, it is much harder to admit wrongdoing.

For Seuss Enterprises, it was an easier decision to admit the mistake and have *no excuses* because their decision was not personal. It was business!

No excuses come when you finally admit to yourself that you have done something wrong as David did. Otherwise, *excuses* will dominate. Seuss Enterprises did the right thing—*no excuses*—because they owned it.

In essence, if a decision involves something that was wrong with our functional self, like the six books needing to be taken off the shelf, it is easier to have *no excuses*. If a decision involves our personal, emotional self, then it is much more difficult to admit wrongdoing. It is the difference between I did something wrong (function), and I am something wrong (emotion).

In family therapy, we call this emotionalism versus functionalism. For example, if you look at why marriages ended in the 50s, you will see that divorce was based on function. "He is not a good provider." Relationships were based more on function. But from the 60s to today when a marriage dissolves, it is more likely to be based on emotion. "We have grown apart. I thought that he would change." This is emotionalism.

Cuomo's dilemma is that he is on shaky ground at both the functional level as people are questioning his handling of the pandemic by not being forthcoming with statistics of deaths in nursing homes. That's a business wrongdoing. He is now accused of sexual harassment. That is more of a personal, emotional decision that is characteristic of emotionalism. It will be difficult for him to recover from that combination, which is why he has many *excuses* coming forward.

Florence Nightingale, the founder of modern nursing, said something about the way that she conducted her life that resulted in her becoming the founder of modern-day nursing. How did she get nurses to function at such a high level that it turned the profession into something at the very heart of healthcare? She was all about functionalism. It's business! She said that she attributed her success to "I never gave or took an excuse!"

I don't think that it is as clear cut as Nightingale's statement. It is usually a blend of emotion/person with the functional/business. The question is which of the two is the bigger player. Paying attention to *excuse* versus *no excuse* can help you assess your response to be the most helpful, responsible, and ethical. Which is under fire? Did I do something wrong, or I am something wrong? If both questions are in play, such as with Cuomo, watch out!

Post 182. Epitaph for a Catastrophe

An article in the *Inquirer* on 3/7/2021 is entitled "Epitaph for a Catastrophe" by Anthony Faiola. The article is about what should be put in a time capsule outside of Washington, DC, that would describe how humanity across the world responded to the pandemic. It was a capsule that would help people never forget what happened during this terrible time of dealing with the enormous challenges created by the virus. Humanity tends to forget. Look at where we are right now. Texas, Florida, Mississippi, and other states have opened up and have made mask wearing optional. In Texas, the governor never checked with his medical officers who did not agree with him. Mayors of big cities remembered when we opened up too early and are encouraging their residents to stay the course and wear a mask and social distance.

Mr. Faiola's article points out countries that did well in their response and countries that did not. We are in the "did not" group because of the failure of the Trump administration to have a proper response. There were great responses from countries, such as New Zealand and Australia, and from businesses, such as the Maryland vodka distillery that changed its operation to produce hand sanitizers. There were many successes in attacking the virus, such as the incredible speed that drug companies produced the vaccine.

However, Faiola's position is that we will be remembered for our colossal failures in our nation to come together under a divisive leader and too many who chose to not wear masks and adhere to the proper guidelines. This failure to respond was seen in some of the wealthiest nations. Many defied guidelines to stay at home because if they didn't, their families would have starved. People on Wall Street continued to make money. People on Main Street continued to struggle for financial stability.

It will not read well for us as the most vulnerable in our country continued to be underserved by vaccinations going to those with more access. We were not good neighbors to the world as we made sure that our people were vaccinated before vaccines were made available to many in those countries. We are like the people who go to the grocery store before the possibility of a big storm and horde as many vital items as we can.

England has memorials for just about everything, but there is very little that has been done to remember the pandemic of 1918, except a stained class tryptic in East London in Whitechapel where there is a church turned into a library.

It was not our finest hour. Vicki and I had a Zoom call with friends from England. Margaret is a retired teacher and Roger is the retired chief architect of the Anglican Church of England. They characterized England's response with mixed reviews. However, England had something that helped them to remember catastrophe as they had the Blitz. During the Blitz, masks were never an issue for the English. They were seen as a patriotic duty. The Brits also came together as a nation because the Blitz was happening on English soil, and they certainly had a robust leader in Churchill. Boris Johnson was not a great leader at first, but his bout with the virus made him an instant convert to change to a more rigorous approach. Our wars were fought on foreign soil. Our civil war on our land never became a reference point for resilience for combatting the virus. It was too much in our distant past and far from our consciousness.

We covered all the usual subjects in the Zoom call, such as the current crisis in the Royal family, but they suggested something at the end of the call which Vicki and I did last night. They suggested that we view something that was released in Britain a week ago. It was a documentary, "Blitz Spirit with Lucy Worsley," and was a time capsule in a way to explain the English response to the pandemic. Recall that the British gave a "jab" (British for a vaccination) to as many people as possible. Our friends will not receive a second shot until April. Their approach made sense to them. Try to vaccinate as one people together. They also had to shut down for a longer period than we did. It was against the law to leave your home.

I wish we could create a documentary of everything that our doctors, nurses, front-line workers, and first responders had to go through, including the death and the despair of families. I am not talking about what we see on the news in short episodes but a full-length documentary and *require* everyone to watch it in the same way that we require people to get their photo for their real identification to replace the driver's license. We could juxtapose that with the governor of Texas' address saying, "Texas is open!" and some video footage of the drinking and partying in large groups of our college students on Spring Break! Do you think it would make a difference? Out of sight would not be out of mind for the governors who have opened up—and the Spring Breakers. Do you think that they would process all who have died and are presently dying? Today I will settle for a maybe!

A Video of "Blitz Sprit with Lucy Worsley" can be found on my blog on my website under the title of "Epitaph for a Catastrophe."

Post 183. The Power of "Yet"

I had a meeting with a hand surgeon in December of 2020 for a surgery that I knew was inevitable. Someone must have complained to her that she did not tell them everything they should have known about the surgery before the procedure. One bone would be removed, and two bones in the central column had to be fused.

In addition, there was a second surgery to remove pressure on the median nerve compressed by the carpal bone. Like those TV ads that are advertising a new medication and all of its possible side effects, she left nothing out and repeated too often the description that "this is a big deal," so choose wisely.

My response was that I don't have a choice. This was a perfect choiceless choice that defines the nature of some hard ethical choices as well. I will simply say that the surgery lived up to all of her descriptions of how it was a "big deal," but I will spare you the details.

Recently I started physical therapy with a certified hand specialist who is terrific. Each session was filled with, "Can you do this or that?" I didn't even realize how often I said in response, *"Not yet."* I am not a very patient person when it comes to this kind of thing, but it dawned on me when I was with the hand specialist and other people that I was very aware of what I could and could not do. To make matters worse, it was my left hand, and I am left-handed.

I recently have become aware of how often the word *yet* has entered into my conversational style without previously thinking much about it. *Yet* is a very powerful word! If you are in a situation such as my hand and me, you find out quickly *yet*'s importance. Everyone is living with something that is going to call *yet* from within them. I went to my usual source of comfort, the Bible, and found something startling. *Yet* is mentioned 365 times in the Good Book. I am in good company. *YET* is a word that can take us from sadness to hope, from struggle to attaining a goal, from something negative to something positive, and from pain to feeling more comfortable to name a few.

We often place our lifetime between one year and another with a hyphen in between. The dates of our birth and death are important, but what is more important is what happens on that hyphen. The word *yet* is a word that acts like the hyphen of our faith as it falls between struggle and hope in God. *Yet* functions as a bridge in our faith where we go from pain and suffering to hope in God and His promises to us that He will always be by our side. The following pieces of scripture are examples of this, "All their captors hold them fast, refusing to let them go. *Yet* their Redeemer is strong, the Lord Almighty is his name" (Jer. 50:33–34), "Father, if you are willing to take this cup from me, *yet* not my will, but yours be done" (Luke 22–42), and "The winds blew and beat against that house, *yet* it did not fall because it had its foundation on the rock" (Matt. 7:25).

The *yet* word offers a very important lesson for life and learning as well. It is one of the key concepts that I have used in teaching and counseling. Failure, *yet* success, will come. Permanent perceptions drag us down. A temporary mindset can open new vistas for us. I will never þe able to ...yet tomorrow is a new day with new possibilities. My mantra for learning has been "learn to fail or fail to learn." *Yet* drives us from failure to success, and from the permanent to the temporary.

In my years of teaching, I have observed that the students who struggle the most are those who have not had a "positive failing experience" from which they have learned and grown. Carol Dweck has a model in her book, *Mindset: The New Psychology of Success*, that is very helpful in framing one's life in a way to address failure and create a positive experience from it. If you have failed a test (or submit where you think that you have failed) and feel that it is a permanent issue for your life, you will find yourself depressed, possessing a negative attitude toward yourself, and the inability to cope with moving forward.

If after failing a test you say to yourself or others, "I am stupid. I will never be able to do well in this course," you lock yourself into that mindset. If, on the other hand, you feel that your poor performance is a temporary condition and that you have identified the issues of why you didn't do well, then you will be able to say to yourself, "I didn't do well on this test, *yet* I know what I need to do to correct things and do well on the next evaluation." This attitude will enable you to see life as a challenge but one that you feel confident in addressing as you move forward. Grab ahold of your *yet*.

People frame life in a temporary way to address issues, taking baby steps. That is one of the key tenets of Alcoholic Anonymous that is still the preferred treatment platform for alcoholism today. They stress the mantra, "Take one day at a time." That approach can also be applied to most problem solving.

The person who has a permanent mindset feels that change is not possible. There is no *yet* there. All of us feel this way from time to time. This mindset destroys hope. Individuals with permanent mindsets take a long-range view that stifles progress. I once met with a parent who was paralyzed by the thought that her child would not be admitted to Princeton. The child was in first grade. Taking the long-haul perspective is not the way to problem solve. It has no *yet*.

The work of Edison and Einstein that led to their scientific discoveries illustrates that even for the greatest problem solvers, baby steps and many failures along the way were the reason they achieved so much. There are few overnight successes in life. The people who seem like overnight successes usually combined years of practice or work that met with good luck or providence! They also had plenty of *yet*.

If you pay close attention, you may find yourself using that pivotal word *yet* in life, in learning, and most important in your faith. It always moves us from something challenging to something that is filled with hope and possibility. When I shared this observation with my hand therapist, she said, "You are way ahead of where you should be, *yet* there is so much more that we can accomplish with your hand and wrist! She reminded me to get my *yet* back!

Post 184. Life Lessons Learned from Harry and Meghan's Interview: Storybook or Playbook

Few things could live up to the hype of Oprah's interview with the Duke and Duchess of Sussex, better known as Harry and Meghan. However, this interview did and then some. We talked about the upcoming interview with our friends from England on a Zoom call. Their perspective was that Queen Elizabeth and Prince Philip were good people, but the press was not. As we watched the interview and various newspaper and tabloid papers' headlines scrolled across the screen, we could see why our English friends came to that conclusion. The headlines targeted Meghan about harassment of her, but the headlines would certainly cause the public to pick up the newspaper to see exactly what happened. Those headlines sold papers.

One of our alumni at EA was a columnist for the *Inquirer*. He made an interesting statement when he addressed our student body on the nature of the newspaper business. He said, "What you want is a response from the public. It doesn't matter if it is good or bad."

When the interview began, I was very skeptical about why this interview was necessary. I knew that Oprah was getting seven million dollars to show it. I assumed that Harry and Meghan were trying to "have their cake and eat it too." In essence, I thought that they wanted to keep the titles and everything that went with it but have an independent life on their terms. Oprah's first comment was to clarify that Meghan wasn't being paid to do the interview.

Boy, was I wrong! Here are some conclusions that I drew from the interview that were themes that relate to the rest of us.

If something is too good to be true, it is usually too good to be true. The world watched the wedding ceremony. There were lots of smiles and "princess bride" implications. Wow! People wished that they could have that kind of life. As it turns out Harry and Meghan were married three days before the event with a private ceremony with the Archbishop of Canterbury. One of the things that I have learned over the years is that there is always a story behind the story. It came with my position as chaplain. I knew many of the backstories of people in our community. Behind smiling faces was a degree of pain. As one rock star, Jim Morrison, put it, "No one gets out alive!" meaning everyone takes a hit along life's way, some more so than others. Rabbi Harold Kushner reminded us in his book, *When Bad Things Happen to Good People*, tragedy doesn't have a ticket into our lives. It has a box seat. It is not a matter of if, it is a matter of when tragedy will cross our path.

Giraudoux, a French novelist, once said, "Once you can fake sincerity, you got it made." I couldn't disagree more. Meghan and Harry's sincerity and authenticity were very evident. Their pain, struggle, and empathy for others were very present as well.

Oprah was the talented interviewer that we know her to be, but even she was shocked by the question raised to Harry who told Meghan, "People are wondering how black our children will be." Oprah literally leaned into that comment, wanting to know who said that. The couple didn't reveal that out of concern for the people who raised it. We do know in an after comment that it was not the Queen or Prince Philip. Before any of this breach with the family, it was made clear that their child would not have a title or protection. If this whole thing wasn't due to racism, I will eat my hat.

Harry and Meghan did not read the culture of the monarchy as well as they should have. They were bought into the storybook and forgot about the playbook, namely what was required of them. We should learn to enhance our social intelligence and read better the situations that we find ourselves in. Remember just one word. That word is *expectations,* for a good deal of anger is based on missed expectations. Think of the last time that you were angry, and I bet that there is a missed expectation nearby.

Harry quickly channeled his experience of his mother. We all channel experiences of formative people in our lives. It is usually our parents, as they are the key players who have the most influence.

Meghan articulated the theme of "It takes courage to ask for help if you need it." Her story may have saved lives as a result of that statement, so we owe them both our prayers and hope for a happier future.

Racism and expectations were the key issues, in my opinion, to what brought the once-royal couple to the interview with Oprah last night.

I have a *wish*, a *hope*, and a *fear*. I wish that there had been a way for someone to interview them with the royal family present before the interview with Oprah. Empathy is getting into someone else's shoes. I know they tried to do this before, but one more time is only going to help. They couldn't say that Meghan and Harry didn't let them know how revelatory the interview would be. It is always good to run sensitive material by people who are going to be affected. They could even do it by letter. I hope no lasting damage has been done because family is family, even a royal one. It is defined as the "place where they always have to take you in." They needed to hear all of this before the world did.

I fear that Meghan and Harry were most concerned about protection above all else. Since racism is alive and well in England and America, I fear that someone may now be empowered to harm them because the world knows that their protection has been removed.

Last, the truth shall set you free, but it may make you miserable in the interim.

Post 185. Do You Speak American?

My family and I have spent some extended time in England and became immersed in UK culture. Language is a big deal in helping and hurting relationships. Regarding the UK, there are some basic challenges in translating the meaning of words. When we returned home, my wife and I made a list of British words and their new meaning to us. You can always tell the nerd travelers. It would take me a long time to list them all, but here is a small sampling: public school is private school, a wanker is an idiot, crisps are chips, the dustbin is a garbage can, football is soccer, a vest is an undershirt, a nappy is a diaper, and so forth. You get the drift.

But the meaning of the words is easy to learn. What is not as easy to learn is the cultural language usage differences between us and the English. What do I mean by cultural language usage differences? I had a student who was from a rather staid Irish Roman Catholic family whose fiancé was Jewish. The happy couple (still married) had a dinner for both families to meet. My student described it as a great high-powered debate with interruptions, loud banter, and certainly little or no silence. My student was use to this as he had dinner with the family many times before. His parents sat there throughout most of the evening in shock. They entered into the conversation when they could in a calm, if not serene, fashion. Their voices were never raised.

My go-to person for all things linguistic is Deborah Tannen, a professor at Georgetown. She wrote an article, "Talking New York." The high-energy Jewish family used a "high involvement conversational style." My student's family used a "high considerate conversational style." Suffice it to say, that the American style of Harry and Meghan would be more "high involvement," whereas the British style and that of the Royal family would be "high-considerate." These are descriptive categories. One is not better than the other. Different cultures have different assumptions and expectations for use of language.

The royals are more "male" in their exchanges. The male use of language is about maintaining status. The Royals can't help that their status is high, for it is built-in. Meghan and Harry are more "female" in their exchanges, wanting to share in intimacy with their family. Let's see how this applies to "trouble talk." When Meghan raised her concerns about her mental health, the Royals might have been baffled, for they may think "Well, that's not a problem for me," which feels like a nonresponse or putdown as they would make little or no response. Meghan and Harry were looking for a different response, like "I am the same way" or "I know how you feel."

Michael Deacon, a reporter for the *Telegraph*, wrote an article after the infamous interview with Oprah. He wrote the article as a response to one of the headlines that were shown to show the harsh nature of the British press. One headline was one of his. His anger at being "outed" was because the article was written eleven months after the couple announced that they were stepping down from a senior royal role. His article didn't drive them out. His article was about the age-old observation that America and Britain are two nations divided by a common language.

Tannen would agree with many of Deacon's points regarding the power of language when expectations are different. As Deacon indicates, "We tend to shy away from emotional language. We are a stiff, socially awkward bunch who communicate via understatement, irony, and sarcasm." If you want to see what this style looks like, watch a Hugh Grant comedy movie. The humor is based on the above fact.

I listed British words and meanings above. Deacon does an analysis of the interview by citing the terms that are used that are emotionally based: humbled, empowered, passionate, inspired, "what was our continued reality going to be?" people she "reached out to," her gratitude to Oprah for "giving us the space" to talk. Oprah mirrored the same use of language back. She asked Meghan how the Royals would think about "hearing you speak your truth?" Oprah followed up with "What is going on with you internally?" The dominant word in the exchanges in the interview was *sharing*. American speech, such as this, is more like the "female conversational style" of seeking connection and intimacy. The British feel that this comes across as "cloying," or excessively sweet.

To make my point, I want you to fantasize for a moment that Meghan bares her soul to the Queen, and the Queen responds with "What I hear you saying Meghan is_____. I am deeply grateful for your sharing! I am humbled by hearing you speak your truth." Prince Philip would enter the conversation by waiting so he doesn't interrupt anyone and declare, "I am inspired by your words and the passion with which you have presented them. Thank you for sharing." He might even slip in a "Hey, dude, I get it!" as an ode to California.

Words lead to understanding, but you got to make sure you have the right ones. As I indicated in an earlier blog, Meghan and Harry came at their new roles as senior royals who understood the storybook but didn't have the playbook firmly in their grasp, for the playbook is about the use of language that leads to understanding, not to hurt, ache, and division.

Post 186. What Tip O'Neill and Joe Biden Know

President Biden's style couldn't be more different from Donald Trump's tweets, character assassinations, and bullying. Tip O'Neill's style has been a base for a lot of my relationships with others. Tip tells the story on himself. When he was a young person, he shoveled a woman's sidewalk, who lived across the street from him during every snowstorm. He did this for free. When he was running for some low-level office, he learned that the woman whose walk he shoveled did not vote for him in that election. He was angry, crossed the street to her house, and asked her why. Her response was a classic, "Tip, everybody likes to be asked. You took my vote for granted." From that comment, Tip developed his attitude towards others. He said, "All politics is local!" which put him on the road to be the Speaker of the House.

I would add, "Treat everybody as though your life depended on it! Someday it just might." I mean that in a figurative sense, but later in life, I found myself dealing with a heart issue and was in the hospital. My doctor was a former student, and my life literally depended on him." He had a heavy patient load as a resident. I would have to encourage him to spend less time with me and more time with others. The point is, people remember.

Biden operates in the same fashion whether it is a SEPTA train employee, a person who has lost a loved one, or someone just down on their luck! Stories about his responses to those in need are legendary. There is a story about Biden being angry with arch-conservative Jesse Helms who would not support a bill to benefit those with disabilities. He let the Senate Majority Leader Mike Mansfield know about his anger. Mansfield, in turn, let him know that Jesse Helms had adopted a child with disabilities. Biden felt like a fool, but he learned a very important lesson. Feel free to question another person's judgment but not their motivations. In essence, you can argue a difference of opinion but never attack the personhood of another.

Always try to find a way to give somebody else the credit or face time. Most of us in a high-profile position get enough recognition. Look around for someone who doesn't. Honor people. When it was thought that Senator Manchin wouldn't support the COVID-19 Relief Bill, Biden went to him, sat down, and simply said, "Joe, you have to do what you think is right!" He leveled no threats that we have been use to for four years. Manchin, on his own, came on board, and the historic bill was passed, and who was there to sign it—Schumer and Pelosi. Biden's name won't be on the stimulus checks either.

People were shocked that Kamala Harris was selected by Biden to be his running mate. She went after him in the debate. Those who know Biden were not. He forgives and doesn't hold grudges. Forgiveness is a key to leadership, and I have found that it is not always easy to do, but for the benefit of all, it must be done. Joe Biden has had plenty of people mad at him, but there is no revenge on his part. One of the Republicans' greatest complaints is that it is hard for the public to be angry at Biden, unlike President Obama, who had many angry with him, which I attribute to his race.

Biden's approach is to make an enemy into a friend. Randy Pausch in his book, *The Last Lecture*, said that everyone has good in them. It may take some time to find it but hang in there. I know that it must be there in our former president, but I still haven't found it. I will keep looking.

Machiavelli wrote in his book, *The Prince,* about the nature of leadership that people should fear you first and then you would get respect from them. Tip, Joe Biden, and I couldn't disagree more. It is respect that can enrich your actions and relationships with others and help you to live a moral life, empowering people to show their better angels. Nothing else can do that!

Post 187. Andrew Cuomo and Sexual Harassment Allegation

Governor Cuomo is in a very difficult position as he has been accused of at least five sexual harassment offenses. Four of those women were part of Cuomo's administration. One was a private citizen who was harassed at a wedding.

It boggles my mind that the New York State Government didn't have a sexual harassment policy in place to respond to at least four of these accusations, along with a sexual harassment officer. Sexual harassment policies empower women and provided much-needed feedback to men or women who may be the offender. I know something about them because I wrote several of them, first dating back to the 90s at EA. These policies are sometimes called Inappropriate Behavior Policies to reach into more general forms of nonsexual harassment. Sexual harassment can be of two forms: (1) targeted behavior, which is directed at a person; and (2) environmental harassment, which means that the environment in which the woman is functioning can make her uncomfortable, such as sexually suggestive posters on walls or sexually explicit conversation that is going on around her.

Harassment policies usually include several important steps. We will assume that it is a woman being harassed by a man. The policy indicates that the first step that a woman should take is to speak directly to the man who is involved and state emphatically that whatever occurred in the exchange made her feel threatened and embarrassed. If the man is in a position of power and she is unable to address him directly because of this difference in status or that she just does not feel that she can do this, she can elicit the support of someone else to go with her for the intervention with the perpetrator.

It is made very clear in the document that any form of retribution would not be tolerated. Hence, there should be someone who is either informed of the conversation or be part of the conversation. This is needed so that someone knows if there is any further harassment of others by the man. For many years that was me, as it should be someone who is not attached to hiring or firing an individual or determining the salary of the man. I later expanded that role to other chaplains at the school since some of the assistant chaplains were women. The important thing is to make it easy for the woman to come forward. If the woman went to another chaplain, I would still need to know so that I had the overall experience of this man with any others.

The goal for this approach was to empower the woman to speak directly to the perpetrator, and for the male to be directly in touch with the woman so that he was not hearing this from someone else. My experience was that once this step was accomplished, the harassing behavior stopped. Resolution occurred. I cannot remember a single occasion where it did not stop unwanted behavior. This sort of policy also speaks to the issue of the "eye of the beholder." It doesn't matter how you thought you acted. It matters how the woman received your comments or gestures. At times, the man knew exactly what he was doing. At other times, it was a learning experience for the man to change his behavior.

It should be a requirement that every employee should read the Sexual Harassment or Behavior Harassment Policy at least once a year and sign the document as testimony that everyone had read it, and that everyone understands the process. Confidentiality was key in having this policy work for both the woman and the man.

A document is a form of consent that everyone in the community had read the document and supported its steps.

Regarding Governor Cuomo and the woman at the wedding, I would hope that being familiar with a policy in his state would heighten his sensitivity to avoid behavior in a public or private venue not directly connected with his office as governor.

Keep in mind that women can harass women, women can harass men, and men can harass other men. My experience with this kind of policy was very helpful in maintaining and empowering the community.

Back to Governor Cuomo for a moment. He has three daughters, Michaela, Mariah, and Cara, who have been involved with curtailing sexual abuse, another human rights, and another regarding worldwide social justice. The three daughters are living with him during this pandemic. Can you imagine the conversations that he is having with his daughters right now? The mother of the girls is a Kennedy, so the apple has not fallen far from the Kennedy's concerns with justice. Cuomo also returned Harvey Weinstein's campaign contribution when it was clear that Weinstein was a serial abuser.

He had so many external forces to make him more aware of his behavior than he exhibited. He is a bully, but I don't think that is based on low self-esteem or a need to belong, which is the usual case. I think that he wants to be seen as a tough guy from Queens. I would love to have a conversation with him regarding how he went off the rails of appropriate behavior. There is much that is good about him and contributions that he could make in the future to benefit others.

Post 188. Why Is Governor Cuomo So Surprised and Shocked?

Let's apply an ethical lens to the possible impeachment of Andrew Cuomo and the growing number of people who have been asking for his resignation. A reporter stated in *New York Magazine,* "I never thought the governor wanted to have sex with me. It wasn't about sex," she wrote. "It was about power. He wanted me to know that I was powerless, that I was small and weak, that I did not deserve what relative power that I had; a platform to hold him accountable for his words and actions."

Let's unpack a complex situation and issue. First, the reporter and another of Cuomo's accusers used the word *accountable*. When we read or hear the word *accountable*, we think of punishment. Accountability is not the same thing as blame or punishment. To be accountable means to take responsibility for results, good or bad. Accountability provides feedback to people who can't see a problem with their behavior that is affecting others. Accountability provides feedback to enable a person to become a more effective person in his or her relationships in and outside of the workplace. Jessica Moyer states, "that if you find yourself delivering consequences to create more accountability, the problem is not your people—it is you."

Accountability requires feedback, which makes it very different from punishment. It may be there, but I have not seen it yet. Who gave feedback to Andrew Cuomo about how his actions made them feel? There has been a cycle that has brought us to a lose/lose situation. Cuomo will lose. The women involved will lose, except for the reporter who identified Cuomo's actions for what they were, an exercise of power over another.

Let me define the lose/lose. Cuomo will lose because he still does not take full responsibility for his power trip over women. He keeps digging the hole deeper for himself by just focusing on his acts as not sexual in nature. That is the manifestation of his power issue. He is saying to himself, "I didn't do anything sexual to these women." The women, on the other hand, as well as various politicos who are calling for his resignation, will be made very uncomfortable by Jessica Moyer's observation that if you find yourself

THIS TOO SHALL PASS

delivering consequences, such as removal from office, the problem is not only Cuomo, it is also you.

The key here is feedback. Truth is in the eye of the beholder. How the women feel is how they feel. That is what is important. But an ethical response would also ask important questions. Was direct feedback ever given to him? If it was given, did he repeat the behavior? The answers to those two questions are critical. I spent a good deal of my chaplaincy dealing with captains of industry. People thought that since they were good at business, they would be good about family relationships. Often that wasn't true! People with power don't necessarily understand how power can be abused when they are doing it. A wife of a top attorney would say, "Smell the coffee; don't try to make the situation a case that you want to prove me wrong!" A husband of a psychologist may say to his wife, "Don't try all that psychology stuff on me!"

You can't just say, "He is the governor. He should know better!" Why? Has he gotten any feedback on his actions? I take it that he has not. If he has and has continued this behavior that is another matter. The dilemma with sexual harassment is that it is sometimes about something else: power. It is the same with other issues, such as eating disorders. They are not about food. They are about control that nobody can take away from you.

At EA, we were evaluated for everything and frequently. We had evaluations of our evaluations. It was crazy but important. I set up the evaluation process with people who I supervised in the following way. None of us should get to the final evaluation phase by receiving any surprises. Feedback as part of daily feedback was welcomed. I also set it up so I would be evaluated by my team in the same way that I evaluated them. During their final evaluation of me, there should be no surprises for me as well. Feedback is about growth, not punishment!

Here are the questions. Was Governor Cuomo ever given feedback on his behavior? If not, why not? Did it repeat itself? Why is it so difficult for him to admit that what he did was sexual harassment?

Was there a sexual harassment policy? Why does he seem so surprised and baffled and feeling like a victim? Answers to those questions could turn this lose/lose into a win/win. Why weren't people interested in making him a better governor by providing a check to behavior that is hurtful to these women and, in turn, to the New York State government?

Post 189. Bioethics in the Big Easy

The Roman Catholic Church in Louisiana is against using the Johnson and Johnson vaccine because it uses a line of cells from fetuses aborted in 1970. This is similar to the ethical dilemma that faced the Church regarding the issue of condom use as a way of preventing AIDS, particularly in Africa. The position of the Roman Catholic Church is that they are against abortion and contraception. There are three things to consider when approaching the bioethics of Johnson and Johnson vaccine use in Louisiana and two teachings in the Roman Catholic Church that apply. The church opposes contraception because every sex act should be open to procreation. Second, the church also teaches that everyone has the right to defend one's life "against mortal danger." Third, eighty-seven percent of Roman Catholics in America do not accept the Church's positions on these two issues.

The bioethical dilemma of vaccine use by Roman Catholics has gotten very little press until the situation in Louisiana put it in the news. Here is the issue. There is great debate in the Catholic Church over accepting vaccines and treatments that use fetal tissue, centering on HEK 293 cells, which were cloned from an aborted fetus in the early 1970s. The cells used now, such as in the Johnson and Johnson vaccine, are not from the original fetal tissue. All vaccines have used lines of tissues from fetuses.

According to the *Inquirer*, "In the case of the COVID-19 virus, the Vatican said that they could be used in good conscience, given the severity of the pandemic since the vaccine's connection to the original abortion is remote. Pope Francis took the Pfizer vaccine."

If the Pope says it is OK, it is OK, right? Not so fast! Dr. John Haas is the president emeritus and senior fellow at the National Catholic Bioethics Center. I know John, as his children attended EA, although he and I have never discussed this particular issue. He is a thoughtful bioethicist, but he and I would have to agree to disagree on various topics. In essence, he is one of the key bioethicist consultants to the Pontifical Counsel.

I will quote some of Dr. Haas' statements that appeared in the *National Catholic Register*. Here is the Roman Catholic Church's position. The standard is "First do no harm, do good and avoid evil, and never do evil that good may come of it." He is also concerned with the consent forms where companies don't mention the "use of a cell line which had its origins in tissue from an aborted child. That does not constitute true informed consent."

The heart of Dr. Haas' position is, "Grave reasons may be morally proportionate to justify the use of such 'biological material.'" Thus, for example, danger to the health of children could permit parents to use a vaccine, which was developed using cell lines of illicit origin, while keeping in mind that everyone has the duty to make known their disagreement and to ask that their healthcare system make other types of vaccines."

Moderna and Pfizer vaccines argue that, although the vaccines weren't produced directly from cell lines derived from aborted babies, their research and production depended on the HEK cell line derived from a baby aborted in the 1970s. Dr. Haas' response was "that it would have been better if there had been no connection, but it was not used for the manufacture of the vaccine, so there would be a very distant connection."

My response to Dr. Haas is simple. Time was of the essence. There were no other vaccines that were available other than those that used the HEK cell lines. There was no choice. If we are going to hold up the value of human life, we need to hold up the value of the living who are attempting to live during this pandemic. He does have a point about consent. Consent always means full disclosure.

In terms of the Catholic guideline of "never do evil that good could come of it," I would put it another way. Abortion is wrong but necessary. The woman should have the right to choose.

The New Orleans Archdiocese has articulated an argument that could be picked up as another reason by the anti-vaxxers not to get vaccinated. Today I asked a Roman Catholic person if he was going to get a vaccine. He said no, "I don't believe in abortion." Vaccines and abortions could be equated as moral equals going forward. That thought could be a reason for some to not get the vaccine at the peril of their own lives. It is wrong, in my opinion, to link abortion and vaccine use as wrong in the context of the deaths due to the pandemic.

Here are two strong arguments about vaccines to simplify the matter for our Roman Catholic brothers and sisters. The Vatican Academy for Life issued a document in 2017 with regards to vaccines using fetal cell lines from the 1960(s) to make rubella, chickenpox, polio, and hepatitis A vaccines. It stated that, "All clinically recommended vaccinations can be used with a clear conscience and that the use of such vaccines does not signify some sort of cooperation with voluntary abortion."

My mentor, Arthur Caplan, now professor of bioethics at New York University School of Medicine told *Science*, "If you are going to say the government shouldn't fund things that a minority of people object to, you will have a very long list of things that won't get funded by this government from research on weapons of war to contraceptive research."

Enough said! Get a vaccine!

Post 190. An Ethical Guideline That Works to Create Justice

It is very difficult for all when you treat one person differently than you treat another. This happens frequently in the world of social ethics. Remember that our first ethical statement as a developing human being is most often "it's not fair." This statement is often made when a very young person feels that they are being treated differently from others. A sense of the importance of justice is one of the two pillars that hold up ethics. The other is the pillar of love.

Therefore, justice demands to be taken seriously. It is also a key ingredient to make us feel uncomfortable when we are accused of treating others differently. Adolescents have very strong feelings about fair and equitable treatment in their moral development. A sense of justice is important to hold society together.

A phrase that has worked well for me over the years is "What you do for one, you have to do for all." I have spent enough time in between two people who feel that injustice has been done to them, such as when EA was perceived as treating a student or parent differently from others. For that matter, it is also true of how faculty, administrators, and alumni/ae will feel anger if injustice is perceived with the phrase, "Well, you didn't do that when _____ did the same thing."

Nationally this is at the heart of much of social ethical debate. The suburban Philadelphia counties feel that they are not getting their fair share of the vaccine as other counties in the state. The mayor of Detroit initially refused the Johnson and Johnson vaccine because he didn't feel it was as effective as other vaccines. Black people across the nation feel that they are not treated in a just way in interactions with police, as well as getting access to the vaccine. Most recently Meghan Markle indicated that she was treated differently as a person of color from someone who was white. *The Telegraph Online Web News Report* provided a rebuttal to Harry and Meghan's complaint with facts and not opinion. The report indicated that Meghan and Harry weren't being fair.

Today Senator Lindsey Graham said that the COVID-19 Relief Bill was giving funds to black farmers, which was a form of reparations and wasn't fair to white farmers who would get nothing. House Majority Whip, James Clyburn, responded with anger that

"Lindsey should know better. He should go to church and get back in touch with Christianity."

The bottom line for all of the above accusations is "You are treating me differently." You name it, such as college admissions policies, the argument remains the same. This is a huge ethical dilemma because people are not hearing "what you do for one, you must do for all." That phrase is tied to ethical precedent. Such and such situations were handled in way X, and now they are being handled in way Y. How can that be? Times may change the reasoning, but that is not often the case. Any action creating justice with our "justice phrase" should stand the test of time.

How can this be corrected? It needs to be engaged at the micro-level and the macro-level all at the same time. Recall the post earlier that I wrote about a way to stop sexual attack was to make asking for permission normal in everyday life. This could spill over in terms of future behavior with sexual interactions. We have lost that important manner and tend to ask "for forgiveness before we ask for permission."

Every time that you are accused of favoritism or that you should treat people in a just manner, recall quickly that phrase, "what you do for one you should do for all" as an important ingredient of creating relationships that are "just" at the personal, national, and global levels. If that phrase does not hold up in describing a situation, work hard to introduce justice and being fair at every level, personal as well as cultural. That is the way we make justice happen. It has always has been that way and will always be that way!

Post 191. You Can Lead a Horse to Water, But You Can't Make Him Think

There are two absolutes about human nature. You can't tell somebody what to do if they have an option not to do it. You can't manipulate people, for it degrades them. Since I got a vaccine shot today, vaccines are on my mind. We are told to get a vaccine and wear a mask. Both of those things work against being told to do them. I use to think that people took this irrational approach because they wanted their freedom. I failed to see what they meant by freedom. Adam Grant's most recent book, *Think Again,* describes what I believe they mean. I am one of those "Don't tell me what to do people!"

Grant's research supports a view that I underscore in developing a new form of counseling called Lever Counseling that is on my website: revsquirecounseling.com. The questions I always raise are what does the person have going for him, and how can I leverage that to help the person change to reach his goals? This relates to people getting vaccines and putting on a mask as well. I will channel Grant's research during this blog. What I call counseling, he calls motivational interviewing. His and my premise is that you can't motivate someone to change. We have to help them find their motivation and way to change.

Think vaccines and mask wearing as changes that we know will help people and us to live through the pandemic. Requiring mask wearing and getting the vaccine has not worked for everybody. It has worked for me and others because we have decided that it is the best way to stay healthy. We have forgotten how much people resist being told what to do, even when their life depends upon it. The more people wouldn't agree with the CDC approach, the more we talked. We need to listen more.

Motivational interviewing or listening means giving people an opportunity to think about why they have their point of view. This type of approach has changed KKK members, anti-vaccinators, and stopped fights of warlords in Africa. It changed them to be better people in society. Let me share with you some of Grant's thoughts and research in *Think Again:*

When people ignore advice, it isn't always because they disagree with it. Sometimes they are resisting the sense of pressure and the feeling that someone else is controlling their decision. To protect their freedom instead of giving commands, a motivational interviewer might say something along the lines of 'here are some things that helped me — do you think any of them might work for you?' Many communicators try to make themselves look smart. Great listeners are more interested in their audiences feel smart. The power of listening doesn't lie just in giving people the space to reflect on their views. It's a display of respect and an expression of care. Listening is a way of offering our scarcest, most precious gift: our attention. Once we've demonstrated that we care about them and their goals, they will be more willing to listen to us.

I know that this approach works in counseling with the most difficult situations.

I always told young faculty members that students won't care about your subject until they know you care about them. It is the same for mask wearing and getting a vaccine.

We just passed the most transformative legislation in the history of our country, which will raise our nation's children out of poverty, save our economy, put food on peoples' tables, will give them jobs to produce income and meaning, and will usher in a future with hope. We can't forget that with all the talk by so many, it was one sentence that brought all of this about. Just one. I don't know how many noticed. Getting a somewhat reluctant Joe Manchin's vote was key. Where other politicians in the past might have pressured him, threatened him, or tweeted about him, Joe Biden said simply to Joe Manchin, "Joe, you have to do what you think is right." He put the decision in Joe Manchin's hands.

Fortunately, we have a President who cares about people and uses this kind of exchange to Manchin. I hope it continues to make its way to those who doubt that the vaccines and masks are signs of hope. As strong as the virus is, nothing beats the strength of Americans who feel listened to and are motivated from within. Take it from me, someone who doesn't like to be told what to do!

Post 192. Tapper and Carlson

Have you ever heard Jake Tapper say that he was wrong about something? Have you ever heard Tucker Carlson say that he was wrong about something? They both are content to be in their one-silo world. No matter what Joe Biden does, one says that he is a terrific leader while the other says that he is leading us down the road of socialism. They are at home in a black-and-white world. The problem is that they are not operating in a transformational world of being a fully human being.

It was F. Scott Fitzgerald who said, "The test of a first-rate intelligence is the ability to hold two opposing ideas in mind at the same time and still be able to function." I would change that statement a bit to what separates people from just living and living fully are those who are in the category of first-rate emotional intelligence. What Fitzgerald was describing has a new label. It is called cognitive dissonance, which means we can hold two conflicting realities together at the same time. One sees the world in black and white and the other sees the world as gray. Tapper and Carlson are content to stay in their lanes and continue to promote what we call confirmation bias. Their antennae are out to find information that supports their point of view. There is a rare group of people who can "walk and chew gum" in a gray world. My wife, Vicki, is one. A friend said something to me recently that is an example of Fitzgerald's point. She said, "I have a sad life right now, but I am a very happy person." If Carlson and Tapper were having a conversation with her, they might not be able to figure out what she was talking about. They would say, "You are sad and happy! You can't be both." However, the great novelist, F. Scott Fitzgerald would very quickly get it and would say that people who can say what she said are in a high group of social/emotional intelligent people.

One of the great things about teaching ethics to older adolescents is that you can see first-hand a change from a black-and-white world to one that may be gray. Some things are always right and always wrong. There are absolutes in our world. But in the course description, I indicated that I wanted students to walk around a problem and see it from many different angles, sometimes requiring the student to hold two conflicting issues or emotions at the same time.

When course evaluations and the evaluations of me come back, I am impressed and sometimes moved by what is said like, "My view of _____hasn't changed, but I didn't know that my classmates could have so many different ways of seeing the issue. I can now get into why they see things the way that they do." To use a sports metaphor, I watch them go from a single play in their playbook, which results in them being limited with the same play being run over and over again to having many plays that they can understand and a multidimensional approach to get the ball in the net meaning a fuller life.

The problem is I don't think that Tapper or Carlson could ever make that statement. People don't tune in to them to get two opposing thoughts. They tune in to them to get what they already believe confirmed. CNN and Fox are confirmation bias stations. This is the way that we are tending to move as a nation, in armed opposing camps. What we need now is people who are just as happy being wrong as they are at being right. Yes, you read that right. That is what is needed now, particularly in a divided nation. Be careful of people who never apologize for something that they have said or done. We need more like my friend who "can have a sad life at this moment but be a happy person." I don't think that Tapper or Carlson would understand that. Our kids need to know that life is not either/or, but it can be both/and.

No one has captured what Fitzgerald's words look like in the religious life that is filled with cognitive dissonance than the Peace Prayer of Saint Francis. I will often tell couples whose marriages I bless to go to the web, find the Prayer of Saint Francis, print it, cut it out, and put it in their wallet. During days when they are trying to hold together the most important aspects of life, they can take it out, find a quiet place, and pray for it. I treasure the feedback I get from them about that request. Rev., I am still getting that Prayer of St. Francis out!

Lord, make me an instrument of your peace;
Where there is hatred, let me sow love;
Where there is injury pardon;
Where there is doubt, faith
Where there is despair hope;
Where there is darkness, light;
Where there is sadness, joy.

O divine Master, grant that I may not so much seek
To be consoled as to console,
To be understood as to understand,
To be loved as to love,
For it is in giving that we receive,
It is in pardoning that we are pardoned,
And it is in dying that we are born to eternal life. Amen

Post 193. A Look Back to Move Forward to Face the Moral Disease

I have attached an article, "Pandemics Kill Compassion, Too," which appeared in *The New York Times*. Take a close look at that date. It was written on March 12, 2020, almost a year ago when we were becoming more familiar with the pandemic. Our family just returned from a trip to Costa Rica. It didn't dawn on us when we said goodbye to two of them that it would be over a year before we could say hello in person.

Brooks' article is a thorough history of how other pandemics were handled by nations long ago. He did not have a crystal ball, but his article of what happened in the past is fairly on target with what happened to us during the past year. We have learned to take history seriously so that we don't repeat how we acted in the past and repeat the same mistakes in the future. The benefit of his article is that it shows us that human nature is very basic. Some things don't change. The way that people handled the pandemic in the past informs the way that we handle that issue today. This is why I thought it was so helpful to see how the British handled the Blitz with grit and perseverance that got translated to their handling of the pandemic. There was a definite difference. They had a great leader who could keep the spirits and the resilience of the British people up. We did not have that kind of leadership that accepts huge challenges and keeps the people informed with the truth.

There are a few points from the article that I want to highlight. Frank Snowden's comment that "Pandemics hold up a mirror to society and force us to ask basic questions: What is possible imminent death trying to tell us? Where is God in all this? What is our responsibility to one another? Imminent death frightened most of us, but some had a death occur in their family that changed their lives forever, so they could appreciate death more. For them, life will not be the same as well. They will appreciate life even more. Others simply denied it as a possibility. This was particularly true for younger people. I am talking about the partygoers during significant events like a holiday such as Spring Break. They will move forward in life, not giving the pandemic a second thought."

Where is God in all of this? He is lived out in the words of the Gospel of Saint Matthew, "When did we see you, Lord? When you helped those in need." God always appears in tragedy in ways known and unknown.

What was our responsibility to one another? When people write about this era of struggle in our lives, I think that they will give us mixed reviews in the same way that the response to past pandemics demonstrates how some rose to the occasion and made us proud of our shared humanity, and some did not. I was struck by Brooks' comment that "This explains one of the puzzling features of the 1918 pandemic. When it was over, people didn't talk about it. There were very few books and plays about it. There was almost no conscious cultural mark." With Trump, we heard nothing about it. With Biden, we remembered publicly what had occurred.

What would those want to be said or written who wrote the flu off as no big deal not worthy of thinking that it could kill them or those who would not care for others by getting a vaccine and wearing a mask? They would want nothing said, written, or done.

The pandemic brought out the best and the worst in us with one exception according to Brooks, "Health care workers. In every pandemic, there are doctors and nurses who respond with unbelievable heroism and compassion." Brooks wouldn't have known that the medical people would be added to by heroic behavior from teachers, grocery store workers, truck drivers, first responders, and all those who put their lives and the lives of their loved ones at risk by coming to work when it would be safer to stay home.

When people talk about the pandemic, they focus on the physical challenges, such as the new variants being found. But it was just as much a moral crisis, seeing what people did and did not do. That needs to be explored as well.

The "Brooks Article" can be found on my blog on my website under the title of "A Look Back to Move Forward to Face Moral Disease."

Post 194. Never Let a Crisis Go to Waste

We normally make anthropomorphic references, giving human characteristics to that which is important. We refer to the stock market as "needing to take a breather," "having a difficult time," or "trying to gain a foothold" on the economy. I have learned that the stock market is taking the pulse of what is going on in corporate America, such as the advancements in technology, the job market, inflation, and how Main Street is doing. But I have learned something else. Even though the stock market is concerned about today, it is just as concerned about what the future holds, so its sights are also set on what may be occurring months ahead. It also pays attention to trends. It looks at today and tomorrow!

By now we have been getting very used to living one day at a time with some days feeling so much like the day before. But we have also been getting used to looking forward to that time when we can be less afraid and go out again with no one coming toward us, who represents a threat by carrying the virus. Our lives may feel like that old movie, *Groundhog Day* where we are dogged by a sense of "sameness." I am not sure that I know a good anthropomorphic image to apply here, but for me, it would be that we are athletes running on a treadmill; some of us are having very different days from one to the other where others are ruled by the tyranny of "the same."

There are several ways that I know that I can improve my own life and do various things, such as writing, doing physical therapy, and exercise to make tomorrow better than today. Having goals helps as well.

I remember after 9/11, another crisis in our nation's history, we were confronted by a similar issue. We lived each day under the threat that it could be our last, but we changed as we moved forward. We know that the pandemic wreaked havoc on our lives, as we were confronted by our own mortality. The pandemic was an equal-opportunity offender as it caused death and destruction regardless of status, class, religion, location, or race.

I have always operated from the premise that one should not let a crisis go to waste and learn something from it. If I gave the pandemic an anthropomorphic description, it would be that it was very Job-like found in Hebrew literature. So why would I use Job to describe us during this time both today and what we could learn about how to see our future? One of the things that happened after 9/11 is that people had soul-searching moments, some of which required monumental changes in their lives regarding how they would live each day and what direction they might direct their attention in future days. Two of my married friends gave up high-powered corporate law careers to become teachers. The pandemic affected Wall Street and Main Street but in a different way that could focus lives on a matter of the spirit in a powerful way.

We shouldn't miss this opportunity to welcome a deepening change in our faith. All of us felt vulnerable and Job-like in never knowing what would come next. We certainly had a lot of questions of God as Job did. Why did my _____ have to die? What is next? What is the price I am paying in living my life now? Is there something in life that would give me more meaning and fulfillment? Where is hope? I saw this search for answers in a very concrete example. After 9/11 admission, applications went up significantly in faith-based schools. Parents wanted their children to have more of a spiritual experience as part of their education. They wanted a school that would take seriously the building or revealing of character in their children.

This is an opportunity for our nation to find a new relationship with our God in the same way that Job attempted to do. Job asked God a lot of reason-based questions, such as where God was when all of this was happening to him and why did this happen to him and his loved ones. When God responded, it was not what Job expected, for He offered a kind of "how dare you ask me" that kind of question. "Then the Lord answered Job out of the whirlwind; Who is this who obscures my plans with words without knowledge? Brace yourself like a man; I will question you and you will answer me. Where were you when I laid the earth's foundation? Tell me if you understand" (Job 38:1–4). The feedback to Job is harsh because God wanted to teach him an important life lesson. You can't live by reason alone. Faith takes over where reason leaves off.

The message given to Job is the same message that we have gotten during the pandemic. Yes, we have to live by reason and science, but we have questions that point out that we can't live now or in our future without faith. In essence, where reason stops on those hard-to-answer spiritual questions, answers are provided not by reason but by our faith as Job found. In the same way that there are no atheists in foxholes with bullets over our heads, we need to reach out to our creator and Lord. How do we get started as Job-like figures?

Last night I had a zoom meeting with a couple whose marriage I will bless in the fall. What an example of coping with the now but looking to their future. I gave them an assignment that they needed some initial help to get started, so I gave them just a few directions. I asked them each to write a statement about their faith. First, write it for *you,* not for me. Both had been through some major heartaches beyond the pandemic? Did God, Jesus, or something else help you to get through that time? What outside of yourselves helped you to cope? Then for the most important piece of advice, which resonated with the couple. It gave them a clear direction to the point that they smiled with insight and recognition. Their eyes said, "We get it." What would each of you ask me to pray for? If you want to discover what is in the heart of someone, ask them that question. Try that question every day. What would you want your prayer to be? Some prayers about today? Some about the future? This is a practice that could change your life! It seemed to make sense to my happy couple on a zoom meeting.

Post 195. The Butterfly Effect

Donald Trump is gone but unfortunately not forgotten. His support of white supremacy is still with us, most recently with the prejudice against Asians, which manifested itself recently in the killing of an Asian woman who was working in a spa. White supremacist propaganda is rising, according to a report by the Anti-Defamation League that has documented an increase in hate messages in 2020. The roots of white supremacy run deep, so increased vigilance is needed as we attempt to determine hate speech.

It is first helpful to define the groups that are included in the word *Asian*. Professors at Clemson University and Lincoln University indicate that Asian refers to people who live in countries such as China, Japan, Indonesia, Korea, Singapore, and Vietnam. The focus now is on China.

Stereotypes have not helped with prejudice against Asian people. I recently saw the movie, *Breakfast at Tiffany's* for the first time. Mickey Rooney, who plays a buck-toothed Chinese man in the film, portrays the negative caricature in such a way that it was uncomfortable for me to watch him in the role. When I and some others think of the Far East, we think of that classic opera, "Madame Butterfly," which is a tragic love story where the woman commits suicide at the end. However, regarding the recent murders in Atlanta, I want to refer to another type of butterfly, the butterfly effect.

The butterfly effect was coined by meteorologist Edward Lorenz who discovered in the 1960s that tiny, butterfly scale changes to the starting point of his computer weather models resulted in anything from sunny skies to violent storms with no way to predict in advance what the outcome may be. In the movie, *Jurassic Park,* Jeff Goldblum's character explains chaos theory that "it simply deals with unpredictability in complex systems. A butterfly can flap its wings in Peking, and in Central Park, you get rain instead of sunshine"

If a butterfly can do that, I shudder to think what long-lasting effects that the toxic four years of Trump will continue to have both here and abroad. Our nation is now concerned with the rise of attacks on Asian Americans. They rose by 150 percent during 2020 when other hate crimes were going down in numbers. This past week Robert Aaron Long, a white man, was charged with fatally shooting eight people, six women of Asian descent, at spas in the Atlanta area on Tuesday night.

The perception of Asian American women as exotic, hypersexual, and submissive can be traced back centuries. One of the earliest examples of prejudice against Asians goes back to the Page Act of 1875 which was a law that was enacted seemingly to limit prostitution, but in reality, it was to prevent Chinese women from entering the US under the bias that they were prostitutes.

Trump resurfaced a bias that was already in the culture. He made a point of referring to the COVID-19 virus as the China Virus and

Kung Flu. He would grit his teeth and emphasize each syllable. It was his classic defense at the expense of others. He wanted to shift blame for the deaths by the virus to Asian Americans to take the blame away from himself. Throwing people "under the bus" was his prevalent defense when his poor leadership caused the spread.

The wings of the Trump butterfly were always moving the air to create "the other," anyone different. The strategy to keep this butterfly effect working was to divide so that people wouldn't have safe places to get to know people who were different from them.

I learned a great deal about the Chinese from one of my assistant chaplains, the Reverend Dr. Peyton Craighill. His parents were missionaries in China. Peyton was fluid in Mandarin and revered the Chinese people, and they, in turn, revered him. He led student trips to China and was our school's unofficial ambassador to that country. Peyton had also taught in China. Students came from China to our school to study for a year. They were smart, talented, hard-working, and polite. I recall at one of Trump's press conferences that he was called out by a reporter who was Asian after he repeated, again and again, the reference to the China Virus. He immediately claimed that the reporter had it all wrong, but he became angry with her and brushed her off in the manner of a schoolyard bully's style that he constantly used.

The butterfly wings of Trump's racism eventually stirred the air in an area near Atlanta in the form of a killer taking the lives of six Asian American women. He still would say, "Don't blame it on me. I am not responsible." Somebody should tell him about the butterfly effect.

The irony is that in the Christian tradition, the butterfly is a symbol of the Resurrection bringing new life. Now, however, the butterfly effect is a symbol of stereotypes, prejudice, harassment, and death for our Asian brothers and sisters.

Post 196. Missteps and Specks

The steps up to Air Force One have been a humbling moment for our leaders. In spite of all the important news that occurred this week, from hate crimes against Chinese Americans to harsh words delivered to Russia and China, it seems that the conservative press, in particular, focused on President Biden's three trips up the steps. He is in good company as President Obama had his misstep moment. President Gerald Ford's misstep coming down the steps was possibly the most dangerous to cause injury. Trump was taped going up the steps with toilet paper stuck to his shoe. While some saw this as an embarrassment of a public official, which seemed to be played over and over. I and others saw it differently. Why?

I began my ministry, being called to be on the staff of Trinity Church in Swarthmore. Among other things, it was made clear to me that I was chosen for my academic credentials and completing a program in counseling at Duke University Medical Center. Trinity Church was a large church that was one of the most socially active in the Diocese. There was diversity in the parish including faculty members and the Religion Department Chair at Swarthmore College. No matter what the diversity, there was one theme that described the people in the parish. They were smart and engaged. They had high standards. After every sermon that I preached, there was feedback. I often referred to my seven years there as a swing through an intellectual jungle gym and I loved every minute of it.

Then it happened! In the middle of preaching a sermon, I lost my place in my manuscript. I had a misstep. It seemed to take forever to sort things out in the pulpit, so I looked up and said to the congregation that "Sorry, but I had lost my place!" They erupted with laughter and applause, which, given my insecurities, I interpreted their response as laughing at me. I was embarrassed. However, I had it all wrong. As people were leaving, they commented, "Thank you for your misstep. It frees us all up to make mistakes."

After I arrived at the Episcopal Academy, during a chapel service, one of my student spiritual leaders was leading the prayers and got lost as well. He simply looked over at me and said, "Rev., I have no idea where I am!" He wasn't just any student. He was that student who did everything right in the classroom and on the sports field and was admired by all. When the congregation heard his plea to me, they too broke into laughter and applause.

Needless to say, I had already had the same gift of a misstep given to me, so I could share my experience with him. He laughed and felt great. The congregation throughout the day indicated how great it was that he could just look over at me and, for all to hear, say, "Rev., I have no idea where I am." It loosened the community up. This was just another example of this student's incredible leadership.

I think that both those who viewed Biden's video tripping up the steps of Air Force One and the EA community hearing a student say that "he was lost" had two ways of viewing these honest missteps. It could be such as the Trinity Church, Swarthmore, congregation made or mire themselves in embarrassment that a mistake had been made that means we aren't perfect. Missteps are important to learning and living. In fact, they should be celebrated. We live in a culture that doesn't support this attitude, and we live in it at our own peril.

A performance culture, which emphasizes production over creativity and emphasizes try and try again, building from one's missteps, has proven to be more productive. We need a switch in our culture from being fearful about mistakes to one that embraces and celebrates them. It is what our greatest inventors, such as Edison and the Wright brothers knew.

We either learn to fail (make missteps) or fail to learn. In the 2018 French Open, Sloane Stephens was defeated by the number one tennis player in the world, Simona Halep. Sloane had a high regard for Halep, and following the match, paid her opponent a great tribute. After taking time to reflect on her performance, Sloane posted an inspiring message, "You win or you learn, but you never lose."

The missteps up the stairs to enter Air Force One taken by President Biden and other presidents is like a cultural Rorschach Test from a leader. We will know that we will be getting closer to a productive, growth-producing nation when those missteps are celebrated, yes even, with applause as opposed to embarrassment by another. When we see our missteps as something that produces learning, we will move to be more open to that which produces a "place" for a sense of psychological safety. It is a fact that we will trip because one thing is sure. We will. That is what makes us fully human.

Recall that biblical axiom in the Gospel of Matthew, "First remove the beam from your eye and then you can see clearly to remove the speck in your brother's eye" (Matt. 7:3). Missteps and specks!

Post 197. Perspectives on Accusations Against Governor Cuomo

There is something about the accusations regarding Governor Cuomo that has not happened. There have been a growing group of women who have accused him of sexual harassment, but I have not seen or heard anyone who has said to him, "What are you doing? Stop!" There is a concern among some that there may be a rush to judgment, which is their perception of what occurred with Senator Franken. Hindsight can offer twenty/twenty vision. Some people feel Franken's removal from Congress was a cautionary tale for other male politicians.

The voters of the state of New York are split 50/50 over their support of the governor. He continues to claim that he wants the process of the investigation to move forward, and then he will accept the outcome. He is known to be a tough politician who has made many enemies along the way, given his bullying style of dealing with people who disagree with him. He was also the poster boy for how to govern during the pandemic, although his nursing home numbers which were lower than they should have been may shed new light on whether he was the model for leadership in times of great struggle.

People have joined the cry to have him removed. Others are saying that nothing was done about Trump's indiscretions. They are referring to the Democrats as too self-righteous.

I have questions and observations. Why wasn't he confronted along the way, which would have been a more empowering response for women? Yes, I know that he is a bully and has exacted revenge on others. But as most sexual harassment statements state, a first step is to confront the person or take someone with you for support to do that. Second, why hasn't anyone asked the governor what he thinks constitutes sexual harassment? He is not stupid. Cuomo's refrain has been that he "never touched anyone in any way or been inappropriate." If that is the case, how does he define sexual harassment?

People have forgotten about a very powerful group with which I have had many conversations about sexual harassment that are just as powerful as the "me too" movement. That group is the mothers of boys. When they look at what is happening regarding the governor, they don't see him; they see one of their sons who they want to protect from similar accusations. People have forgotten about how emotional this issue is for mothers of sons as seen in a letter sent to the *Notre Dame Newspaper* (March 29, 2019) after Maryann White attended a Mass at Notre Dame. A group of young women all clad in tight, clingy Spandex and short tops, were sitting directly in front of her and her family. "I thought of all the other men around and behind us who couldn't help but see their behinds," the self-described Catholic mother of sons wrote. What happened next is a microcosm of what may be happening across our nation as people read about the harassment allegations against Governor Cuomo. She begged female students to "think of the mothers of sons the next time you go shopping and consider choosing jeans instead." No one should fail to see what response was coming. One thousand students indicated that they planned on showing up to class in their leggings following the publication of her letter. It gets better as Mrs. White went on to say, "We don't go naked because we respect the other people who must see us. I'm fretting both because of unsavory guys who are looking at you creepily and nice guys (her sons) who are doing everything to avoid looking at you."

The students' response was just as strong and indicated that Mrs. White's letter perpetuated a narrative central to "rape culture." Other strong responses indicated that the leggings are "comfortable," and others challenged Mrs. White to know if her sons went shirtless at all because chests and abs are something that women found attractive.

Let's not miss the larger lesson. Black parents sent their sons out into the world after "the conversation." So do parents of daughters have "the conversation" with them as well about challenges they may face, and so do parents of boys. All have strong feelings about the precarious world their children are entering where one misstep can lead to terrible consequences. Remember that these people are watching how Cuomo is treated and the plight of the women.

I have already raised the questions that relate to Governor Cuomo. Here is an exercise that students in my ethics class found meaningful and helpful. Put yourself in the shoes of a parent of black sons. Put yourself in the shoes of parents of daughters as well as the parents of boys. Put yourself in the shoes of parents of both girl and boy children.

As you are hearing about all the information about Governor Cuomo, how would you react if you were in one of these three groups? How does it change or confirm your perspective? What would that hypothetical letter that you wrote to the *Notre Dame Newspaper* look like? What would it say?

Post 198. Hidden in Plain Sight

Before immigration at the border became such a controversy, there was a puzzle that most of us grew up knowing. As the puzzle goes, there was a man who was constantly carrying a load of goods in a wheelbarrow from the US side of the border into Mexico. He was crossing time after time, and the officials at the border knew that he was smuggling something, but they never could discover what it was. One of the border officers finally said, "You win! We know that you are smuggling something, but we can't figure out what it is. What are you smuggling?" The man replied, "Wheelbarrows!" Two things were in operation here. One is an expectation as they never expected that wheelbarrows were the issue. They were looking elsewhere! Second, what the smuggler did was outrageous.

I was thinking about these two words, *expectation* and *outrageous*, when I read a column in the *Inquirer* (March 24, 2021) by Julie Coleman. The title of the article is "Antique Doors Stolen Off Hinges." This has become a bit of a crime wave in our fair city for two reasons. The thieves take them off the hinges during the day in the sight of all those who walk by or live in the neighborhood. No one bothers to stop and ask them what they are doing. They look like your average worker doing some handyman work. The doors are worth quite a bit of money, $10,000 for some. They don't expect a criminal to be doing such a crime in broad daylight. The act is so outrageous that it defies the belief that such a crime is being committed.

We are approaching Holy Week in the Christian tradition which begins with Palm Sunday and ends with the celebration of Easter, the Day of Resurrection. As we approach this Holy Week, I think that it is important to have in mind these two words, *expectation* and *outrageous*. Jesus had been making more and more claims in public, with such questions and answers as, "Are you the Messiah? His answer is, "You say that I am!" He was healing people, which had attracted a lot of attention, and His teachings had certainly become threatening to the Pharisees and the Sadducees, members of the priestly caste. He alluded to the fact that He is the Son of God, which is an outrageous and an unbelievable thing to say. He did not hide except for humankind's ability to let outrageous things and expectations stand in the way of seeing Him for all that He said about who He was.

The disciples were no better than the man in the street, for they could buy into the outrageous part as they had witnessed those events of healing. However, their expectation of who He was lacked real insight. Their expectation clouded their "faith sight." They were jockeying for position in His new government. They were looking for a political messiah who would set the people free from the Romans. They thought that He was a political messiah despite his outrageous acts.

This notion of hidden in plain sight is the backdrop for this Holy Week. He was making everyone notice, even the ones who stated to Jesus on the Cross, "If you are the son of God, come down from that cross!" Most of us during this Holy Week know how this greatest story ever told will end, but the danger is to blame the disciples and others for being clueless. If we were there, we would certainly have known that Jesus was the Son of God, *but to make Holy Week really real,* we need to do the following.

During this week, all Christians need to be reminded of outrageous expectations and antique doors, and a wheelbarrow for Jesus was hidden in plain sight. They wouldn't admit it, but some secretly believe that we would have acted differently. We would have known who He was. We would, however, have acted no differently than the disciples, even if we are convinced that we would. That is the power of being hidden in plain sight. If we want Holy Week to be holy and take us to a deeply spiritual place, that is what is needed to be driven home. We hear that question in the Good Friday hymn, "Were You There When They Crucified My Lord?" We can't get to Easter without answering, "Yes, I really would have been there, filled with my hopes and fears and faith and doubts."

Post 199. Is It Ethical to Jump Ahead in Line for the Vaccine?

Dr. Sanjay Gupta put this question to Dr. Art Caplan, a one-time bioethicist from Penn, who is now a bioethicist at the New York University Goodman School of Medicine. Art has been my mentor, so I was surprised by some of his responses but not by all. There were parts that I would have stated differently.

First, Dr. Caplan acknowledged what a difficult and complex problem that Dr. Gupta raised. The full interview is below, but I want to summarize some of his key points and then get to how I think we should go about making sure things are ethical by proposing a different approach.

Here is some background that will help you know what informed my "better way." My wife and I got both shots from our health provider. They called us, as we fit the categories that were now OK to receive the vaccines. All worked out well as it did for our family members who live in different parts of the country. Vicki and I live in the suburbs of Philadelphia in one of the counties that did not get their fair share of the vaccine. Senators and members of the House of Representatives were very much involved in our plight. The state kept saying that we were getting what was fair, but everyone knew that wasn't the case as the numbers were being made public by the press.

But that is not what became tempting for us to cheat. Before we got our vaccines, we started to hear from people we knew, such as Vicki's sorority sisters in North Carolina. Most had already gotten their second shot before we got our first. We also heard about the extraordinary way that some people "cut in line" to get their vaccine. Of course, Philadelphia put the distribution of the vaccine in the hands of a twenty-two-year-old college graduate who became the leader of the distribution in the city. He took some home for his friends and didn't know what he was doing. Everybody was wondering how he got the job in the first place. We were living in a situation where everyone around us had adopted the principle of "everyone for themselves." It was classic Machiavelli where the ends (getting the vaccine) justify the means (anything goes). There was a touch of Social Darwinism as well where "only the strong or connected survive."

Dr. Caplan cited stories to address the question indirectly. He said sometimes jumping ahead is OK, but at other times it isn't. This is an Ethic of Relativity that usually begins with those magical three words, "It all depends." He cites other issues, such as it is not only about getting in line. It is also where the vaccine is. He thought that the problem was that there was still not a universal approach. His feeling was that the first thing that needed to be done in the future is for all the governors to meet in the beginning and come up with a strategy. We know they met on a zoom call, but can you imagine all the governors agreeing on an approach. Think Texas!

Dr. Caplan felt that part of the problem was that there were no consequences to those who did jump in line. He thought that might help. There needed to be a punishment. It is at that point that I disagreed with him. It is time for our superhero to enter the scene and his name is Nudge Theory. I didn't think that I would ever agree with Rand Paul who is always taking on Dr. Fauci in an impolite, know-it-all sort of way, but he did say something that could move us forward. When Dr. Fauci said that we need to continue to mask because of the variants, Paul shot back that people need a reward! In the words of the *Sopranos* TV show, "Bada, Bada, Bing!" I think he is on to something, although not what he means by reward.

Nudge Theory was invented by two behavioral economists, one of whom won a Noble Prize for coming up with Nudge Theory. Their names are Thaler, who won the Nobel Prize, and Sunstein. These are two high-powered academics, one at the University of Chicago and the other at Harvard Law. Nudge Theory persuades people to act in their own and others' best interests. I have included their ideas in a new form of counseling that I have developed found at my website, revsquirecounseling.com.

Nudge theory takes seriously what is going on around you. Some examples will help. When I was traveling from my home to another town, I was speeding and got a ticket. The next time I was speeding along that road, I encountered one of those blinking signs that tell you how fast you are going. Without thinking, I immediately slowed down. I was nudged to change speed and slow down.

There was a town in England that was having a difficult time collecting taxes. They sent out scary penalty letters to the residents threatening punishments. It didn't change a thing. Then they sent out a letter, which told how many people were paying their taxes in a timely matter so others could compare what they were doing with those who were being responsible. They made it more local and therefore more immediate. Taxes started rolling in at a super speed.

If everybody around you (which was the case for Vicki and me) is sharing stories of others getting the vaccine earlier or in a suspect fashion, your tendency is going to be to enter the arena of "anything goes." Those numbers on the evening news are too global and don't touch us literally where we live. They don't make us aware of who is following the guidelines, and they don't tell us the percentage of people who are doing things the "right" way and are not jumping ahead in line. Social behavior is a powerful force. It is not necessarily a reward, but it is rewarding those who are doing the right thing. Interview people for the evening news, who are doing things right. Subtract the deceased from the total population in a county. Give the numbers of those who are living. One problem! That doesn't sell the news. Fear doesn't change people. Showing who is doing it right and the results of that behavior will change them.

I know people who could have gotten the shot illegally and those who didn't. Jumping ahead in the line occurs when we are desperate and when we feel that we are the only ones following the rules. Nobody likes the role of "outlier." Let them know that they have some good neighbors to model appropriate behavior. I assure you that will reduce the line jumping. You don't get a Nobel Prize for something that doesn't work in many different situations.

"Dr. Sanjay Gupta's Interview of Dr. Art Caplan" can be found on my blog on my website under the title of "Is It Ethical to Jump Ahead in line for the Vaccine."

Post 200. The Great Oxford Comma Debate and Holy Week

If you are not a journalist, English teacher, writer, or lawyer, then the Oxford Comma Debate may not be something that would catch your interest, but it is something as small as a comma and big as a ten-million-dollar lawsuit, clarification of an ethical or religious issue, or anything else where you would want to see clarity.

The Oxford comma is the comma that is placed between the last two items or three or more at the end of a sentence. An example of the need for the Oxford comma would be the following, "I admire my parents, Martin Luther King and Kamala Harris. If there isn't a comma between King and "and," someone might think that Kamala Harris and Martin Luther King are your parents. The Oxford Comma gives that sentence total clarity such as if we say, "I admire my parents, Martin Luther King, and Kamala Harris.

Oakhurst Dairy in Maine did not include a comma between the last two descriptions of what constituted overtime. The judge ruled that because of the lack of clarity in that part of the job description, he awarded the workers ten million dollars in that case. He found the statement to be ambiguous; therefore, he had to rule in favor of the workers. He wanted to see the Oxford comma rule otherwise.

Opponents of the Oxford comma find it redundant, stuffy, and pretentious. If you are in the newspaper or magazine business, it takes up valuable space.

I am aware of a recent legal dispute where one party used the expression something X or something Y, which implies that either could be true. But another reading of the law said that something X, or something Y (with the comma), is true. You have to choose between the somethings as they are each independent items. It is further clarity given to the same legal statement. But what is the debate really about? In my opinion, it is about whether you can live with ambiguity when the comma isn't used or clarity when it is. Most of our lives are divided into that which is clear and that which is ambiguous.

Are you a gray-area person who thrives in ambiguity, or are you a black-and-white person who thrives in the world of the absolute? Are you a little of both? Situation ethics is derived from a modern-day interpretation of Existentialism which is a philosophical theory that thrives on ambiguity. The mother of contemporary Existentialism is Simone de Beauvoir whose classic book is *The Ethics of Ambiguity*. Situation Ethics declares, for example, that the situation determines what is right or wrong. The classic example is that we have been taught not to lie. You are living in Nazi Germany, and a stormtrooper comes to your door and asks if there are Jews hiding in your basement. Do you tell the truth or lie, knowing that it would be certain death for those you are hiding if you are truthful?

Kantian ethics, on the other hand, believe that there are a set of universal moral standards that apply to all human beings, regardless of context or situation. But let's posit the thought that you agree with F. Scott Fitzgerald's comment that "the truest sign of intelligence is the ability to entertain two contradictory ideas simultaneously." This gives rise to the notion of cognitive dissonance which is defined in the same way.

Where would you put that Oxford Comma at that end of a sentence between two things that mean a great deal to you? Should they be seen as one where you would not necessarily add the comma or two separate entities that don't necessarily go together and need a comma? Let's consider some important dyads in our lives such as:

Hope and despair
Faith and doubt
Strength and weakness
Happiness and meaning
Joy and sorrow
Wisdom and intelligence
Soul and psyche
Failure and learning

As we approach Holy Week, there are two pieces of cognitive dissonance that we must reflect on to make the week as powerful as it could possibly be in terms of living in the day-to-day and becoming more and more spiritual. They are the following:

Death and Resurrection
Teacher and Savior
God and Son

Who would have thought that such a small piece of punctuation could cause such big ripples in how we see important aspects of our lives? When you think about it, the Oxford Comma defines how you will go through Holy Week. Keep in mind that the disciples and the women at the tomb did not have the benefit of 20/20 hindsight. Like so many of us, they went quickly into the world of ambiguity, attempting to reach clarity of who this man on a cross and no longer in a tomb was. That is the ongoing theme in our spiritual lives.

Post 201. Sadie the Wonder Dog Is Scared to Death of Me

Sadie the Wonder Dog is scared to death of me. How do I know this? Yesterday when I was standing at our kitchen counter, she got right next to me with her paws on the counter, looking at me with those brown eyes that asked, "Where are the treats? I am counter surfing! Remember yesterday?" When I said, "Get down," she did just that. Yesterday I made a ham and cheese sandwich, put it on the counter, and left to get something from my office. In two seconds, it was half-eaten. I managed to save the other half. I don't believe in yelling or hitting a dog, so that is the price I pay. In fact, I yell at people who yell at her. My family says that I spoil her. I prefer to see it as following the Dr. Spock of dog treatment after the very progressive treatment that he recommended in treating young children. He campaigned against "Spare the rod and spoil the child." Sadie greets me every morning at the bottom of the stairs with her tail wagging, not because she loves me but because she knows that I will give her a biscuit then. I am not fooled.

The above paragraph is true with one exception, that Sadie is scared to death of me which may have been the hook to read this far in the first place. It is called "bait and switch." It got some interested enough to see some more. Stores, car dealers, and websites are notorious for the "bait and switch." Stores usually advertise something of great value that is reduced in price, and when you get there, they no longer have that item. They do, however, have many more expensive items to show you. This approach is not legal in some states.

It is legal on websites. The only website that I read daily is CNN Breaking News. As you are reading the news, there are all sorts of advertisements to keep you reading with a "catch and bait" style. Today on the CNN Breaking News were "29 Google Street View Photos That Raise Eyebrows." When you look at the "catch," the "bait" is hardly eyebrow raising, but there are plenty of sales ads to look at. Another was "Red Carpet Falls We Will Never Have Enough Of." The results when you click on the title don't deliver much, but they do have ads for various skin products and clothing lines.

Such titles mislead us to more interruptions like subscriptions, known as popups to the *Wall Street Journal* or *The Washington Post*. You can't get them off the page to read an article. The result is frustration, feeling stupid, a failed expectation, and anger.

So why start a blog with a total lie and a piece of irony? It has a lot to do with Holy Week and perhaps the greatest "bait and switch" in the history of humankind. It all has to do with Jesus' death and resurrection. Some feel that it was the Jews who killed Jesus. This evil lie has been a root of a great deal of anti-Semitism. Others feel it had to be a jealous caste of the priesthood, the Sadducees and the Pharisees. There is not enough proof in Rabbinic theology to prove that one. Who killed Jesus? You and I did. It was the general population of the day!

The central theme leading to Jesus' death is "bait and switch" and a failed expectation. The Romans were oppressing the people. The people yearned for a political messiah as depicted in Hebrew literature. That was what they thought they had, someone to lift the foot of oppression off their necks. Why else would there be such a triumphant entrance into Jerusalem with the crowd waving palm branches and declaring "Hosanna! Hosanna!" The crowds of people created their own "bait" in the form of Jesus. They were going to catch, through Him, their freedom from oppression. We forget that freedom was a big hunger for the people. A big parade means a big hunger for something they didn't have, much like the parades in a city after a team has lost for many years. We forget an important phrase. "They were desperate for a political messiah. That is what they yearned for."

Jesus, through His words and actions, says, "That's not me!" I am here for something bigger. I am here for something that will change history. I am here for your very soul. I am here to quench your thirst and give life to you now and for all eternity. You will never be thirsty again. I am a spiritual Messiah." The crowds' vision was a near-sighted faith, meaning they could only see what was close by, driven by immediate gratification. This near-sighted faith was blurry, so they could not see in the distance the meaning of the cross and the empty tomb. No one else did the bait and switch. They did it to themselves, driven by a relentless need for power now. We can't forget this during this week that we deem holy, or nothing else makes much sense.

Post 202. Unreasonable Reasonable Person Standard

Just when we thought we heard it all regarding the "stop the steal" false statements that were coming from Trump's camp, we hear from one of Trump's attorneys and allies who made a statement that defines yet another example of the bizarre behavior of his loyal fans. His attorney and super fan, Sidney Powell, is being sued by Dominion, owner of the ballot-counting machines, for an outrageous sum of money because of the damage that she has caused as a result of lies that she talked about the election and their machines which counted the ballots. Powell said, "Reasonable people wouldn't believe my election fraud claims."

What a great example of an unethical and illegal statement. Ms. Powell was attempting to get near enough to the Reasonable Person Standard to use that as her last-ditch defense of her actions. The Reasonable Person Standard is one that "the amount of care and caution that an ordinary person would use in a given situation." It is sometimes described as follows. If you put an average group of people together in a room and they are hearing a case, they would all conclude that an act was right or wrong.

This is getting to be a popular defense from the far right as Dominion has been in the driver's seat, suing one after the other of people who lied about how the votes in the last presidential election were counted. Fox (I won't say Fox News.) had lawyers who said that "no reasonable person thinks tuning in to Tucker Carlson is expecting to hear real news. They are there for his opinions." The other thing that Ms. Powell is attempting to do is to demonstrate that her words were a parody like *Saturday Night Live* and shouldn't be taken seriously.

Sorry, but none of the above is going to fly because one six-letter ethical and legal word that is going to throw Ms. Powell into fear and trembling is *intent*. When you think about it, intent can make an action right or wrong. You may intend one thing, but the result may be something very different. Ethical and legal action, however, gives weight to that six-letter word. The other term which plays a role is *carelessness*. Was the person careless in their deliberations?

The easiest way to see how intent makes a difference is to see it in its extreme. Murder involves thinking before the crime that results in death. Manslaughter is most often seen as accidental and has, at times, carelessness as part of the criminal description.

Under California law, for example, carelessness may cause death to occur. In some cases, when manslaughter occurs, the defendant consciously disregards the risk involved, and that act results in the death of others. Intent and degree of carelessness will determine what degree of manslaughter occurred.

From an ethical and legal standpoint, Ms. Powell and her attorneys may have made her case worse, for there are two things that can convict her: one, that she made a false statement, and (2) that she knew the statement was false when she made it. In her defense, she is admitting that she knew what she was doing was wrong but did it anyway.

I would anticipate that the first question from the prosecution's statement would be "What did you intend to achieve by making false statements?" January 6 will demonstrate the carelessness resulting from her words and actions. Ironically the Reasonable Person Standard will be what convicts her in the end. Justice, one of the two pillars of ethics, will prevail.

Post 203. Dry Ice

The first time I ever heard of dry ice is when I needed it for a project for a science fair. I built a Wilson Cloud Chamber, which is a way to see both waves and particles as a description of matter in Planck's Law. You set a metal plate with a hole in the middle underneath a cylinder surrounded by two copper strips adhered to the cylinder that can be electrified with regular current. The whole mechanism sits on a square block of dry ice. When the copper bands are charged, you can look down through the top and see a radioactive source (thumbtack scraped on a radioactive watch hour number). Coming out of it in a cloud are particles that change to waves that change back to particles. I never bothered to ask how dry ice, which was the key ingredient in the experiment, was made. I did, however, adhere to the directions not to touch it or you would stick to it.

Yesterday, I found out more about dry ice in an article entitled, "Dry ice, the unsung hero of the COVID-19 rollout, explained," by Tom Avril. I will summarize focusing on a particular word that he used. Dry ice is formed when pressure is applied to CO_2 gas. It goes directly from a gas state to a solid with no liquid in between those steps. It is one of the reasons that it worked so well with transporting the vaccines. It also can maintain super low temperatures. Avril stated, "It gets its nickname from a chemical that is fairly described as sublime. It does not melt, but sublimates— going straight from a solid to gas, no messy liquid involved. And because the solid form has a temperature of negative 109 degrees Fahrenheit, it cools everything nearby like a champ."

Sublimation, another variation of the word *sublimate*, is a very important process in counseling. In fact, it is needed to help a person move forward to achieve a goal of more wholeness and integration of the psyche and soul. Sublimation works by channeling unacceptable negative impulses into ones that are positive and socially acceptable. A simple example is a student whose mother came to see me and said, "He is all yours. I can't get him to do anything on time." To make matters worse, he was standing right next to her. I was embarrassed for him. She was partly right! He waited until the last minute to do assignments and would get them in just under the wire. He loved to push deadlines to their limit, but he always met them.

In our meetings, I asked him why he always waited until the last minute. He wasn't trying to drive his mother crazy. He liked the pressure. He liked knowing that he had to get things done with not much time for wiggle room. What do you do with a person who loves the thrill of deadlines when that is probably not a good study habit in a high-powered secondary school environment? This student had heard "manage your time" from his teachers until he was dreaming about it. Liking the thrill of the deadline was a core piece of who he was, so I didn't want him to change that as long as he got things in on time and wasn't being penalized. To make a long story short to make a point, he is now an editor of a newspaper in

Vermont and thinks that he has died and gone to heaven with dead-lines galore. His mother was angry with me at first, but the deal was as long as he got his assignments in on time, I would support him in the thrill of victory that he found in this endeavor.

Stock brokerage firms know about sublimation. When I ask my former students, who were great athletes, what they enjoy in that field, they have a response that is pure sublimation. They like the money. They like helping others, but above all else, they like the competition.

Few people want you to change a practice or a way of life that is at their core. They will resist and never move forward. Many, how-ever, are interested in changing a practice that is working against them to something positive. My role is to leverage that piece in such a way that they see and experience how it can work for them and others around them. It's what great presidents in the past, such as Lincoln and Franklin Roosevelt did and what Joe Biden is cur-rently doing. He had taken his grief over the loss of his wife and daughter and, more recently, his beloved son, Beau, and subli-mated it to be more caring, kind, and helpful to those who have experienced loss. Who better to go to Atlanta and be our Consoler in Chief for the community of Atlanta and the families of the six Asian women who were recently murdered?

Dry ice was the unsung hero of the COVID-19 rollout. Sublimation is the unsung hero of the counseling process. Maybe I will put some dry ice in the corner of my office. Perhaps someone coming to see me for help will ask the question, "What is that? Why is it there?" My response would be, "I thought you would never ask! Have you ever heard of sublimation?"

Post 204. Hold Still

Hold still. Don't move. Then the moment is captured by a click of the camera or touch of a phone. They can be different types of photos, some candid photos, some school pictures, and the classic family photo. We want to preserve the moment.

In a major study, people were asked if there was a fire in their home, what would be the thing that you value the most to carry out of the fire. A large proportion of people said the "family photo album" because it is not replaceable. Today it might be a change to our iPhone since a good number of photos are there. Many people want to capture the moment. When you view the photo, it takes you back through time to perhaps where you were told to "Hold Still."

I couldn't resist writing about the title, *Hold Still*. It is the name of the book by Kate Middleton who took pictures of the events of the pandemic. It is usually the other way around where the author of a book or article writes a book or an article, and then the title emerges from that.

I was equally inspired by what the Duchess wrote in her book, "When we look back at the COVID-19 pandemic, we will think of the challenges that we all faced—the loved ones we lost, the extended isolation from our families and friends and the strain placed on our workers. But we will also remember the positives; the incredible acts of kindness, and helpers and heroes who emerged from all walks of life, and how together we adapted to a new normal."

I can't think of taking pictures without thinking about Christy DiSilvestro Rivard. Christy was my senior student spiritual leader of the Vestry, a group of students who planned chapel services and shaped the moral culture of our school. She went on to Harvard University where one spring morning in her freshman year, she went to bed as a Harvard water polo player and woke up the next morning unable to walk because of a double hip injury. She underwent surgeries and navigated the campus for two years on crutches. She was in great pain during a good part of her time at Harvard, took exams standing up, and graduated with her class. We connected by phone. She was on our daily chapel prayer list. She was a person of faith and prayer, and she was chosen as the Class Day speaker at her graduation in 2014.

Her address to the Harvard community was about the "Album of Us." She talks about those important moments in our lives that a "selfie" records, and those important moments when a photo is never taken. She shares a series of life lessons that brought her to the day that she graduated amid Facebook, iPhone, and Instagram. It is what every one of us needs to know to live a full life. A link to the audio version of her address is at the end of this article.

A year or so after her graduation, I received a call from her asking me to bless her marriage. When I asked her who was the lucky guy, she said, "Do you remember me telling you about that guy who carries me all over campus? It's him." She is married to Laurent Rivard, one of the greatest basketball players in the history of Harvard, and one of the most humble, unassuming people one could meet.

We don't hold still for narcissistic moments although many do. We hold still for those memories that can be summoned from a deep place that bring tears, a quick smile, a reminder of courage, compassion, or a hearty laugh.

There is an irony in the Duchess' title, *Hold Still*. We may hold still, but what we remember is all the action that touches places in the heart. It is the reason that parents carry pictures of their loved ones in their wallets. We take photos, not for the still moment, but for all that led up to it, was contained in it, and happened since we captured that moment. As I sit here typing this blog and look around my office, I notice that is filled with many photos of important moments in my life, some filled with joy and some filled with sorrow. There are faces and places that transport me right to that emotion-filled moment when we "held still."

If you could take just one picture that would mean the most to you, what would it be? Why? What picture would you take with you from your home if you had to leave quickly and could never go back? Hold still for those moments, look at them and listen to how they would speak to you! What story would they tell?

"Harvard Class Day Address by Christy Rivard" can be found on my blog on my website under the title of "Hold Still."

Post 205. Next Man Up

March Madness and Easter coincide this year. One of the friendships that I have valued over the years is my connection to Jay Wright and his family. His children attended EA, and one of those children, Colin, was a key student spiritual leader in our school. Villanova was recently eliminated from the competition, having gone deep into the finals. What is more impressive is that Jay's team lost twenty-three days of practice due to the COVID-19 virus, and his two captains were injured and could not play in the March Madness games.

There was not one "Woe is me" statement from Coach Wright to the press. He was sad the captains would miss this key part of their basketball lives, but he went immediately to what any great coach would do. He said, "Next man up!" and pulled from his bench and had a successful ending to a crazy year. I am sure that he will enter the Basketball Hall of Fame, perhaps even this year, not only for being a great coach but also for being a great mentor of young men. Some of his players are entering the "transfer" window or the window into the pros. His reaction is to help them in any way that he can. Their gain will be his loss.

I have played sports most of my life, although I am left now with just the ability to run, so my view of mentoring is to be a good coach. I have been blessed to work with student leaders, particularly in the area of their leading in developing the spiritual life of our school. I like the diversity of students who are elected as the spiritual leaders called the Vestry. Some questioned who were elected as not "being good enough," but the Holy Spirit has never provided me with a student who was not just right to grow in that position, which was a highly valued part of the community. During elections, it wasn't unusual to have twenty-four students run for four positions.

I don't see any distinction between being a coach or a mentor. The opportunities are the same. "Next man up!" is an important part of developing a leader or player. It communicates that everyone is valued and may be required to take on the important task of making a difference.

To mentor others, you must talk less and listen more. I measured the success of any Vestry meeting by the few words that I had to speak. A mentor or coach is a resource who enters the conversation when a perspective or change of plan is needed. I always believed that student leaders should be just that, real leaders in real situations that require tough decisions. Keep in mind that Jay Wright is not going to play in the game; his players are. He takes a time out when a change of plan or strategy is needed and "trusts" the team to execute it. If someone asked Jay who are the most important people on the team, he would not respond with "me.' He would say the players. I felt the same way. I would say the student spiritual leaders.

We had a very successful and meaningful chapel program that always got high marks when evaluators from the outside came in to look at the entire school. They got the message that it wasn't me that made it great; it was the student leaders. That is the truth. It is why a coach or mentor has to be humble. There is that old adage that says, "There is nothing that you can't achieve, if you let other people take the credit."

The student spiritual leaders gave up quite a bit of their time having luncheon and evening meetings. It was a commitment. Each student who runs for the office has to give a short address in chapel about why they are running. They reflect on the commitment and their faith. If they are going to be with each other so much, it is the mentor or coach's job to be make sure they enjoy their time with one another, particularly as they take on a large negative piece of feedback from someone in the community as chapel addresses were available on the school website. The mentor helps them jell. Jay always communicates to the press what a great group of guys he has on his team. Vestry meetings were a high point in my day for the same reason.

Students' time is precious, and so is practice time particularly during the pandemic. Everyone should leave a meeting or practice feeling that their time was not wasted. They have to feel that it was valuable. Time is a gift. One year when the seniors were leaving at the end of the academic year for college, the other members of the team gave them each a pocket watch with the inscription, "Watch Your Time! Rev." I never realized how often I made that statement. It is one of my core life ingredients. Never waste a moment! It became the title of my first book, *Watch Your Time*, about the ethical life.

Stop. Listen. You can hear it in your soul! "Alleluia! Alleluia! He is risen! He is risen indeed!" But listen; there is more. "Go into all the world and preach the gospel to all creation" (Mark 16:15).

"Next men and women up!"

Post 206. The Thinker

Have you read the new Georgia Voting Law which disenfranchises many members of the Democratic Party, particularly people of color? What were they thinking—or perhaps not thinking? They need to have Rodin's sculpture, The Thinker, placed in the Georgia Capitol instead of Jim Crow. I think that it is terrific that so many businesses have made it known that the Georgia Voting Law is a law of suppression. That has been followed by MLB pulling the All-Star Game from Atlanta. That old Reasonable Person Standard sinks this bill underwater quickly. Who would you choose as the most reasonable: 150 captains of industry and a professional sports organization, or a bunch of white men signing a voting bill with the backdrop of a large portrait of a Georgia plantation behind them that was notorious for its crimes against slaves?

Speaking of reason, let's turn to scientific thought and logic, which are used in ethics as well, and put the bill up for ethical evaluation. You cannot offer drink or food to people in line waiting to vote. There is another Latin phrase in ethics referred to as the *Reductio ad Absurdum* argument that can start us off. It means obviously to reduce to the absurd. They reason that it should only be poll workers and not political groups who may influence the voters. I have voted a gazillion times. I have never seen a Democrat, Republican, or Independent try to offer up a bribe to me of food or water. Maybe they think that this is not needed to cope with the long lines due to the suppression. In the words of our esteemed president, "Give me a break!"

There are three types of reasoning in science and ethics to bring understanding to a matter: deductive, inductive, and abductive. Spoiler alert: abductive reasoning is going to kill the law quickly.

Deductive reasoning starts with a general premise and moves to a specific action. For example, all men are going to age. Jim is a man; therefore, he is going to age. The problem for Governor Kemp is that the original general premise has to be true, and there was no basis or need for change since the investigations into voting fraud proved to find none.

Inductive reasoning moves to broad generalizations that can be made from individual data. We make observations that form a pattern, which can lead to an explanation. Often this can lead to the wrong conclusion. For example, Jim is a father. Jim has a nice head of hair. Therefore, all fathers have a nice head of hair. There are too many ingredients in the bill that lead us to believe that it is not about election integrity but voter suppression. A lawmaker who didn't think about what he was saying made the statement that "we (Republicans) will never win another election if we don't get this bill passed." You can't make this stuff up!

Now we go to the "closer" line of reasoning, our friend and hero, abductive reasoning. This type of reasoning starts with an incomplete group of observations and proceeds to the most likely explanation, based on the best information available. For example, I left a delicious sandwich on a low table and left the room. My lab, Sadie, was in the room when I left. My wife was in the room as well. She had a friend over who was in the room. Most of us, particularly me, would conclude that Sadie was the culprit who ate my sandwich, not my wife or the friend. I could try to accuse my wife or her friend to a group of reasonable people, but I think that they would choose Sadie as the culprit, particularly when she couldn't get the taste of mustard out of her mouth.

An old adage holds true for this kind of reasoning. If it looks like a duck, sounds like a duck, and walks like a duck, it is probably a duck! The Georgia Voting Bill is a duck! By all logic, ethical, and scientific thought, we don't need to see the noses of the governor and his colleagues to know that they are growing longer with each moment.

Now, here is an additional piece of logic. Trump created the "Big Lie" about the election. Trump lies. Therefore, his public statement that everyone should boycott the companies and the MLB is the wrong thing to do.

Obama is a model of integrity. His actions speak to that character trait. Obama just tweeted to thank the MLB for standing up for all to have the right to easily vote. Obama is right.

Get that statue of The Thinker into that Georgia Assembly Lobby so they see it as they come and go! We could hope for a different outcome!

Post 207. Less Is More

This past week, I watched *Hamilton* again for the third or fourth time. Each time I watch it, lines stand out. Recently I was struck by the words of Aaron Burr to Alexander Hamilton regarding how to be successful. Burr said, "Talk less. Smile more." The wisdom of "less is more" has its origin in the final verse of the 1855 poem by Robert Browning, "Andrea del Sarto," named after the Italian painter. "Well, less is more, Lucretia, I am judged." The wisdom of that short phrase is a piece of wisdom for the ages. We have a variation of it in the biblical record in the book of Proverbs 15:16, "Better a little with the fear of the Lord than great wealth in turmoil." For me, it has more to do with how to live life than it has to do with contrasting levels of wealth.

Coco Chanel once advised about the outfits that women wear and their accessories, which became the secret to her success, "Before you leave the house, look in the mirror and take one thing off."

The phrase is most associated with the architect Ludwig Mies Van Der Roche, who worked in the early and middle of the twentieth century and ushered in modern architecture. I worked with Robert Venturi, one of the greatest architects of the twentieth century, in designing the Class of 1944 Chapel on the Newtown Square Campus of EA. I learned that his motto was "less is poor," but the chapel that he and his wife, Denise Scott Brown, created was a perfect example of less is more. There was not a square inch of wasted space with an economy of design. In addition, no one could say, "I saw something like this before."

Keep in mind the axiom that "God gave us two ears and one mouth" so that we would know to listen twice as much as we speak. One of the best ways to honor another person is to adhere to this simple but important strategy for a rewarding life. It is one of the first things that you learn in advanced experiences in counseling for it is the foundation upon which a helping relationship is born.

What if "less is more" was a truth for the training of police officers? These three words are a theme that is seen clearly during the trial of Derek Chauvin. He had six incidents of excessive force before he put his knee on the neck of George Floyd.

There is a similar pattern to other deaths of black men and women. The mantra seems to be "shoot to kill." That is the theme in almost every death of a black person. Somehow that has been ingrained into some police in our nation. There has been important research highlighted in Malcolm Gladwell's book, *Blink*. When the police fire a gun at another human being, it is traumatizing to the police officer. It is not like what we see on the silver screen. It is also one of the reasons for post-traumatic stress disorder in our armed forces fighting abroad.

There are incidents where the police have to use deadly force when they have a real threat to their lives, but that is not the pattern that we see addressed in the Black Lives Matter movement. They are trained to shoot first and then ask questions later. Let's reverse that so that instinctively we train and put before police signage at every turn that "Less Is More." If Chanel in the fashion world can do it and if the world of architecture can adopt it, why not the world of law enforcement.

Dan Ariely, a professor of psychology and behavioral economics, is the founder of the Center for Advanced Hindsight at Duke. One of my students, David Cornell '88, reflected on Ariely's research in a chapel address that "reminders of morality right at the point where people are making a decision appear to have an outsized effect on behavior. According to Ariely's experiments, his observations arise from hard data that supports a contention that having regular, recurring reminders of what 'to do' are far more effective than being told what NOT to do."

Imagine at police training, at police headquarters, and in squad cars having the reminder for people to see that "Less Is More." The world of sports knows how a message right before a game shapes an athlete's attitude. That is why each Notre Dame football player touches the sign over the doorway as they exit to the stadium which reads, "Play Like a Champion Today."

Ninety percent of the police in England do not carry guns. Their motto is "Working Together for a Safer London." In 1955 the Los

Angeles police force had a contest for their members to come up with a motto for the department. Officer Joseph S. Dorobek won the contest. His submission for a motto was, "Protect and Serve."

Chauvin's trial is summarized by "less is more" to stand against the excessive force used against George Floyd. What a perfect time to remind the police that "less is more." Less force, more safety. Less times a gun is fired, more lives are saved. Less perceived as the enemy, more times perceived the police are regarded as friends. Three small words with a big idea! *Black lives matter! Less is more!* Makes sense to me!

Post 208. I Am Not Going to Compete with Your Toothpaste

I know someone who has been going through the toughest of times. She is not someone who readily asks for help, as she is an independent person. When she reaches out to someone, you know that she needs support. Recently, she called a friend. She could tell that the person on the other end of the line was multi-tasking. When she inquired about what she was doing, her friend responded, "I am picking up my dog's prescription toothpaste." The individual who needed to connect with someone and talk responded, "I am not going to compete with your toothpaste."

Her friend was multi-tasking, which is an admirable trait. Gender studies indicate that women do this much better than men, so to give the benefit of doubt to the person picking up her dog's toothpaste, she probably slipped into the mode of multi-tasking as a path of least resistance instead of really responding to the call with her full attention. I am a multi-tasker. I frequently watch television with a computer on my lap, a cell phone parked on the arm of a couch, and one or two books at my side. The yellow pad for notes would be there as well. Vicki will sometimes ask, "Are you watching this show or not?" I rarely read one book at a time, but I learned something very important from working with young people for so many years about important conversations.

First, if you want to see a relationship in its clearest form, pay attention to what is important to a high school student. Adolescents live out loud, so it is easy to see what works for people in general by seeing what works for them. When someone wants to talk with you about a matter, assume that it is not the easiest thing for them to do. Few young people reached out to me, who was in a tough spot, who didn't need to talk. The other thing that we humans do when we reach out to others is to assume incorrectly that what we need to talk about is not as bad as we thought it was. I would often hear a person who called or came to my office utter that famous opening line, "Look, this is no big deal, but …" Then they would proceed to tell me something that would bring me or others to our knees. There is a tendency to understate our pain. It's a coping mechanism. Kids do it all the time.

If you don't want to hear, "I don't want to compete with your tooth-paste," then make sure that you are available to the other person. We live in a culture of looking past people who need to talk. Think of the last time that you were in an important conversation with someone, and you were thinking more about how you were going to respond, rather than listening to their plight. We all do it, but the opposite is very much needed. Listen first, then talk. An approach that I have found to be helpful is that after an important exchange whether it is with someone on the phone or in my office, I will take a moment, reflect on the conversation, and ask myself how I could have been more helpful. I learn a lot from those moments. That was the nature of how I was trained.

We had something called verbatims at Duke, which is writing down an exchange with someone that you are counseling and have the supervisor go over it from an objective standpoint. It also forced me to remember everything that I could about an encounter. It would force me to listen carefully until it became a positive habit. My supervisor would then tell me how I could have done it better. Not easy on the ego, but easy on getting better in being of help. The key issue is focus. The person you are helping needs to be the only person in the world at that moment. Recall the famous line of

Gandhi, "You may be only one person in the world but you may be the whole world to one person." That is always the goal.

People who need help reach out to people who they feel will understand the *emotional world in which they are living*. When parents discovered that their son or daughter came to me first to talk about a problem and not them, their feelings would be hurt even though one of my goals in any exchange was to get the young person in communication with their parents. Young people go to friends or an adult whom they think will understand because they are living in that world 24/7. Students knew that I understood that they were hard working and under constant evaluation and pressure. Most parents have a reference point of their time in school. That can be the same as their children, but often it is not.

Human beings love others to inconvenience themselves for them. They may resist this truth. The friend who had focused on her dog's toothpaste could have said, "Whoa! I am here to pick up some toothpaste, but let me get back in the car and focus on you, for you never call unless it is important." How different that experience would have been for the person seeking a listening ear.

Students knew that I had a crazy schedule, but their games, theater, and musical productions were important to them, so I showed up because I genuinely loved watching the result of a lot of their hours of preparation. They saw this as me inconveniencing myself for them. They would always thank me the next day if we ran into one another. It's not hard to find the clerical collar in a crowd. I don't know about you, the reader, but if someone inconveniences themselves for me, *they have a friend for life*.

Life isn't perfect! Sometimes I get a call when I am driving and have to take it then. I could be in a store or public place as well. The next time that someone calls me from their car, however, when it is convenient for them and they are multi-tasking to scratch me from their mental list, I may just say, "I am not going to compete with your toothpaste." It will give them something to think about,

scratch their head in confusion, and perhaps inconvenience themselves for someone else. One can only hope!

Post 209. Why Can't a Woman Be More Like A Man? Or?

Deborah Tannen, who is my resource person in gender issues and
understanding how gender affects ethical action, states that any
time that two men are in conversation, competition tends to power
the exchange as two men compete for status. When two women
are in conversation their exchanges usually attempt to make a connection as they use language to connect and support. Women tend
to listen more as they are building a connection with one another.
Men will bounce around on issues, seeking to gain the upper hand.

Gender issues, like race, are not biological. They are derived from
the culture in which we were raised as well as the culture in which
we find ourselves today. Women can have the male conversation pattern, and men can have the female conversation pattern. I
believe that the above patterns are the reason that it is so difficult to
achieve a bipartisan decision in Congress. John Boehner, a former
Speaker of the House, is making this point in his recent book, *On
the House*. The people who he describes in government are cari-
catures of men seeking status.

Trump is now the head of the Republican Party that is seeking a
way to regain its status of the good old days. It is Trump's culture
now. If we want to see the dynamic of men in conversation in the
extreme, just think of Trump's exchanges with others. "Only I can
make America great again." Women who follow him are quick
to accept this competition style. The women in the Republican
Party are meeting this weekend in Florida with none other than
Matt Gaetz addressing the group, a person alleged to have been
involved in the sex trafficking of women. There was a backdrop
of a photograph of the January insurrection attempt for all to see
as they entered the women's conference. They see that event as a
patriotic act even now. They unfortunately have adopted the male

way of seeing the world. Think for a moment. Were those people, men and women who were attacking the Capitol, seeking connection or status?

We hear shades of that classic line in *My Fair Lady*, "Why can't a woman be just like man?" If that happens, we will never see bipartisan actions in Washington.

If ethics is based on the pillars of justice and love, who is most likely to enter into a conversation that achieves those two ethical principles? Clearly, Biden operates more from a support and connection mode of conversation, and Mitch McConnell and Nancy Pelosi both seem to be interested in power and status as a way to achieve those two pillars. For a brief moment, Mitch forgot that times have changed when he told business to stay out of politics. This was certainly a move to get the upper hand and status. Business' reaction was to spank him until he finally said that "he didn't express his thinking well." It's a new day, Mitch! Pelosi, on the other hand, has figured out that sometimes getting into a spitting contest with men doesn't work.

When I was in graduate school for counseling psychology, my group had group therapy several times a week to determine how we came across so that we could adopt more enabling interpersonal conversation styles. This was a hard-hitting experience. People would leave a session in tears because a hard truth about how others perceived them came their way. Since my mother may have invented group therapy as she would always confront anyone with whom she differed, I was very comfortable with the whole process. This was the world in which I was raised, with a mother who was very male in a conversational style and a father who was very female in a conversational style.

My supervisor was a very skilled and tough guy. He and I clashed regularly. There is a song that I hear on the radio called "I won't back down!" performed by Tom Petty in 1989. One of the lyrics is, "You can stand me up at the gates of hell, but I won't back down." Every time I hear it, I begin to smile because of a truth I learned

413

about myself from my supervisor of the group. In one of our one-on-one meetings, he said, "Jim, competition! It's my issue too! You and I have to stop competing with one another for who is going to run the show!" I learned the hard way how much status and competition entered my conversational style with other men.

There are three big thinkers in political ethics. Politics is about the distribution of power, who has it, and how can I get it. We have to come to a fundamental understanding of how people are built, which we see in their style of communication. Thomas Hobbes said that humankind is competitive and glory-seeking, with one person having the power, the Leviathan, a mortal God. Locke, on whom our government is based, saw people as basically cooperative with a desire to help one another, and Rousseau saw humankind as not only good but great, giving us that guideline that "the government that governs best, governs least." Since you can trust us to do the right thing, we don't need much government. He called us the "noble savage."

If we want to have less gridlock in Washington, perhaps we need to change the question in that musical, My Fair Lady, to "Why can't a man be more like a woman?" That conversational style that grows out of the cooperative spirit could lead to the support of one party for another as well as co-operation, justice, and love defined as "willing the neighbor's good." However, there is also an important ingredient in gender issues that we could use in fewer amounts. Tannen says that "Women never forget an injustice. Men, on the other hand, get quick closure and move on." We saw that clearly in Biden's choice of Harris who went after him in the Democratic Debate. He said, "I don't hold grudges!"

Can you imagine if politicians in Washington understood these principles! The underlying principle of group therapy is that once you become aware of how you are acting that is unhelpful, you do less of it. Certain situations, however, will bring it out again. My supervisor and I never challenged one another after he pointed out how too much competition and a quest for status can be counter-productive for me and others! It is like having a wild horse locked in a stable that only comes out when I need to ride it! We all have a variation of that, men as well as women. What's yours?

Post 210. Candid Camera and Inflection Points

Those of a certain age grew up laughing at the antics of people caught on the TV show, *Candid Camera*, which was hosted by Allen Funt. Pictures may be worth a thousand words, but video and photos also speak most profoundly in capturing moments that define a generation.

We have such a candid video that has been seen over and over during the past year, weeks, and days that will be a defining moment for the next generation that sits on the brink of changing hearts and minds in combatting institutional racism. It is the video by Darnella Frazier that captured the murder of George Floyd by Derek Chauvin. In my opinion, it was a seventeen-year-old girl who filmed that horrible crime, who single-handedly created the most important evidence in convicting Derek Chauvin. I know many agree. Her action underscores how one person can really make a culture-changing difference in the world. It also underscores the courage that it took for her to take out her phone and record that moment. It also points out that each of us may have such a moment someday in our future when we least expect it.

It has been said that greatness in anything takes 10,000 hours of practice. We practice correcting injustice by paying close attention to what is going on around us and repeating our moral interventions until they become, as Socrates said, "Habits of the heart."

We see that "readiness to act" in two other pieces of film that capture the moral imagination of my generation. First, was the Abraham Zapruder film which captured the assassination of President John Kennedy. Zapruder used an 8mm color home motion-picture camera. It too was shown over and over until it was part of the national consciousness. It ushered in the time of violence of an unpopular war in Vietnam, and the killing of Robert Kennedy, Malcolm X, and Dr. Martin Luther King.

Last May, Mary Ann Vecchio watched the video of the death of George Floyd. She was reminded that fifty years earlier, someone took a picture of her kneeling on the ground with a Kent State student in her arms. As the person that she held was dying, she looked up in anguish, pleading, and asking for help with outstretched arms. She was not a Kent State coed as many mistakenly thought. She was a fourteen-year-old runaway who didn't even know the person she was holding. She realized in disbelief that the National Guard was firing on fellow Americans. Sixty shots were fired in thirteen seconds. Four people died, and nine were wounded. The Vietnam War had come to America. John Filo who was just an ordinary Kent State student knew injustice was occurring in front of his eyes. His picture of Mary Ann Vecchio holding the student who was shot defined a generation and won a Pulitzer Prize.

Darnella Frazier, Abraham Zapruder, Mary Ann Vecchio, and John Filo were ordinary people, ordinary citizens, who performed extraordinary ethical actions that focused the nation and the world on the moral purpose of showing the world the importance of justice.

We cannot unsee the video of the death of George Floyd. When I was watching the addresses of people who were thanking others after the verdict of guilty of all charges was announced, I couldn't help but remember that it was one girl, who with courage and the right instincts to notice injustice when she saw it, was really at the heart of the verdict. When we think about it, it has always been the little-known, ordinary people, the seemingly unimportant, who usually are behind the most extraordinary acts. That has always been the case.

According to *The Guardian*, April 21, 2021, "Ma'Khia Bryant, sixteen, was shot and killed by a police officer in Columbus, Franklin County, about twenty minutes before the former Minneapolis police officer Derek Chauvin was convicted of murdering George

Floyd. Michael Woods, Columbus interim police chief, said that a caller said females were trying to stab them and put their hands on them. Police played a ten-second body cam video at a news conference on Tuesday that appeared to show the girl wielding a knife as she grappled with another person. A police officer opens fire, and a girl drops to the ground. The Ohio Alliance for Innovation in Population Health released a study that determined the rate of black people killed by police was 339 percent higher than white fatalities.

It is past time for us all to do justice and for it to become second nature. The Prophet Micah said it best, "And what does the Lord require of you? To act justly and to love mercy and to walk humbly with your God" (Mic. 6:8). Nothing is ambiguous about that call to identify habits of the heart. We probably will never take an iconic video or photo, but we do have eyes to see and ears to hear. The picture of moral action is taken with eyes and action that will be developed in the darkroom of our hearts and souls. All of us need to be ready! Inflection points are moments that change the culture for good or bad. We need to be part of those moments that call for good change that will lead to justice for all.

A "Picture of Mary Vecchio at Kent State Shooting" can be found on my website on my blog under the title of "Candid Camera and Inflection Points."

Post 211. Believe

I have known Pat Croce since he was a nobody. When I first met him, I was taken by his "can do" spirit, his overwhelming energy as I thought that he was about to leap out of his skin, his motivation, and his concern for the physical fitness of people who weren't taking that seriously at the time. I was always on the hunt for speakers who would inspire the students at EA, so I asked him to come and speak to the community. He was a motivational speaker then, so he readily agreed. There is no way that I could describe what he did on the stage in our theater, but suffice it to say that the people who heard him and saw him in action thought that they could run through walls when he had finished. He refused any honorarium.

The next year I called him again to give us a "booster shot." He was on his way to being somebody. He said, "Jim, I am sorry but I just signed with an agent, and I can't do anything without him approving, and there is a hefty fee attached." I thanked him, we had a great conversation, and off he and I went.

Since I returned to the Philadelphia area after school in the Northeast and South, I saw his career take off. He became a physical therapist, started Novacare, sold it for $40 million, and became a minority owner and president of the 76ers. I lost track of him after he had a motorcycle accident that almost cost him a leg, although I was also aware that he had bought some restaurants in Key West, one of my favorite spots.

Yesterday, I opened my email to read an article in the *Philadelphia Citizen* by Larry Platt. I was shocked to discover in the article that for the past six years, Croce has been on a spiritual quest based on meditation and being still. Since Croce recently learned of his diagnosis of lymphoma, he has now launched an approach for the American Cancer Society that focuses on science as well as what he has learned on his spiritual journey. Keep in mind that if there was a category in his high school yearbook for the person who was least likely to achieve or be still, it would be Pat Croce.

The point of Platt's article is that the nation could use some chan-neling of Croce. We need to turn inward to our spiritual selves and clean up all of that stuff that continues to get in the way of being helpful to ourselves and others. As I reading the article I was struck about how much, you the reader, have seen in my memoir and posts that was me channeling some of Croce. We should replace, "What is in it for me?" to "How can I help you be all that you want to be?" and it starts with soul work.

Here are some areas where Croce and I connected as per the article by Larry Platt. Croce reached a point in his life where he raised an important question. In my opinion, it is an important question to start looking at the soul work that you, I, and the nation should examine. That question is, "How did I get here from there? Who and what helped me along the way?" My memoir is obviously about me, but that is the least important part of the book. It is really about chasing that question, "How did I get here from there? Who or what helped me along the way?" What am I doing here?" Spoiler alert: I don't even mention that until the last page of the book. The book is a head fake to encourage others to go after that question.

Everybody loves the guy who "is a resilient underdog from the other side of the tracks." That is Croce and that is me. Who would put their money on a kid such as me with a father with a sixth-grade education and a mother graduating from high school, living in a depressed, blue-collar community with not much encouragement for education beyond high school? Why do people like that story? Why did they love Rocky? I believe that it is because it lets us see not Rocky or me but the tacit dimension of who and what helped along the way. They are the really important people. Nobody does it on their own, although erroneously, people may come away with that impression. Maybe I would hope that folks see the role that Rocky's trainer and girlfriend have in helping him to make it. For Croce, it was his wife, Diane. If you read my book or blog, you will see mine.

Croce taught the city of Philadelphia to believe again in themselves, albeit, through a sports team. We need to believe in ourselves, our neighbor, and our nation more fervently to begin to have the thought that changes our souls, "Think of the other person first." I received a text out of the blue yesterday that read, "How about _____ getting into that great university for graduate school? You'll get partial credit for that." My response was, "The secret is that I treated him as someone who would do great things. More important it was the role of you and _____. I got my money on you inspiring him for a long time." There isn't anyone who doesn't want someone to believe in them, and we as a nation need to get on board that pivotal notion. Believing in others and acting on it is at the heart of reducing the COVID-19 virus and Black Lives Matter succeeding. In Christianity and other world religions, it is formed in the golden rule: "Treat others the way you want to be treated."

In a few days, I will preside at the memorial service of one of the great surgeons in the Philadelphia area, who died too young of a brain tumor at fifty-seven. I was asked how I would approach things to celebrate his life. I responded by saying that "Dr. Gary Rosato was a great guy who was real. The motto of our school is *Esse Quam Videri,* to be rather than to seem to be. Be real. Be authentic. I will speak about a statement that we need to change about our souls. "Gary doesn't have a soul. He is a soul." This implies the definition of religion, which means to connect to self, others, and God. It comes from the Latin root, *ligare,* which means to connect. This doctor spent a great deal of time with his skilled hands as a surgeon dealing with various body parts and ligaments, also a word derived from *ligare.* We need to know the soul work that we and our nation need to claim. "Believe!"

Recommended Readings and Resources

Abbott, Edwin A, *Flatland: A Romance of Many Dimensions*, First Warbler Classics Edition, 2019.

Albom, Mitch. *Tuesdays with Morrie*. New York: Doubleday, 1997.

Arendt, Hannah. *The Origins of Totalitarianism*. San Diego: Harcourt, Inc, 1976.

Arendt, Hannah. *On Violence*. San Diego: Harcourt, Inc, 1970.

Ariely, Dan. *The Truth About Dishonesty*. San Diego: Harper Perennial, 2013.

Becker, Ernest. *The Denial of Death*. New York: Simon and Schuster. 1973.

Before And After video regarding ethical decision-making. https://www.imdb.com/title/tt0115645/

Bettleheim, Bruno. *The Uses of Enchantment*. New York: Vintage Books, 2010.

Bonhoeffer, Dietrich. *The Cost of Discipleship*. New York: Touchstone, 1995.

Bonhoeffer, Dietrich. *Letters and Papers from Prison*. New York: Touchstone, 1997.

Bogle, John. *Enough: True Measures of Money, Business, and Life*. Hoboken, New Jersey: Wiley, 2008

Brooks, Arthur C. *Love Your Enemies*. New York: Harper Collins, 2019.

Browning, Robert. *Andrea del Sarto*. Watham Saint Lawrence, England: Golden Cockeral Press, 1925.

Buckley, William F. *On the Firing Line: The Public Life of our Public Figures*. New York: Random House, 1989.

Burklo, Jim. "Mindful Christianity." Huffpost, 2014.

Bush, George W. *Decision Points*. New York: Crown Publishers, 2010.

Bush George W. *Portraits of Courage*. New York: Crown Publishers, 2017.

Callahan, David. *The Cheating Culture*. San Diego: Harcourt Publishing Company, 2004.

Carey, Alice. *Poems of Alice and Phoebe Carey*. London: (Classic Reprint) Forgotten Book, 2018.

Chessick, Richard. *How Psychotherapy Heals*. Cincinnati, Ohio: Science House, 1965

Curry, Bishop Michael. *Love Is the Way*. New York: Penguin Random House, 2020.

Csikszentmihalyi, Mihaly. *Flow: The Key to Unlocking, Creativity, Peak Performance and True Happiness*. Canada: Harper Collins, 2008

Clayton, Eric and Jennings, Will. *Tears of Heaven*. Warner Brothers, 1992.

Coleman, John. *Blue Collar Journal: A College President's Sabbatical*. Philadelphia: Lippincott, 1974.

Collins, Larry and Lapierre, Dominique. *Or I Will Dress You in Mourning: The Story of El Cordobes and the Spain He Stands For*. New York: Simon and Schuster.

Cousins, Norman. *The Anatomy of An Illness As perceived By The Patient*. New York: W.W. Norton and Company, 1979.

Crosby, John with Richard Caruso. *Built to Help Each Other*. New York: Radius Book Group, 2019.

Dweck, Carol. *Mindset: The New Psychology of Success*. New York: Random House Publishing Group, 2006.

DeBeavior, Simone. *The Ethics of Ambiguity*. New York: Citadel Press, 1948.

Diangelo, Robin. *White Fragility*. Boston: Beacon Press, 2018.

Duckworth, Angela. *Grit*. New York: Scribner, 2016.

Fletcher, Joseph. *Situation Ethics*. Louisville, Kentucky: Westminster John Knox Press, 1966.

Frankl, Victor. *Man's Search for Meaning*. Boston: Beacon Press, 2006.

Fink, Sheri. *Five Days at Memorial Hospital*. First Edition, New York: Crown Publishers, 2013.

Gattica, Movie Released October 24, 1997, Director: Andrew Niccol.

Geisel, Theodore. 10 Quotes to Live By on His 113th Birthday. Website.

Goodwin, Doris Kearns. *Leadership in Turbulent Times*. New York: Simon and Schuster, 2018.

Goodwin, Doris Kearns. *A Team of Rivals*. New York: Simon and Schuster, 2005.

Grant, Adam. *Give and Take: Why Helping Others Drives Our Success*. New York: Penguin Books, 2013.

Grant, Adam. *The Originals*. New York: Penguin Books, 2014.

Grant, Adam. *Think Again*. New York: Penguin books, 2021.

Gwande, Atul. *Better: A Surgeon's Notes on Performance*, New York: Henry Holt and Company, 2007.

Hepburn, Audrey. Video Film and Fashion Icon. https://www.youtube.com/watch?v=thRD7XVy_Xs

Hong, Harry V. *The Essential Kierkegaard*. Princeton: Princeton University Press, 1995.

Jastrow, Robert. *God and the Astronomers*. New York: W.W. Norton and Company, 1992.

Johnson, James and J. Rosamond Johnson. *The Book of American Spirituals*. New York: Viking Press, Inc., 1925.

Kabat-Zinn, Jon. *Full Catastrophe Living*. New York: Random House, 1990.

Kendi, Ibram X. *How to Be an Anti-Racist*. New York: Random House, 2019.

Kidder, Tracy. *House*. New York: First Mariner Books Edition, 1999. www://kinginstitute.edu/king-papers/documents

Kierkegaard, Soren. *Fear and Trembling*. London, England: Penguin Books, 1985.

Koresh, David. Koresh: The Final 24 A Full Documentary https://www.youtube.com/watch?v=65rUlirPCjI

Kushner, Harold. *When Bad Things Happen to Good People*. New York: Random House, Inc.,1981.

Larson, Erik. *The Splendid and the Vile*. New York: Random House, 2020.

Latourette, Kenneth Scott. *A History of Christianity*. New York: Harper and Brothers, 1953.

Lewis, C. S. *The Four Loves*. San Diego: Harcourt, Brace, and Company: First American Edition, 1960.

Machiavelli, Niccolo. *The Prince*. Oxford, England: Oxford World Classic Series, 2020.

Mahler, Gustav. *Symphony #2 Der Grosse Apelle, the Great Calling, the Resurrection*, 1895.

Markle, Sandra. *Wounded Brains: True Survival Stories*. Minneapolis, Minnesota: Lerner Publishing Group, 2011.

McNamee, John P. *Diary of a City Priest*. London, England: Sheed and Ward, 1995.

Mower, O Hobart. Sheldon B. Kopp. *If You Meet the Buddha on the Road, Kill Him!* Palo Alto, California: Science and Behavior Books, Inc., 1972.

Obama, Michelle. *Becoming*. New York: Crown Publishing Group, 2018.

Oluo, Ijeoma. *So You Want to Talk about Race.* New York: Hatchett Book Group, Inc, 2018.

Pocock, George. Htttp://www.youtube.com/watch?v=oYaveihFIXk https://www.youtube.com/watch?v=oYaveihFlXk Website

negrospirituals.com. www.negrospirituals.com

New Revised Standard Version of the Bible. Washington, D.C.: National Council of Churches, 1989.

Nietzsche, Friedrich. *Maxims and Arrows, Twilight of the Idols: How to Philosophize with a Human.* Oxford: Oxford University Press, 2016.

Paine, Thomas. *Common Sense.* Originally published on January 10 1776. Coventry, England: Coventry House Publishing, 2016.

Parks, Dr. Colin Murray. *Bereavement: Studies of Grief in Adult Life.* Routledge: New York, NY, 2010.

Pausch, Randy. *The Last Lecture.* Hyperion Books, 2008 Video https://www.youtube.com/watch?v=ji5_MqicxSo.

Pink, Daniel. *When: The Scientific Secrets of Perfect Timing.* New York: Riverhead Books, 2018.

Potok, Chaim. *The Chosen.* New York: Simon and Schuster, 1967.

Riemer, Jack. "Perlman Makes Music the Hard Way." *The Houston Chronicle*, February 10, 2001.

Rilke, Ranier Maria. *Letters to a Young Poet.* New York: W. W. Norton and Company, 1934.

Rogers, Carl. *Client Centered Therapy.* Boston: Houghton Mifflin, 1951.

Roosevelt, Theodore. "Citizen in a Republic." Scotts Valley, California: Create Space, 2014.

Sandberg, Sheryl and Grant, Adam. *Option B.* New York: Alfred A. Knopf, 2017.

Sartre, Jean-Paul. *Existentialism Is Humanism.* New Haven, Connecticut. Yale University Press, 2007.

Sartre, Jean-Paul. *No Exit.* New York: Vintage International, 1989.

Schwartz, Barry. *The Paradox of Choice: Why Less Is More*. New York: Harper Perennial, 2005.

Seligman, Martin. *The Circuit of Hope*. New York: Public Affairs, 2018.

Seligman, Martin; Raiton, Peter; Baumeister, Roy F.; Sripada, Chandra. *Homo Prospectus*._Oxford, England: Oxford University Press, 2017.

Shahar, Tal Ben. *Happier: Learn the Secrets to Daily Joy and Lasting Fulfillment*. New York: McGraw-Hill, 2007.

Skloot, Rebecca. *The Immortal Life of Henrietta Lacks*. New York: Crown Publishers, 2010.

Shahar, Tal Ben. *The Pursuit of Perfect: How to Stop Chasing Perfection and Start Living a Richer, Happier Life*. New York: McGraw-Hill, 2009.

St. Augustine of Hippa. *Confessions*. Brewster, Massachusetts: Paraclete Press, 2011.

Squire, James R. *Watch Your Time*. Scotts Valley, California: Create Space, 2017.

Squire, James R. *The Times of My Life*. Maitland, Florida: Mill City Press, Inc, 2019.

Squire, James R. Website. https://www.revsquirecounseling.com

Stephens, Sloan. Htttp://ftw.usatoday.com/2018/06/sloanstephens-tennis-french-open-inspiring-message-loss-simona-halep

Sunstein, Cass R., Thaler Richard H. *Nudge*. New Haven, Connecticut: Yale University Press, April 8, 2008.

Tavris, Carol and Aronson, Elliot. *Mistakes Were Made But Not By Me*. New York: Houghton Mifflin Harcourt Publishing, 2007

Tatum, Beverly Daniels. *Why Are All the Black Kids Sitting Together in the Cafeteria?* New York: Basic Books, 1997.

Teilhard de Chardin, Pierre, *The Phenomenon of Man*. New York: Harper Perennial Modern Thought, 2008.

Thaler, Richard H. and Sunstein, Cass R. *Nudge*. New York: Penguin Books, 2009.

Verde, Guiseppe. *Nabucco, Va Pensiero*. Inspired by Psalm 137, 1842.

Walker, Alice. "Sunday School Circa 1950," *Revolutionary Petunias and Other Poems*. New York: Harcourt, Brace, and Jovanovich, Inc, 1973.

Watson, Robert P. *The Nazi Titanic*. New York: Da Capo Press, 2016.

Weathers, Beck. *My Journey Home from Everest*. New York: Bantam Books Trade Paperback Edition, 2015.

West, Cornel. *Race Matters*. New York: Vintage/Random House, 1993.

Wiesel, Ellie. *Night*. New York: Hill and Wang, A Division of Farrar, Straus and Giroux, 2006.

Williams, Margery. *The Velveteen Rabbit*. New York: George H. Doran Company, 1922.

Wilkerson, Isabel. *The Warmth of Other Sons*. New York: First Vintage Books Edition, 2011.

Wilkerson, Isabel. *Caste*. New York: New York: Random House, 2020.

Worsley, Lucy. The Blitz Spirit with Lucy Worsley, 2021 https://www.youtube.com/watch?v=r_v8kBvRVSg

Wright, Jay. *Attitude*. New York: Ballantine Books, 2017.

Zung, Rebecca. Real Leverage Against a Narcissist https://www.youtube.com/watch?v=BCmCZnEguxQ

Works Cited

Abbott, E. A. (1992). *Flatland: A Romance of Many Dimensions*. Dover Publications, Inc.

Arendt, H. (1973). *The Origins of Totalitarianism*. Harcourt Brace Jovanovich.

Ariely, D. (2019). *Amazing Decisions: The Illustrated Guide to Improving Business Deal and Family Meals*. Hill & Wang.

Ariely, D. D. (2012). *The Honest Truth About Dishonest: How We Lie to Everyone-Especially Ourselves*. Harper.

Avildsen, J. G. (Director). (1976). *Rocky* [Motion Picture].

Beauvoir, S. d. (2000). *The Ethics of Ambiguity*. Citadel.

Becoming. (2018). *Michelle Obama*. Crown.

Berg, P. (Director). (2006). *Friday Night Lights* [Motion Picture].

Bettelheim, B. (1977). *The Uses of Enchantment: The Meaning of Importance of Fairy Tales*. Vintage.

Bezos, J. (2020). *Invent & Wander: The Collected Writings of Jeff Bezos*. Hatchette Book Group, Inc, Inc.

Bok, S. (1999). *Lying: Moral Choice in Public and Private Life*. Vintage.

Bonhoeffer, D. (1995). *The Cost of Discipleship*. Touchstone.

Boyle, C. (2018). *The Inquirer*.

Brooks, A. C. (2019). *Love Your Enemies: How Decent People Can Save America from the Culture of Contempt*. Broadside e-books.

Brown, R. (1855). *Andrea del Sarto*. Men and Women.

Buber, M. (1971). *I and Thou*. New York: Charles Scribner's Sons.

Callahan, D. (2004). *The Cheating Culture: Why More Americans Are Doing Wrong to Get Ahead*. Mariner Books.

Cameron, J. (Director). (2009). *Avatar* [Motion Picture].

Collins, J. (2005). *Good to Great and the Social Sectors: A Monograph to Accompany Good to Great*. Harper Business.

Crow, J. F. (2001). Unequal by Nature: A Geneticist's Perspective on Human. *Daedalus Journal*.

Cukor, G. (Director). (1944). *Gaslight* [Motion Picture].

Danforth, J. (2015). *The Relevance of Religion: How Faithful People Can Change Politics*. Random House.

Donne, J. (1997). *No Man is an Island*. Folio Society.

Duckworth, A. (2016). *Grit: The Power of Passion and Perserverance*. Collins.

DuVernay, A. (Director). (2014). *Selma* [Motion Picture].

Dweck, C. S. (2006). *Mindset: The New Psychology of Success*. Random House.

Fandos, N. (2020). Frustration and Fury As Rand Paul Holds Up. *New York Times*.

Fink, S. (2013). *Five Days at Memorial: Life and Death in a Storm-Ravaged Hospital*. Crown.

Frankl, V. E. (2006). *Man's Searching for Meaning*. Beacon Press.

Garfunkel, S. &. (1966). Scarborough Fair.

Gladwell, M. (2002). *The Tipping Point: How Little Things Can Make a Big Difference*. Back Bay Books.

Gladwell, M. (2007). *Blink: The Power of Thinking Without Thinking*. Back Bay Books.

God's Minute: A Book of 365 Daily Prayer Sixty Seconds Long for Home Devotion. (`943). The John C. Winston Company.

Goodwin, D. K. (2006). *Team of Rivals: The Political Genius of Abraham Lincoln*. Simon & Schuster.

Goodwin, D. K. (2018). *Leadership: In Turbulent Times.* Simon & Schuster.

Grant, A. M. (2021). *Think Again.* Viking Books.

Grimm, B. (n.d.). *The Girl Without Hands.*

Hemingway, E. (1940). *For Whom the Bell Tolls.* Scribner.

Johnson, L. (Director). (2016). *Elvis & Nixon* [Motion Picture].

Joncas, M. (n.d.). On Eagle's Wings.

Kendi, I. X. (2019). *How to Be an Antiracist.* One World.

Kennedy, J. F. (2003). *Profiles in Courage.* Harper.

Khazan, O. (2020). Why White Men Love Trump's Coronavirus Response. *The Atlantic.*

Kierkegaard, S. (2006). *Fear and Trembling.* Penguin Books.

Kiern, D. (Director). (2009). *Journey to Everest* [Motion Picture].

King James Bible. (2008).

Kropp, S. B. (1982). *If You Meet the Buddha on the Road, Kill Him!* Bantam.

Landon, A. (2018). *White Fragility: Why It's So Hard for White People to Talk About Racism.* Beacon Press.

Larson, E. (2020). *The Splendid and the Vile: A Saga of Churchill, Family, and Defiance During the Blitz.* New York: Crown.

Lee, P. (n.d.). Is That All There Is?

Levinson, B. (Director). (1988). *Rain Man* [Motion Picture].

Lewis, C. (2017). *The Four Loves.* HarperOne.

McCain, J. (2004). *Why Courage Matters: The Way to a Braver Life.* Random House.

Miranda, L.-M. (2015). *Hamilton.* New York.

Morries, T. W. (2000). *Mitch Albom.* Warner.

New International Bible. (1985). Zondervan Publishing. The National Council of Churches. New Revised Standard Version of the Bible. (1989)

Oluo, I. (2018). *So You Want to Talk About Race*. Seal Press.

Orwell, G. (2013). *1984*. Houghton Mifflin Harcourt.

Pausch, R. (2008). *The Last Lecture*. Hachette Books.

Piper, W. (2006). *The Little Engine That Could*. Platt & Munk.

Platt, L. (2020). *Philadelphia Enquirer*.

Platt, L. (2020). Defund the FOP. *The Philadelphia Citizen*.

Pressley, E. (1960). Are You Lonesome Tonight.

Ramis, H. (Director). (1993). *Groundhog Day* [Motion Picture].

Reimer, J. (n.d.). *The Houston Chronicle*.

Rodgers, R. (1949). *South Pacific*. New York.

Salovey, P. (2020). Address to the Class of 2020. *Yale Alumni Magazine*.

Sartre, J.-P. (1989). *No Exit*. Vintage.

Schroeder, B. (Director). (1996). *Before and After* [Motion Picture].

Schwartz, B. (2005). *The Paradox of Choice: Why More is Less*. Harper Prerennial.

Sheldon, C. M. (2016). *In His Steps: What Would Jesus Do?* CreateSpace Independent Publishing Platform.

Skloot, R. (2010). *The Immortal Life of Henrietta Lacks*. Crown Publishing Group.

Song. (n.d.). Retrieved from Negro Spirituals: www.negro spirituals.com

Squire, J. R. (2017). *Watch Your Time: An Interfaith Spiritual and Psychologival Journey*. CreateSpace Independent Publishing Platform.

Squire, J.R. (2019) *The Times of My Life*. Mill City Press.

Talbot, J. M. (1997). Be Not Afraid.

Tatum, B. D. (2017). *Why Are All the Black Kids Sitting Together in the Cafeteria?* Basic Books.

Tavris, C. (2007). *Mistakes Were Made (But Not by Me): Why We Justify Foolish Beliefs, Bad Decisions, and Hurtful Acts.* Houghton Mifflin Harcourt.

The Man in the Red Bandana (n.d.). [Motion Picture].

The Power of Positive Thinking. (2019).

Various. (2020-21). *Philadelphia Inquierer.*

Viorst, J. (1998). *Necessary Losses: The Loves Illusions Dependencies and Impossible Expectations That All of us Have.* Simon & Schuster.

Wang, D. (2015, July 11). *Scalia/Ginsberg.* (D. Wang, Performer) Castleton Festival, Castleton, Virginia, United States of America.

Watson, R. (2016). *The Nazi Titanic: The Incredible Untold Story of a Doomed Ship in World War II.* Da Capo Press.

West, C. (1994). *Race Matters.* Random House.

Whitford, E. (2020). Notre Dame President Under Fire for Not Wearing a Mask at White House. *Inside Higher Ed.*

Wilkerson, I. (2020). *Caste: The Origins of Our Discontents.* Random House.

Wolfe, T. (2004). *The Right Stuff.*

Woodward, B. (2020). *Rage.* Simon & Schuster.

Wright, J. (2017). *Attitude.* Ballantine Books.

Wujec, T. (1988). *Pumping Ions.* Main Street Books.

Zacharia, J. (2015). The Bing "Marshmallow Study": 50 Years of Continuing Research. *Distinguished Lecture Series, Stanford.*